CORPORATE GOVERNANCE IN THE SHADOW OF THE STATE

Over recent decades corporate governance has developed an increasingly high profile in legal scholarship and practice, especially in the United States and the United Kingdom. But despite widespread interest, there remains considerable uncertainty about how exactly corporate governance should be defined and understood. In this important work, Marc Moore critically analyses the core dimensions of corporate governance law in these two countries, seeking to determine the fundamental nature of corporate governance as a subject of legal enquiry. In particular, Moore examines whether Anglo-American corporate governance is most appropriately understood as an aspect of 'private' (facilitative) law, or as a part of 'public' (regulatory) law. In contrast to the dominant 'contractarian' understanding of the subject, which sees corporate governance as an institutional response to investors' market-driven private preferences, this book defines corporate governance as the manifestly public problem of securing the legitimacy – and, in turn, sustainability – of discretionary administrative power within large economic organisations. It emphasises the central importance of formal accountability norms in legitimating corporate managers' continuing possession and exercise of such power, and demonstrates the structural necessity of mandatory public regulation in this regard. In doing so it highlights the significant and conceptually irreducible role of the regulatory state in determining the key contours of the Anglo-American corporate governance framework. The normative effect is to extend the state's acceptable policy-making role in corporate governance, as an essential supplement to private ordering dynamics.

CONTEMPORARY STUDIES IN CORPORATE LAW

Corporate law scholarship has a relatively recent history despite the fact that corporations have existed and been subject to legal regulation for three centuries. The modern flourishing of corporate law scholarship has been matched by some broadening of the field of study to embrace insolvency, corporate finance, corporate governance and regulation of the financial markets. At the same time the intersection between other branches of law such as, for example, labour law, contract, criminal law, competition, and intellectual property law and the introduction of new inter-disciplinary methodologies, affords new possibilities for studying the corporation. This series seeks to foster intellectually diverse approaches to thinking about the law and its role, scope and effectiveness in the context of corporate activity. In so doing the series aims to publish works of high intellectual content and theoretical rigour.

Titles in this series

Working Within Two Kinds of Capitalism: Corporate Governance and Employee Stakeholding: US and EC Perspectives
Irene Lynch Fannon

Contracting with Companies
Andrew Griffiths

The Jurisprudence of the Takeover Panel
Tunde Ogowewo

The Law and Economics of Takeovers: An Acquirer's Perspective
Athanasios Kouloridas

The Foundations and Anatomy of Shareholder Activism
Iris H-Y Chiu

Corporate Governance in the Shadow of the State

Marc T Moore

·HART·
PUBLISHING
OXFORD AND PORTLAND, OREGON
2013

Published in the United Kingdom by Hart Publishing Ltd
16C Worcester Place, Oxford, OX1 2JW
Telephone: +44 (0)1865 517530
Fax: +44 (0)1865 510710
E-mail: mail@hartpub.co.uk
Website: http://www.hartpub.co.uk

Published in North America (US and Canada) by
Hart Publishing
c/o International Specialized Book Services
920 NE 58th Avenue, Suite 300
Portland, OR 97213-3786
USA
Tel: +1 503 287 3093 or toll-free: (1) 800 944 6190
Fax: +1 503 280 8832
E-mail: orders@isbs.com
Website: http://www.isbs.com

British Library Cataloguing in Publication Data
Data Available

ISBN: 978-1-84946-008-8

Typeset by Hope Services, Abingdon
Printed and bound in Great Britain by
Lightning Source UK Ltd

To my family (present and soon-to-be),
and to John Parkinson

Preface

This was originally supposed to be a book about the global financial crisis. I first thought up the basic idea for the book in late 2008, in the wake of the major banking collapses that occurred in the United States and United Kingdom around this time, and the extensive government action that they entailed. My initial aim was to provide a critical analysis of corporate governance law and theory in these countries in light of the issues that recent events had exposed, especially concerning the essential role of the state in the private sector of the economy. In the intervening four years, though, much ink has been spilt on this general topic, and many people – myself included – have grown tired of reading and talking about the ubiquitous 'c' word ('crisis', that is!). Accordingly, while the experience of the crisis remains highly pertinent for the discussion that follows, this has in fact turned out to be a book about Anglo-American corporate governance more generally. Specifically, it is a book that is concerned principally with how we, as academics and scholars, *think* about the respective bodies of laws relating to corporate governance in the United States and United Kingdom. This is in distinction from, but by no means entirely detached from, the practical questions about how those laws operate within the relevant jurisdictions.

Above all, this book aims to make sense of, and also challenge, the underlying assumptions that we commonly bring to bear on our studies of Anglo-American corporate governance – particularly with respect to the supposedly 'private' nature of the phenomenon, and the limited involvement of the state therein. In approaching this task, I have tried – as best as possible – to adopt a 'neutral' point of view, by analysing the relevant laws and their underpinning theoretical rationales at face value and on their own terms – that is to say, without any particular normative predisposition or bias. Of course, the fallibility of the human condition is such that no scholarly account of any social-scientific phenomenon can ever be truly 'colourless' in this regard, although I hope that my standpoint is sufficiently impartial to elicit the attention of readers from across the political spectrum.

As will become clear fairly early in the following discussion, it has long been my belief that the dominant way of thinking about corporate governance laws in the United States and United Kingdom – namely, the 'contractarian' or 'nexus of contracts' paradigm of the subject – is in many respects not entirely satisfactory. In particular, I feel that the particular ideological 'picture' that contractarian theorists seek to present in their work – emphasising the primacy of (market-determined) private ordering over (state-determined) public policy in propelling the law's evolution – is, to a significant extent, out of keeping with the 'real' nature and content of its subject-matter. At the same time, I am cognisant of the immense value of this particular school of thought in aiding the teaching and learning of both corporate governance and corporate law more generally. Indeed, few would deny that the contractarian paradigm, for all its arguable faults and limitations, is largely creditable for the status that corporate governance enjoys today as a respectable and intellectually rigorous field of academic enquiry. With this consideration in mind, I am wary about engaging in the practice of 'contractarianism-bashing' that has become popular within progressive varieties of corporate law scholarship over the past two decades. At the same time, though, I believe that there remain some fundamental – and, as yet, unresolved – issues concerning the empirical and logical validity of the contractarian approach, which risk either obstructing – or, at worst, *derailing* – the continuing constructive development of legal scholarship in this field.

Although the actual writing of this book took place exclusively over the last two years, the ideas and thinking behind it have been many years in the making. Since I began teaching my graduate course in Anglo-American corporate governance some seven years ago, it has been my intention to present the subject to students as a subject of distinctly *legal* enquiry. To this end, I have consistently encouraged students to understand and evaluate the key laws and institutions in this field in accordance with what are, at root, characteristically legal criteria. I have always believed that corporate governance – viewed from a law (as opposed to economics or business) student's perspective – should be concerned at least as much with the legalistic concepts of power, accountability and legitimacy, as it should be with the economistic criteria of efficiency, profitability, and regulatory cost-effectiveness. I hope that, in the discussion that follows, I am – at the very least – able to impart this method of thinking about corporate governance to some students and scholars outside the walls of my seminar rooms, regardless of whether they agree with everything that I have to say about the subject.

In researching and writing this book, I have been fortunate to have benefitted from the assistance of a number of people who were kind enough to share their valuable time and expertise with me over recent months and years. I am especially indebted to Iris Chiu, David Kershaw, Harry McVea and Edward Walker-Arnott, for their insightful comments on some earlier draft chapters. I have presented parts of this book at various conferences and workshops over the past few years in both the United Kingdom and United States. I am thankful for invitations, comments, criticisms and words of encouragement received from participants at all of these events. Special thanks in this regard are due to John Armour, Brian

Cheffins, Blanaid Clarke, Paul Davies, Simon Deakin, Alan Dignam, Paddy Ireland, Ciaran O'Kelly, Andreas Kokkinis, Chris Riley and Sally Wheeler. I am also thankful for conversations with Roger Barker, Carrie Bradshaw, Pat Capps, Anna Donovan, Nick Gould, Claire Moore, Antoine Reberioux, Arad Reisberg and William Wright, which have likewise helped to shape my thinking in many important respects. Of course, in acknowledging the above individuals, I am in no way suggesting that they would personally endorse any of the views expressed in this book – on the contrary, I suspect that one or two may strongly disagree with certain aspects of what I have to say!

Thanks also to Panos Koutrakos, for initially encouraging me to get my idea for this book off the ground. I am furthermore grateful to all of the excellent company law and corporate governance students at both UCL and Bristol with whom I have had the privilege of discussing the ideas in this book over the course of my teaching career. And I must make special mention of my JD Business Entities class at Seattle University in spring term 2011, for their willingness to be taught the finer points of US corporate law by a rambling and somewhat idiosyncratic Scotsman!

I wrote a significant part of this book during a four-month spell in early 2011 at the Adolf A Berle, Jr Center on Corporations, Law & Society, based in the Seattle University School of Law. I am grateful to Chuck O'Kelley for inviting me to work at the Center, and also for the many informative and inspiring conversations that we've had about corporate governance, law and political economy both during and since then. My understanding of the complexities of US corporate law would not be what it is without the benefit of Chuck's superb knowledge, insights and time-generosity. I am further indebted to Bob Menanteaux from the Seattle University Law Library, for his generosity in securing for me various pieces of obscure literature from across the US northwest on inter-library loan. These sources turned out to be central to the research that I conducted whilst at the Berle Center. I am also thankful to Randall Thomas, for inviting me to present my work to the corporate law students at Vanderbilt University in spring 2011 – an experience from which I benefited greatly.

Fortunately, a recurrent theme in my career has been the inexplicable willingness of many important people to put their faith in me, despite having little-to-no tangible evidence to justify those beliefs! This list includes John Lowry, my former head of department and current company law teaching colleague at UCL, and also Richard Hart, who as a publisher has consistently been enthusiastic, encouraging and understanding about this project, despite my running over our initially agreed deadline for the book. In this regard, I must also mention the late John Parkinson, who agreed to accept me as his PhD supervisee at the University of Bristol in 2001 on the basis of a five-minute telephone conversation, and with no more than an undergraduate law degree to my name! I am indebted to John for being such a patient, open-minded and inspirational supervisor to me, up until his tragic and untimely death in early 2004. In my opinion, John's classic 1993 work *Corporate Power and Responsibility* remains one of the most pioneering and conceptually sophisticated works in the history of corporate law academia. I only hope that I have done justice to John's legacy by producing a work that in some way comes close to meeting his high standards, although whether he would have agreed personally with my approach and arguments herein is quite another matter! I must also pay my thanks to Charlotte Villiers, for being a constant source of support and inspiration in her multi-faceted role as my LLB dissertation supervisor at the University of Glasgow, my 'stand-in' PhD supervisor at Bristol after John's death, and – latterly – a valued academic colleague and friend more generally.

Finally, I must thank the two people in the world who have done the most to make this work a reality. First, I am eternally thankful to my mother and friend Catherine McGee, who has contributed in more ways than could be imagined to enabling me to follow my chosen career. Without her persistent self-sacrifices throughout the most testing of circumstances, I would no doubt be in a very different place. Secondly, I am forever grateful to my wife Emily, who has been a constant source of love and support throughout the past 13 years, despite having to deal with some tremendous personal and professional challenges of her own during these times. More recently, Emily has very patiently put up with my many solitary hours over the past months spent in the study, while acting as the best (and worst paid!) research assistant that an author could possibly wish for. I can say in all sincerity that without Emily, this book (like so many other things in our life) would not have existed.

Last but certainly not least, thanks to George – for keeping me sane over the past year in his own unique little way!

Marc Moore
27 July 2012, London

Contents

Table of Cases

Table of Legislation

United States

European Union

1

Introduction

I. WHAT IS THIS BOOK ABOUT?

I N THIS BOOK, I will attempt to answer the following question: *what is the fundamental nature of the laws relating to the governance of public corporations in the United States and United Kingdom?*

Above all, I will examine whether so-called 'Anglo-American' corporate governance is more appropriately characterised as an area of *private* or facilitative law, or else as an aspect of *public* or regulatory law. This question is not just an academic one in the pejorative sense. On the contrary, it is arguably the most important issue confronting those who study or teach the subject of corporate governance in any level of depth or analytical rigour.

The way in which scholars and students characterise a phenomenon academically is of enormous – and often underappreciated – significance, especially when it comes to aspects of the law. How we characterise an area of law – or, in other words, what the dominant academic *paradigm* of that subject is – affects how we customarily think about it, write about it and teach it. Crucially, it also affects our *normative* perspective on that subject. That is to say, it determines what we regard to be its strengths and weaknesses, its 'rights' and 'wrongs', and the appropriate course of its future development. The opinions and attitudes that are shaped in legal monographs, law review articles and law school classrooms don't just echo around the proverbial ivory towers of elite academic institutions. Ultimately – albeit often very gradually – they trickle down into the so-called 'real world' either when former students of the law later become influential practitioners of it, or when leading academic texts are used by judicial or policy-making figures to help shape their critical understanding of challenging legal issues.

Within the Anglo-American environment, the dominant academic characterisation of corporate governance – and indeed corporate law generally – is as an aspect of private or facilitative law. As such, corporate (or company[1]) law is conventionally bracketed alongside other traditional

---

[1] Whereas the term 'corporate law' is ordinarily used in the US, in the UK it is still customary to refer to the law of incorporated business entities as 'company law'. On the historical origins of this semantic distinction, see below ch 5 of this volume, fn 11 and accompanying text. For purposes of authorial convenience, I will tend to use the former of these terms in this book.

private law subjects such as contract, property,[2] equity, agency and trusts law. Accordingly, the efficacy of the various laws and regulations concerning corporate governance in the United States and United Kingdom is ordinarily judged by reference to how responsive those rules are to the supposed private preferences of key corporate participants or 'contractors'. For the most part, this category is normally restricted to include – in the last place – the common or ordinary shareholders who supply the corporation's equity or risk capital; and, by necessary implication, the managerial officers (including directors) who are appointed to make executive policy decisions on shareholders' collective behalf. It follows from this premise that the core and motivating purpose of corporate governance laws should be to reflect or 'mimic' the governance 'terms' that shareholders and managers would be inclined to agree upon with one another privately, in the hypothetical scenario where no antecedent laws exist and therefore all norms stand to be determined by private negotiation alone.[3] This is what is commonly known as the 'contractarian' or 'nexus of contracts' theory of corporate law.

Correspondingly, corporate law is ordinarily *not* characterised as an aspect of 'public'[4] or regulatory law, in the way that subjects like tort,[5] or

---

[2] Although property law is unquestionably part of private law, whether it is a 'facilitative' area of law in the sense of the other topics in this list is open to question. Arguably, property law is more correctly understood as a *market-constitutive* (and thus *pre-facilitative*) area of law insofar as it delineates the set of social relations that are conventionally understood to constitute ownership, on which basis productive exchange becomes possible. However, for purposes of argumentative convenience, I will regard this function of property as being facilitative in itself, thereby justifying property law being viewed on the same plane as these other, notionally private law subjects. In any event, one may make a similar claim about contract law, on the basis that modern social exchange relations are arguably not innate or pre-ordained in a proverbial state of nature, but rather are artificially constituted by judicial doctrines that define the essential features of an enforceable promise. As important as these concerns are for lawyers, though, they lie outside of the scope of the present study. For an authoritative exposition of the concept of property as an artificial and juridically constituted 'bundle of rights', see WN Hohfeld, 'Some Fundamental Legal Conceptions as Applied in Judicial Reasoning' (1913) 23 *Yale Law Journal* 16; WN Hohfeld, 'Fundamental Legal Conceptions as Applied in Judicial Reasoning' (1917) 26 *Yale Law Journal* 710. For an excellent critical perspective on these issues, drawing on the work of the American legal realist Robert Lee Hale, see P Ireland, *Property and Contract in Contemporary Corporate Theory* (2003) 23 *Legal Studies* 453, 486–91.

[3] The most comprehensive and influential statement of this conception of corporate law is provided by Easterbrook and Fischel's now classic work, *The Economic Structure of Corporate Law* (Cambridge MA, Harvard University Press, 1991).

[4] To clear up any potential confusion amongst readers, I am not using the term 'public law' here in its conventional doctrinal sense, which tends to denote areas of law that govern the relationship between individual citizens and the state, including constitutional and administrative law. Rather, I use the term here essentially to refer to 'non-private' or regulatory areas of the law that affect the activities of business corporations, and for want of a better word for this purpose.

[5] No doubt many English private lawyers will dispute my inclusion of tort law within the 'non-private' category of legal topics. However, insofar as tort law is designed to regulate the ex post facto risk-distributive outcomes of economic activity, and thus only indirectly affects the ex ante prudential motivations therefor, it is in my opinion more appropriately situated within this latter list. In view of the fact that the vast majority of tort claims (espe-

criminal, environmental, antitrust (or competition) and securities law[6] are. That is to say, unlike the above areas of law, corporate law – including corporate governance law[7] – is typically not perceived as being designed to coerce social-behavioural change, or to bring about direct distributional outcomes within society whether in terms of risk, power or wealth. Therefore academic characterisations of corporate governance normally do not seek to portray the laws and norms in this field as exhibiting such characteristics, which would run counter to their purportedly facilitative – and thus fundamentally *non*-socially-determinative – nature.

Just as the purpose of an artistic caricature is to accentuate the most distinctive or noteworthy features of a person rather than portray her every physical detail, the objective of an academic characterisation is to emphasise and draw on the key distinguishing features of a subject rather than to document that phenomenon in all of its complexity. Inevitably, therefore, the process of academic characterisation – in law as elsewhere – involves some marginal degree of papering over the empirical cracks. That is to say, the occasional outlying or idiosyncratic feature is conveniently (and quite acceptably) elided so as not to detract from the essential qualities of the subject that the writer is seeking to accentuate.

Therefore an academic characterisation of an area of law, like an artistic caricature, need not be 100 per cent comprehensive in documenting a subject, nor sensitive to its every empirical nuance. As a minimum requirement, however, the characterisation must be capable of incorporating *all materially significant* features of its subject-matter, or else the ensuing model will lose its essential representational quality.

Moreover, the process of academically characterising a subject – and especially an area of law – involves not just an empirical but also a normative dimension. These two elements necessarily overlap and reinforce one other. Inevitably, the answer to the empirical question – that is, what essentially *is* a given phenomenon? – affects our answer to the ensuing normative question – that is, what essential form or qualities *should* that phenomenon embody? Thus in any field of social science, constructive academic debate involves scholars providing competing characterisations of the essential (empirical) nature of a thing on a definitional level, in

---

cially concerning large businesses) are settled on a negotiated 'out of court' basis, there is an argument to say that tort law is best understood as a market-*facilitative* area of law designed to provide a framework for the retrospective 'purchase' by a tortfeasor of the victim's right not to be wrongfully harmed. On this, see PS Atiyah, *The Rise and Fall of Freedom of Contract* (Oxford, Clarendon Press, 1979) 750. Accordingly, in categorising tort law in the above way, I do not deny being guilty of a degree of deliberate conceptual over-simplification.

[6] On the (somewhat arbitrary) substantive distinction that is customarily drawn between corporate law and securities (or, in Europe, capital markets) law, see below ch 6 of this volume, pt II.C–E.

[7] On the distinction between corporate *governance* law and corporate law more generally, see my introduction to ch 3 of this volume below.

order to establish (or change) the points of reference in accordance with which the efficacy or desirability of that phenomenon can subsequently be judged from a more critical perspective.

In short – in law as in elsewhere – '*ought*' judgements are ultimately dependent to a large extent on '*is*' judgements, because in order to be able to critically evaluate a subject we must first of all understand its key attributes and qualities.[8] It follows that, where a particular characterisation of an area of law lacks adequate empirical foundations (in the sense of failing to represent any materially significant features of the relevant subject-matter), any normative conclusions that are drawn on that basis are either void – or, at the very least – become subject to further questioning as a precondition to their continuing acceptance by others.

In the field of corporate governance, the main 'is' dispute concerns the alleged 'private' v 'public' nature of the laws in this field – that is, to what extent can corporate governance laws properly be regarded as the outcome of decentralised market or civil society bargaining, in contrast to centralised regulatory state imposition? Or, to put the issue another way: is corporate governance law at its core an organic ('bottom-up') or synthetic ('top-down') creation? Where one adopts the former view as regards the fundamental nature of corporate governance law, one is ordinarily led to the ensuing normative position that the relevant laws in future *should* rightfully be developed along the same basic path: that is, law-making in this field should be *responsive to* private preferences, rather than determinative of such.[9]

Conversely, proponents of the latter (synthetic) view of corporate governance law tend consequently to arrive at the contrary normative position. That is, that the laws in this field should be coercive and socially-determinative, aimed at eliciting direct change in the behavioural patterns and relative resources of key corporate participants in line with general democratic opinion in society, and irrespective of whether or not such regulatory outcomes are consistent with the affected participants' (especially shareholders') private preferences.[10]

---

[8] At the same time, it may conversely be said that 'is' judgements are to a large extent dependent on preceding 'ought' judgements, insofar as it is impossible to make sense of any social phenomenon without first having a preordained sense of its perceived purpose or objective. On the 'is–ought' distinction in legal discourse generally, and also the distinction between (i) sheer physical facts and (ii) institutional facts as interpreted – and thus given meaning – through the lens of a given normative order, see N MacCormick, *Institutions of Law: An Essay in Legal Theory* (Oxford, Oxford University Press, 2007) chs 1 and 2; N MacCormick, *Questioning Sovereignty: Law, State, and Nation in the European Commonwealth* (Oxford, Oxford University Press, 1999) ch 1.

[9] On this, see JE Parkinson, *Corporate Power and Responsibility: Issues in the Theory of Company Law* (Oxford, Oxford University Press, 1993) 25–32.

[10] On the distinction between socially-determinative and non-socially-determinative conceptions of the purpose of corporate law, see D Millon, 'New Directions in Corporate Law: Communitarians, Contractarians, and the Crisis in Corporate Law' (1993) 50 *Washington and Lee Law Review* 1373.

As will be demonstrated in later chapters, to a significant extent the contractarian characterisation is supported – albeit it in different ways – by the actual form and substance of corporate governance law as it exists in both the United States and United Kingdom.[11] However, a comparatively significant body of existing Anglo-American corporate governance rules and principles would – at first sight anyhow – appear to undermine or at least challenge the dominant contractarian portrayal of the law in this area as being purely facilitative, by suggesting that corporate governance law is in fact imbued with a heavily 'public' or regulatory impetus.[12] In particular, the fact that many fundamental norms of Anglo-American corporate governance are determined on a mandatory (and thus contractually irreversible) basis – either directly or indirectly at the behest of the regulatory state – sits uneasily alongside the dominant contractarian portrayal of corporate laws as being the flexible, instrumental and *non*-socially-determinative outcome of private selection methods based on rational (shareholder and managerial) choice.

The most problematic feature of mandatory rules from a contractarian perspective is the fact that they are necessarily subject to universalistic or 'across the board' application, and hence by definition *cannot* be responsive to individual preferences or firm-specific circumstances that might merit the occasional exception from the regulatory norm. Accordingly, consideration for collective conformity on a macro (ie system-wide) basis effectively trumps any conflicting concern for respecting private ordering at the micro (ie individual firm) level. Insofar as the permissible ambit of private ordering in corporate governance is in this way restricted by externally-imposed regulatory boundaries, it can consequently be said that the process of legal-institutional evolution in corporate governance is one which – although in many respects organic and quasi-contractual in nature – nonetheless operates substantially *in the shadow of* the interventionist regulatory state.

Against this background, if the contractarian position is to retain its normative argumentative force, it must be capable of providing a convincing explanation for the significant presence of prima facie regulatory laws within the corporate governance field. In fairness, defenders of the contractarian paradigm of corporate governance have been acutely cognisant of the conceptual difficulties which mandatory rules pose for the continuing validity of their empirical and, in turn, normative claims. In my view, though, the principal arguments that have been advanced by contractarians in response to these difficulties have – with limited exception – been at

---

[11] On the principal manifestations of the contractarian paradigm within the doctrinal frameworks of US and UK corporate governance law, see below chs 4 and 5 of this volume respectively.

[12] On the principal 'public' or regulatory dimensions of Anglo-American corporate governance law, see below ch 6 of this volume.

best unconvincing, and at worst fundamentally *paradoxical* (and thus self-defeating).[13]

However, whilst identifying the weaknesses in the contractarian rationalisation of mandatory rules is one thing, providing an alternative positive explanation for the widespread regulatory features of Anglo-American corporate governance law is quite another. To this end, I will attempt towards the end of the book to develop what I believe to be a more convincing explanation for the somewhat peculiar combination of facilitative and regulatory rules that together constitute the key laws of corporate governance as they apply in the United States and United Kingdom respectively.[14] The counter-explanation that I will offer for the prevailing structure of the law in this field is, I believe, at root consistent with the basic impetus of the contractarian position. However, in contrast to contractarianism, it involves recognising the inherent limitations to effective private ordering of corporate governance at the individual firm level, and the consequent inevitability of regulatory state interventionism as a necessary means of achieving the core objectives of the law in this area.

Finally, I will outline the normative consequences that acceptance of this position tends towards. Essentially, it entails accepting a significantly wider ambit of regulatory state involvement in the development of governance norms at the macro level, as a logically necessary precondition to the effective functioning of Anglo-American corporate governance as a whole.

II. THE PLAN FOR THE BOOK

Accordingly, the 'road map' for the discussion in this book is as follows. In chapter two, I will attempt to define corporate governance as a subject of legal-academic enquiry, which is a necessary preliminary to the subsequent analysis of its fundamental nature as an area of law. Here I will argue that, whatever one's specific view as to the fundamental (facilitative or regulatory) nature of corporate governance law, there are certain core aspects of the subject that are constant and, moreover, intrinsic to the subject by virtue of its very nature.

Thus any corporate governance system is, ultimately, designed to ensure that those who possess and exercise *power* within the corporate structure (namely managers) are perceived by those who are directly subject to such power (principally shareholders) as being effectively held *accountable* for their exercise of that power, so as to *legitimate* the former group's continuing possession and exercise of such power in the eyes of

---

[13] On this, see below ch 7 of this volume.
[14] See below ch 7 of this volume, pt V.

the latter. The three core and irreducible elements of any framework of corporate governance law, accordingly, are: (i) power, (ii) accountability, and – ultimately – (iii) legitimacy.

Essentially, *power* represents the initial corporate governance problem, with *accountability* being the solution, and *legitimacy* the consequence which follows from successful resolution of the corporate power problem. I will submit that the answer to the question of how effectively managerial accountability is achieved inevitably differs depending on how one perceives the fundamental nature of corporate governance law. However, regardless of one's particular theoretical perspective, the above trichotomy of factors is – in my opinion – a necessary constant of *any* meaningful corporate governance debate.

In chapter three, I will examine the dominant contractarian characterisation of corporate governance law in detail. Above all, I will seek to demonstrate how the contractarian paradigm is dependent on a peculiarly passive-instrumentalist understanding of corporate law as a phenomenon that is in the last place *determined by*, rather than determinative of, the private preferences and bargains of individual corporate participants (principally shareholders and managers).

In seeking to (empirically) demonstrate and (normatively) defend the purported 'privity' of corporate law – including corporate governance law – in the sense of its inherently private or transactional nature, contractarianism implicitly denies any effective role for regulatory state interventionism in determining the legal ordering of internal corporate affairs. Rather, effective managerial accountability, and – in turn – the legitimacy of managers' continuing possession and exercise of power, is believed to be most appropriately determined on a decentralised, micro level in accordance with firm-specific governance norms and institutions.

Corporate governance is thus presented as a contractual rather than regulatory creation. The purpose of the 'regulatory' state within this model, meanwhile, is merely to supply the most popular governance 'terms' to corporate participants on an 'off-the-shelf' basis, so as to save participants (principally shareholders) the extensive transaction costs that would otherwise be involved in devising such norms from scratch. Over and above this base facilitative level of involvement, however, the state is perceived as having no further material role to play in engendering effective managerial accountability within public corporations.

In chapters four and five, I will demonstrate the main respects in which the contractarian paradigm of corporate governance law is actually manifested within the US and UK frameworks of corporate governance law respectively. I will explain how the prima facie contractual nature of both systems has (empirically) reinforced – and in turn been (normatively) reinforced by – the popular contractarian understanding of corporate law.

The principal doctrinal embodiments of the contractarian tradition within US corporate governance are the commodified 'opt-out' and 'choice' traditions of corporate law design that persist at State (especially Delaware) level, and also the long tradition of judicial deference to the internal contractual autonomy of corporations as manifested in the business judgment rule at common law. Both of these phenomena will be explored in chapter four.

In the United Kingdom, by comparison, the influence of contractarian logic is demonstrated most conspicuously in the significant degree of regulatory deference apparently afforded to so-called 'soft law' norms that are promulgated outside of government and which depend mainly on market pressures, rather than the binding force of state sanction, for their effectiveness in eliciting managerial behavioural change. Meanwhile, judicial deference to internal corporate autonomy likewise persists in the English common law environment under the doctrinal label of the 'internal management' doctrine. This rule, together with the comparably longstanding contractual principle that underpins the juridical character of the corporate constitution, has operated so as to affirm the characteristic 'privity' of UK corporate law in the sense of its inherently *facilitative* and *non*-regulatory nature. These issues will be analysed in chapter five.

A key theme that I will seek to draw out from these two chapters' doctrinal analyses is the extent to which – and variety of ways in which – the regulatory state has taken a proverbial 'back seat' when it comes to establishing effective managerial accountability mechanisms at the micro level. In many respects, both legislators and courts have restricted their respective law-making functions to the provision of broad procedural standards and mechanisms, which provide a facilitative framework for private ordering within individual companies. This has ultimately left corporate participants with a material degree of self-regulatory 'space' in which to determine directly, and on an individual firm basis, which substantive accountability norms will govern their ongoing governance relationships with one another. Such a finding has the effect of affirming – to a considerable extent – the empirical validity (and, in turn, normative persuasiveness) of the contractarian characterisation of corporate governance law.

As against this, however, in chapter six I will seek to demonstrate that the contractarian paradigm – in spite of its substantial descriptive accuracy in the above ways – is nonetheless significantly limited empirically in a number of other comparably important respects. For a start, the growing compliance costs encountered by Anglo-American (and especially US) public corporations in adapting to a continuously expanding corporate governance regulatory agenda over the past decade have put into question the contractarian claim that legal rules in this area are primarily the result of flexible private ordering rather than coercive state sanction.[15] On a more fundamental level, meanwhile, the extent to which both US and UK corporate governance law is – and has for a long time been – pervaded by significant mandatory elements would appear, at least on first inspection, to undermine seriously the forcefulness of the theory's normative claims about the rightful form and content of the law in this field. Therefore, insofar as many core managerial accountability norms are determined not at the individual firm level, but rather on a centralised and universalistic basis, some further explanation is required in order to demonstrate that such outcomes are driven principally by private-contractual – rather than public-regulatory – pressures.

Accordingly, in chapter seven, I will critically evaluate the main contractarian rationalisations of mandatory corporate governance rules. In other words, how have defenders of the contractarian paradigm sought to justify their 'private ordering' conception of corporate governance in spite of the fact that, in many crucial respects, the basic (mandatory) structure of the relevant legal rules prima facie lends credence to a public-regulatory understanding of this area of law? Here I will attempt to demonstrate that all of the main contractarian explanations for mandatory rules in corporate governance, in spite of their undeniable intellectual sophistication, are nonetheless highly problematic on either an empirical or logical level.

I will therefore attempt in the final part of chapter seven to provide a more convincing and defensible rationalisation of the prevailing (dual facilitative and regulatory) structure of Anglo-American corporate governance law today. In essence, I will seek to highlight the impossibility of engendering an effective – and thus legitimate – framework for formal managerial account-giving within widely-held public corporations on a decentralised, micro basis. I will argue, rather, that effective accountability in corporate governance, and the resultant sustainability of the Anglo-American governance system as a whole, are necessarily dependent on the interventionist regulatory state as an active and ever-present corporate governance participant at the macro level. Additionally, I will explore the most notable normative consequences that tend to follow from acceptance of my re-characterisation of corporate governance law. Essentially, I will argue that scholars and students of Anglo-American corporate governance law must in general be considerably more willing than they have been in the past to embrace the (essential) regulatory dynamics of their subject.

---

[15] On this issue generally (viewed from a US perspective), see L Ribstein, 'International Implications of Sarbanes-Oxley: Raising the Rent on US Law' (2003) 3 *Journal of Corporate Law Studies* 299; A Barden, 'US Corporate Law Reform Post-Enron: A Significant Imposition on Private Ordering of Corporate Governance?' (2005) 5 *Journal of Corporate Law Studies* 167; R Romano, 'The Sarbanes-Oxley Act and the Making of Quack Corporate Governance' (2005) 114 *Yale Law Journal* 1521; S Bainbridge, 'Dodd-Frank: Quack Federal Corporate Governance Round II' (2010) UCLA School of Law, Law-Econ Research Paper No 10-12, available at: ssrn.com/abstract=1673575.

Finally, in chapter eight I will summarise the conclusions of the book as a whole, and also make some suggestions for future avenues of enquiry that that would be constructive either in developing or testing the hypotheses advanced herein.

III. PROVISOS TO THE FOLLOWING DISCUSSION

Before continuing, two important substantive provisos should be noted at this point. First, given the extraordinary significance of the managerial power phenomenon as it operates within widely-held corporate ownership environments, the following study – in contrast to standard accounts or analyses of company law – will be concentrated exclusively on *public* corporations: that is, companies whose shares are traded on a public equity market and which consequently exhibit the characteristic known popularly as the separation of ownership and control.[16]

Although I acknowledge the potential (albeit limited) applicability of some of this book's insights concerning power, accountability and legitimacy to larger-scale private or closely-held companies, I can only say by way of defence that concern for the length and thematic consistency of the book have necessitated the imposition of a substantive 'cut-off point' in this regard; and the public/private company divide – while admittedly imperfect – appeared to be the most logical and, correspondingly, least arbitrary such threshold to adopt.

Secondly, the scope of the discussion that follows is, for pragmatic reasons, restricted exclusively to the so-called 'Anglo-American' environment: in other words, to the corporate governance systems of the United States and United Kingdom. Insofar as both these systems share basically similar institutional features[17] and also a broadly comparable – albeit by no means equivalent – politico-economic climate,[18] their common analysis is in my opinion both appropriate and mutually reinforcing. That said, it is imperative to be aware of the significant differences between these two countries' respective legal, market and political environments, and throughout this book it is my intention to avoid the common trap of obfuscating these distinctions via blunt and inconsiderate usage of the 'Anglo-American' label.[19]

---

[16] On this notion generally, see AA Berle and G Means, *The Modern Corporation and Private Property*, 4th edn (New York, Harcourt, Brace & World, 1968) (first published 1932).

[17] Most notable amongst these are widely-held and liquid equity ownership, a unitary and non-pluralist board model, and a mutual common law heritage.

[18] Common politico-economic characteristics of the two systems include liberal democracy, financial capitalism, and a relatively non-interventionist approach to national industrial policy.

[19] For an excellent account of the key differences between the US and UK corporate governance systems, including relevant distinctions between the two countries' respective

In an increasingly globalised and interlocking industrial, financial and regulatory environment, it is understandable that such a western-centric focus as that adopted in this book might be regarded by some readers as rather antiquated and parochial. Undoubtedly the recent (US-originated) financial crisis and ongoing shift in the global balance of politico-economic influence towards the rapidly industrialising BRIC nations[20] have together called into question the purported comparative advantage of western corporate and financial norms. As against this, however, it remains the case that – for all its alleged systemic flaws and social injustices – the Anglo-American system of financial capitalism, with its underpinning framework of corporate governance, remains highly influential on an international level.[21] For this reason, its exclusive treatment within an academic work of this nature is in my view justified.

Furthermore, if the general theoretical themes developed in this work prove to have some (albeit limited) relevance in other corporate ownership environments and legal cultures beyond the particular geographic scope of the present study, this can hardly be regarded as a weakness of the book. On the contrary, such a finding would indicate the wider international applicability of the ideas and arguments developed herein.

Before getting ahead of oneself, though, there remains the small matter of tackling the initial job at hand: that is, convincing readers to accept my claims as valid and sustainable within their immediate Anglo-American context. It is to this task that I will now turn.

---

political cultures, see C Bruner, 'Power and Purpose in the "Anglo-American" Corporation' (2010) 50 *Virginia Journal of International Law* 579.

[20] Brazil, Russia, India and China. The BRIC thesis posits that of these four emerging economies, China and India will by the middle of the 21st century become the world's dominant suppliers of manufactured goods and services, respectively, while Brazil and Russia will become similarly dominant as suppliers of raw materials.

[21] For a comprehensive comparative analysis of the Anglo-American system of corporate governance set within its broader global and macro-economic context, see A Dignam and M Galanis, *The Globalization of Corporate Governance* (Farnham, Ashgate, 2009).

2

Defining Corporate Governance as a Subject of Legal Enquiry

I N ORDER TO understand the fundamental nature of an area of law, one must first determine its essential substance. Therefore as a necessary preliminary to tackling the core thesis of this book, it must initially be established: what actually *is* corporate governance as a subject of legal-academic enquiry?

Over recent decades, the topic known as 'corporate governance' has become an increasingly high-profile aspect of legal scholarship and practice, especially within the Anglo-American environment. In the process, it has risen from being a specific sub-topic of business entities law to a legitimate and popular subject of study in its own right. A growing number of graduate law courses are now dedicated exclusively to corporate governance,[1] and mainstream company law textbooks are devoting ever more attention to major governance issues including independent boards, institutional shareholders and financial risk oversight.[2] On a practical level, meanwhile, the corporate governance advisory profession has grown in direct correlation with corporate boards' ever-increasing governance responsibilities, and is now recognised as a distinct City sub-industry alongside traditional sectors such as commercial law and investment banking.[3]

---

[1] A Dignam and J Lowry, *Company Law*, 6th edn (Oxford, Oxford University Press, 2010) 373.

[2] For instance in the UK, the 8th edition of *Gower and Davies' Principles of Modern Company Law* (London, Sweet & Maxwell, 2008) devotes 115 pages to corporate governance issues alone (see chs 14 and 15 thereof). Other notable examples are B Pettet, J Lowry and A Reisberg, *Pettet's Company Law: Company and Capital Markets Law*, 3rd edn (Harlow, Longman, 2009) ch 7 and pp 60–64; Dignam and Lowry, ibid, chs 15 and 16; B Hannigan, *Company Law*, 2nd edn (Oxford, Oxford University Press, 2009) chs 15 and 16; D Kershaw, *Company Law in Context: Text and Materials* (Oxford, Oxford University Press, 2009) chs 5–8. The above excerpts exclude those chapters of the relevant books that are devoted to directors' duties, which arguably also constitute part of corporate governance law.

[3] On the role and influence of corporate governance advisory firms generally today, see below ch 4 of this volume, fns 117–19 and accompanying text; M Kahan and E Rock, 'Embattled CEOs' (2010) 88 *Texas Law Review* 987; MT Moore, '"Whispering Sweet Nothings": The Limitations of Informal Conformance in UK Corporate Governance' (2009) 9 *Journal of Corporate Law Studies* 95, 122–23.

Despite this widespread interest, there remains considerable uncertainty about how exactly 'corporate governance' should be defined. When viewed from a purely formalistic (or 'black letter') perspective, corporate governance comes across as a heavily procedural and bureaucratic field of study, involving the painstaking perusal of a burgeoning body of codes, committee structures and consultation documents. At the same time, though, corporate governance is commonly regarded to be a theoretical and largely *extra*-legal subject, involving open-ended engagement with questions as to the nature and rightful beneficiaries of corporations within a wider social context.[4] From this point of view, corporate governance is frequently contrasted with company law: the former dealing with the conceptual 'big issues' from a radical or reformist standpoint, and the latter with the doctrinal minutiae of business entities regulation viewed in (small 'c') conservative terms.[5]

In this book, I will use the term 'corporate governance' in neither of the above senses. Rather, for the purpose of the discussion that follows, I submit that corporate governance – analysed from a distinctly *legal* perspective – is first and foremost an enquiry into the causes and consequences of the allocation of *power* within large economic organisations.[6] Indeed, understood in its traditional state law context, the concept of 'governance' is conventionally perceived as relating to the ways and means by which the authority and decisions of powerful political office-holders are

---

[4] The conceptual foundations of the Anglo-American 'corporate governance' debate – as understood from this perspective – are widely believed to be traceable to the landmark 'Berle v Dodd' debate in the 1932 edition of the *Harvard Law Review*. See E Merrick Dodd, 'For Whom are Corporate Managers Trustees?' (1932) 45 *Harvard Law Review* 1145; AA Berle, 'For Whom Corporate Managers *Are* Trustees: A Note' (1932) 45 *Harvard Law Review* 1365; WW Bratton and ML Wachter, 'Shareholder Primacy's Corporatist Origins: Adolf Berle and "The Modern Corporation"' (2008) 34 *Journal of Corporation Law* 99, 100–105 and 122–35. On this general trend in US corporate law scholarship, see H Wells, 'The Cycles of Corporate Social Responsibility: An Historical Retrospective for the Twenty-first Century' (2002) 51 *Kansas Law Review* 77. In the specific context of the UK, the seminal academic work on 'corporate governance' in the above sense is commonly regarded to be John Parkinson's pathbreaking book, *Corporate Power and Responsibility: Issues in the Theory of Company Law* (Oxford, Oxford University Press, 1993).

[5] As one commentator has remarked: '[a]cademic company lawyers in the UK have not generally been noted for their fascination with theory. On the contrary, they have long displayed something of an aversion to the important questions about the nature of companies, separate corporate personality and shareholder rights which underlie company law, preferring to busy themselves with more immediately practical, if less foundational matters'. See P Ireland, 'Property and Contract in Contemporary Corporate Theory' (2003) 23 *Legal Studies* 453, 453. On this, see also BR Cheffins, 'Using Theory to Study Law: A Company Law Perspective' (1999) 58 *Cambridge Law Journal* 197, 208; M Stokes, 'Company Law and Legal Theory' in W Twining, *Legal Theory and Common Law* (Oxford, Blackwell, 1986) 155, 155.

[6] MT Moore and A Rebérioux, 'Revitalizing the Institutional Roots of Anglo-American Corporate Governance' (2011) 40 *Economy and Society* 84, 85. On this, see also D Tsuk Mitchell, 'From Pluralism to Individualism: Berle and Means and 20th-Century American Legal Thought' (2005) 30 *Law and Social Inquiry* 179; SR Bowman, *The Modern Corporation and American Political Thought: Law, Power and Ideology* (PA, Penn State University Press, 1996).

checked, counterbalanced, or otherwise rendered legitimate from the perspective of those who are subject to the powers in question.[7]

Correspondingly, *corporate* governance can be defined as the social problem of holding powerful decision-makers in large *economic* organisations accountable for their actions, in order to legitimate their continuing possession and exercise of power. Therefore, in the same way that constitutional and administrative law seek to achieve this outcome within the public governmental domain, corporate law (or, at least, those aspects of corporate law concerned with governance matters) is designed to ensure that the powers and decisions of key economic functionaries in the private sector are in general acquiesced in by those persons who are principally affected by them.

Given the extent to which corporate governance issues pervade the general field of corporate law today (especially in the US), it is not uncommon for the terms 'corporate (or company) law' and 'corporate governance' to be used in an almost interchangeable manner. However, it is not my intention to do this in the present book. Rather, I understand the specific field of corporate governance law, at least as it is known in the Anglo-American environment, to refer only – or at least substantially – to the legal and other institutional components that comprise *the corporate equity relation*: that is to say, the so-called 'agency' relationship between the management and ordinary shareholders of a public or widely-held corporation.[8]

I fully acknowledge that a considerable proportion of the broader field of corporate (or company) law exists principally to safeguard the interests of unsecured creditors and other potentially vulnerable 'third parties' in society, whose incentives are on occasion misaligned with those of shareholders and – consequently – managers. This is especially so at times when the financial solvency of the firm is threatened.[9] However, since creditor protections in corporate law (unlike many shareholder protections) tend – at least in the ordinary course of things – *not* to entail direct

---

[7] For an analysis of the concept of governance within a wider institutional context, see O De Schutter and J Lenoble, *Reflexive Governance: Redefining the Public Interest in a Pluralist World* (Oxford, Hart Publishing, 2010).

[8] On the so-called 'agency' (or 'agency costs') model of corporate governance, see M Jensen and W Meckling, 'Managerial Behavior, Agency Costs and Ownership Structure' (1976) 3 *Journal of Financial Economics* 305; EF Fama, 'Agency Problems and the Theory of the Firm' (1980) 88 *Journal of Political Economy* 288, 288–97; EF Fama and M Jensen, 'Separation of Ownership and Control' (1983) 26 *Journal of Law and Economics* 301. For a critical analysis of the limitations of agency theory, including its inconsistency with core legal principles of Anglo-American corporate governance law, see Moore and Rebérioux, 'Revitalizing the Institutional Roots', above n 6, 90–93. In the current discussion, I refer to the corporate equity relation as an 'agency' relationship for reference purposes only, and do not wish to convey any of the normative implications that acceptance of the agency model tends to give rise to.

[9] On the likelihood of shareholders' and creditors' respective incentives becoming misaligned when a company is insolvent (or when its solvency is under threat), together with the implications for the design of directors' duties, see R Grantham, 'The Judicial Extension of Directors' Duties to Creditors' (1991) *Journal of Business Law* 1.

regulation of the firm's internal executive decision-making procedures or dynamics;[10] they consequently tend to be placed outside of the normal scope of corporate *governance* in the sense in which that term is ordinarily understood. For this reason, and also in light of concern for the length of this book, I have intentionally excluded consideration of creditor protections in corporate law from the scope of the present study.

Before proceeding, it is necessary to deal in advance with a potential substantive criticism of the material that follows. At first sight, the conceptual portrayal of corporate governance presented in this chapter might be dismissed by some readers as overly abstract, and thus divorced from the day-to-day realities of how large business firms operate. Above all, it may appear to company lawyers of an orthodox inclination that the esoteric values of power, accountability and legitimacy have no constructive part to play in an area of activity where instrumental criteria such as efficiency, efficacy and cost-effectiveness have traditionally prevailed as the principal currency for determining the desirability of any given law or institution.

As against this, however, I would argue that for too long corporate governance scholars, and indeed corporate lawyers generally, have – whether deliberately or unintentionally – maintained an implicit blind spot when it comes to the normative dimensions of their subject. In particular, I believe that academic corporate lawyers of a contractarian bent (even if they have not expressly acknowledged themselves as such) have, at times, unjustifiably foreclosed the disciplinary boundaries of their subject by focusing on the functionality of laws and norms in a purportedly economic or 'practical' respect, to the exclusion of other – arguably more fundamental – issues of legal concern.

Therefore if the tone of the discussion that follows comes across either as peculiar or outside of the normal corporate lawyer's comfort zone, it is

---

[10] The frequency and significance of the (theoretically) extraordinary instances where creditors' interests become an exclusive or core concern of management should not, however, be underestimated. Such instances include, inter alia, situations where the wrongful trading rule under section 214 of the Insolvency Act 1986 is invoked within UK companies facing imminent business failure, whereupon creditors collectively become the sole proper focus of the board's attention. On this, see A Keay, 'Wrongful Trading and the Liability of Company Directors: A Theoretical Perspective' (2005) 25 *Legal Studies* 431; T Cooke and A Hicks, 'Wrongful Trading – Predicting Insolvency' [1993] *Journal of Business Law* 338. A further notable category of exceptions to the general pattern of creditors standing outside of internal firm governance processes are those cases where professional lenders invoke contractual self-help remedies, which provide for intrusive intervention in corporate governance (including, in some cases, appointment of a creditor representative on a debtor company's board of directors) on the occurrence of a specified credit event. Whilst such outcomes are – strictly speaking – attributable purely to private contractual stipulation rather than any rules of corporate law itself, their significance to the corporate governance dynamic in financially troubled firms cannot be denied. On this, see DG Baird and RK Rasmussen, 'Private Debt and the Missing Lever of Corporate Governance' (2006) 154 *University of Pennsylvania Law Review* 1209.

because it is intentionally so. Indeed, an important subsidiary objective of mine in writing this book is to contribute towards the development of a new conceptual 'language' or set of reference points for analysing corporate governance from a legal-academic perspective, irrespective of whether readers agree with the specific normative conclusions that I intend to draw at the end of the book.

This is not to deny the continuing importance of economic-instrumental concerns such as efficiency and cost-effectiveness in evaluating the overall social desirability of laws – indeed, such considerations figure very heavily within the book. The key point, though, is that these factors are not teleological 'ends' of corporate governance debate in themselves, but rather form part of a wider discourse aimed – in the last place – at determining the conditions under which the possession and exercise of corporate-managerial power is rendered legitimate from the perspective of those who are principally subject to it.

The discussion in this chapter is thus structured as follows. In part I, I will begin by outlining the essential problem that underlies Anglo-American corporate governance as a whole, which is the inevitable existence of managerial *power*. Here I will highlight the distinctiveness of managerial power within the corporate context, and also demonstrate the parallels between executive-organisational power as it exists within the public-governmental and private-corporate environments respectively. I will further explain here how *shareholders* represent the principal subjects of managerial power, insofar as the equity relation[11] by nature necessitates an investor sacrificing her contractual autonomy in order to grant management both allocative and appropriative control over her capital.

In part II, I will emphasise the structural imperative of legitimating management's continuing possession and exercise of power from a general investor perspective, in order to sustain the basic structure of the equity relation. I will also explain here the central importance of formal managerial accountability norms in securing the legitimacy of corporate-managerial power, in the sense of maintaining the acquiescence of equity investors as a whole in the perpetuation of the (functionally necessary) management-shareholder power imbalance.

In part III, I will tackle what some readers may perceive as the proverbial 'elephant in the room' in this discussion, which is the as-yet unacknowledged question as to why, in the Anglo-American environment at least, equity should be regarded as the exclusive direct beneficiary of managerial accountability norms. In particular, one may legitimately query why *labour* – which, as a corporate constituency, is likewise exposed to corporate-managerial power in the sense defined below – is not directly

---

[11] That is, the legal and economic relationship – both collective and individual – between ordinary (or common) shareholders and corporate management.

and formally answerable to by management in the same basic way as ordinary shareholders are. Here I will attempt to provide an explanation for this state of affairs, for the purpose of the present study.

I. THE PROBLEM OF CORPORATE-MANAGERIAL POWER

A. The Multifarious Nature of Power as a Social Phenomenon

Power is a ubiquitous phenomenon: it has been said that 'next to sex and love, [it] is perhaps the oldest social phenomenon in human history'.[12] However power is also an opaque and contested phenomenon,[13] and '[f]ew words are used so frequently with so little seeming need to reflect on their meaning'.[14]

Constructing an objectively defensible definition of power is a highly difficult – some might say intractable – intellectual challenge.[15] To a Marxist, the notion of power denotes that prevailing economic, political and legal institutions are inextricably linked to bourgeoisie class domination over industrial society. Feminist or critical theorists, meanwhile, frequently rely on the concept to refer to overt or tacit forms of societal domination stemming from other underlying factors such as gender, race or technology.

Even within the specific *corporate* domain, the origins, nature and significance of power remain largely ambiguous issues. While law and economics scholars typically conceptualise power in the narrow and relationship-specific guise of 'agency costs',[16] progressive theorists have advanced a broader understanding of corporate power in terms of 'social decision-making power':[17] that is to say, the discretion that socially significant corporations enjoy to 'make private decisions which have public results'.[18] Indeed corporate power has been described as 'one of the great enigmas of political science . . . [a] complex phenomenon possessing economic, legal, political, and social significance'.[19]

---

[12] AA Berle, *Power Without Property: A New Development in American Political Economy* (New York, Harcourt, Brace & World, 1959) 77.

[13] Parkinson, *Corporate Power and Responsibility*, above n 4, 8.

[14] JK Galbraith, *The Anatomy of Power* (Boston MA, Houghton Mifflin, 1983) 1.

[15] Interpreted in its most general sense, power can be defined as 'the ability of A to cause B to behave in a manner intended by A that B would not have done without A's intervention'; insofar as 'A has some form of control over B, or at least a strong bargaining position that enables A to score a "victory" over B'. See Parkinson, *Corporate Power and Responsibility*, above n 4, 8. Beyond this basic level, however, obtaining universal agreement on the precise meaning of power is an impossible task.

[16] See the papers cited above n 8.

[17] See Parkinson, *Corporate Power and Responsibility*, above n 4, 10.

[18] Ibid.

[19] Bowman, *The Modern Corporation*, above n 6, 1.

In recent social-scientific literature, corporate power has been categorised as taking two distinct but overlapping forms, namely 'internal' and 'external' power. According to Bowman, the internal dimension of corporate power denotes power arising from the contractual or quasi-contractual control relationships intrinsic to the functioning of the firm as a productive entity. This is in distinction from the external dimension, which encapsulates the power wielded by corporations within the broader framework of society including their political lobbying power and consequent influence over the governmental policy-making process.[20]

Given the complexity and substantive indeterminacy of corporate power, any rigorous academic account of the concept must inevitably adopt a degree of selectivity in defining its subject-matter. In this chapter I will therefore focus exclusively on *internal* corporate power. This type of power is of particular interest from the perspective of the book, in that it pertains directly to the corporate equity relation which – as explained above – is generally acknowledged to lie at the heart of corporate governance law in the United States and United Kingdom.[21]

B. The Distinctiveness of Corporate-Managerial Power

The most comprehensive and renowned academic exponent of the power phenomenon (at least within the English-speaking world) as it exists in the economic-organisational context is the economist John Kenneth Galbraith. For this reason, Galbraith's definition of power represents the most appropriate theoretical starting point in any enquiry into the nature of corporate power viewed from a legal perspective.

Fundamentally, Galbraith understood power in Weberian terms as enabling the imposition by some person or group of 'its will and purpose or purposes on others, including on those who are reluctant or adverse'.[22] Galbraith observed that *all* organisations – economic or otherwise – are by their very nature sources of power in this sense, insofar as the essence of an organisation is 'a number of persons or groups . . . united for some purpose or work'.[23] This presupposes that the relevant individuals 'in one degree or another, have *submitted to* the purposes of the organization in pursuit of some common purpose' (emphasis added).[24]

However the business corporation – in comparison to other non-corporate organisational forms – is possessed with an extraordinary

---

[20] See ibid, esp chs 2–4.

[21] This is not to deny, though, that the scope of external power wielded by a corporation vis-à-vis wider society is affected *indirectly* by its internal legal constitution of power.

[22] Galbraith, *The Anatomy of Power*, above n 14, 2.

[23] Ibid.

[24] Ibid, 55.

capacity to impose its will and purposes on others in the Galbrathian sense. This is on account of a phenomenon that I will term *discretionary administrative power* (or DAP), which is largely (albeit not wholly) distinct to the corporate form of economic organisation. In essence, DAP denotes the capacity that public corporations enjoy to collect and administer the resources or funds of others in the pursuit of autonomously determined objectives that the contributors may *or may not* commonly share.

DAP arises where an organisation collects and administers externally contributed economic resources from investors on a centralised and substantially autonomous basis, and in an endeavour that the external resource providers retain a common material interest in. Thus DAP necessarily entails the sacrifice by an individual investor of her autonomy or freedom of action with respect to a given asset or resource, in the expectation that this will ultimately bring about a net gain in her material welfare. The situation can basically be rationalised in accordance with social contract logic, insofar as a group of individuals submit part of their individual freedom of action over economic affairs to centralised organisational control, in return for the benefits that they each stand to derive as passive beneficiaries of some greater collective scheme.[25]

The concept of DAP in the above sense is manifested most extensively in the governmental context, where social services and/or productive functions are administered within the bureaucratic state apparatus using public economic resources. In a communist command economy, the primary economic resource advanced by citizens in this regard is their labour or human capital. In the archetypical case, such capital is allocated and coordinated by government unilaterally in the service of centrally-determined social objectives, the most common of which is the generation of a sufficient quantity of essential goods and services to satisfy projected public need. In a liberal market economy, on the other hand, the main economic resource collected by government is public taxation revenues. These revenues are then used to purchase human and physical capital on free and decentralised labour and goods markets in the pursuit of objectives that are, in the last place, determined democratically.

---

[25] The original exponent of this concept in political philosophy was Thomas Hobbes. See T Hobbes, *The Leviathan*, Penguin Classics edn (Harmondsworth, Penguin, 1968) (first published 1651). In this classic work, Hobbes explained that only by sacrificing his natural right to all things in a state of nature could man acquire any real freedom of action whatsoever, so that civil society institutions – including the rule of an absolutist sovereign monarch – were justifiable on the basis that they allowed a citizen only 'so much liberty against other men as he would allow other men against himself' (p 271). Accordingly, the sovereign monarch could be regarded as a centralised enforcer of the terms of citizens' implicit mutual pact over the basic terms of their relations with one another, thus legitimating the monarch's entitlement to wield absolute sovereign power over his subjects (as being in the latter group's ultimate collective interest). For an excellent analysis of this argument, see PS Atiyah, *The Rise and Fall of Freedom of Contract* (Oxford, Clarendon Press, 1979) 42.

In both instances, however, the basic point stands that a collectivised process of resource accumulation – and subsequent administration – is taking place. The only differences are the identity of the principal resource that is being accumulated by government (whether human or financial capital), and the extent of the public accumulation process as a proportion of overall national economic activity: such proportion typically being much higher in command economies than in market economies.

When one moves from the public to the private sector of a market economy, a fundamentally similar tendency can be observed within the corporate form of economic organisation. In the same way that the dual institutions of taxation and executive government permit the centralised administration of public resources, the significant powers vested by law in *corporate* controllers enable the collectivisation of privately-invested capital *outside of* the democratic state apparatus. The existence of DAP in the corporate setting accordingly provides the basis for a form of non-statist quasi-taxation, whereby formally private office-holders wield substantial discretion in appropriating and allocating economic resources outside of the reach of direct proprietary or democratic control.[26]

There are two distinct but interlocking components of DAP that together constitute the basis of the corporation's characteristic autonomy in this regard. The first of these is *allocative* power, which relates to the range of uses or 'ends' to which an invested (financial or non-financial) resource can legitimately be devoted *without* the specific agreement of the resource provider. The second constituent component of DAP is *appropriative* power, which denotes the legal capacity of corporate controllers to determine the rate of return on an externally provided resource *without* seeking the direct consent of the resource provider thereto. In this way – as I will explain below – appropriative power gives a corporation considerable latitude to establish its current rate of capital accumulation, and also the extent to which such accumulation will be financed at the collective expense of its external resource providers.

Moreover, whilst DAP in the above sense exists – to varying extents – in all corporate governance relations – the concept has special (although not exclusive) relevance in the context of the corporate equity relation. The reasons for this will likewise be discussed below.

C. Power Imbalance in the Corporate Equity Relation

It is well-accepted by law and finance scholars that equity or 'risk' capital represents a unique form of investment, especially in the context of busi-

---

[26] On the common fundamental features of the centralised resource accumulation process within communistic and capitalistic-corporate organisations, see Berle, *Power Without Property*, above n 12, 151, discussed further below n 70.

ness enterprise. While debt is a largely 'fixed' or contractually determinate method of financing in terms of durability, price and terms of advancement, equity on the other hand is inherently 'open-ended': that is to say, it is contractually *indeterminate* with regard to its longevity, compensatory rate of return, and also the substantive conditions under which its productive use in enterprise is sanctioned.[27]

From this premise, it is commonly argued that the technical incapacity of equity investors to exercise effective control over their capital by orthodox contractual means necessitates that they be protected instead via extra-contractual hierarchical rights over the productive venture in which that capital is used.[28] It follows that equity investors should be granted ultimate power of direction over the *entire enterprise* in which their capital is invested,[29] together with the corresponding entitlement to appropriate surplus cash flows in excess of the firm's fixed contractual liabilities to other (non-equity) investors.[30] This reasoning purportedly explains why equity (as opposed to debt or human) capital in the ordinary case 'owns' the business firm, in the sense of enjoying residual control and distributional rights in it, as compensation for standing last in line in the event of any periodic or terminal distribution of its funds or assets.[31]

In the case of *unincorporated* business entities the above logic could certainly be said to hold true. In such instances, the equity investor's peculiar contractual vulnerability can be regarded as a quid quo pro trade-off for the exclusive management and agency rights that she enjoys in respect of the running of the firm's business, whether individually (as a sole proprietor) or collectively (as a partner). It can accordingly be said that the equity investor here gives up full ex ante control over her capital in return

---

[27] See OE Williamson, *The Mechanisms of Governance* (Oxford, Oxford University Press, 1996) ch 7; OD Hart, 'Incomplete Contracts and the Theory of the Firm' (1988) 4 *Journal of Law, Economics and Organization* 119.

[28] See G Kelly and J Parkinson, *The Conceptual Foundations of the Company: A Pluralist Approach* in A Gamble, G Kelly and J Parkinson (eds), *The Political Economy of the Company* (Oxford, Hart Publishing, 2000) ch 6, 120.

[29] Oliver Williamson has argued that debt 'works almost entirely out of (contractually-fixed) rules' whereas 'equity governance allows much greater discretion' in terms of the degree of control that it permits an asset-financier to exercise over firm operations. Williamson claims that equity finance, in particular, 'contemplates intrusive involvement in the oversight of a project' in a manner that is 'akin to administration'. See *The Mechanisms of Governance*, above n 27, 567, 579.

[30] Within the latter group are included not only professional and unprofessional (ie trade) debt investors, but also human capital investors (ie employees).

[31] In this context, the term 'ownership' is deployed in a purely technical sense to denote the purported status of equity investors as exclusive collective bearers of the residual risk of firm underperformance or failure. It thus does not seek directly to infer or convey any of the moral-political qualities associated with property ownership in the traditional sense of the term (although it may, of course, have the indirect or unintended effect of doing so). For an authoritative examination of these broader dimensions of the concept of ownership, see AM Honore, 'Ownership' in AG Guest, *Oxford Essays in Jurisprudence* (Oxford, Clarendon Press, 1961) 107.

for pervasive proprietary powers of direction, appropriation and disposal over the firm as a whole including its unsecured assets and cash flows.[32]

In the corporate[33] setting, however, such structural reciprocity is not present in the equity relation. Indeed, the essence of *corporate* governance as an organisational activity is that it necessarily entails submission by equity investors of executive authority to a substantially autonomous central body (namely the board of directors), which is charged with coordinating the various inputs of external resource providers in pursuit of internally-formulated objectives and strategies.[34] More fundamentally, since independent corporate personhood acts as a formal ownership partition between the respective assets of the corporate entity and its shareholders, the act of *corporate* equity investment consequently demands outright submission by investors of any proprietary entitlement to their capital whether in money or physical asset form.[35] Instead, equity investors acquire the relatively limited and artificially prescribed bundle of rights consequent to their shareholding in the company,[36] with the curious effect that *no one* – except for the corporate entity itself – can be said to own the company in either a juridical or beneficial sense.[37]

[32] Notably, Grossman and Hart draw a distinction between specific contractual rights and open-ended residual rights, with the proprietary rights traditionally afforded to equity falling in the latter category. The authors explain equity's residual rights of control in accordance with the following logic: 'When it is too costly for one party to specify a long list of the particular rights it desires over another's party's assets, it may be optimal for that party to purchase *all the rights except those specifically mentioned in the contract*' (emphasis added). See SJ Grossman and OD Hart, 'The Costs and Benefits of Ownership: A Theory of Vertical and Lateral Integration' (1986) 94 *Journal of Political Economy* 691, 692.

[33] My use of the word 'corporate' in this context – in parallel with the slant of the book as a whole – is used to refer specifically to *public* or widely-held corporations. In private or closely-held incorporated firms, the common dual capacity of equity investors as shareholder-directors, or at least close associates or overseers of management, frequently gives them the effective status of 'quasi-partners' (and thus quasi-owners) irrespective of their formal legal control rights over the firm. This is evidenced, inter alia, by the traditional equitable jurisdiction of the English courts to order the just and equitable winding up of a quasi-partnership company (under what is today section 122(1)(g) of the Insolvency Act 1986) where a shareholder's exclusion from management undermines the fundamental basis of his relationship with the other quasi-partners, irrespective of the parties' formal legal rights *inter se*. See *Ebrahimi v Westbourne Galleries Ltd* [1973] AC 360 (HL).

[34] On this generally, see SM Bainbridge, 'Director Primacy: The Means and Ends of Corporate Governance' (2003) 97 *Northwestern University Law Review* 547.

[35] On the dual corporate legal attributes of 'defensive' and 'affirmative' asset partitioning, see H Hansmann and R Kraakman, 'The Essential Role of Organizational Law' (2000) 110 *Yale Law Journal* 387.

[36] For an influential judicial exposition of the Hohfeldian concept of the corporate share as a 'bundle of rights', see *Borland's Trustee v Steel Bros & Co Ltd* [1901] 1 Ch 279, 288 (Farwell J): 'A share is the interest of a shareholder in the company measured by a sum of money for the purpose of liability in the first place, and of interest in the second, *but also consisting of a series of mutual covenants entered into by all the shareholders inter se* . . . The contract contained in the articles of association is one of the original incidents of the share' (emphasis added).

[37] As the English company lawyer Len Sealy explains, whereas '[a] share in a partnership reflects the partner's proprietary interest in the partnership assets: the assets are jointly owned by the partners . . . [i]n the case of a company, *it is not the shareholders but the company*

It logically follows that no external resource – *even equity* – is legally entitled to usurp the board's constitutional prerogative to control the company's business affairs and transact on its behalf (whether directly or, in the more common case, indirectly by delegated managerial authority), except in the specific ways (if any) that are provided for in advance by the corporate constitution.[38] Indeed, a fundamental trade-off at the heart of any large-scale organisation, including business corporations, is that the freedom of action of the organisation itself is – in large part – contingent on the denial of formal executive influence to individual organisational participants. In other words, corporate autonomy is – by its very nature – paradoxically predicated on the collective *loss of* individual autonomy by corporate resource providers in determining the direction of the enterprise in which their capital is invested.[39] The inherent tension between individual and corporate autonomy stems from the fact that, where bureaucratic scale and complexity render egalitarian methods of rule impractical or inefficient, effective organisational control necessitates prioritising hierarchy over accountability as the principal criterion of governance effectiveness.[40]

Therefore, in contrast to the situation with unincorporated entities, the sacrifice by corporate equity investors of determinative control over their capital is *not* matched by the corresponding acquisition of control over the

that owns the corporate assets, and the concept of a share serves somewhat different functions' (emphasis added). See LS Sealy, *Cases and Materials in Company Law*, 7th edn (London, Butterworths, 2001). For judicial dictum to this effect, see *Short v Treasury Commissioners* [1948] 1 KB 116 (CA) 122 (Evershed LJ): 'shareholders are not, in the eyes of the law, part owners of the undertaking'. See also *Gramophone and Typewriter Co v Stanley* [1908] 2 KB 89; *Macaura v Northern Assurance Co* [1925] AC 619 (HL). Similarly, Paddy Ireland describes a corporate share (from a more critical normative perspective) as 'a particular and distinctive form of money capital; property in the form of a claim on the company's profits'. See P Ireland, 'The Myth of Shareholder Ownership' (1999) 62 *Modern Law Review* 32, 47.

[38] See *Automatic Self-Cleansing Filter Syndicate Co v Cunninghame* [1906] 2 Ch 34 (CA); *John Shaw & Sons Ltd v Shaw* [1935] 2 KB 113. The US corporate lawyers Margaret Blair and Lynn Stout have exploited this legal feature of the corporation as the basis for their influential 'team production' theory of the firm, which essentially portrays the corporate board as a 'neutral mediating hierarch' – entrusted with the responsibility of combining and compensating the respective productive inputs of a corporation's various resource-providers (including shareholders, creditors and employees) on a centralised discretionary basis, and in a way that is calculated to maximise the overall wealth-creating capacity of the business entity for the mutual benefit of its participants as a whole. See M Blair and LA Stout, 'A Team Production Theory of Corporate Law' (1999) 85 *Virginia Law Review* 248. Notwithstanding the undoubted normative appeal of Blair and Stout's model, whether it provides an accurate *descriptive* representation of the existing framework of US corporate law is arguably questionable. On this, see Bainbridge, *Director Primacy*, above n 34, 592–605.

[39] Adolf Berle explained how an individual citizen, if and to the extent that he agrees to subject himself to the command structure of an organisation, in effect yields to the central source of that organisational power 'some part of his individual freedom to do as he pleases'. See Berle, *Power Without Property*, above n 12, 81.

[40] On this, see SM Bainbridge, 'Director Primacy', above n 34, 1745–47; KJ Arrow, *The Limits of Organization* (New York, Norton, 1974) 68–70. For a further discussion of this issue, see below ch 3 of this volume, fns 69–71 and accompanying text.

productive enterprise in which their invested capital is mobilised. The consequent incapacity of equity investors to constrain the exercise of the board's managerial prerogative whether contractually or hierarchically means that – in contrast to other corporate resource providers – equity investors are *entirely subjected* to the discretionary administrative power of the corporation and its controlling officers. The effect is to render the corporate equity relation uniquely indeterminate and vulnerable from the investor's perspective insofar as both the rate of return on equity, and also the uses to which such capital is put, are inherently uncertain and susceptible to ongoing variation by management on a unilateral (ie non-negotiated) basis.[41]

D. The Legal Foundations of Power Imbalance in the Corporate Equity Relation

Both the allocative and appropriative dimensions of the DAP possessed by a corporation vis-à-vis its equity investors are attributable to the corporation's unique structural characteristic of centralised board decision-making. This feature is in its turn principally dependent on two fundamental and interlocking corporate law principles.

The first of these is the principle of board primacy,[42] which entitles the board of directors (or, more commonly, its managerial delegates) to make executive policy decisions with respect to the internal allocation of corporate cash flows unimpeded by interference from shareholders or other 'outside' parties. The second such principle is that of board control over corporate dividends, whereby the board of directors is vested with exclusive constitutional power to set the uppermost limit on the extent to which the corporation's periodic profits will be distributed to shareholders, as opposed to being appropriated by management internally in the form of retained earnings.

---

[41] Moreover, to the extent that an ordinary shareholder's expected rate of return on equity is contingent on the prospect of capitalising future cash flows 'externally' via disposal of her investment on a liquid securities market, rather than on appropriating current cash flows 'internally' via receipt of profit distributions, the degree of reciprocal imbalance in the equity relation is further exacerbated. Berle and Means regarded this phenomenon as the basis of shareholders' effective structural externalisation from the public corporation. See AA Berle and G Means, *The Modern Corporation and Private Property*, revised 4th edn (New York, Harcourt, Brace & World, 1968) (first published 1932) 247–48.

[42] I have deliberately used the term 'board primacy' in distinction from Stephen Bainbridge's term 'director primacy'. However, both terms should be regarded as essentially equivalent in meaning. I deviate from Professor Bainbridge with respect to terminology in the personal belief that the former term better depicts the collective (as opposed to individual) nature of the executive decision-making authority that is vested in corporate directors. On Bainbridge's concept of director primacy, see 'Director Primacy', above n 40.

Under the law of the US State of Delaware, where the majority of larger listed US corporations are registered, the executive primacy of the board is established by section 141 of the State General Corporation Law, which affirms that '[t]he business and affairs of every corporation . . . shall be managed by or under the direction of a board of directors'.[43] The same basic position is established within UK company law by article 3 of the governmentally-prescribed Model Articles, which provides that '[s]ubject to the articles, the directors are responsible for the management of the company's business, for which purpose they may exercise all the powers of the company'.[44] Under the law of both the above jurisdictions, moreover, the board's supreme managerial function is constituted not just as a responsibility but, more significantly, as a constitutional *right* (or, more accurately, a set of constitutionally guaranteed powers) that is consequently defensible by the board against any outside party or group – including equity – which seeks to challenge or displace the board's executive prerogative in any regard.[45]

Within the traditional US legal model of corporate governance, the principle of board primacy is carried to its logical extreme insofar as the board's powers are, at common law, deemed to be 'original and undelegated . . . in the sense of being received from the State in the act of incorporation'.[46] According to this logic, 'the individual directors making up the board are not mere employees, but [rather are] a part of an elected body of officers constituting the executive agents of the corporation'.[47] Furthermore, a company's constitutional charter is purportedly vested with the force of law by virtue of the act of incorporation alone, with the effect that the corporate governance arrangements established in the charter – as supplemented by generally applicable corporate laws – are perceived to emanate directly from the State as the formal grantor of corporate status.[48] It follows that, insofar as the corporate charter and general

---

[43] Delaware General Corporation Law, § 141(a).

[44] The Companies (Model Articles) Regulations 2008 (SI 2008/3229) Sch 3 ('Model Articles for Public Companies') art 3.

[45] On this, see the sources cited above n 38.

[46] *Hoyt v Thompson's Executor* 19 NY 207, 216 (1859) (Court of Appeals of New York) (Comstock J). Judge Comstock further emphasised (ibid) that '[t]he recognition of this principle is absolutely necessary in the affairs of every corporation whose powers are vested in a board of directors. Without it the most ordinary business could not be carried on, and the corporate powers could not be executed'.

[47] *People ex rel Manice v Powell* 201 NY 194, 201 (1911) (Court of Appeals of New York) (Chase J).

[48] Underlying this position is the traditional adherence of US courts to the so-called 'concession' theory of corporate law, whereby the (state-derived) act of incorporation, rather than (contractually-derived) act of initial business association, is regarded as the principal factor to which the legal existence of the corporation is attributable. On this generally, see WW Bratton, 'The New Economic Theory of the Firm: Critical Perspectives from History' (1989) 41 *Stanford Law Review* 1471; Parkinson, *Corporate Power and Responsibility*, above n 4, 25–32.

law (at individual State level) vest executive authority for the running of the business in the hands of a company's board (as opposed to its shareholders), then the board's constitutional discretion over executive affairs can be regarded as sovereign and absolute, subject only to compliance with minimal fiduciary standards of honesty, loyalty and decision-making rationality (what in US corporate law jurisprudence is known as 'the business judgment rule'[49]).[50]

Thus shareholders of Delaware corporations, inter alia, have no right to give any legally binding directions – whether specific or general – to the board regarding the running of the business,[51] or to acquire any broader constitutional authority over managerial affairs absent the assent thereto of the board itself.[52] More fundamentally, section 141 arguably establishes the

[49] For an examination of this important legal doctrine from the perspective of the thesis in this book, see below ch 4 of this volume, pt IV. For a general critical rationalisation of the rule, see SM Bainbridge, 'The Business Judgment Rule as Abstention Doctrine' (2004) 57 *Vanderbilt Law Review* 83.

[50] The early doctrinal evolution of the board primacy principle in the above sense was effected by the New York Court of Appeals in a line of landmark nineteenth-century decisions (on which, see above nn 46–47 and accompanying text; see also *Olcott v Tioga Railroad Co* 27 NY 546 (1863); *Continental Securities Co v Belmont* 206 NY 7 (1912)). Moreover, with the subsequent rise to prominence of New Jersey – and, latterly, Delaware – as the country's corporate law jurisdiction of choice, the board primacy principle was further developed throughout the twentieth century so as to extend considerably the scope of boards' exclusive executive prerogative. On this, see Bowman, *The Modern Corporation*, above n 4, 131–32; GC Lodge, *The New American Ideology* (New York, Knopf, 1975) 135. In consequence, the board primacy principle as constituted under Delaware law today applies not just to strategic or operational matters, but also to more fundamental structural concerns including the initiation of charter amendments and the issuance of new corporate stock including voting equity capital. The latter dimension of the doctrine is particularly problematic from a political perspective, in that it effectively empowers directors – within the wide ambit of their fiduciary capacity – to influence the distribution of shareholder voting power on which their continuing constitutional entitlement to hold office depends. This significantly limits the democratic force of the shareholder franchise by providing scope for managerial self-perpetuation, even in situations (such as a contest for corporate control) where the a priori balance of shareholder opinion may be overall averse to the prospect of an incumbent board remaining in office. On the regulation of managerial takeover defences under Delaware law, see below ch 4 of this volume, pt V.C. On the contrasting British approach towards regulating so-called 'stock dilution' tactics by corporate managers, see below ch 5 of this volume, pt III.D.

[51] On the contrasting position of UK corporate law in this regard, see the Model Articles, above n 44, art 4.

[52] See LA Bebchuk, 'The Case for Increasing Shareholder Power' (2005) 118 *Harvard Law Review* 833, 844–45. While shareholders admittedly have joint authority (alongside the board) under Delaware law to initiate changes to the corporation's bylaws, the necessary invalidity of any bylaw provisions that contradict the superseding charter of incorporation (which only the board may initiate amendments to) renders this power of limited practical effectiveness. See section 109(b) of the Delaware General Corporation Law, which provides that '[t]he bylaws may contain any provision, *not inconsistent with law or with the certificate of incorporation*, relating to the business of the corporation, the conduct of its affairs, and its rights or powers or the rights or powers of its stockholders, directors, officers or employees' (emphasis added). On this, see Bebchuk, ibid, 845. In light of such considerations, Adolf Berle remarked in a still highly relevant passage from *Power Without Property* that shareholders 'have the right to receive only. The condition of their being is that they do not interfere in management. Neither in law nor, as a rule, in fact do they have that capacity'. See above n 12, 74.

board's executive prerogative as an inalienable phenomenon, meaning that shareholders are necessarily precluded from revoking the board's decision-making supremacy within the corporate-organisational hierarchy.[53]

Therefore, whereas in unincorporated firms, equity has hierarchical superiority over (delegated) management; in Delaware corporations, this lexical order is reversed so that equity is hierarchically subordinated to the board, with the latter constituting the supreme executive and rule-making organ within the corporate-constitutional framework, and the former representing little more than an economic functionary with no 'sovereign' governance status.[54] Moreover, as a result of Delaware law's underlying presumption in favour of management control, the board – and, indirectly, its managerial delegates – are in effect vested 'by default' with any corporate functions or powers not specifically reserved for shareholders.[55]

It is thus arguable that residual legal 'ownership' of US corporations – if it can be said to rest with any particular constituency – resides squarely in *the board* (and, indirectly, senior management) rather than the shareholders.[56] This position is, of course, contrary to the orthodox portrayal of equity's formal status within the firm as expounded within law and finance literature.[57] And, significantly for present purposes, it serves to highlight the extensive degree of discretionary administrative power with which US boards – and, in turn, managers – are formally vested in allocating equity as a corporate resource.

---

[53] Delaware's extensive regulatory disempowerment of shareholders in the above respects has been rationalised judicially by recourse to the so-called 'cardinal precept . . . that directors, rather than shareholders, manage the business and affairs of the corporation'. See *Aranson v Lewis* [1984] 473 A 2d 805 (Del) 811. The modern Delaware approach to this matter would appear to be inspired by the preceding New York judicial position to the effect that '[t]he board of directors [and not the general body of shareholders] represent the corporate body', so that 'recommendations by a body of stockholders can only be enforced through the board of directors [itself], and indirectly by the authority of the stockholders to change the personnel of the directors at a meeting for the election of directors'. See *Continental Securities Co v Belmont*, above n 50, 16 (Chase J).

[54] In addition to their structural exclusion from managerial affairs in the above ways, shareholders moreover have no legally guaranteed power under Delaware law to remove directors without cause before expiration of office. Rather, the 'default' statutory right that shareholders enjoy in this regard can be disapplied (or 'opted out of') by a corporation on the voluntary classification of its board. The effect is to render the directors of many Delaware corporations formally irremovable throughout the period of their official tenure. On this, see ch 4 of the volume, pt II.

[55] On the development of US (and particularly Delaware) corporate law's general presumption in favour of managerial (over shareholder) control, see Bowman, *The Modern Corporation*, above n 6, ch 3.

[56] Indeed, Berle and Means inferred this very point back in 1932, claiming that the 'traditional logic of profits' supports distribution of residual firm wealth to *management* (rather than shareholders), in order to induce the continuing efficient use of the company's capital. See *The Modern Corporation and Private Property*, above n 41, 302. See also Moore and Reberioux, 'Revitalizing the Institutional Roots', above n 6, 94.

[57] See, eg the sources cited in nn 27–32 above.

The British legal model of corporate governance is commonly portrayed as being much more shareholder-centric than its US counterpart, and in some specific regulatory respects (which will be examined in chapter six below) this is undoubtedly true. However, the most fundamental conceptual difference between the two systems is the fact that, under UK corporate law, the corporate constitution – including any corporate governance arrangements established therein – is vested with the formal status of a private (and thus alterable) contractual agreement binding together a company's 'members' or shareholders.[58]

Prima facie, the exclusive quasi-membership entitlement of shareholders to act as signatories to the notional corporate-constitutional 'contract' might be thought to confer a corresponding degree of hierarchical supremacy over a company's controlling officers. However, the foundational English case law on the division of corporate decision-making power makes clear that the legal relationship between a company's shareholders and board of directors is a reciprocal one between contracting equals, as opposed to a hierarchical relation founded on any sense of either group – whether shareholders or the board – enjoying constitutional supremacy over the other.[59]

This position was put most emphatically by Greer LJ in *John Shaw & Sons v Shaw*, who explained the doctrinal nature of the board primacy principle at common law in the following (resolutely *non*-hierarchical) terms:

> [i]f powers of management are vested in the directors, they and they alone can exercise those powers. The only way in which the general body of shareholders can control the exercise of the powers vested by the articles in the directors is by altering the articles, or, if the opportunity arises under the articles, by refusing to re-elect the directors of whose actions they disapprove. *They cannot themselves usurp the powers which by the articles are vested in the directors any more than the directors can usurp the powers vested by the articles in the general body of shareholders* (emphasis added).[60]

It follows that shareholders have no subjective power over the corporation or its management under English law, in the sense of any general capacity to demand deference to their expressed interests.[61] On the con-

---

[58] See the Companies Act 2006, s 33. For a theoretical analysis of the contractual principle in UK corporate law, including its implications for corporate governance, see below ch 5 of this volume, pt I.

[59] For an examination of the principal authorities to this effect, see below ch 5 of this volume, pt II.B.

[60] *John Shaw & Sons v Shaw* [1935] 2 KB 113, 134.

[61] It may be argued that managerial deference to shareholders' interests is compelled by the director's general statutory duty of loyalty under section 172 of the Companies Act 2006, which requires directors to promote the success of their employer company for the benefit of its shareholders as a whole. However, the duty of loyalty – like all directors' general duties – operates exclusively on an ex post facto basis as a response to conduct already committed

trary, UK corporate law – like its Delaware counterpart – ultimately affirms the discretionary administrative power of the board (and, indirectly, management) by establishing that shareholders are, in the ordinary course of things,[62] formally *subject to* the executive prerogative of the board with respect to the allocation of corporate cash flows – including externally invested equity – in the service of centrally determined organisational objectives.[63]

Accordingly, whereas in the United States – as explained above – management's allocative power vis-à-vis equity derives at root from the board's exclusive and statutorily-entrenched prerogative over internal corporate affairs; in the United Kingdom, by comparison, such power is understood to derive from the notional mutual agreement of shareholders and directors regarding the proper allocation of decision-making powers within the corporate-constitutional framework. Structurally, however, the basic doctrinal result – namely *board primacy* – is the same in both environments.[64]

The board primacy doctrine is supplemented and reinforced by the second major legal principle underpinning DAP in the corporate equity relation, which is the principle of board control over corporate dividends. This latter principle is the doctrinal source of the board's traditional and continuing authority to divert corporate cash flows to capital accumulation, most notably via unilateral retention of dividends. As such, it represents – in conjunction with the more general board primacy doctrine – the formal foundation of the significant *appropriative* power that exists in the corporate equity relation.

Under Delaware law, the board is vested with ultimate constitutional control over the declaration and payment of dividends as a default statutory rule, with the effect that shareholders have no formal power to displace directors' collective determination in these regards.[65] While UK law by contrast vests the default power to declare dividends in the shareholders by way of ordinary resolution, any resolution to declare a dividend is necessarily contingent on the board first recommending the amount of dividend that is to be declared.[66] Crucially, shareholders are in the ordinary course of things prohibited from declaring a dividend higher than the amount that is recommended by the directors.[67] The effect of the above

or proposed by directors, and in any event defers wide subjective discretion on the board (and, indirectly, management) in conducting the company's business affairs.

[62] That is, at least pending usurpation of the board's managerial powers by collective amendment of the articles under section 21 of the Companies Act 2006, which in a public company is both highly impractical and also counter to the basic logic of the corporation as a business entity characterised by centralised control and oversight. On the technical possibility of this occurrence, see below ch 5 of this volume, fns 11–12 and accompanying text.

[63] See Moore and Reberioux, 'Revitalizing the Institutional Roots', above n 6, 97–99.

[64] Ibid, 99.

[65] Delaware General Corporation Law, § 170(a).

[66] Model Articles, above n 44, art 70(2).

[67] Ibid.

provision is that, in virtually all US and UK public corporations, share-holders are formally excluded from the important periodic decision as to whether a company's free cash flow should be retained and reinvested within the business internally, or else distributed to shareholders for sub-sequent reinvestment or consumption on a macro (ie economy-wide) level. This is the essence of the appropriative power phenomenon as it operates within the wider social context.[68]

The concept of appropriate power has historically been the most con-spicuous and, consequently, controversial dimension of DAP within the corporate decision-making framework. One of the most noted critics of this aspect of corporate power was Adolf Berle, who observed that its effect is to vest a company's directors with unchecked discretion over 'whether and to what extent its profits shall be distributed, and to what extent these profits shall be dedicated to capital formation'.[69] The most worrying implication of appropriative power, according to Berle, is its tendency to permit 'perpetual accumulation' by corporations with 'no top limit' thereon.[70] Berle described the practice of discretionary corporate

---

[68] It may be argued in response to this claim that, over recent decades, managers' de facto control over the corporate distributional process has been mitigated significantly following the development – and subsequent practical implementation within corporations – of free cash flow theory. This influential neo-liberal doctrine, associated most commonly with the work of the financial economist Michael Jensen, emphasises the important role of dividends, share repurchases and debt finance as governance mechanisms, and advances the external capital markets as disciplinary mechanisms for reducing managerial control (or 'slack') over internal corporate earnings. The essential claim is that, in firms that commit to high financial-distribution schedules in either or all of the above ways, managers will continually be compelled to 'disgorge' cash reserves in excess of immediate needs in order to satisfy the expectations of outside capital providers. The ultimate effect is to render corporate managers subject to the control and imperatives of the market at all times, even in situations where resort to external capital is not necessary to sustain the continuing operations of the firm. See MC Jensen, 'Agency Costs of Free Cash Flow, Corporate Finance, and Takeovers' (1986) 76 *American Economic Review* 323; FH Easterbrook, 'Two Agency-Cost Explanations of Dividends' (1984) 74 *The American Economic Review* 650 (however, for a critical perspective on this school of thought, see W Lazonick, 'The Quest for Shareholder Value: Stock Repurchases in the United States' (2008) 74 *Louvain Economic Review* 479). On the basis of the above logic, it may thus be concluded that managers' discretionary administrative power vis-à-vis shareholders has been substantially eradicated in the modern financial-capitalist era. However, the flaw in this argument is its failure to take into account the nature of corporate cash flow distributions as *a source of corporate-managerial power in itself* – that is to say, a source of what John Kenneth Galbraith has termed 'compensatory power' – ie the power that a person or organisation enjoys in effect to 'buy' the submission of others to their personal or economic purposes. In the corporate financing scenario, management's extensive access to retained earnings permits its use of corporate funds (in the form of internally-determined levels of dividend and/or share repurchase) to cause shareholders to continue in future to submit their capital under managerial control on unspecified terms and for an unspecified return. The fact that share-holders have other investment opportunities available to them reduces the extent of the com-pensatory power that any individual firm enjoys over them, but nevertheless it does not negate the existence of this type of power in itself, which is a common structural feature of large corporations in general. On the notion of compensatory power generally, see Galbraith, *The Anatomy of Power*, above n 14, ch 5.

[69] Berle, *Power Without Property*, above n 12, 52.

[70] Ibid.

earnings retention as a form of 'forced savings' imposed by managers on both shareholders and consumers (to whom the benefits of corporate profitability are consequently not passed on), which is tantamount to 'a sales tax whose proceeds were ticketed for capital expansion of the corporation' without prior public consultation.[71]

II. THE STRUCTURAL IMPERATIVE OF LEGITIMATING CORPORATE-MANAGERIAL POWER

A. The Centrality of Power-Legitimacy in Sustaining Power Imbalance

In any organisation where the power of senior office-holders rests on the consent of the direct subjects of that power, the formal accountability of office-holders to subjects is of key importance in securing the *legitimacy* of the former group's possession and exercise of executive power. 'Legitimacy' is understood here to denote a general and inherent quality of public 'rightness'.

In the context of social organisations and power structures (including business corporations), such rightness derives from a popular understanding 'that the holders of power are considered by the community to be justified in their tenure of it', so that 'the system conforms to the general consensus on a moral base'.[72] Basic social contract logic dictates that the holder of power should not be free to exercise it in her own interest, but rather in the interests of those affected by it. Hence the distinctive feature of a non-totalitarian governance system is that the centralisation of power, which is necessary for administrative efficiency, is counterbalanced by 'checks' placed on that power.[73]

Where the use of power is subjected, by appropriate institutional checks, to the collective will of the subjects of that power, the resulting governance framework can be referred to – in the words of the liberal

---

[71] Berle, *Power Without Property*, above n 12, 148. Berle noted the fundamental parallels between this process and the system of arbitrary conscription of productive capital by the state in the command economy of the Soviet Union. However, he believed that in the American system, the process of 'capital gathering . . . is better since the taking is painless, is acquiesced in, and provides comfortably for future development, while the Soviet system is obviously marred by compulsion' (ibid, 151). Moreover, it may be said that in instances where retained earnings are dedicated not to capital formation but rather to other more socially objectionable forms of corporate expenditure (eg managerial enrichment or 'empire building'), the politically problematic character of the practice is exacerbated. This is because, in such cases, the community is effectively being 'taxed' for the support of activities or projects that – unlike industrial capital formation – it cannot be said to have acquiesced in even in the broadest possible sense, thereby establishing a material democratic deficit at the level of society as a whole.

[72] AA Berle, *The American Economic Republic* (New York, Harcourt, Brace & World, 1963) 42.

[73] Moore and Reberioux, 'Revitalizing the Institutional Roots', above n 6, 94.

political philosopher Alan Gewirth – as a 'hierarchy of authority'.[74] That is to say, the possession and exercise of discretionary administrative power is legitimately authorised – or at least widely acquiesced in – by those who are principally affected by it.[75] It follows that the individual contractual autonomy or freedom[76] of those subject to the relevant power is not undermined, or – at least – where it is, any such loss of autonomy can be regarded as a generally acceptable trade-off for the material benefits that follow from submission to the authority structure in question. Consequently in such cases, organisational and individual autonomy can legitimately (and thus feasibly) co-exist even though the pursuit of collective corporate objectives will inevitably entail curtailment of the pursuit of individual goals by the subjects of authority.

On the other hand, where these conditions are in large part absent from an organisation's governance framework, the organisation in question is more appropriately termed a 'hierarchy of power'.[77] In such instances, the absence of subordinate authorisation for the possession and exercise of power by senior office-holders means that the latter's position and privileges are incapable of deriving legitimacy from representational criteria.[78] Accordingly, the dual phenomena of organisational and individual autonomy will be incapable of co-existing in a legitimate manner, insofar as sacrifice of individual freedom of action will be widely regarded as an

---

[74] See A Gewirth, *The Community of Rights* (Chicago IL, University of Chicago Press, 1996) 271.

[75] Ibid. This institutional characteristic is most clearly manifested in liberal-democratic political systems, where the dual phenomena of free contested elections and the rule of law ensure that incumbent office-holders' lack determinative control over their successors to government, and also over the constitutionally established scope of their executive powers – both of which are, in the last place, determined at the collective behest of citizens.

[76] My understanding of the often-nebulous term 'freedom' in this context is premised on Gewirth's understanding of freedom as individual autonomy. In Gewirthian political philosophy, freedom is explained as a logically necessary precondition of action and successful action in general as a prospective purposive agent. Accordingly 'all persons have a generic right to freedom, which consists in controlling one's behavior by one's unforced choice while having knowledge of relevant circumstances'. See Gewirth, *The Community of Rights*, above n 74, 18–19, 266. Admittedly, this very short summary can in no way do justice to the intellectual richness and complexity of Gewirth's theory of rights and his Principle of Generic Consistency (PGC).

[77] Ibid.

[78] This is on the commonly-held understanding within liberal-democratic political economies that '[p]ower (aside from its crude or brute form) cannot exist apart from some idea or principle justifying it and, therefore, entitling holders of it to expect allegiance and cooperation'. See Berle, *Power Without Property*, above n 12, 100. However, this is notwithstanding the fact that, within *non*-representational governance frameworks, popular elections may comprise at least a nominal part of the formal leadership selection process and a formal source of the system's public legitimacy. A notable example of this is the political system of the People's Republic of China, whereby the principle of universal franchise is constitutionally guaranteed in form, albeit substantially meaningless in practice given the ruling Communist Party's pervasive control over the electoral process.

unjustifiable concession on the part of those subject to the unauthorised power in question.

Crucially, the fact that a particular organisational power structure may, as a matter of fact, be overall efficient or utility-maximising from an economic point of view does not eliminate the possibility that its conditions may still fail to secure the acquiescence of those directly subject to the relevant power.[79] On the assumption that organisational participants operate under conditions of bounded rationality (and consequent informational incompleteness), there will inevitably be an informational disparity between 'inside' (managerial) office-holders and (non-managerial) 'outsiders' insofar as the former group – by virtue of its innate positional advantage – will have greater access than the latter group to organisation-relevant knowledge and expertise. This renders it impossible for outsider participants to determine reliably whether their submission to internal organisational goals represents an acceptable price to pay in return for the material benefits that are expected to flow from organisational membership. It follows that some degree of formal accountability (or checks) on the exercise of executive power is an essential structural precondition to securing widespread membership 'buy-in' to the ensuing power imbalance, in the absence of complete or equal informational access between organisational participants.[80]

[79] Parkinson has noted the traditional idea that 'corporate decision-making power should be accepted as the price of efficient wealth creation', which infers that 'if we [as a society] want the benefits of efficient wealth creation it must be acknowledged that companies will inevitably possess power'. At the same time, though, Parkinson has observed that 'at least beyond a certain level of prosperity, increases in wealth do not compensate for, cannot be traded-off against, the accumulation of power'. This is because '[t]he corollary of the possession of power by companies is that [those] affected by it suffer a lack of control over the conditions which determine how they live their lives'. According to Parkinson, '[an] alternative vision of human flourishing to that which underlies wealth maximization as a social goal ranks *autonomy* above continued increases in material well-being, and thus calls into question the legitimacy of non-participative organisations' (emphasis added). See Parkinson, *Corporate Power and Responsibility*, above n 4, 48–50. Writing over three decades earlier, Adolf Berle made a similar point in observing that '[a]lmost inevitably, in the end, all societies will demand organization of power sufficient to realize the economic potential. The issue is whether they will also demand self-restraint and guidance of that power sufficient to permit the self-determination of men'. See *Power Without Property*, above n 12, 158.

[80] In this regard, Bowman has observed (writing in the context of US society) that '[t]he conception of *balance* as a remedy for concentrated power permeates the fabric of American institutions and informs the distinctive development of American liberalism'. The logic of Madisonian Republicanism dictates that, so long as organisational power is politically 'checked' by a 'systemic balance of forces' to prevent it from straying out of its proper functional bounds, such power can be exercised both legitimately *and* largely autonomously within those bounds – thus functioning in effect as a form of 'limited oligarchy' (emphasis added). On this, see Bowman, *The Modern Corporation*, above n 6, 217.

B. Cost of Capital as the Principal Criterion of Managerial Power-Legitimacy

In the democratic governmental context, the legitimacy of senior executive office-holders' continuing possession and exercise of discretionary administrative power (what may be referred to in shorthand as 'executive power-legitimacy') is, in general, manifested in their popular mandate to hold office as reflected in periodic election outcomes and ongoing opinion polls. Vice versa, revocation of the mandate to govern is manifested in the withdrawal of public support for incumbent office-holders, which renders their continuing possession and exercise of executive power normatively unsustainable.

However, given the general informational disparity between governmental and non-governmental actors, and the resultant incapacity of 'outsider' citizens or representatives to exert effective control over the executive allocation of public revenue streams via executive appointment alone; it follows that other supplementary accountability (or checking) mechanisms are called for in order to secure the continuing acquiescence of citizens in the centralised possession and exercise of discretionary administrative power within the state-organisational framework. Hence the preponderance of transparency requirements, committee structures and other formalised review mechanisms, which have the collective effect of ensuring that, in any developed democratic state, public-governmental powers are possessed and exercised in a manner that – broadly speaking – is acquiesced in by the subject citizenry as a whole.

In the corporate context, meanwhile, executive power-legitimacy is, in general, manifested in a criterion that can crudely be termed 'cost of capital'. For the purpose of the argument at hand, cost of capital should be understood as denoting the general willingness of outside investors to purchase a firm's securities (especially equity) on primary and secondary markets. Such willingness is contingent not just on the perceived risk-adjusted return that an investor expects to make by purchasing the firm's securities, but also on the opportunity cost of that investment: that is, the return that an investor expects to receive from an alternative investment at the same price and with the same risk exposure. It follows that the firm (or, specifically, its management), by reducing the perceived risk exposure of its securities (all other factors being equal) will effect a reduction in its cost of capital insofar as an alternative lower-risk investment will have lower projected net returns than an alternative higher-risk investment (after accounting for risk), thereby increasing the relative attractiveness of the firm's securities and – in turn – the market valuation of its equity.[81]

---

[81] On this concept generally, see F Modigliani and M Miller, 'The Cost of Capital, Corporation Finance and the Theory of Investment' (1958) 48 *American Economic Review* 261.

To the extent that the continuing survival of a firm is ordinarily contingent to some extent on access to outside investment, maintaining a low cost of capital can be regarded as a central managerial goal in its own right. However, cost of capital is for the most part a means to an end from managers' perspective, in that an exceptionally low demand for a particular firm's securities – and the consequent devaluation in equity that this entails – can prompt the displacement of the incumbent management team via revocation of its continuing investor license to hold office (as manifested most typically in the case of a proxy contest aimed at ousting the incumbent board of directors).[82]

Given the inherent informational disparity between managerial and non-managerial actors, outside investors are generally incapable of exerting effective control over the executive allocation of *private* revenue streams via securities selection (coupled with occasional managerial displacement) alone.[83] It follows that other supplementary accountability (or checking) mechanisms are called for in order to ensure the continuing acquiescence of investors (and, in particular, equity) in the centralised possession and exercise of discretionary administrative power within the *corporate*-organisational framework. Hence the extensive collection of legal governance mechanisms that will be discussed in chapter six below, which have the collective effect of ensuring that, in any capitalistic corporate enterprise, *private*-governmental powers are possessed and exercised by managers in a manner that – broadly speaking – is acquiesced in by the subject shareholders as a whole.

As the following discussion will show, in order to secure the legitimacy – and corresponding acquiescence of equity investors – in the continuing possession and exercise of DAP by management, the key quality that a corporate governance system must engender is *accountability*. That is to say, managers must be continuously and formally called upon to give an account of themselves to those who are directly subject to their executive power (namely shareholders), as a precondition to obtaining the latter's acquiescence in the underlying power imbalance inter se.

Of course, greater managerial accountability – absent other factors – will not in itself engender enhanced corporate performance, or eliminate scope for managerial diminution of shareholder wealth in other ways. The key

---

[82] On this, see HG Manne, 'Mergers and the Market for Corporate Control' (1965) 73 *Journal of Political Economy* 110.

[83] The body of literature on the informational limitations of securities markets is voluminous, and the structural limitations of securities markets as a medium for generating and reflecting firm-relevant information are widely accepted today by scholars. See, eg A Shleifer, *Inefficient Markets: An Introduction to Behavioral Finance* (Oxford, Oxford University Press, 2000); RJ Shiller, *Irrational Exuberance*, 2nd edn (Princeton, Princeton University Press, 2012); LA Stout, 'The Mechanisms of Market Inefficiency' (2005) 14 *Journal of Financial Transformation* 95.

point, however, is that where bounded rationality[84] inhibits the capacity of outside investors to evaluate the diversity of variables determining the overall riskiness of a firm's securities, the *accountability* of its senior executive office-holders is likely to be perceived as an important – albeit imperfect – bulwark against misappropriation or wastage of shareholder wealth. At the very least, formal accountability serves to legitimate the basic structure of the equity relation within any corporation, which – as explained above – is essential to the firm's ongoing capacity to raise and allocate capital on terms that – prima facie at least – are fundamentally deteriorative of the continuing contractual autonomy of external equity providers.

C. Accountability as the Key Factor in Legitimating Power Imbalance

Accountability has been described as 'one of the most powerful symbols in modern politics and administration',[85] and – more fundamentally – as something intrinsic to the moral character of a human being.[86] Understood in its simplest and most general sense, accountability entails 'the giving and demanding of reasons for conduct',[87] and as such is 'a chronic feature of daily conduct'[88] derived from the innate nature of human beings as 'reason seeking / giving animals'.[89] A relationship of accountability by definition involves at least two actors (namely the account-giver and account-recipient(s)), and the key relational quality of accountability practices are their intended effect in enabling the 'settling up or getting right' of a matter between the account-giver and account recipient(s).[90]

[84] On the dual concepts of bounded rationality and inherent uncertainty as developed within behavioural economics literature generally: see HA Simon, 'Theories of Decision-Making in Economics and Behavioral Science' (1959) 49 *American Economic Review* 253; AA Alchian, 'Uncertainty, Evolution, and Economic Theory' (1950) 58 *Journal of Political Economy* 211; Williamson, *The Mechanisms of Governance*, above n 27, 55–57.

[85] MJ Dubnick and HG Frederickson, *Public Accountability: Performance Measurement, the Extended State, and the Search for Trust* (Dayton OH, The Kettering Foundation, 2011) 3.

[86] In his *Theory of Moral Sentiments* (1759, III, 1), Adam Smith famously proclaimed that '[a] moral being is an accountable being' (cited in Dubnick and Frederickson, above n 85, 52). As interpreted by Dubnick and Frederickson, 'Smith believed that any and all social interaction is judged not only by an individual's immediate self-interest, but also by the judgments of an "impartial spectator" that inhabits one's character' (ibid, 52–53).

[87] J Roberts and R Scapens, 'Accounting Systems and Systems of Accountability – Understanding Accounting Practices in their Organisational Contexts' (1985) 10 *Accounting, Organizations & Society* 443, 447. On this, see also A Sinclair, 'The Chameleon of Accountability: Forms and Discourses' (1995) 20 *Accounting, Organizations & Society* 219.

[88] A Giddens, *Central Problems in Social Theory: Action, Structure, and Contradiction in Social Analysis* (Berkeley CA, University of California Press, 1991) 57; cited in Roberts and Scapens, above n 87, 448.

[89] Quote from well-known American sociologist Professor Charles Tilly, cited in MJ Dubnick, '*Sarbanes-Oxley* and the Search for Accountable Corporate Governance' in J O'Brien (ed), *Private Equity, Corporate Governance and the Dynamics of Capital Market Regulation* (London, Imperial College Press, 2007) ch 9, 246.

[90] Dubnick and Frederickson, *Public Accountability*, above n 85, 3.

In this regard, an 'account' is – essentially – 'a statement made by a social actor to explain unanticipated or untoward behavior – whether that behavior is his own or that of others'.[91] An account can take one of two basic forms, namely either a *justification*, in which 'one accepts responsibility for the act in question, but denies the pejorative quality associated with it; or, alternatively, an *excuse*, whereby 'one admits that the act in question is bad, wrong, or inappropriate but denies full responsibility'.[92] Where an account is 'honoured' (ie accepted as reasonable by the account-recipient), its effect is to restore 'equilibrium' in a relationship, thereby ensuring that the relevant relationship is preserved (at least for the time being).[93]

The most direct and conspicuous form of reason-giving in society is what the sociologist Melvin Dubnick has termed 'performative accountability'. This involves 'explicit and direct acts of account giving' between two or more parties, usually via 'the social act of 'reason giving' and 'as a functional and appropriate reaction to some error or faux pas'.[94] However, Dubnick has observed that, in practice, most forms of accountability instead take the form of 'presumptive accountability'.[95] This means that they 'occur *in anticipation* . . . *of* the need or requirement to engage in performative accountability' (emphasis added).[96] As such they are geared to pre-empting the performative accountability stage, via a potential account-giver taking appropriate remedial action to resolve the supposed concerns of the prospective account-recipient(s) in advance of being called to account by them directly.

It has been observed that 'modern governance – public as well as private – is at its core based on some form of accountability [in the above sense]'.[97] Drawing on historical evidence of the governance of embryonic nation-states in the late mediaeval period, Dubnick has observed that – from a governance perspective – the principal value of accountability processes resides in their capacity to enable rulers 'to maintain and sustain authority over autonomous subjects who were becoming increasingly aware of [the rulers'] capacity for discretionary action'.[98] In other words, formal accountability processes evolved historically as a natural counterbalance to discretionary administrative power, and as an essential means

---

[91] MB Scott and SM Lyman, 'Accounts' (1968) 33 *American Sociological Review* 46, 46.

[92] Ibid, 47. Scott and Lyman further explain that '[e]xcuses [in the specified sense] are socially approved vocabularies for mitigating or relieving responsibility when conduct is questioned'.

[93] Ibid, 52.

[94] Dubnick, '*Sarbanes-Oxley*', above n 89, 246.

[95] Ibid.

[96] Ibid, 247.

[97] Ibid, 228.

[98] Ibid.

of legitimating and sustaining such power in the face of potential resistance by those who were subject to it.[99]

The functional value of the act of account-giving, in improving the overall quality of individual – and, in turn, organisational – action and decision-making, is normally taken for granted. Above all, account-giving is valuable insofar as an account-giver – when making a particular proposal or decision – is compelled 'to give reasons that make the proposal acceptable to others who cannot be expected to regard [her] preferences as sufficient reasons for agreeing'.[100] Consequently, account-giving necessitates that a person objectify or universalise the implications of her actual or proposed course of action to some extent, by appreciating how it may be felt or perceived by the account-recipient(s), and – if necessary – seeking to alleviate any adverse impacts or concerns thereon. The phenomenon has been described in the following terms:

> [T]o be held accountable for one's actions serves to sharpen one's sense of self and one's actions. The practice of accountability . . . acknowledges and confirms self, and the fact that one's actions make a difference. Conversely in the absence of being held accountable there is the possibility of a weakening and blurring of one's sense of self and situation.[101]

Aside from the above, though, the act of account-giving is also highly significant on a normative or political level, especially when it occurs within relationships or organisations that are characterised by relative power disparity between participants. In the public-governmental environment, it has been said that '[n]othing is more fundamental to representative democratic government than is political accountability to citizens', to the extent that 'we commonly equate democracy with accountable governance – and vice versa'.[102] However, within any organisational context – governmental or otherwise – the extent to which senior decision-makers are rendered accountable to those principally subject to or affected by their decisions or actions is normatively crucial on both an individual and collective level.

First, effective accountability mechanisms are central to protecting the individual autonomy of those parties subject to DAP, in that where individual preferences are formed by deliberative processes and not simply by 'external circumstances' (eg relative distributions of power and influence), they can be regarded as emanating first and foremost from the 'power of

[99] On the general concept of institutional counterbalance via 'countervailing power', see JK Galbraith, *American Capitalism: The Concept of Countervailing Power* (Boston MA, Houghton Mifflin, 1952).

[100] J Cohen, 'Deliberation and Democratic Legitimacy' in A Hamlin and P Pettit, *The Good Polity: Normative Analysis of the State* (New York, Blackwell, 1989), ch 2.

[101] J Roberts, 'The Possibilities of Accountability' (1991) 16 *Accounting, Organizations & Society* 355, 356.

[102] Dubnick and Frederickson, *Public Accountability*, above n 85, 18.

reason' as opposed to being imposed or manipulated by dominant organisational interests (eg senior executive office-holders).[103] Secondly, effective accountability mechanisms are essential in establishing the legitimacy of the relevant organisation as a whole, by demonstrating the *non-inconsistency* of its internal power imbalance(s) with the basic democratic principle of fair collective representation.

This is because the procedural requirement of account-giving, based on the elicitation of reasons that are generally acceptable to an organisation's participants, in effect 'neutralises' any underlying power imbalance(s) by ensuring that (objective) reasons 'trump' (inter-subjective) relative influence or resources as the principal determinant of fundamental, important or controversial organisational decisions.[104] As a result, the basic representational inclination of organisational controllers is – in outward appearance at least – not impaired by the fact that the vast majority of their decisions are made on a centralised and autonomous basis. This preserves the aforementioned link between collective (organisational) and individual (participant) autonomy that is a precondition to executive decision-makers' continuing ability to possess and exercise power on *legitimate* – that is to say, generally acquiesced in – terms.

D. Power and Accountability as *Non*-Mutually-Reducing Phenomena

It should be noted that, where organisational participants operate under the condition of bounded rationality (and, in turn, informational disparity between managerial and non-managerial actors) power and accountability are *not* mutually reducing phenomena. That is to say, an increase in accountability to subjects of power does not necessarily equate to a reduction in the underlying organisational power itself; and, conversely, an increase in internal organisational power need not necessarily entail a corresponding diminution in the external accountability of office-holders. This is because the primary function of formal accountability mechanisms – as explained above – is not to eradicate or mitigate the presence of discretionary administrative power in organisations. Rather, their function is simply to 'check' executive organisational power in the sense of ensuring that such power is exercised on terms that are broadly acquiesced in by those directly subject to it.

[103] Cohen, 'Deliberation and Democratic Legitimacy', above n 100.
[104] In the so-called 'ideal' speech scenario envisaged by the social theorist Jurgen Habermas, 'no force except that of the better argument is exercised'. See J Habermas, *Legitimation Crisis* (Boston MA, Beacon Press, 1975) 108. The basic logic here is described succinctly by Joshua Cohen in the following passage of his excellent paper 'Deliberation and Democratic Legitimacy': 'Deliberation is *reasoned* in that the parties to it are required to state their reasons for advancing proposals, supporting them or criticizing them. They give reasons with the expectation that those reasons (and not, for example, their power) will settle the fate of their proposal' (above n 100, 22).

This demonstrates that, contrary to what has been argued by one leading corporate law scholar,[105] the power of ex post facto *review* of organisational decisions is *not* equivalent to – or even tantamount to – the ex ante power of executive decision-*making*.[106] Rather, the widespread availability of formal decision review procedures is an essential structural precondition to the continuing legitimacy – and, in turn, sustainability – of senior office-holders' possession and exercise of power to initiate high-level allocative and appropriative decisions. In other words, far from undermining centralised and autonomous organisational decision-making, effective outside accountability mechanisms make the sustainable exercise of such power *possible* in the presence of bounded rationality and unequal access to information.

It follows that, in the corporate governance context, the principal function of legally-constituted managerial accountability mechanisms such as disclosure regulation, rights of occasional shareholder review of high-level executive decisions, and the equitable fiduciary principle,[107] is not to reduce the permissible ambit of the board's – and, indirectly, management's – executive prerogative. Rather, and less controversially, it is simply to maintain the structural conditions under which the widespread and necessary centralisation of organisational decision-making power is perceived as legitimate from a general investor perspective. The ultimate and intended outcome is to ensure public corporations' continuing access to outside equity capital on broadly favourable terms, notwithstanding

[105] Stephen Bainbridge has asserted that 'giving investors the power of review [of managerial decisions] differs little from giving them the power to make board decisions in the first place', on the basis that '[e]ven if investors are not inclined to micromanage portfolio corporations, vesting them with the power to review board decisions inevitably shifts some portion of the board's authority to them'. Moreover, according to Bainbridge, 'this remains true even if the review entails only major decisions'. See Bainbridge, 'Director Primacy and Shareholder Disempowerment', above n 34, 1749–50.

[106] In conflating the respective activities of decision-*making* and decision-*review*, Bainbridge (ibid) could arguably be said to elide an important distinction between what Alan Gewirth has referred to as 'occurrent' and 'dispositional' control. The former type of control, according to Gewirth, comprises 'the direct exercise of decision making', whereas the latter 'consists in having the longer-range background ability to exercise occurrent control *without actually exercising it*'. Crucially, Gewirth explains that '[d]ispositional control is had by persons or groups who have the final authority over binding decisions, *without necessarily making those decisions themselves*' (emphasis added). On this, see Gewirth, *Community of Rights*, above n 74, 271. The characteristic futility of retroactive decision-review processes – in effecting meaningful change to the executive decisions at which they are directed – is perhaps best summed up in the following quote by the twentieth-century American public intellectual Walter Lippmann: 'Outside the rather narrow range of our own possible attention, social control depends upon devising standards of living and methods of audit by which the acts of public officials and industrial directors are measured. We cannot ourselves inspire or guide all these acts, as the mystical democrat has always imagined. But we can steadily increase our real control over these acts by insisting that all of them shall be plainly recorded, and their results objectively measured'. See W Lippmann, *Public Opinion* (New York, The Free Press, 1965) (first published 1921) 197.

[107] For a critical evaluation of these legal phenomena from the perspective of the thesis of this book, see below ch 6 of this volume.

the considerable loss of individual contractual autonomy that the corporate equity relation necessarily entails from an investor point of view.

My central claim here should now hopefully be clear. To reiterate, it is that the function of formal managerial accountability norms in Anglo-American corporate governance law is *not* to empower shareholders in corporate decision-making at the expense of the board (and, in turn, managers). On the contrary, the purpose of legal account-giving processes within corporate governance is – in the last place – to *reaffirm* centralised corporate-managerial power by subjecting it to (limited) formal limitations. The result is to secure the continuing acquiescence of investors (and especially equity) in the continuing possession and exercise of such power by management. In short, formal accountability is a necessary structural precondition of executive power-legitimacy.[108]

E. Accountability as a 'Double-Edged Sword'

The above explanation of executive accountability – as a necessary precondition of legitimate organisational decision-making – suggests that, within any organisation (all other things being equal), greater accountability of

---

[108] I fully acknowledge that some readers may interpret the above argument as attributing a somewhat cynical quality to corporate governance as a general social practice – that is, as a phenomenon designed to 'gloss over' the realities of managerial power so as in effect to help 'dupe' unwitting investors into putting themselves in a position of economic vulnerability. Such a depiction of corporate governance – and of the position of corporate equity investors in particular – would undoubtedly be significantly out of sync with the sophisticated and institutionally-dominated capital markets of the contemporary era. In any event, it is not my intention to portray the role of managerial accountability norms in this way. Rather, as the discussion in the previous part of this chapter should hopefully have demonstrated, I regard formal accountability mechanisms as fulfilling a crucial function in recalibrating the relational dynamic between managers and shareholders of public corporations in the latter constituency's favour, albeit not in a way that is likely to empower shareholders materially in an executive capacity. I believe that my understanding of how the phenomenon of managerial accountability operates within corporate governance (in both the US and UK contexts) bears certain parallels with Walter Lippmann's understanding of the origins of political democracy in the United States. Lippmann regarded the political enfranchisement of individual citizens principally as a method for establishing the legitimacy of centralised and autonomous federal-governmental control, which was in general deemed to be a practically preferable form of government relative to disparate control by various dispersed local bodies. However, according to Lippmann, the actual grant of self-expression to individual citizens – while providing the normative underpinning to democracy – was on a practical level *not* the original motivating rationale for enfranchisement. Lippmann believed that the original problem as conceived by the founding fathers of the US constitution was how 'to restore government *as against* democracy', so as to prevent '[t]he collisions and failures of concave democracy, where men spontaneously managed all their own affairs'. The outcome, Lippmann highlighted, was Hamiltonian republicanism – which emphasised equilibrium and balance of power while, at the same time, retaining a significant ambit of centralised federal sovereignty. On this basis, Lippmann rejected as 'a great conservative fiction' the Jeffersonian understanding of the US constitution as a democratic instrument in any meaningful functional sense. See Lippmann, *Public Opinion*, above n 106 at 176, 179 (emphasis added).

decision-makers is always preferable to lesser accountability from the point of view of non-managerial participants. In reality, however, the correlation between formal accountability and power-legitimacy is more complex than one of simple direct variation.

As anyone accustomed to taking bureaucratic decisions within a complex organisation can testify, where accountability processes are concerned it is possible to have 'too much of a good thing'. In other words, accountability can often become *excessive* in nature, in the sense that, beyond a given 'equilibrium' level of accountability, the bureaucratic costs to the organisation – and, in turn, its external resource providers – of any further increase in formal executive accountability to the latter group will *exceed* the corresponding benefit to the organisation (and, indirectly, its resource providers) from enhanced executive power-legitimacy.[109]

Bureaucratic costs in the above sense can take either of two basic forms: namely *compliance* costs or *maladaptation* costs. Compliance costs comprise the direct expenses incurred by an organisation in establishing and implementing accountability mechanisms or procedures, including – inter alia – the cost of employing additional supervisory, accounting or reporting personnel, and also the cost of installing new technologies or employee training systems to support such practices.[110] Maladaptation costs, meanwhile, comprise the administrative inefficiencies that arise *after* the implementation of new accountability norms within an organisation. Such costs are the result of structural, cultural or social 'mismatches' between the new mechanisms or procedures, and pre-existing organisational practices or dynamics.[111]

---

[109] The phenomenon of excessive (and thus self-reducing) accountability is recognised by organisational theorists in the concept popularly referred to as 'red tape'. For an academic rationalisation of this concept, see B Bozeman, 'A Theory of Government "Red Tape"' (1993) 3 *Journal of Public Administration Research and Theory* 273; H Kaufman, *Red Tape: Its Origins, Uses, and Abuses* (Washington DC, Brookings Institution, 1977). Bozeman refers to 'red tape' (albeit it in the public-governmental context) as comprising 'guidelines, procedures, and forms that are perceived as excessive, unwieldy, or pointless in relation to official decisions and policy' (ibid, 276, borrowing from the definition of 'red tape' advanced previously by RA Rosenfeld in 'An Expansion and Application of Kaufman's Model of Red Tape: The Case of Community Development Block Grants' (1984) 37 *The Western Political Quarterly* 603). Examples of cost-*effective* formalisation within organisations, on the other hand, are referred to by Bozeman under the (non-pejorative) descriptor of 'white tape'. See Bozeman, ibid, 276.

[110] Notable examples of corporate governance regulatory reforms that have given rise to significant compliance costs in this sense are the internal financial control requirements introduced under the US Sarbanes-Oxley Act of 2002, and the internal anti-corruption control requirements prompted by the introduction of the Bribery Act 2010 in the UK. For a discussion of the former set of reforms as viewed from the perspective of the thesis of this book, see ch 6 of this volume, pt I.A.(i).

[111] An example of a corporate governance regulatory initiative giving rise to material maladaptation costs in this sense is the affirmative recommendation in 2003, for the first time, of US-style majority-independent boards and independent chairmen in larger listed companies in the UK, under the post-Enron reforms to the UK's Combined Code on Corporate Governance (now known as the UK Corporate Governance Code). On this, see Moore, 'Whispering Sweet Nothings', above n 3, 107–17.

The difficulty of attempting to strike an optimal balance between the conflicting criteria of executive power-legitimacy and bureaucratic cost-effectiveness is exemplified most conspicuously in the public-governmental context, where the common outcome is an effective 'no win' scenario for executive decision-makers. On the one hand, a perceived scarcity of formal checks on discretionary decision-making power is liable to result in executive office-holders being castigated as 'mini-dictators' or megalomaniacs. On the other hand, an apparent excess of formal account-ability measures is liable to result in the same individuals being derided as 'box tickers', 'paper pushers' or other such pejorative titles indicative of alleged over-bureaucratisation.

In the corporate environment, in instances where the marginal bureau-cratic costs of an extra unit of managerial accountability exceed the marginal legitimacy gain therefrom, there results the perverse scenario where the compliance and maladaptation costs to the firm (and, in turn, investors) of increased managerial accountability *outweigh* the ensuing reduction in cost of capital at the micro level. In this scenario, investor wealth is overall *lower* than it would be if the extra accountability measures were absent. Moreover, as explained above, the purpose of formal account-ability norms is to compensate in part for investors' bounded rationality, by acting as an effective proxy for reduction in shareholder risk exposure. However, in the same way that bounded rationality prevents investors from assessing the underlying riskiness of securities, it also prevents inves-tors from assessing the *actual* cost-effectiveness of managerial accountabil-ity norms, in the sense of whether the accountability mechanisms that a firm has in place are excessive relative to their risk-reducing effect.

The result is that, just as an apparently *under*-burdensome system of checks on managerial discretion will be perceived as a source of unac-countability (and thus executive power-illegitimacy), a prima facie *over*-burdensome accountability framework will be perceived as a source of unjustified (and hence unauthorised) bureaucratic costs for the corpora-tion and, in turn, its shareholders. In this latter situation, the legitimacy of the relevant framework of managerial accountability norms itself is called into question – but in this case, not because discretionary administrative power has gone formally unchecked, but – contrarily – because the bureaucratic framework to which management is subject *cannot by its nature* be regarded as something that rational investors would be liable to acquiesce in. This is what I will refer to as the problem of *bureaucratic illegitimacy* – which, somewhat paradoxically – arises from a perceived *surplus* rather than lack of formal account-giving requirements applicable to executive office-holders. The element of 'illegitimacy' here stems from the fact that, in such instances, the requisite condition of collective inves-tor authorisation is again absent – albeit that, in this case, the problem inheres in an absence of authorisation for *the relevant corporate governance framework itself*, rather than the underlying problem of power-illegitimacy in response to which that framework has been constructed. Thus, on the whole, the putative cure (ie accountability) has the effect of *exacerbating* the underlying problem (ie illegitimacy) that it is designed to remedy.

Since – as explained above – the actual cost-effectiveness of accountability norms is incapable of reliable external assessment, the notionally 'optimal' or equilibrium level of accountability within any complex organisation is indiscernible under real world conditions. However, there is still an equilibrium level of *perceived* accountability: that is, a level of accountability sufficiently high to provide credible assurance to external resource providers against the risk of diminution of organisational resources via maladministration, but sufficiently low to provide credible assurance against risk of diminution of the same resources via cost-ineffective bureaucracy (ie 'red tape'). It follows from this that, under conditions of bounded rationality, organisational accountability levels (all other things being equal) will tend towards an equilibrium 'normal' or median level. Accordingly, lower than normal accountability will tend to create an outside presumption of increased maladministration risk, while higher than normal accountability will – conversely – be indicative of over-bureaucratisation (or 'red tape') risk.

It is for this reason that, in complex organisational contexts (eg public companies) at least, executive accountability is most appropriately depicted in terms of a 'double-edged sword'. The challenge for an effective system of corporate governance law is thus to establish the appropriate institutional conditions under which each corporation is best positioned to approximate the equilibrium level of managerial accountability that is applicable on a micro (ie individual firm) level. In this way, corporate governance law contributes to securing the legitimacy – and, in turn, sustainability – of discretionary administrative power as it exists within complex private sector organisations.

III. WHY SHAREHOLDER EXCLUSIVITY?

A. The *Non*-Exclusivity of Equity as the Collective Subject of Corporate-Managerial Power

If one accepts that the phenomenon of corporate-managerial power – as outlined above – represents an issue of material concern for corporate governance law, then it follows that one must also consider the wider existence of such power within the corporation *beyond* the immediate context of the equity relation.

In particular – as will be demonstrated below – the concept of discretionary administrative power developed in this chapter also inheres to a significant extent in *the employment relation* as constituted at common law. For this reason, any systematic analysis of the problem of corporate-managerial power necessarily entails examining the principal ways in which discretionary administrative power is manifested not just in the 'core' shareholder-management relation, but also in the legal relationship existing – on both an individual and collective level – between management and employees.

B. Power Imbalance in the Employment Relation

The seminal – and arguably most influential – social-scientific rationalisation of the impact of discretionary administrative power in the employment context is Ronald Coase's path-breaking 1939 article 'The Nature of the Firm'.[112] In this work Coase observed how, contrary to what had previously been the accepted orthodoxy in economic thinking, the dual phenomena of 'firms' and 'markets' are not part of the same institutional phenomenon. Coase claimed that the firm and the market are in fact logically distinct features of a capitalist economy, and fulfil markedly separate economic functions from one another in the coordination of productive activity.

Accordingly the entrepreneur or producer, by deciding to carry out business through the medium of a firm, in effect takes the decision to opt out of the decentralised market system and instead organise his productive activities by way of a centralised, extra-market command structure. Coase explained how, on a formal level, the command structure within the firm is achieved by the intrinsic structural features of the common law employment relation, and – in particular – the basic and peculiar concept of employee subordination to the reasonable orders of the employer. Thus the entrepreneur, rather than entering into numerous discrete contracts every time she requires a particular productive or administrative service performed, instead establishes one unifying contract 'whereby the factor [ie employee], for a certain remuneration (which may be fixed or fluctuating), agrees to obey the directions of [the] entrepreneur *within certain limits*'.[113] It follows that within the typically broad limits stated in the employment contract, the entrepreneur is free to direct and organise the employee's work in accordance with her own discretion and in light of the perceived exigencies of the business, without the need either to seek the assent of the employee to each ordered task or to negotiate the latter's compensation for each task on an ongoing basis.

As Coase expressly acknowledges, this essential characteristic of the firm derives from the peculiarly vague and somewhat lop-sided nature of

---

[112] R Coase, 'The Nature of the Firm' (1937) 4 *Economica* 386.
[113] Ibid, 391.

the Anglo-American employment relation, which has its roots not in the orthodox law of (exchange) contract but rather in pre-industrial master and servant law. According to Coase:

> [i]t is this right of control or interference, of being entitled to tell the servant when to work (within the hours of service) and when not to work, and what work to do and how to do it (within the terms of such service) which is the dominant characteristic in this relation and marks off the servant from an independent contractor, or from one employed merely to give to his employer the fruits of his labour.[114]

The employment relation is commonly perceived today to be an example of conventional market exchange relations as regulated under the law of contract. For this reason, it is commonly associated with classical laissez faire notions such as reciprocal exchange and contractual freedom, especially within modern neo-liberal thought.[115] However, in the common law environment, the pervasiveness of these tenets in the context of *non-employment-based* exchanges was traditionally not carried over into the labour relations field. Indeed, as is the case with the concept of discretionary administrative power in the context of the equity relation, DAP is not a structurally innate or pre-ordained feature of labour exchange relations. It is, rather, attributable to certain distinct, longstanding and somewhat idiosyncratic Anglo-American legal principles derived at root from pre-industrial master and servant law.

As Simon Deakin has observed, the peculiarity of the employment relation relative to other types of exchange is attributable to the fact that, historically, the master-servant relation was based on *status* rather than orthodox exchange contract. Thus master and servant law, as originally constituted by the English courts, was regarded as a facet of the 'law of persons' rather than the 'law of things'. On a jurisprudential level, the effect of this categorisation was to portray the servant – conceptually speaking – as offering his 'whole person' to the master for exploitation at the latter's discretion, rather than as providing any distinct labour 'commodity' that could be regarded as independent of, and thus separable

---

[114] Ibid, 404.

[115] See, eg AA Alchian and H Demsetz, 'Production, Information Costs, and Economic Organization' (1972) 62 *American Economic Review* 777, who argued (incorrectly) that the ability of an employer firm to enforce or terminate his employment agreement was qualitatively no different from the ability of a consumer to sue, or terminate a relationship with, his grocer by refusing to continue purchasing goods from the latter. Accordingly, the authors claimed, '[t]o speak of managing, directing, or assigning workers to various tasks is a deceptive way of noting that the employer continually is involved in renegotiation of contracts on terms that must be acceptable to both parties' (ibid, 777). See also FA Hayek, *The Constitution of Liberty* (London, Routledge, 1960) 136: 'The individual provider of employment cannot normally exercise coercion, any more than can the supplier of a particular commodity or service. So long as he can remove only one opportunity among many to earn a living, so long as he can do no more than cease to pay certain people who cannot hope to earn as much elsewhere as they had done under him, he cannot coerce, though he may cause pain'.

from, the servant's inherent personhood.[116] In other words, '[t]he servant was seen as contributing personal service, conceived not as specific labour duties but as a general contribution to the needs of the enterprise, be it household, farm or workshop'.[117] There was thus an assumption that '[i]n some vague but important sense . . . *the whole person* was committed to the relation'.[118]

The original hierarchical understanding of the employment relation within the English legal tradition was subsequently carried through to the industrial era. Therefore,

> [a]lthough contract theory ostensibly gave full discretion to the parties in defining the nature and scope of authority, in fact the law imported into the employment contract a set of implied terms reserving *full [and unilateral] authority of direction and control to the employer* (emphasis added).[119]

And, although labour market mobility via legally unimpeded 'exit' from employment became possible from the early twentieth century, the modern idea of a universal employment contract was not recognised in Britain until after World War II, in the context of the post-1945 construction of the welfare state.[120]

Even today, however, important remnants of the traditional status-based master-servant model remain within the common law employment relation, particularly in the form of the employee's implied duties of care,

[116] See S Deakin, 'Legal Origin, Juridical Form and Industrialization in Historical Perspective: The Case of the Employment Contract and the Joint-Stock Company' (2009) 7 *Socio-Economic Review* 35.

[117] A Fox, *Beyond Contract: Work, Power and Trust Relations* (London, Faber, 1974) 185. As Deakin and Morris further observe, this position was reinforced by the subjucating effect of early English master and servant legislation, which (inter alia) rendered breach of contract – via either disobeying the master's orders or absconding from service altogether – as an offence punishable under criminal law (in the case of absconding, by 3 months' imprisonment) in a magistrates' court. Even after the repeal of the Master and Servant Act in 1870, contractual damages still took the form of fines and were enforceable in a magistrates' court. Notably, 'white collar workers' such as managers, agents and clerks were traditionally regarded as 'employees', and thus had a fundamentally contractual employment relation. By contrast, manual workers such as industrial and agricultural labourers, and domestic servants, had no contractual relation with their employer in the commonly-accepted sense of the term. Interestingly, the civil law systems of France and Germany, from the initial stage of these countries' industrialisation, contrarily recognised the employment relation as being essentially contractual in nature. As such, it was understood in the more modern sense in which it is depicted within neo-liberal scholarship today, essentially as 'a relationship of exchange between juridical equals' (Deakin, 'Legal Origin', above n 116, 44). See S Deakin and GS Morris, *Labour Law*, 5th edn (Oxford, Hart Publishing, 2009) 19–20.

[118] R Selznick, *Law, Society and Industrial Justice* (New York, Russell Sage Foundation, 1969) 124, cited in Fox, *Beyond Contract*, above n 117, 185. In a sense, this echoes Karl Marx's classical depiction of the labour exchange as a relation of 'human flesh and blood'. On this, see KW Wedderburn, *The Future of Company Law: Corporate Governance, Fat Cats and Workers* (London, Institute of Employment Rights, 2004) 31.

[119] Fox, *Beyond Contract*, above n 117, 187–88.

[120] See Deakin and Morris, 'Labour Law', above n 117, 20–21.

obedience to, and cooperation with, his employer.[121] A notable consequence of the above is that the practice of 'working to rule' in a strike
action, denoting the rigid adherence by employees to the express terms of
their employment contract, in fact constitutes a breach of contract on
grounds of failure to render a requisite level of obedience and cooperation
to the employer's interests.

It can thus be said that, in a critical sense, the employee's contractual
commitment to the firm and its management is substantively *infinite*.[122]
This is because the effect of management's legally-constituted prerogative
within the employment relation is to render the labour relation open-
ended in the sense that human capital (ie wage labour) becomes susceptible – like equity capital – to manipulation by managers in unspecified
ways and for the purpose of generating an unspecified level of return on
that capital.[123] Such unilateral open-endedness (or 'diffuseness') of the
employment relation creates a significant degree of *allocative* power in
favour of management vis-à-vis labour, on both an individual and collective level.[124]

The common law employment relation is furthermore conducive to the
establishment of considerable *appropriative* power on management's
behalf, albeit that this dimension of DAP is rather less conspicuous than
the former one. The phenomenon can be described as follows. While the
rate of return on human capital is normally fixed in monetary terms, the
employee's implied duty of obedience to and cooperation with his

---

[121] See Deakin, 'Legal Origin', above n 116, 46. For an illustration – and influential judicial
rationalisation – of the degree of self-sacrificial loyalty that is expected of an employee in
carrying out his duties, see the US federal Court of Appeals decision in *Community
Counselling Service v Reilly*, 317 F 2d 239 (1963) (United States Court of Appeals, Fourth
Circuit), analysed in C O'Kelley and R Thompson, *Corporations and Business Associations:
Cases and Materials*, 6th edn (New York, Aspen, 2010) 21–25.
[122] The extent of the employer's authoritative right of direction is arguably most prevalent in
the context of 'rank and file' or low-discretion (from the employee's perspective) work structures, such as the Fordist/Taylorist mass production and scientific management practices of
the early-to-mid-twentieth century. Such practices typically entailed the substantial substitution of command over consensus as a means of achieving entrepreneurial co-ordination of firm
– and, in particular – human resources. As Fox explains: 'In low-discretion work structures the
problems are considered to have been foreseen and planned for already by higher authority
through the means of technological and workflow design and/or of bureaucratic discipline'. It
follows from this that coordination requires 'highly restricted interaction and communication
patterns between lower and higher ranks', so that 'social control rests less on consensus and
more on the power of management to enforce compliance to the rule system'. Fox, *Beyond
Contract*, above n 117, 28; see also R Blauner, *Alienation and Freedom: The Factory Worker and His
Industry* (Chicago IL, University of Chicago Press, 1964) 177–78, cited in Fox, ibid, 28.
[123] Fox, *Beyond Contract*, above n 117, 190. On this generally, see SE Masten, 'A Legal Basis
for the Firm' (1998) 4 *Journal of Law, Economics and Organization* 181.
[124] As Alan Gewirth has observed, '[t]he workers' equal rights to freedom are violated
because they are subjected in the workplace to hierarchic controls whereby managers or
employers tell them what to do and how to do it, so that the workers are at the bottom end
of an authoritarian chain of command in which they are required to execute orders given
from above, with no participation or control on their part'. See Gewirth, *Community of Rights*,
above n 74, 258–59.

employer means that his input is – at the same time – formally manipulable by management within relatively wide contractual bounds. The consequence is that management has the capacity *indirectly* to vary the employee's rate of return on human capital in real terms, either by altering the level and/or rigour of work expected in return for the same level of money compensation, or else by maintaining employees' prevailing contractual rate of money compensation notwithstanding the existence of price inflation or other forms of material increase in the cost of living (so that employees' real rate of return on human capital is reduced). This is a particular risk for employees during periods of market or organisational transition, which can give rise to a perceived need for large-scale reorganisation of employee task allocation or established work methods or patterns.[125]

C. Collective Adversarialism as a Legitimating Counterbalance to Employer Power

The above discussion has highlighted that, in certain important respects, the basic power dynamic of the employment relation – as it is legally constituted within the common law environment – is, at root, *not dissimilar* to that of the corporate equity relation. In particular, both relationships involve the sacrifice by one party (whether employee or ordinary shareholder) of substantial contractual autonomy in the ordering of her individual economic affairs, at least for the duration of that person's dealings with the firm.

At the same time, within both relationships the ongoing contractual autonomy of the firm (and, in turn, management) itself is preserved and – moreover – *enhanced*, insofar as the relevant counterparty's rights against the firm are at once both prescribed and restricted on a formal basis (whether under the corporate constitution or via an extraneous contract of employment), thereby creating a reciprocal imbalance of allocative and appropriative power in management's favour.[126] It follows that in both the above cases, there is a need for corresponding institutional countermeasures that are capable of legitimating – and, in turn, sustaining – these relations notwithstanding their characteristic (and normatively destabilising) features of reciprocal imbalance and unilateral discretionary power.

---

[125] The legally-constituted ambit of discretionary prerogative that an employer enjoys in these regards is arguably the principal institutional factor underpinning the practice of surplus value extraction, which Marx regarded as intrinsic to the basic structure of the employment relation within capitalistic systems of production and exchange. On this, see K Marx, *Capital: A Critique of Political Economy*, Penguin Classics edn (Harmondsworth, Penguin, 1976) (first published 1867) vol I, book 1, ch 7.

[126] On the concept of reciprocal imbalance in the employment relation (and to whom this term is attributable), see generally Fox, *Beyond Contract*, above n 117.

The effect of formal managerial accountability norms in securing the legitimacy of the corporate equity relation has already been noted above. But are any similar such institutional countermeasures to corporate-managerial power evident in the context of the employment relation?

At least insofar as the US and UK corporate governance systems are concerned, the answer to the above question – broadly speaking – is 'no'. That is to say, legally-invoked managerial account-giving to employees has traditionally *not* been perceived as an appropriate institutional response to the problem of managerial (or employer) power in the corporate employment relation, at least in the same way that it has in the context of the corporate equity relation.[127] Rather, within the Anglo-American environment at least,[128] the orthodox institutional response to corporate-managerial power as it exists in the employment relation has been invocation of a practice that can be referred to in general terms as *collective adversarialism*.[129]

Collective adversarialism is less a means by which management formally accounts for its exercise of discretionary power vis-à-vis employees; and more a method by which employees directly and collectively curtail the scope of such discretionary power ex ante. The essential dual feature of collective adversarialism, as its name suggests, are: first, that it involves the *collective* representation of labour in its dealings with management in concentrated masses (as represented by, and coordinated via, trade unions); and, secondly, that any engagement by collective labour representatives with a firm's management is conducted on an *adversarial* basis – that is to say, on an 'arm's length' and fundamentally *non*-cooperative manner, most commonly via the trade union-initiated practice of collective bargaining. Accordingly, management and labour each seek to elicit the best possible bargaining outcome from their own partisan perspec-

---

[127] On the general lack of political support in the UK (even from the left) for corporate-organisational reforms aimed at internalising the influence of workers within internal firm decision-making dynamics, see B Clift, A Gamble and M Harris, 'The Labour Party and the Company' in Parkinson, Gamble and Kelly, *The Political Economy of the Company*, above n 28, ch 3.

[128] On the contrasting traditional position of German and Japanese corporate governance in this regard, see, respectively: S Vitols, 'Varieties of Corporate Governance: Comparing Germany and the UK' in PA Hall and D Soskice (eds), *Varieties of Capitalism: The Institutional Foundations of Comparative Advantage* (Oxford, Oxford University Press, 2001) 337; T Hoshi, 'Japanese Corporate Governance as a System' in KJ Hopt, H Kanda, MJ Roe, E Wymeersch and S Prigge (eds), *Comparative Corporate Governance: The State of the Art and Emerging Research* (Oxford, Clarendon Press, 1998) 847. On the Germanic concept of (cooperative and non-adversarial) management-employee communications as a mechanism for 'building social side-purposes into economic action', see G Teubner, 'Corporate Fiduciary Duties and their Beneficiaries: A Functional Approach to the Legal Institutionalization of Corporate Responsibility' in KJ Hopt and G Teubner, *Corporate Governance and Directors' Liabilities: Legal, Economic and Sociological Analyses on Corporate Social Responsibility* (Berlin, de Gruyter, 1985) 149, esp 160–64.

[129] On this concept generally, see Galbraith, *American Capitalism*, above n 99, ch 9.

tive, treating the other party as a 'pure' contractual counterparty rather than a common interest-sharing 'partner' in the relationally richer sense.[130]

The institution of collective adversarialism is premised on the understanding that legitimation of corporate-managerial power in the employment relation via managerial accountability norms at the micro (ie individual firm) level is for the most part impossible, or at least highly impracticable. The reason for this is that effective managerial account-giving can only be engendered where there is a credible background threat to management in the event of its failure to conform to presumptive accountability norms on an ongoing basis.

In the context of the corporate equity relation, this negative disciplinary pressure is provided by the external capital market. Therefore, as explained above, the market-determined criterion of cost of capital in effect represents both the principal reflection of managerial power-legitimacy in this context, and also the principal incentive for effective managerial account-giving to shareholders on an ongoing basis. This means that, where managerial account-giving processes operate in the context of the corporate equity relation, they do so against the conspicuous background possibility that a perceived lack of accountability to shareholders will bring about a corresponding rise in a firm's cost of capital (together with the adverse managerial repercussions that are prone to follow from this).

The capacity of capital market pressures to provide an effective negative incentive for managerial accountability to shareholders at the micro level is premised on the largely unique nature of the corporate equity relation. In particular, it is dependent on the extraordinarily low displacement costs incurred by the relevant resource providers (ie shareholders) in 'exiting' their individual economic relationship with any firm. However, in other firm relationships (most notably the employment relation) where the displacement costs of exit to a resource provider are materially higher, the practicability of collective counterparty exit is significantly restricted.[131] As

---

[130] For an influential exposition of the adversarialist understanding of management-employee engagement in corporate governance, see O Kahn-Freund, 'Industrial Democracy' (1977) 6 *Industrial Law Journal* 65, 76. In Kahn-Freund's opinion, the interests of the company (as represented by management) were, in the ordinary course of things, 'irreconcilably opposed to that of each member of the employee group'. See also P Davies and Lord Wedderburn of Charlton, 'The Land of Industrial Democracy' (1977) 6 *Industrial Law Journal* 197, 211, who referred to the 'reality of *conflict* between workpeople and capital', which necessitated increasing the collective bargaining powers of workers via the trade union machinery (emphasis added).

[131] As Parkinson has highlighted, '[d]ismissal imposes costs on the employee, in terms of lost income, severance of social relationships at work, and the inconvenience involved in finding another job, that the employee will wish to avoid and which have no equivalents when relationships between customers and grocers break down'. Moreover 'in periods of high unemployment, and especially in areas or occupations in which the current employer is in a dominant position, the threat of discharge is a potent weapon'. Parkinson concludes that '[t]he attempt to assimilate the employment relationship to one of continuous contractual

a result, the possibility of mass revocation of individual employees' acquiescence in the relational power-imbalance vis-à-vis management is limited.
It will therefore be unlikely to provide a credible negative incentive for
effective managerial account-giving to employees at the micro level. The
probable outcome of this is that the management-labour power imbalance
– at least in the absence of other countervailing checks or counterbalances
– will be rendered *illegitimate* from labour's perspective, causing employees
in effect to dissent to being subject to management's discretionary administrative power, at least in the absence of condign[132] or economic[133] compulsion to do so.

Against this background, the intended governance function of collective
adversarialism – from labour's perspective – is two-fold. First, collective

renegotiation is therefore unconvincing'. See *Corporate Power and Responsibility*, above n 4, 9.
From a similar point of view, Gewirth has objected to Alchian and Demsetz's aforementioned
'grocer' analogy for the employment relation (see 'Production, Information Costs, and
Economic Organization', above n 115) on the basis that 'it ignores the more general context
wherein there is an asymmetry rather than a symmetry of power, bearing on the divergent
abilities to control the consequences of breaking or modifying the contract'. Accordingly, 'if
workers refuse to do as the employer directs, they may be fired . . . [b]ut if the employer
refuses to do as the workers ask, they are hardly in a position to fire the employer'. Whilst of
course 'they may quit their jobs', they 'thereby . . . usually suffer far more than does the
employer' due to 'the far fewer alternatives that are open to them'. Workers 'therefore suffer
from the forced choices that are antithetical to freedom' in that 'they are compelled to choose
between severely undesirable alternatives set by employers who have superior bargaining
power'. See Gewirth, *Community of Rights*, above n 74 at 258–59, 268.

[132] Of course, where labour is compelled on a condign basis – that is to say, at the risk of
direct punishment (eg via physical force) in the event of failure to conform to the employer's
demands – the resulting relationship would be one of slavery, rather than employment. As
such, it would be both illegal and morally reprehensible within a liberal society.

[133] It should be noted that where either: (i) the choice of available alternatives open to a
contractor (eg an employee) is restricted to the extent that they are effectively compelled (by
material circumstances) to enter into a particular relation, or (ii) the transaction costs of
informing themselves about the nature and/or extent of contractual power to which they
would be subject are inhibiting; it follows that any reciprocal power imbalance between
management and the relevant contractual counterparty can justifiably fail to command the
latter's free and/or informed acquiescence, despite being prudentially 'acceptable' on a
basic contractual level as an individually rational response by that person to current economic exigencies. In such instance, management's possession and exercise of DAP vis-à-vis
that person will likely remain illegitimate (or, at least, of questionable legitimacy) from the
latter's perspective, in spite of that person prima facie signalling assent to his subjection
thereto by tendering his labour on the contractually 'agreed' terms. This important normative point has been noted by Galbraith, who observed that where alternative employment
opportunities available to an employee are significantly limited, the situation is almost tantamount to that where the employer is able to exercise *condign* power over the employees –
that is to say, power exerted by means of the infliction or threat of physical force – on the
basis that termination of employment will in effect deprive the employee of his continuing
livelihood and subsistence. Therefore like condign relations, such relations are 'sustainable'
only at the most base and primitive level of human association, so that their perpetuation
can be regarded as not just morally reprehensible, but also as *economically inefficient* insofar
as such an arrangement cannot reasonably be regarded to be the product of a consensual –
and thus presumptively mutually-beneficial – bargain between the associating parties. Such
economic interactions are consequently indefensible even from an orthodox contractarian
perspective. On this, see Galbraith, *The Anatomy of Power*, above n 14, 109.

adversarialism entails the mass coordination – under centralised (normally union-initiated) direction – of employees' respective individual decisions over whether to withdraw their human capital from the firm's productive process. Absent such centralised coordination, the mass withdrawal of human capital is rendered impracticable within large business enterprises. This is on account of the obvious collective action impediment thereto, coupled with the typically significant displacement costs to individual employees resulting from the structural inequality of labour markets. That is to say, since a typical (albeit not universal) characteristic of labour markets (all other things being equal) is the tendency to generate a surplus of supply (ie number of prospective employees) over demand (ie number of prospective employers),[134] it follows that the displacement costs to employees consequent upon termination of their employment are more likely than not to exceed significantly the corresponding replacement costs to their employer firm.[135] Such costs for the employee include the loss of regular income – and potentially even material livelihood – along with the social, psychological and other costs that loss of employment typically entails. For the employer firm, on the other hand, the ready availability of alternative personnel on the labour market (at least in the typical case) has the effect of mitigating the firm's – and, in turn, management's – replacement costs in the event of unilateral termination of the relationship by the employee.[136]

As against this, however, collective adversarialism – by posing the realisable threat of wholesale (and reversible) human capital withdrawal in the event of a successfully implemented strike – has the effect of significantly increasing the prospective displacement costs to management in the event of failure to secure labour's continuing acquiescence in the former group's possession and exercise of discretionary administrative power vis-à-vis employees. Thus, by concentrating labour's reactive capacity, and resultant bargaining power vis-à-vis management en masse, collective adversarialism effects an equalisation – or, at least, moderation – of the relative bargaining power of the contracting parties in employees' favour.[137]

A second important dimension of collective adversarialism as a governance device is its effect in mitigating the aforementioned problem of

---

[134] On this, see D Ricardo, *On the Principles of Political Economy and Taxation*, 3rd edn (London, Murray, 1821) (first published 1817) ch 5.

[135] On this, see above n 131.

[136] An important component of the economic argument for worker empowerment in corporate governance is the notion of 'co-dependency' between the firm and its employees, which infers that the replacement costs to both parties of the other's unilateral termination are roughly comparable. See Kelly and Parkinson, *The Conceptual Foundations*, above n 28, 123–27; MM Blair, *Ownership and Control: Rethinking Corporate Governance for the Twenty-First Century* (Washington DC, Brookings Institution, 1995) ch 6. However, while this argument has a certain theoretical appeal, few would regard it as being representative of more than a minority of niche (typically high-skilled) employment sectors, where ordinary labour market conditions (that is, a structural surplus of supply over demand) do not apply.

[137] On this, see Galbraith, *The Anatomy of Power*, above n 14, 137.

reciprocal imbalance in the employment relation, by enabling the effective reduction of the unilateral diffuseness of employees' contractual commitments to the firm. In this regard, an important function of adversarial practices such as collective bargaining is to reduce – via the extraction of improved (or, at least, more substantively definite) contractual terms with respect to money compensation, working conditions and work patterns – the allocative and appropriative power that management would otherwise enjoy by virtue of its discretionary administrative prerogative as an employer.[138]

Therefore, in the above ways, the persisting management-employee power imbalance is legitimated not so much by any perceived imperative of frequent managerial account-giving to employees, but instead by the commonly acknowledged fact that corporate-managerial power vis-à-vis labour is exercised against the effective background threat of unilateral revocation of the latter's collective acquiescence therein. Such threat is realisable in the case of strike or other adversarial methods of collective mobilisation of human capital.

D. Why has Collective Adversarialism been the Preferred Structural Response to Employer Power?

In the case of the corporate equity relation, as noted above, the relative ease with which shareholders can dispose of their equity interests on a liquid capital market makes practicable the collective revocation of shareholder acquiescence in management's continuing executive prerogative. This gives equity the unique capacity to influence its collective availability as a corporate resource on an ongoing basis, given that – on a liquid and efficient market at least – the cost of equity capital is relatively sensitive to changing individual investor perceptions of the legitimacy of management's continuing possession and exercise of DAP vis-à-vis shareholders.[139]

It follows that management has a rational incentive to hold itself continuously and conspicuously to account to shareholders and also the wider public investor community, concerning the ongoing exercise of its executive discretion and the consequences thereof for shareholder wel-

---

[138] See Gewirth, *Community of Rights*, above n 74, 268.

[139] At the same time, the limitations of equity disposal alone as an effective countervailing pressure to management's executive prerogative should not be overestimated. Actual or threatened use by a shareholder of her individual 'exit' right in itself amounts only to an effective (and on its own limited) right of veto over managerial policies or norms, and does not convey the further positive power to determine alternative executive initiatives ex ante, at least in the absence of further specific regulatory powers to this effect. On the concept of 'market veto' (albeit as applied in the consumer rather than shareholder context), see Parkinson, *Corporate Power and Responsibility*, above n 4, 13.

fare. This in turn gives rise to a significant negative incentive for the establishment of robust managerial accountability norms (in favour of shareholders) at the micro level. By contrast, in the context of the corporate employment relation, individual revocation by employees of acquiescence in management's executive discretion by means of unilateral termination of the relationship is highly impracticable. As discussed above, such impracticability is attributable to the typically high displacement costs to an employee of such termination, coupled with the innate structural imbalance of employer v employee bargaining power under typical labour market conditions.

Consequently, the cost of *human* capital is typically *in*sensitive (and, in the extreme case, *static*) to changing individual employee perceptions of the legitimacy of management's continuing possession and exercise of DAP vis-à-vis labour at the micro level. As a result, management has *no* rational incentive to hold itself either continually or conspicuously to account to employees, whether on an individual or collective basis, concerning the ongoing exercise of its executive discretion as it affects *worker* welfare at the micro level. Conversely, employees' general awareness that management has no such incentive will cause labour rationally to discount the credibility and reliability of any representations that management *does* actually make to labour concerning its actual or intended exercise of executive decision-making power. The likely result is – in the 'best' case scenario, communicative stagnancy; and, in the worst case, outright mutual distrust and hostility between the communicating parties.[140]

The only appreciable exception to the above is in occasional and exceptional instances of wholesale firm restructuring or transfers of control that elicit subsequent demands for systemic change in employment arrangements. This is because collective industrial action, and any corresponding employee demands for managerial account-giving, by nature occur on an (extraordinary) episodic rather than (ordinary) continuous basis, so that human capital is only collectively 'costed' in any appreciable way in instances of extraordinary industrial crisis or dispute, such as the aforementioned scenarios. Therefore since the collective cost of human capital

---

[140] This arguably helps to explain the almost complete lack of interest shown by UK-based employees and trade unions in voluntarily invoking the collective informational and consultation rights available at EU level under the Information and Consultation of Employees Regulations and Works Council Directive. This is in spite of the initial high hopes that were placed in these reforms as a means of transforming the UK's national industrial relations culture, towards a more cooperative and mutually beneficial management-employee settlement. On this, see H Collins, 'Flexibility and Empowerment' in T Wilthagen (ed), *Advancing Theory in Labour Law and Industrial Relations in a Global Context* (Amsterdam, Royal Netherlands Academy, 1998) 117, esp 119–20; KD Ewing and GM Truter, 'The Information and Consultation of Employees Regulations: Voluntarism's Bitter Legacy' (2005) 68 *The Modern Law Review* 626; S Wheeler, 'Works Councils: Towards Stakeholding?' (1997) 24 *Journal of Law and Society* 44.

is, like the individual cost of human capital, ordinarily *not* sensitive to changing employee perceptions of managerial power-legitimacy; it follows that – at least in the normal course of industrial affairs – there are *no* incentives for managerial account-giving to labour on an ongoing basis at the micro level. At the same time, the incentives for continuous managerial account-giving at both the macro and meso (industry- or sector-wide) levels are likewise significantly limited for fundamentally similar reasons.

Therefore, to the extent that corporate governance laws are responsive in any material degree to corporate participants' rational private preferences (as the contractarian paradigm of corporate governance avers), it follows that such laws will *not* be inclined to prescribe formal managerial accountability norms within the context of the corporate employment relation. The above analysis demonstrates rather that, in the Anglo-American environment at least,[141] the legitimacy of management's possession and exercise of discretionary administrative power vis-à-vis labour is more appropriately and effectively safeguarded via the regulatory protection of employees' collective capacity to withdraw their labour unilaterally. In this way, strikes and other adversarial forms of industrial action can be mobilised as effective expressions of dissent to the reciprocal imbalance of power between management and labour within the corporate structure, together with any adverse material outcomes for employees that are perceived to result therefrom.[142] Far from impeding the efficient purchase and sale of labour by contributing to structural rigidities in employment markets (as neo-liberal analyses of labour relations often suggest), the perpetual possibility of collective industrial action is, for the above reasons, an essential precondition of securing the continuing legitimacy – and, in turn, sustainability – of the discretionary power with which employer firms (and, in turn, managements) are vested in allocating and compensating labour as a corporate resource.

However, the statutory immunities and other collective employment protections that are structurally essential for the effective implementation

---

[141] The traditionally corporatist-consensual industrial relations systems of many continental European countries (most notably Germany and The Netherlands) lie outside the scope of the present study. For present purposes, though, it suffices to stress the need for caution when considering the applicability of my arguments in this part to corporate governance systems outside of the immediate Anglo-American context. On these broader considerations, see A Dignam and M Galanis, *The Globalization of Corporate Governance* (Farnham, Ashgate, 2009) esp chs 7–8.

[142] At the same time, though, it is important to acknowledge the arguably diminishing socio-economic relevance of collective adversarialism as a meaningful institutional force today, particularly in view of the steady diminution in trade union membership levels over recent decades, especially amongst private sector workers. However, further examination of this issue lies beyond the scope of the present work. On this trend in the US context, see JG Pope, P Kellman and E Bruno, '"We Are Already Dead": The Thirteenth Amendment and the Fight for Workers' Rights After EFCA' (2010) 67 *National Lawyers Guild Review* 110, 110. On the same trend in the UK context, see N Brownlie, *Trade Union Membership 2011* (London, UK Department for Business Innovation and Skills, 2011) esp 9–10.

of employee adversarialism[143] are conventionally perceived as lying *outside* of the scope of corporate governance, at least as this subject is conventionally understood within the Anglo-American environment. For this reason, their further detailed analysis is beyond the scope of the present study, although – in light of this chapter's insights – the extent to which collective employment rights *should* be integrated into mainstream academic accounts of Anglo-American corporate governance law is, at the very least, a live issue for future debate.

---

[143] Both the general right of association via collective organisations, and also the more specific right to strike, have been authoritatively recognised on a transnational level by the International Labour Organization (ILO). To these ends, the ILO's Freedom of Association Committee has asserted (inter alia) that '[w]orkers should have the right to establish the organizations that they consider necessary in a climate of complete security irrespective of whether or not they support the social and economic model of the Government, including the political model of the country'; and also that 'the right to strike by workers and their organizations [is] a legitimate means of defending their economic and social interests' and, indeed, 'one of the essential means' by which they may do so. See *Freedom of Association: Digest of Decisions and Principles of the Freedom of Association Committee of the Governing Body of the ILO*, 5th edn (Geneva, International Labour Organization, 2006) paras 213, 521, 522. At the domestic level, it could be said that the basis of a right of collective association – and arguably, by implication, a right to strike – exists in the United States under the Thirteen Amendment, which provides that '[n]either slavery nor involuntary servitude, except as a punishment for crime whereof the party shall have been duly convicted, shall exist within the United States'. It has accordingly been claimed that: 'Every human being has under the Thirteenth Amendment to the Constitution of the United States an inalienable right to the disposal of his labor free from interference, restraint or coercion by or on behalf of employers of labor, including the right to associate with other human beings for the protection and advancement of their common interests as workers, and in such association to negotiate through representatives of their own choosing concerning the terms of employment and conditions of labor, and to take concerted action for their own protection in labor disputes'. See Pope, Kellman and Bruno, '"We Are Already Dead"', above n 142, 112. However, on the general reluctance of trade unions to assert their purported 'right to strike' within the country's contemporary political climate, see the same piece at 114–15. By contrast, the absence of a positive right to strike at English common law means that, as a general rule, the unilateral withdrawal of labour by an employee constitutes a breach of contract, thereby entitling the employer correspondingly to terminate the employment contract and dismiss the striking employee(s). As against this, however, the UK (Labour) government in the late 1990s introduced a limited form of statutory unfair dismissal protection for employees who participate in industrial action (under s 238A of the Trade Union and Labour Relations (Consolidation) Act 1992, as inserted by Schedule 5 of the Employment Relations Act 1999, and subsequently amended by ss 26–28 of the Employment Relations Act 2004), which applies where (inter alia) it can be shown that the employee's taking of industrial action was the principal reason for his subsequent dismissal. On this, see T Novitz and P Skidmore, *Fairness at Work: A Critical Analysis of the Employment Relations Act 1999 and its Treatment of Collective Rights* (Oxford, Hart Publishing, 2001) 39–42 and 130–33. The dual collective labour rights of association and strike are, furthermore, affirmed at the pan-European level under article 28 of the European Charter of Fundamental Rights, which provides that '[w]orkers and employers, or their respective organisations, have . . . the right to negotiate and conclude collective agreements at the appropriate levels and, in cases of conflicts of interest, to take collective action to defend their interests, including strike action'. See Charter of Fundamental Rights of the European Union ([2000] OJ C364/01), available at: www.europarl.europa.eu/charter/pdf/text_en.pdf .

IV. SUMMARY

In this chapter, I have attempted to provide an objective definition of corporate governance as a subject of legal-academic enquiry, as a necessary preliminary to examining the fundamental nature of this subject in the remainder of the book. I have submitted that, at its core, corporate governance essentially comprises three irreducible elements, on which all thinking and debate in this field is either expressly or implicitly dependent. These three elements are: (i) power, (ii) accountability, and (iii) legitimacy.

The first of these component parts of corporate governance, namely *power*, I defined in part II in terms of the discretionary administrative power wielded by senior executive office-holders in appropriating – and thereafter allocating – externally provided economic resources in the service of internally (ie managerially) determined corporate goals. I further highlighted how the internal contractual autonomy of the corporation and its managing officers is predicated – somewhat paradoxically – on the sacrifice of individual contractual autonomy by external corporate resource providers (especially equity investors) in determining the application of their capital by management on an ongoing basis.

In part III, I examined the concept of executive power-*legitimacy*: that is to say, the general public 'rightness' of management's continuing possession and exercise of discretionary administrative power, as determined by the collective willingness of equity investors to acquiesce in the ensuing management–shareholder power imbalance. In practice, executive power-legitimacy is both reflected in, and prompted by, the market-determined criterion known as 'cost of capital', which essentially denotes the general willingness of investors to purchase a firm's securities relative to other potential outlets for their capital.

I explained that, ultimately, executive power-legitimacy – and, in turn, ready corporate access to external equity capital – is dependent on whether the exercise of managerial discretion is subject to appropriate formal checks as determined by shareholders in their capacity as the principal collective subject of such power. The objective of formally checking the exercise of executive power in this way is to ensure that the possessors of such power exercise it in a manner that is generally acknowledged by shareholders to be *accountable*. The *accountability* of executive decision-makers is a central concern of any effective corporate governance system. By nature it cannot be an end in its own right, although from a general investor perspective the existence of formal checks on managerial discretion is – under conditions of bounded rationality and consequent informational limitation – the best available proxy for assessing the likely riskiness of corporate securities. This in turn requires the establishment of effective managerial accountability norms, by which executive office-holders are required to provide objectively-verifiable reasons in support of their discretionary decisions, and also resolve – whether presumptively or directly – any actual or supposed shareholder concerns arising therefrom.

Accordingly, it can be said that effective managerial account-giving processes are a necessary institutional precondition to securing the legitimacy – and, in turn, sustainability – of management's continuing possession and exercise of discretionary administrative power, at least from the perspective of the principal collective subjects of such power. A key motivating function of corporate governance *law*, therefore, is to formulate and make available a set of formal managerial accountability norms that are effective in bringing about the above outcome across corporations generally.

However, whilst the presence of robust managerial accountability norms is – from an investor prospective – a broadly positive institutional characteristic, it is nonetheless possible for a corporate governance system to be conducive to *too much* managerial accountability. 'Excessive' accountability occurs where the bureaucratic costs to the firm of formal managerial account-giving – as measured by both compliance and maladaptation costs – outweigh the corresponding benefits to the firm in terms of increased executive power-legitimacy and, in turn, reduced cost of capital. In such instances, the perceived legitimacy of the firm's actual *corporate governance framework* will be called into question, on the commonly acknowledged basis that shareholders logically cannot be deemed to have acquiesced in the possession and exercise of discretionary administrative power by management on cost-*ineffective* terms. But given that the overall cost-effectiveness of accountability norms is impossible (or, at least, highly impracticable) for non-managerial actors to determine extraneously, it follows that – under conditions of bounded rationality – prevailing levels of managerial accountability within individual firms will tend towards a median level that is indicative of neither a material shortage nor a material surplus of micro-level accountability norms.

Therefore the effectiveness of any system of corporate governance law as a whole must ultimately be judged in terms of its capacity to achieve this overall result. That is, to enable individual corporations to strike an effective balance between, on the one hand, engendering a sufficient level of perceived managerial accountability to secure executive power-legitimacy, while, on the other, ensuring that the institutional measures that are put in place to achieve the above goal do not impose a cost-ineffective bureaucratic burden on the firm – and, indirectly, its shareholders – so as to secure the bureaucratic legitimacy of the corporate governance framework itself.

In part IV, I diverted slightly from the above line of enquiry to examine what may be perceived by many as the proverbial 'elephant in the room' issue in this debate: in other words, a basic but often unarticulated presumption on which much of the discussion in this chapter is built. That is the notion that *only shareholders* have a rightful entitlement to be the direct collective beneficiary of managerial accountability norms in corporate governance law, on the basis that they are the constituency principally affected by the corporation's internal power dynamic.

However, as the discussion in this part established, equity as a group is not the exclusive collective subject of corporate-managerial power in the above sense. Rather, reciprocal power imbalance also persists to a significant extent in the management-employee relationship as a result of the peculiar hierarchical nature of the employment relation at common law, coupled with the innate structural imbalance of labour markets in favour of employers as (generally scarce) purchasers of (generally non-scarce) human capital.

On the consequent understanding that the corporate equity and employment relations are *not* fundamentally dissimilar from one another in terms of their underlying power dynamic, I proceeded to query why – in the Anglo-American legal environment at least – only shareholders are ordinarily recognised as the rightful beneficiary of managerial accountability norms. In answer to this question, I attributed the traditional non-empowerment of labour within corporate governance law to the absence of rational incentives, on the part of both management and labour, to engage in any effective continuous process of managerial account-giving.

This is on account of the general insensitivity of the cost of human capital – unlike equity capital – to changing investor (ie employee) perceptions of executive power-legitimacy. Therefore both management and labour ordinarily lack adequate prudential incentives to seek to legitimate corporate-managerial power via the establishment of formal managerial accountability norms in the context of their relationship. Instead, employees as a general interest group have a rational incentive to invoke collective bargaining and other adversarial means of counterbalancing and – ultimately – mitigating corporate-managerial power, in order to secure the continuing legitimacy (and, in turn, sustainability) of the reciprocal power imbalance at the heart of the employment relation. This largely explains the persisting principle of shareholder exclusivity that underpins the basic doctrinal and normative slant of Anglo-American corporate governance law as a whole.

Having established the basic substance and parameters of corporate governance as a subject of legal-academic enquiry, I will now proceed to examine the fundamental nature of the phenomenon that is under scrutiny in this book. To this end, in the following chapter I will critically examine the most influential academic characterisation (or 'paradigm') of corporate governance within the Anglo-American environment today. That is the contractarian or 'nexus of contracts' theory of corporate governance.

Picking up on the core themes from this chapter, a principal focus of my analysis in chapter three will be how the contractarian paradigm has sought (with considerable success) to demonstrate that the central corporate governance problem of establishing the legitimacy of management's continuing possession and exercise of discretionary administrative power is, in the presence of appropriate legal and other institutional conditions, readily resolvable by recourse to private ordering methods alone. In this way, as I will seek to further establish, the contractarian paradigm succeeds in effectively 'reasoning away' any material regulatory role for the interventionist state in determining the appropriate contours of corporate governance law at the macro (ie system-wide) level. As such, contractarianism emphatically rejects the proverbial 'shadow of the state' as an appreciable corporate governance force.

3

The Contractarian Paradigm of Corporate Governance Law

I N THIS CHAPTER, I will examine the key features of the contractarian or 'nexus of contracts' paradigm of corporate governance that holds prominence within the United States and United Kingdom. In part I, I will introduce a key theme in this book, which is the purported 'privity' of Anglo-American corporate law: that is to say, its common perception as an aspect of 'private' or transactional law in contrast to 'public' or regulatory law. The importance of the contractarian understanding of corporate law in maintaining this orthodox understanding of the subject will also be highlighted. In part II, I will provide a brief account of the historical and intellectual background to the initial emergence of the contractarian paradigm in the United States.

In part III, I will describe how the three most prominent legal-institutional features of Anglo-American corporate governance are conventionally rationalised within the contractarian frame of analysis. These features are: (i) the status of shareholders as the exclusive collective beneficiary of managerial accountability norms; (ii) the executive primacy of the board of directors; and (iii) the pivotal status of independent directors, and the monitoring board generally, to the overall functioning of corporate governance as a managerial accountability system.

On this basis – and following on from the claims made in the previous chapter about the essential substance of corporate governance as a subject of enquiry – I will examine in part IV what I understand to be the principal normative dimensions of the private ordering paradigm. Here I will pay particular attention to the underlying tendency of contractarian scholarship to assert the purported superiority of private and decentralised methods of ordering intra-firm governance affairs at the *micro* (ie individual firm) level. Correspondingly, as I will show, contractarianism denies that there is any justifiable role for the interventionist regulatory state as an active determinant of prevailing managerial accountability norms at the *macro* (ie system-wide) level.

The most notable respects in which the contractarian paradigm – as analysed in this chapter – is manifested in the actual doctrinal structure of corporate governance law in the United States and United Kingdom will subsequently be the focus of the next two chapters.

I. THE PURPORTED 'PRIVITY'[1] OF ANGLO-AMERICAN CORPORATE LAW

For much of the past century, corporate law scholars in the United States and United Kingdom have developed the academic contours of their subject as an essentially private, functional and politically 'colourless' field of enquiry.[2] The precise jurisprudential trajectories along which these developments have occurred on each side of the Atlantic bear their own unique characteristics.[3] Nonetheless, a common and fundamental feature of the so-called 'Anglo-American' corporate law system is the dominant scholarly perception of the subject as a dynamic and self-determinative aspect of *private* law lying beyond the meddling reach of the 'public' or interventionist regulatory state. Thus, as mentioned earlier in this book,[4] corporate law is still conventionally rationalised and taught within the English-speaking world as an offshoot of 'building blocks' private law subjects such as contract, agency, equity and trusts. A uniting feature of all these areas of law, and the root of their purportedly 'private' nature, is their common focus on giving legal effect (or conversely non-effect) to the terms and essential substance of arrangements constituted by decentralised persons acting on their own behalf, whether in an individual or private-organisational capacity.

Hence, in commercial environments, legal rules are commonly regarded as providing little more than a structural vessel – whether in the form of a legally-binding agreement or legally-recognised relationship or business entity – into which the participating parties remain free to pour their own substantive content as reflected in the (literal or notional) bargains that

---

[1] I fully acknowledge that, to English private lawyers of an orthodox slant, my (mis)use of the word 'privity' in this context may be perceived as a serious terminological error. I am well aware that, in ordinary legal usage, the term is used to denote the traditional 'private-ness' (in the sense of non-effect on third party rights) of individual contractual agreements, rather than the private-ness (in the sense of non-regulatory nature) of an overall area of law. Notwithstanding, I use the term in this different and broader sense merely for want of a more appropriate word to describe the essential nature of the phenomenon that I will be discussing in this part.

[2] On the tendency of legal formalist thought (particularly in the United States) more generally to portray private law as being apolitical and thus purely instrumental in nature, see MJ Horwitz, 'The Rise of Legal Formalism' (1975) 19 *The American Journal of Legal History* 251; MJ Horwitz, 'The Emergence of an Instrumental Conception of American Law, 1780–1820' (1971) 5 *Perspectives in American History* 287; N Duxbury, 'The Origins of Modern American Jurisprudence, Part I: The Birth of Legal Formalism', University of Manchester Faculty of Law Working Paper No 6 (January 1991).

[3] On this, see below chs 4 and 5 of this volume respectively.

[4] See above ch 1 of this volume, fns 1–7 and accompanying text.

they autonomously strike with one another. Even those aspects of private law doctrine that could be said to exhibit a normative or value-laden quality, such as the notions of good faith, implied terms or fiduciary capacity, tend in general to denote principally procedural standards of fair dealing in any given bargaining context. As such, private law (including corporate law) logic is characteristically averse to concepts of substantive justice or fairness that seek directly to effect distributional outcomes between the participants in a freely (ie honestly and non-coercively) constituted agreement or organisation.[5]

In contrast – and as likewise mentioned earlier[6] – those subjects which are usually placed within the ambit of 'public' or regulatory law, including tort, criminal, antitrust and tax law, are inherently interventionist and redistributive (whether monetarily or in terms of distribution of risk or market power) in nature. In commercial environments, these areas of law seek in differing ways from one another to regulate directly the social outcomes of business activity via the super-imposition of externally-determined standards or norms, over and above the actual or imputed preferences of contractors or business associates.

From an orthodox legal formalist[7] perspective, the functional disparity between the private (contractual) and public (regulatory) spheres of business law is unproblematic so long as each dimension respects the other's legitimate regulatory space. Accordingly, it is asserted that the 'public' aspects of business law should be restricted to setting and enforcing the external 'rules of the game' within which commercial actors or organisations operate. This is with a view, inter alia, to preserving proximately competitive market conditions and also mitigating the uncompensated infliction of social costs on third parties (especially environmental interests) who are incapable of seeking a priori contractual protection or compensation.[8] Ultimately, though, the internal content or structure of each agreement, association or entity that is privately formed – including the motivating goals and objectives of business activity itself – should be left to the realm of spontaneous and decentralised contractual order, as governed exclusively by private law doctrine.[9]

---

[5] Rawls refers to this concept as 'pure procedural justice', whereby 'there is no independent criteria for the right result', but rather 'a correct or fair procedure such that the outcome is likewise correct or fair, whatever it is, provided that the procedure has been properly followed'. See J Rawls, *A Theory of Justice*, revised edn (Oxford, Oxford University Press, 1999) (first published 1971) 75. It follows from this logic that in any transaction 'the outcome is just, whatever it is, in virtue of the contract that produced it'. See M Sandel, *Liberalism and the Limits of Justice*, 2nd edn (Cambridge, Cambridge University Press, 1999) (first published 1982) 108.

[6] See ch 1 of this volume, text to fns 1–7.

[7] On the influence of this important jurisprudential tradition more generally, see above n 2.

[8] See M Friedman, *Capitalism and Freedom* (Chicago IL, The University of Chicago Press, 1962) ch 2.

[9] In this regard, Bowman explains that regulation 'is not simply a coercive tool' but 'is also a method of achieving a desired result by defining the boundaries of self-regulation', in that

In the specific context of corporate law (including, in particular, corporate *governance* law), the influence of neo-classical legal formalism weighs very heavily within the Anglo-American environment under the guise of what is variously termed the 'contractarian', 'nexus of contracts', or 'private ordering' theory of the firm. Originally an invention of US-based financial economists in the 1970s,[10] contractarianism has expanded in depth and influence over recent decades to become the dominant conceptual and normative lens through which the corporation and its constituent laws are conventionally studied across the English-speaking world.

On a jurisprudential level, contractarianism in effect instils the logic of private law into the internal structure and functioning of modern business corporations, by asserting that 'public' or widely-held corporate entities – in spite of their typically enormous organisational scale, extensive social impact and peculiar ownership/control dynamic (including the lack of any distinct proprietary or entrepreneurial presence) – should be regarded as essentially private and quasi-contractual institutions, which are subject to qualitatively similar market dynamics and pressures to those affecting orthodox (ie closely-held) business entities.[11] In particular, contractarian scholars emphatically refuse to afford any conceptual significance to the corporation's formal legal autonomy or 'personhood', instead regarding the incorporated firm as a mere structural convenience that serves the collective, contractually communicated interests of its various human participants at any given point in time.[12]

Moreover, since the aforementioned public-private law dichotomy attempts to put purportedly 'internal' corporate affairs beyond the reach of deliberate state determination, it follows that questions concerning the inherent goals of the corporation are both an unnecessary and inappropriate question for governments directly to concern themselves

by 'prohibiting specific forms of behaviour [it] implicitly sanctions other behaviour'. See S Bowman, *The Modern Corporation and American Political Thought: Law, Power and Ideology* (PA, Penn University State Press, 1996) 139.

[10] On the seminal works underpinning this school of thought, see below n 22.

[11] On this, see generally P Ireland, *Property and Contract in Contemporary Corporate Theory* (2003) 23 *Legal Studies* 453; P Ireland, 'Defending the Rentier: Corporate Theory and the Reprivatisation of the Public Company' in J Parkinson, A Gamble and G Kelly, *The Political Economy of the Company* (Oxford, Hart Publishing, 2000) ch 7.

[12] See, eg BR Cheffins, *Company Law: Theory, Structure and Operation* (Oxford University Press, Oxford, 1997) 31–41. According to Cheffins: 'the history of [the joint stock company] indicates that even without laws providing for incorporation, business enterprises can be organized along much the same lines as the modern corporation. It follows that companies legislation has had in and of itself only a modest impact on the bargaining dynamics which account for the nature and form of business enterprises. Thus, *analytically an incorporated company is, like other types of firms, fundamentally a nexus of contracts*' (emphasis added). See ibid, 41. See also FH Easterbrook and DR Fischel, *The Economic Structure of Corporate Law* (Cambridge MA, Harvard University Press, 1991) 8–15. Easterbrook and Fischel claim (at 12) that '[t]he "personhood" of a corporation is a matter of convenience rather than reality'.

with.[13] Rather, the social desirability of any corporate objective that emanates from existing legal and market mechanisms – in particular, the widely-accepted Anglo-American managerial norm of shareholder wealth (or 'value') maximisation[14] – can be inferred a priori from its very pervasiveness and continuing widespread acceptance both by investors and other corporate participants today.[15]

In respect of any adverse social outcomes that follow from the systematic pursuit by corporations of this objective, the proper remedy is said to lie in the bounds of *non*-corporate (regulatory) law rules – especially tort, criminal and tax law – that use punitive and disincentive measures to reduce or render negative the ultimate monetary 'pay-offs' to corporations of engaging in certain harmful or socially undesirable kinds of activity.[16] The resultant norm is one of 'shareholder wealth maximization within the (extraneous) law'.[17] This approach could be said to respect the internal organisational autonomy of corporations by treating incorporated entities as akin to human individuals, entitled to form their own life plans and objectives subject only to compliance with the universal laws to which *all* (corporate and non-corporate) behaviour in a liberal society is subject.[18]

The principal normative achievement of the contractarian paradigm, as will be explained further below, has been its remarkable success in *alleviating* formerly widespread academic discontent[19] about the continuing relevance and legitimacy of corporate law's privity: that is to say, the traditional treatment of corporate law as an essentially *pre*-political and

---

[13] See M Friedman, 'The Social Responsibility of Business is to Increase its Profits' in T Beauchamp and N Bowie (eds), *Ethical Theory and Business* (Upper Saddle River, Pearson, 2004) (first published 1979); article originally published in *The New York Times Magazine* (1970).

[14] On this phenomenon generally, see SM Bainbridge, 'In Defense of the Shareholder Wealth Maximization Norm: A Reply to Professor Green' (1993) 50 *Washington & Lee Law Review* 1423; MJ Roe, 'The Shareholder Wealth Maximization Norm and Industrial Organization' (2001) 149 *University of Pennsylvania Law Review* 2063.

[15] For an argument to this effect, see Easterbrook and Fischel, *The Economic Structure of Corporate Law*, above n 12, 35–39.

[16] For further discussion and analysis of this so-called 'negative externalities' argument for (limited) regulatory state interventionism in private ordering, see below ch 7 of this volume, pt II. The academic progenitor of this argument is the English economist Arthur Cecil Pigou. See AC Pigou, *The Economics of Welfare*, 4th edn (London, Macmillan, 1932) (first published 1920) pt II.

[17] In using this term I am indebted to John Parkinson, who – in his classic work *Corporate Power and Responsibility* – identified and criticised what he regarded to be the orthodox normative formula in corporate law scholarship of 'profit maximization within the law'. See J Parkinson, *Corporate Power and Responsibility: Issues in the Theory of Company Law* (Oxford, Oxford University Press, 1993) 42–43.

[18] This can be regarded as the standard neo-liberal position with respect to the proper responsibilities of both corporations and corporate law within wider society. For a fuller exposition of this argument, see Friedman, 'The Social Responsibility of Business', above n 13; FA Hayek, 'The Corporation in a Democratic Society: In Whose Interest Ought It and Will It Be Run?' in HI Ansoff (ed), *Business Strategy* (Harmondsworth, Penguin, 1969) 266.

[19] On this, see below pt II.

market-instrumental facet of private law, rather than a publicly-infused dimension of regulatory law concerned with the objectives and substantive outcomes of corporate organisations within the wider fabric of economy and society. It is therefore unsurprising that the contractarian theory of the firm tends, like traditional legal formalism, to display a strong anti-regulatory hue.[20]

Before examining the specific parameters of the contractarian paradigm in detail, it is important to appreciate the historical and intellectual background from which this highly influential school of thought on corporate law and governance first emerged.

II. (A BRIEF)[21] HISTORICAL AND INTELLECTUAL BACKGROUND TO CORPORATE CONTRACTARIANISM

The contractarian paradigm of corporate governance (or 'corporate contractarianism') was developed initially by US financial economists and corporate lawyers over the course of the late twentieth century,[22] as part of a more general ideological transition in the Anglo-American political economy: from the mid- and post-war consensus of state-centric corporatism, towards the market-centric neo-liberalism that became an increasingly pervasive reference point for intellectuals and policy-makers in the century's latter half. As a not-insignificant microcosm of this wider institutional paradigm shift, corporate contractarianism represented a crucial antidote to the modern business corporation's progressive intellectual removal over previous decades from the orthodox field of economic analysis.[23]

The peculiar institutional features of the widely-held or 'public' corporation – in particular, the substantial separation that it entails between beneficial equity ownership and executive control over business affairs –

---

[20] On the prevalence of this characteristic within legal formalist jurisprudence more generally, see the sources cited above n 2.

[21] For a longer and more detailed account of the historical development of contractarian thought, see Ireland, *Property and Contract*, above n 11.

[22] The seminal works of this school of thought include AA Alchian and H Demsetz, 'Production, Information Costs, and Economic Organization' (1972) 62 *American Economic Review* 777; MC Jensen and WH Meckling, 'Theory of the Firm: Managerial Behaviour, Agency Costs and Ownership Structure' (1976) 3 *Journal of Financial Economics* 305; EF Fama, 'Agency Problems and the Theory of the Firm' (1980) 88 *Journal of Political Economy* 288; EF Fama and MC Jensen, 'Separation of Ownership and Control' (1983) 26 *Journal of Law and Economics* 301; FH Easterbrook and DR Fischel, 'The Corporate Contract' (1989) 89 *Columbia Law Review* 1416; Easterbrook and Fischel, *The Economic Structure of Corporate Law*, above n 12. Although the foundational piece of scholarship in the contractarian tradition is commonly regarded to be Ronald Coase's landmark article 'The Nature of the Firm' (1937) 4 *Economica* 386, this work is arguably better regarded as a significant influence for the (later) contractarian movement, rather than as a constituent part of that movement itself.

[23] For a statement of intent to this effect by two early protagonists of the contractarian position, see Jensen and Meckling, 'Theory of the Firm', above n 22, 307.

had hitherto posed significant difficulties for academic social scientists. Most pertinently, the so-called separation of ownership and control within the modern large-scale corporation entailed the absence of any distinct entrepreneurial presence whose initiative and self-interest could be relied on to drive continuing advances in business operations. This signified a breakdown in the proverbial 'invisible hand' mechanism that had previously provided a utilitarian link between business profit-taking and the perceived advancement of society's material welfare.[24] Accordingly, in the view of progressive social scientists such as Adolf Berle, John Maynard Keynes and John Kenneth Galbraith, it made little sense any more to regard a company's shareholders as the rightful recipients of residual corporate profit streams, at least beyond the minimal level required to encourage their continuing investment in industry.[25] This was because shareholders' lack of effective entrepreneurial control or influence meant that any financial returns paid to them in excess of this level would lead to little improvement in business operations and thus would constitute a substantial waste of corporate resources.[26] At the same time, the specialisation of corporate management as a novel profession in itself (in distinction from classical owner-enterprise) arguably called for a new 'technocratic' breed of corporate controller whose technical expertise and organisational planning skills, rather than wealth or creative impulse, represented the primary determinant of corporate success.[27]

On a wider, macro level, the enormous expansion of business operations made possible by the collective pooling of middle-class savings in joint-stock enterprise led to the significant concentration of key industry sectors such as automobile manufacture and public utilities[28] within highly capitalised oligopolies.[29] This purportedly served to remove public corporations from orthodox constraints of product market competition, enabling

[24] See AA Berle and G Means, *The Modern Corporation and Private Property*, 4th edn (New York, Harcourt, Brace & World, 1968) (first published 1932) 9; AA Berle, *The American Economic Republic* (New York, Harcourt, Brace & World, 1963) 43.

[25] See, eg Berle and Means, ibid, 299–302; JM Keynes, 'The End of Laissez Faire' (1926) in JM Keynes, *Essays in Persuasion* (London, Macmillan, 1931) 312, 314–15; JK Galbraith, *Economics and the Public Purpose* (London, Andre Deutsch, 1973) ch 9.

[26] Berle and Means, *The Modern Corporation and Private Property*, above n 24.

[27] On this, see Galbraith, *Economics and the Public Purpose*, above n 25, chs 9–11; JK Galbraith, *The New Industrial State*, paperback edn (Princeton, Princeton University Press, 2007) (first published 1967).

[28] Two of the most notable examples of the significant product market concentration that took place in the first half of the 20th century were the US industrial giants General Motors and General Electric.

[29] On this, see Galbraith, *Economics and the Public Purpose*, above n 25, 81–109; AA Berle, 'Modern Functions of the Corporate System' (1962) 62 *Columbia Law Review* 433, 434; AA Berle, *The Twentieth Century Capitalist Revolution* (New York, Harcourt, Brace & World, 1954) 46; HG Manne, 'The "Higher" Criticism of the Modern Corporation' (1962) 62 *Columbia Law Review* 399, 407; J Strachey, *Contemporary Capitalism* (London, Victor Gollancz, 1956) 21, 24; AD Chandler, *Scale and Scope: The Dynamics of Industrial Capitalism* (Cambridge MA, Belknap, 1990).

corporate managers to formulate quasi-governmental industrial plans geared to stabilising production, pricing and attendant employment conditions over long time periods.[30] Meanwhile, the ability of oligopolistic enterprises to generate significant levels of retained earnings from stable production runs under long-term industrial plans reduced the dependence of corporations on outside financiers as a continuing source of capital, resulting in the further diminution of the external capital markets as an institutional constraint on managers' administrative discretion.[31]

Even to the extent that corporations were compelled to turn to external equity investors to fund the maintenance or expansion of business operations, the general passivity and informational limitations of private shareholders, coupled with their incapacity to take collective action against recalcitrant managers, meant that corporate managers possessed considerable freedom to mobilise shareholder funds in the pursuit of internally-determined corporate goals.[32] Accordingly, by the mid-to-late twentieth century there had developed a popular social-scientific belief in the United States that the raising and allocation of industrial capital (what in today's parlance would be termed 'corporate finance') had become a substantially *internalised* organisational function, so that business corporations now operated largely in autonomy from 'external' securities markets with both institutions fulfilling distinct and separable socio-economic objectives from one other.[33]

As a result of all the above factors, during the post-war period it was widely felt to be no longer appropriate for large-scale business corporations in the United States to be perceived as economic institutions governed by private market processes. On the contrary, corporations were becoming more analogous to statist institutions insofar as the nature, scale and autonomy of their administrative operations were concerned,[34] only without the liberal-democratic checks and balances to which the exercise

---

[30] See Galbraith, *The New Industrial State*, above n 27; AD Chandler, *The Visible Hand: The Managerial Revolution in American Business* (Cambridge MA, Harvard University Press, 1977).

[31] See AA Berle, 'Property, Production and Revolution: A Preface to the Revised Edition' (1967) in Berle and Means, *The Modern Corporation and Private Property*, above n 24, xv; Berle, 'Modern Functions', above n 29, 440.

[32] Berle and Means, *The Modern Corporation and Private Property*, above n 24, 7, 116; AA Berle, *Power Without Property: A New Development in American Political Economy* (New York, Harcourt, Brace & World, 1959).

[33] See, eg Berle, 'Property, Production and Revolution', above n 3, xv, xxi, xxiv; Berle, 'Modern Functions', above n 29, 448; Galbraith, *Economics and the Public Purpose*, above n 25.

[34] On this, see Berle, 'Property, Production and Revolution', above n 3, xxvi; D Tsuk Mitchell, 'From Pluralism to Individualism: Berle and Means and 20th-Century American Legal Thought' (2005) 30 *Law and Social Inquiry* 179. In the context of the UK, meanwhile, John Maynard Keynes had earlier likened the modern large corporation to a semi-autonomous public body in the vein of the Bank of England or the Universities, leading him to opine that the 'so-called important political question' of whether or not Britain's industries should be nationalised was now rendered largely unimportant. See Keynes, 'The End of Laissez Faire' above n 25, 316.

of public decision-making power is ordinarily subject.[35] Therefore it was increasingly regarded as imperative within the corporatist politico-economic climate of the mid-twentieth century that corporations seek to conform to public service expectations as part of their core operational activities, and as an essential pre-condition of maintaining their implicit licence to hold and exercise quasi-public power outside of the formal democratic state framework.[36] The function of regulation, meanwhile, was to solidify and enforce the perceived public interest in economic organisation in situations where corporations were insensitive to the developing climate of opinion as to what constituted socially acceptable corporate conduct.[37]

In short, therefore, the US corporation was, by the mid-to-late twentieth century, in general no longer perceived as an economic institution in the classical sense of the term. Rather, the corporation was widely recognised by social scientists as a historically peculiar, quasi-public institution whose characteristics and effects were more appropriately deciphered through the lens of political as opposed to economic theory. Against this historical and intellectual background, contractarianism essentially sought to reinvigorate the business corporation as a subject of orthodox economic analysis, and thus to portray the modern 'public' corporation as being continually subject to the 'invisible hand' of market governance as opposed to the 'visible hand'[38] of technocratic managerial or state control. In this regard, the theory can be regarded as a key and characteristic component of the more general turn in western social science referred to earlier,[39] which essentially sought – ultimately with widespread success – to assert the purported superiority of decentralised markets over technocratic organisations (both statist and non-statist) in achieving effective control over modern economic activity.[40]

---

[35] As Mary Stokes has observed: 'The effect of changes brought about by the growth of corporate enterprise was that the market could no longer be viewed as regulating and thereby legitimating the exercise of corporate power', with the result that '[t]he power conferred upon corporate managers by the business community was potentially unchecked and hence illegitimate within the framework of liberal democracy'. See M Stokes, 'Company Law and Legal Theory' in W Twining, *Legal Theory and Common Law* (Oxford, Blackwell, 1986) 155, 159.

[36] See Berle, *Power Without Property*, above n 32, 91–92; Berle and Means, *The Modern Corporation and Private Property*, above n 24, 310–13.

[37] Berle, *Power Without Property*, above n 32, 114–15.

[38] This latter term is attributable to Chandler, *The Visible Hand*, above n 30, who developed it as a modern counterpoint to the well-known former notion as developed in Adam Smith's classical economic text *The Wealth of Nations* (1776).

[39] See above nn 22–23 and accompanying text.

[40] The foundational academic texts in this tradition are commonly regarded to be Milton Friedman's *Capitalism and Freedom*, above n 8, and Friedrich von Hayek's *The Road to Serfdom* (London, Routledge, 1944), although as a political force the movement did not begin to attain significant influence until the 1970s.

The influence of contractarianism has undoubtedly been most profound within the United States, where for the past three decades it has constituted the mainstream scholarly take on corporate governance (and, indeed, corporate law in general) as a subject of academic enquiry.[41] At the same time, the spread of influential US-inspired contributions to British scholarship over recent decades[42] coupled with a shortage of viable home-grown counter-theories[43] have together ensured the prevalence of American-esque contractarian logic to a significant extent within UK corporate law thinking and policy-making today.[44]

Indeed, in the UK environment, contractarianism has not only permeated the national academic psyche, but has conspicuously manifested itself even within the realm of governmental policy-making on corporate law. In this regard, the former Labour government's Company Law Review Steering Group – in formulating its recommendations for widespread reform that prefaced the enactment of the Companies Act 2006 – proceeded on the explicitly contractarian basis that 'the role of company law [is] to *facilitate the exercise of effective business choices* so as to maximise wealth and welfare . . . *without public policy intervention*' (emphasis added).[45] Continuing these fundamental themes of free contractual choice and institutional diversity, the Steering Group explained that since '[t]here is an almost infinitely diverse range of businesses and business philosophies', it follows that 'there needs to be a correspondingly wide variety of systems of company governance'.[46] Accordingly, the Steering Group asserted that '*company law must encourage, not suppress, this variety and flexibility*'; and, moreover, that '[w]hen [regulatory state] intervention is necessary it should be designed, so far as possible, to *avoid inhibiting freedom of choice and flexibility for development*' (emphasis added).[47]

Whatever one's personal view on the normative merits or drawbacks of the contractarian perspective, the above discussion establishes one objectively indisputable fact: that the contractarian paradigm is unquestionably

---

[41] Amongst the most influential academic expositions of this model of corporate law and governance are Easterbrook and Fischel, *The Economic Structure of Corporate Law*, above n 12; Kraakman et al's *The Anatomy of Corporate Law: A Comparative and Functional Approach*, 2nd edn (Oxford, Oxford University Press, 2009) (first published 2004), and Stephen Bainbridge's *The New Corporate Governance in Theory and Practice* (New York, Oxford University Press, 2008).

[42] Most notably Brian Cheffins' excellent book *Company Law: Theory, Structure and Operation*, above n 12; and, more recently, David Kershaw's *Company Law in Context: Text and Materials* (Oxford, Oxford University Press, 2009).

[43] One notable exception to this general trend is John Parkinson's *Corporate Power and Responsibility*, above n 17, which provides a comprehensive and path-breaking critical polemic on corporate law theory in a British context.

[44] Ireland, *Property and Contract*, above n 11, 454.

[45] Company Law Review Steering Group, *Modern Company Law for a Competitive Economy: Developing the Framework* (London, Department of Trade and Industry, 2000) ch 2, para 2.4.

[46] Ibid, para 2.6.

[47] Ibid.

the dominant ideological reference point within the field of Anglo-American corporate law and governance today. Moreover, it looks likely to remain so for the foreseeable future notwithstanding growing dissatisfaction with neo-liberal ideologies within broader political and social-scientific discourse.

With the above consideration in mind, a systematic analysis of the key contours of the contractarian paradigm is justified at this point.

III. HOW DO CONTRACTARIANS RATIONALISE THE MOST PROMINENT FEATURES OF ANGLO-AMERICAN CORPORATE GOVERNANCE?

A. The Conceptual Starting Point: The Corporation (or 'Firm') as a Nexus of Contracts

The conceptual starting point of corporate contractarianism is at first sight somewhat paradoxical. In essence, contractarianism asserts that, analytically, the institution known as the business corporation is not an 'institution' at all in any meaningful metaphysical sense.[48] Rather, a corporation (or 'firm') is from a practical point of view composed of nothing more than the particular collection of individuals who are at any one time involved in the carrying on of its productive operations.[49] These individuals will typically include equity and debt investors, workers (including directors and managers), trade creditors and customers. If the firm deserves any independent recognition as a 'thing' in itself, it is merely the notional 'nexus' or 'hub' around which these various micro-agents contract with one another,[50] each offering their respective 'inputs' to the production process (eg equity, debt, physical or human capital) in exchange for a corresponding 'output' (eg dividend, interest, price or wage).[51]

---

[48] P Ireland, 'Recontractualising the Corporation: Implicit Contract as Ideology' in D Campbell, H Collins and J Wightman (eds), *Implicit Dimensions of Contract* (Oxford, Hart Publishing, 2003) 255, 260.

[49] In this regard, the contractarian model of the firm could be said to bear a certain parallel with Margaret Thatcher's famous (or, depending on one's political perspective, *infamous*) adage that 'there is no such thing as society . . . [only] individual men and women'. Ireland refers to this conceptual phenomenon as 'the corporate vanishing trick'. See P Ireland, 'The Myth of Shareholder Ownership' (1999) 62 *Modern Law Review* 32, 56.

[50] See Easterbrook and Fischel, *The Economic Structure of Corporate Law*, above n 12, 11–12. For this reason, corporate contractarianism is commonly referred to in the alternative as 'nexus of contracts' theory. Although now a generic term of reference, the literal phrase would appear to be attributable to the financial economist Eugene Fama, who coined it in his 1980 article 'Agency Problems and the Theory of the Firm', above n 22, 290.

[51] In reality, of course, the 'nexus' or 'hub' will be represented by the firm's senior management team, being the one party that is (at least theoretically) common to the negotiations with all input-providers. However, managers are ultimately themselves no more than mere input-providers to the firm's production process (insofar as they supply their human capital) like everyone else, so that it arguably makes no sense at all to speak of 'the corporation' in

Accordingly, the key analytical characteristic of contractarianism is its capacity to explain the structure and operation of the firm anatomically in terms of the collective pattern of economic incentives motivating its various individual participants. Through this neo-classical economic lens, it becomes possible to ascribe theoretically rational behavioural modes to a corporation's various constituent groups based on the conceptual framework of an implicit and ongoing 'bargain' over their respective entitlements to share in the wealth generated by the firm's productive operations.[52] Allied to this contractual bargaining hypothesis of corporate governance is a passive-instrumental conception of corporate law, whereby legal rules and structures are essentially flexible and facilitative 'tools' – reflective of the commercially expedient arrangements that corporate participants would otherwise tend to establish with one another via private transacting, and correspondingly not as coercive embodiments of moral-political norms established via public consensus and teleological debate.[53]

Having established this basic conceptual bargaining framework, the next issue for contractarians to deal with is what particular corporate governance norms and other arrangements notional corporate 'contractors' will tend to agree upon, in establishing the terms on which they are mutually willing to invest (whether financially or non-financially) in productive enterprise with one another. In understanding the contractarian rationalisation of prevailing corporate governance laws, an important preliminary point to note is that within this frame of reference, corporate law is typically imbued with an inherently contingent and flexible character. It follows that, in general, no substantive feature of corporate governance should be proverbially 'set in stone' on a universal basis, but rather should be freely manipulable at the micro level depending on the specific circumstances and challenges facing individual firms.

Therefore, when rationalising the most prominent legal-institutional features of Anglo-American corporate governance, the principal objective of contractarians is to explain *why* these arrangements tend to exist in the vast majority of cases, while at the same time fully acknowledging the justifiability of the occasional outlying case. As I will explain further below, the

---

the sense of an autonomous, reified institution 'in itself'. Rather, in the words of Jensen and Meckling, the corporation is ultimately just a 'legal fiction which serves as a nexus for contracting relationships'. See Jensen and Meckling, 'Theory of the Firm', above n 22, 311. See also Cheffins, *Company Law*, above n 12, 31–41.

[52] See Fama, 'Agency Problems', above n 22, 289.

[53] As Easterbrook and Fischel explain: 'The corporation and its securities are products in financial markets to as great an extent as the sewing machines or other things the firm makes. Just as the founders of a firm have incentives to make the kind of sewing machines people want to buy, they have incentives to create the kind of firm, governance structure, and securities the customers in capital markets want'. See *The Economic Structure of Corporate Law*, above n 12, 4–6.

normatively significant aspect of this analysis is not that it seeks to imbue prevailing corporate governance norms with the purported quality of innate optimality or universal 'rightness', but rather that it simply queries why existing governance arrangements should *not* be regarded as preferable to all available alternatives, when they have evidently been selected – and, moreover – sustained over time by corporate contractors within a competitive economic environment.[54]

With this proviso in mind, the contractarian rationalisation of the three most prominent legal-institutional features of Anglo-American corporate governance can now be examined. These three features are: (1) shareholder exclusivity; (2) the executive primacy of the board of directors; and (3) majority-independent boards.

B. The Three Most Prominent Features of Anglo-American Corporate Governance

(i) Shareholder Exclusivity

Arguably the most prominent legal-institutional feature of Anglo-American corporate governance, at least in comparison with many developed non-Anglo-Saxon systems, is the perceived special importance that is afforded to the interests of shareholders relative to other corporate participant groups. It is thus commonly said that the US and UK systems of corporate governance – and, indeed, of corporate law generally – are dedicated to the notion of 'shareholder primacy'.[55] This is in contrast to the perceived 'stakeholder' governance model that has become emblematic of countries such as Germany and Japan over recent decades.[56]

The notion of shareholder primacy in corporate governance, however, is something of a misnomer. In fact, shareholder *primacy* – at least as understood in the proper sense of the term – does not exist as a feature of *any* developed system of corporate law or governance, whether in the Anglo-American environment or elsewhere. The word 'primacy' – used in its accurate sense within a governance context – tends to denote the superior-

---

[54] See, eg the argument to this effect advanced by Stephen Bainbridge in his article 'Director Primacy and Shareholder Disempowerment' (2006) 119 *Harvard Law Review* 1735.

[55] See, eg A Keay, 'Company Directors Behaving Poorly: Disciplinary Options for Shareholders' (2007) *Journal of Business Law* 656, 656: 'Generally speaking, Anglo-American corporate law embraces a principle that has been expressed in one of the following ways: *shareholder primacy*, shareholder wealth maximisation or shareholder value' (emphasis added).

[56] Arguably the most well-known academic juxtaposition of the so-called 'shareholder' and 'stakeholder' national models of corporate governance is contained in Hansmann and Kraakman's provocative article 'The End of History for Corporate Law' (2001) 89 *Georgetown Law Journal* 439.

ity of decision-making power enjoyed by a person or group, in relation to other persons or groups within an organisation. As my earlier analysis of the corporation's internal power dynamic has demonstrated, though, decision-making *primacy* within the corporate structure (with very limited exceptions) resides squarely in *the board of directors* – and, indirectly, senior managers – rather than the general body of shareholders.[57]

However, what shareholders collectively *do* enjoy within the Anglo-American corporate governance framework is the quality of structural *exclusivity*: that is, the entitlement to be regarded as the ultimate beneficiary of the accountability norms to which the board – and, indirectly, management – are ordinarily subject in exercising their executive discretion. The two principal and most fundamental managerial accountability norms that together put shareholders' interests at centre-stage within Anglo-American corporations are: first, the collective ex ante right of appointment (and re-appointment) that ordinary shareholders are entitled to exercise over the board of directors at specified intervals; and, secondly, the (limited) right that shareholders have to remedy managerial misconduct on an ex post facto basis in court, by means of the equitable fiduciary principle in corporate law.[58]

On the presumption that shareholder exclusivity *must* be preferable to alternative possible determinations of ultimate legal-beneficial status within the firm, contractarians are faced with the ensuing question as to why this particular allocation of appointment and fiduciary rights is agreed upon by the firm's various participants (or 'contractors') as a whole. While it is fairly obvious why shareholders themselves would notionally opt for such a distribution of governance entitlements, it is less readily obvious – indeed, at first sight, somewhat perplexing – why other participant groups in the firm, especially employees and trade creditors, would agree in a hypothetical bargaining scenario to sacrifice their own potential entitlement to legal-beneficial status within the firm, so as to vest it in shareholders alone.

Moreover, given the defining characteristic of the Anglo-American corporation as a managerially (and, correspondingly, *not* proprietary or entrepreneurially) controlled institution, a further awkward question arises as to why shareholders continue in general to enjoy exclusive profit and governance rights in public corporations. This is in spite of the commonly acknowledged fact that shareholders of public corporations in the United States and United Kingdom generally fulfil no distinct ownership or even control function within the firm, having been substantially externalised

---

[57] See above ch 2 of this volume, pt I.D. On this, see also Bainbridge, 'Director Primacy', above n 54; Bainbridge, *The New Corporate Governance*, above n 41, ch 5.

[58] Easterbrook and Fischel, *The Economic Structure of Corporate Law*, above n 12, 91; Bainbridge, *The New Corporate Governance*, above n 41, 71. For an analysis of the latter phenomenon from the perspective of the thesis of this book, see below ch 6 of this volume, pt IV.

from the productive process by a combination of both legal and market factors. Accordingly, Adam Smith's classical 'invisible hand' theorem – on which market-liberal assumptions about the general social instrumentality (and consequent social acceptability) of profit-seeking entrepreneurial activity have traditionally been founded – has no readily obvious application within the modern corporate-organisational context.

In providing a normative explanation as to why the principle of shareholder exclusivity retains prominence within managerially-controlled public corporations, contractarian theorists seek to reinvent the classical economic concept of entrepreneurial risk-taking in a revised form appropriate to the characteristics of modern *corporate* – as opposed to individual – enterprise.[59] Hence contractarianism portrays the modern corporate equity investor as a 'residual risk-bearer', who voluntarily undertakes the risk of periodic business underperformance by entering into a notionally 'incomplete' contract with the firm under which her periodic economic returns are unspecified. By contrast, other corporate constituent groups, notably workers and lenders, are (in theory at least) usually able to specify in advance their economic return from the firm plus the conditions upon which they agree to advance their respective input to the firm's production process.[60]

As compensation for bearing the 'down-side' risk of receiving little or nothing in the event of the firm being loss-making, it is said that the equity investor will rationally bargain for the corresponding 'up-side' entitlement to the whole of the 'residual' profit generated by the firm over a successful period: that is to say, for any outstanding net returns remaining once all other factors of production (eg employees, lenders, suppliers) have been paid their respective fixed contractual entitlements.[61] Furthermore, in order to exert a degree of influence over how managers use their invested funds, equity investors as a group will tend to demand the two principal (ex ante and ex post facto) managerial accountability norms described above.

Meanwhile, other corporate constituent groups will in the typical case be able to achieve satisfactory protection for their various investments under their respective 'complete' contracts with the firm, thus making

---

[59] On the inappositeness of classical entrepreneurial concepts as a means of rationalising large-scale corporate enterprise, see D Campbell, 'Adam Smith, Farrar on the Company and the Economics of the Corporation' (1990) 19 *Anglo-American Law Review* 185.

[60] For a concise summary and critical analysis of the dual notions of residual risk-bearing and incomplete contracting within corporate-contractarian theory, see G Kelly and J Parkinson, 'The Conceptual Foundations of the Company: a Pluralist Approach' in J Parkinson, A Gamble and G Kelly, *The Political Economy of the Company* (Oxford, Hart Publishing, 2000) 113, esp 114–21.

[61] Fama and Jensen, 'Separation of Ownership and Control', above n 22, 302–03. As Easterbrook and Fischel put it, '[i]nvestors bear most of the risk of business failure, in exchange for which they are promised most of the rewards of success'. See *The Economic Structure of Corporate Law*, above n 12, 11.

hierarchical governance rights unnecessary.[62] Moreover, non-shareholder groups will be prepared to concede governance entitlements to equity investors on the understanding that this arrangement will on the whole prove to be mutually beneficial for them. This is because equity investors are uniquely placed to diversify their capital on an economy-wide basis and thus 'hedge' against the risk of individual firm failure, meaning that the failure of any one firm in which a shareholder has invested will generally not be catastrophic for her overall economic position.[63]

Equity investors are consequently much more capable than other groups of absorbing the occasional losses resulting from risky but potentially path-breaking ventures which, although liable to increase temporarily the likelihood of firm failure, if successful will generate long-term economic benefits for the firm and its participants as a whole. However other corporate constituent groups, such as workers and suppliers, are by nature 'over-invested' in specific firms in the sense that they usually stand to lose considerably in the event of individual corporate failure. Such groups, therefore, if vested with corporate governance rights would arguably not be prone to support risky strategies by management even where they promise positive risk-adjusted returns for the firm.

Furthermore, to the extent that making boards of directors answerable to multiple constituencies is arguably likely to engender conflicts of interest and thus undermine consensus decision-making, it is universally preferable from the viewpoint of the corporation's participants as a whole to establish a system of clear and unitary directorial accountability to one single, roughly homogenous group.[64] And, for the above reason, shareholders generally stand out as the most desirable collective candidate in this regard. It follows therefore that a company's various participants will typically have a mutual incentive to agree to the vesting of corporate governance entitlements in shareholders *exclusively*, as this is the only distribution of rights within the firm that is consistent with the advancement

---

[62] Although for an influential counter-argument to the effect that *all* contracts entered into by a firm's various factors of production are to differing extents incomplete, see OE Williamson, *The Mechanisms of Governance* (New York, Oxford University Press, 1996) ch 7. Williamson's work has provided a crucial intellectual foundation stone for the popular 'stakeholder' theory of corporate governance, which essentially argues for a wider distribution of residual control rights in the firm – notably to certain types of employees as well as shareholders – on the basis that the irreducible residual risk of firm failure is in many cases borne by the former group as much as the latter. On this, see generally Kelly and Parkinson, 'The Conceptual Foundations of the Company', above n 60; MM Blair, *Ownership and Control: Rethinking Corporate Governance for the Twenty-First Century* (Washington DC, Brookings Institute, 1995).

[63] Fama, 'Agency Problems', above n 22, 291; Easterbrook and Fischel, *The Economic Structure of Corporate Law*, above n 12, 29.

[64] See Easterbrook and Fischel, *The Economic Structure of Corporate Law*, above n 12, 38; Bainbridge, *The New Corporate Governance*, above n 41, 66–67; MC Jensen, 'Value Maximisation, Stakeholder Theory, and the Corporate Objective Function' (2001) 7 *European Financial Management* 297, 301.

of the productive dynamism and overall wealth-generating capacity of its business.

Accordingly, corporate contractarianism succeeds in establishing an instrumental rationale for the principle of shareholder exclusivity in corporate governance law, based on the logic of implicit bargain and private ordering. In doing so, it seeks to highlight the purportedly key corporate function of equity investors in effectively underwriting entrepreneurial risks, notwithstanding the typical absence of direct shareholder involvement in the internal executive affairs of Anglo-American public corporations.

(ii) The Executive Primacy of the Board of Directors

However, by theoretically resolving one dilemma by reference to private ordering rationality, contractarianism serves only to throw up another. If it is indeed correct to regard shareholders' exclusive entitlement to internal governance rights as stemming from an implicit bargain with other corporate participants, and as part of the notional 'price' for performing their unique risk-underwriting function within the firm, then one may legitimately query why this entitlement is in the standard case *so heavily restricted*.

As discussed in the previous chapter, one of the most fundamental legal principles of Anglo-American corporate governance is the decision-making primacy of a company's board of directors, meaning that the board has not just the responsibility but also the legally defensible *right* to manage the company's business free from outside interference, even from shareholders.[65] Moreover, in the United States, from where the contractarian theory of the firm initially derives, shareholders' powers to intervene in corporate decision-making are significantly restricted,[66] to the extent that the US corporation has been described by Lucian Bebchuk as 'a purely representative democracy', with directors as its appointed 'heads of state'.[67] But given the supposed centrality of their risk-underwriting function to the corporate wealth-generating process, why would shareholders rationally agree to such an attenuated level of formal involvement in firm decision-making?

The most comprehensive contractarian response to this question is provided by Professor Stephen Bainbridge, who explains the prima facie disempowered status of shareholders vis-à-vis directors in terms of the practical necessity to ensure centralised authority (or 'fiat') within large and complex corporate organisations. Bainbridge explains that in such

---

[65] On this, see above ch 2 of this volume, fns 42–50 and accompanying text.

[66] On this, see above ch 2 of this volume, fns 51–53 and accompanying text.

[67] LA Bebchuk, 'The Case for Increasing Shareholder Power' (2005) 118 *Harvard Law Review* 833, 850.

environments, effective consensus decision-making by shareholders is impossible due to their informational limitations and also the difficulty of uniting the likely conflicting interests of such a large group of participants. It accordingly makes sense for shareholders to agree amongst themselves to vest decision-making authority for the running of the firm in the hands of a centralised body in the form of the corporate board.[68]

Bainbridge observes that, while directors are ultimately accountable to shareholders by means of the voting process and fiduciary principle, within these wide bounds US law vests boards with virtually unconstrained administrative discretion over high-level strategic affairs.[69] Even those limited decision-making powers that shareholders actually are traditionally vested with under US law – namely their right to vote on the re-election of corporate directors and to approve or veto proposed constitutional changes and certain other extraordinary categories of board initiative ex post facto[70] – are not regarded by contractarianism as having any direct use value other than in the most exceptional of instances.[71] In particular, given the aforementioned informational and collective action impediments to the effective functioning of the shareholder franchise within large corporations, it is for the most part purportedly irrational for shareholders to do anything other than endorse those candidates proposed by the board itself for periodic election or re-election as directors.[72] Likewise, within the contractarian paradigm it makes little sense for shareholders to attempt collectively to second-guess the strategic decisions of management even on major issues such as proposed mergers or corporate restructurings, given the latter's superior awareness and understanding of the complex factors underlying such initiatives.[73]

The only situation in which shareholder voting rights are expected to be directly instrumentalised vis-à-vis management as a matter of course is in

[68] See Bainbridge, *The New Corporate Governance*, above n 41, 38–44.

[69] Building on the economist Kenneth Arrow's work on the practical value of authority and hierarchy within large and complex organisations, Bainbridge argues that '[a] complete theory of the firm requires one to balance the virtues of discretionary fiat on the part of the board of directors against the need to ensure that this power of fiat is used responsibly'. See *The New Corporate Governance*, above n 41, 19. On this, see also SM Bainbridge, 'Director Primacy: The Means and Ends of Corporate Governance' (2003) 97 *Northwestern University Law Review* 547. A significant institutional factor underpinning the wide sphere of discretion typically vested in US corporate boards is the almost watertight degree of judicial protection that the business judgment rule affords to board decisions which are carried out on an informed, loyal and good faith (ie non-self-interested) basis in the context of disputes over the application of directors' fiduciary duties. On this, see below ch 4 of this volume, pt IV.

[70] On this, see Bebchuk, 'The Case for Increasing Shareholder Power', above n 67, 844–47.

[71] Bainbridge argues that '[p]roperly understood, shareholder voting . . . is not an integral aspect of the corporate decision-making structure, but rather an accountability device of last resort to be used sparingly, at best'. See *The New Corporate Governance*, above n 41, 235.

[72] Easterbrook and Fischel, *The Economic Structure of Corporate Law*, above n 12, 87.

[73] Bainbridge, *The New Corporate Governance*, above n 41, 43–44; Easterbrook and Fischel, above n 12, 67.

the extraordinary case of a hostile tender offer or proxy fight, where a third party attempts to gain control over a firm's voting franchise (whether by outright acquisition of its share capital or by soliciting the voting rights of existing shareholders) as a prelude to ousting its incumbent board from office.[74] While such instances are uncommon and usually restricted to egregious cases of managerial underperformance, the very possibility of shareholders' votes being aggregated in this way is sufficient to imbue the shareholder franchise with significant 'threat' value. In this indirect capacity, shareholders' voting rights theoretically operate as a tacit but nevertheless crucial disciplinary mechanism insofar as they compel corporate managers to maintain the market value of a firm's equity, via promotion of the general shareholder interest, so as to pre-empt any potential contest for control and the associated likelihood of displacement.[75]

Besides the market for corporate control, there are other important market-institutional pressures acting on corporate managers within the contractarian paradigm that further remove the perceived need for direct shareholder involvement in a firm's business affairs. As a precondition of ensuring the continuing provision of capital to the firm on favourable terms, it is argued that managers will rationally be driven to establish institutional 'bonding' mechanisms that provide credible assurances to outside investors against the risk of misappropriation of their funds or other forms of mismanagement. These mechanisms include the voluntary formation (by managers) of independent boards staffed by a majority of outside (ie non-executive) directors. As explained further below, independent or 'outsider' boards are typically vested with the principal responsibility of supervising high-level managerial decisions and conduct in the interests of shareholders, as backed up by the collective board power to remove managers in the event of underperformance.[76]

Additionally, such bonding devices include the voluntary establishment (by managers and/or independent boards) of performance-related remuneration systems (eg executive stock options) that render managerial compensation sensitive to changes in the firm's share price, so as theoretically to provide the further assurance to shareholders that managers will be motivated proactively to maximise shareholder wealth on a continuing basis.[77] Furthermore, corporate managers are purportedly subject at all

[74] Bainbridge, *The New Corporate Governance*, 235; Easterbrook and Fischel, 'The Corporate Contract', above n 22, 1444. On the regulation of managerial responses to hostile tender offers under Delaware corporate law, see below ch 4 of this volume, pt V.C.

[75] On the (at least theoretic) role of the so-called market for corporate control as a market-disciplinary device within the contractarian frame of logic, see HG Manne, 'Mergers and the Market for Corporate Control' (1965) 73 *Journal of Political Economy* 110.

[76] On this, see below pt III.B.(iii).

[77] On the (theoretic) role of managerial performance compensation as a contractual 'gap-filling' device within the contractarian model, see MC Jensen and KJ Murphy, 'Performance Pay and Top-Management Incentives' (1990) 98 *Journal of Political Economy* 225. For a critical

times to labour market pressures operating both within and outside of the firm, which can be said to reinforce the above mechanisms by ensuring the availability of competent substitute personnel in the event of an incumbent's removal from office.[78]

Finally, the equitable fiduciary principle discussed above[79] – itself a purported manifestation of shareholder agreement within the contractarian paradigm – acts as a crucial contractual 'gap-filling' device by encouraging continual deference by directors (and, in turn, managers) to the collective shareholder interest, even in developing or unforeseen circumstances that could not reasonably be provided for in advance via explicit private ordering.[80]

For a combination of the above reasons, then, contractarians perceive the executive primacy of the board of directors – and, indirectly, management – within the corporate decision-making framework as being entirely consistent with private ordering rationality. This is insofar as the mutual vesting by shareholders of discretionary administrative power in the board is deemed to be an acceptable voluntary trade-off in return for the ensuing collective benefits to shareholders. At the same time, shareholders are said to retain the capacity to exert effective ultimate control over the board via a combination of the various purported 'self-help' measures documented above.

(iii) The Majority-Independent Board

A board of directors sits at the heart of every business corporation. Its members are formally appointed by shareholders and it bears collective responsibility as a group for the success or failure of the company's business. To many new students of Anglo-American corporate governance, the typical structure of a listed company's board is a source of some surprise, not least the fact that a majority of members of the board – including its chairman – typically are 'outsiders', who work formally on a part-time basis and have no executive office within the firm. Given that the board is the ultimate locus of power within the corporate structure and the institutional bridge between the company's top managers and its multitude of shareholders, the fact that most board members are non-executive 'part-timers' is a concept that is initially difficult for observers to grasp.

---

perspective on Jensen and Murphy's 'optimal contracting' portrayal of the managerial compensation-setting process, see LA Bebchuk, JM Fried and DI Walker, 'Managerial Power and Rent Extraction in the Design of Executive Compensation' (2002) 69 *University of Chicago Law Review* 751.

[78] On this, see Fama, 'Agency Problems', above n 22, 292–93.
[79] See above n 58 and accompanying text. See also below ch 6 of this volume, pt IV.
[80] See Easterbrook and Fischel, *The Economic Structure of Corporate Law*, above n 22, 91.

In their landmark 1932 study that first established the parameters of corporate governance as a field of academic enquiry,[81] Berle and Means placed little faith in the capacity of corporate boards (as distinct from managers) to represent an effective governance force. In Berle and Means' opinion, directors of the largest US companies were effectively appointed by – and thus de facto accountable to – the company's senior executive officers as a result of managerial domination of the corporate proxy election system.[82] The authors believed that, as a consequence of this, incumbent boards under management control had acquired the effective capacity to perpetuate their own existence so that corporate managers were acquiring the status of 'economic autocrats'.[83] Shareholders, meanwhile, had been substantially externalised from the corporate control process and thus eliminated as a meaningful governance force. Berle and Means therefore sought to exploit the resulting control deficit at the heart of the modern corporation via the radical reform of boards' responsibilities in the wider public interest.[84]

Over four decades later, however, the institution of the corporate board was reinterpreted by US law and finance theorists in a profoundly different ideological light, consistent with the changing politico-economic landscape of the 1970s and early 1980s. For the new school of conservative-contractarian thinkers, contrarily, the perceived motivation of corporate governance scholarship was the challenge of devising incentive and disciplinary structures that would have the effect of *mitigating* (as opposed to exploiting) the arguably subversive socio-economic consequences of managers' lack of accountability to shareholders. Within this revised frame of reference, the institution of the corporate board was presented as an effective (albeit imperfect) 'solution' to the control deficit endemic to the modern public corporation, rather than as a mere manifestation of managerial hegemony, as Berle and Means had earlier averred.[85]

The original exponents of the monitoring board hypothesis were Michael Jensen and Bill Meckling, who initially developed the concept in their pioneering 1976 paper on managerial 'agency costs'.[86] According to Jensen and Meckling, agency costs comprise the economic loss incurred by shareholders ('principals') as a result of corporate managers ('agents') failing to serve their interests in an honest and diligent manner. The overall loss suffered by shareholders of any one firm comprises three key ele-

---

[81] See Berle and Means, *The Modern Corporation and Private Property*, above n 24.

[82] On this, see below ch 4 of the volume, fn 72 and accompanying text.

[83] Berle and Means, *The Modern Corporation and Private Property*, above n 24, 116.

[84] Berle and Means, ibid, 316–17.

[85] On this point generally, see MT Moore and A Reberioux, 'Revitalizing the Institutional Roots of Anglo-American Corporate Governance' (2011) 40 *Economy and Society* 84, esp 85–90.

[86] See Jensen and Meckling, 'Theory of the Firm', above n 22.

ments: first, the costs to shareholders of directly supervising managers on an ongoing basis (monitoring expenses); secondly, the costs to the firm (and, in turn, to its shareholders) of any ex ante measures that managers put in place to provide assurance to current and potential securities holders that their investment will be productively utilised (which are known as bonding expenses); and, thirdly, any outstanding losses incurred by shareholders as a result of either of the above mechanisms failing to detect continuing corporate mismanagement (residual loss).[87]

It is an accepted fact that, in any large organisation (including a public corporation) where key decision-makers do not bear a major share of the economic consequences of their decisions, some degree of agency costs will be inevitable. However, this is tolerable on the condition that the economic gains to the enterprise resulting from specialisation of entrepreneurial (ie managerial) and risk-taking (ie equity holding) inputs continue to outweigh the corresponding losses to owners caused by the above expenses and residual loss.[88] The challenge for corporate governance, accordingly, is to ensure that levels of agency costs are kept sufficiently low so as to: (a) preserve the continuing economic viability of this separation of functions, and also (b) enhance the ability of the firm to continue to attract investments at minimal cost in the competitive market for new corporate capital.

In a world of zero transaction costs, where the tasks of information-gathering and monitoring are unencumbered by practical difficulties, the reduction of agency costs would result automatically from the basic functioning of the various market forces to which a company's managers are subject at any point in time. Thus, where the value of a corporation to shareholders was reduced as a result of dishonest or incompetent management, the source of mismanagement could be detected automatically by investors, who would refuse to buy the company's securities unless offered a compensatory reduction in price. Under 'real world' conditions, though, monitoring of management and detection of managerial misconduct or underperformance are typically costly activities, especially for outsiders such as minority equity investors who have limited knowledge of or involvement with any individual company's business. Moreover, economic theory (and, it may generally be said, empirical observation) dictates that rational investors will choose to spread their risk by holding a diversified portfolio of securities, thereby providing limited incentives for proprietary engagement on a micro level.[89]

If, however, it was somehow possible for investors to appoint a specialist monitoring body located *within* the hierarchical structure of each

[87] Ibid, 308.
[88] Fama and Jensen, 'Separation of Ownership and Control', above n 22, 301–2.
[89] On this, see Fama, 'Agency Problems', above n 22, 293.

individual firm, then supervision of management could be carried out in a less costly and more effective manner than is possible via direct oversight by shareholders. While it would be technically possible for shareholders to choose these internal corporate monitors directly, the realities of dispersed minority ownership on liquid capital markets renders this impracticable. Accordingly, it makes sense for managers themselves to install a group of specialist supervisors at the apex of the company's hierarchy, thereby directly subjecting their conduct and decisions to ongoing scrutiny so as to project credible assurances to securities holders against the risk of expropriation or loss of any current or future investments in the firm. In this way, the board of directors evolves as a managerially-created bonding device which, although fairly costly to maintain from the firm's (and, in turn, shareholders') perspective, is nevertheless cost-saving on the whole given that it mitigates the extensive monitoring expenses and residual losses that would otherwise accrue to shareholders directly in the absence any effective intra-firm supervisory mechanism.[90]

As regards the identity of the individuals who should comprise the company's internal monitoring board, Eugene Fama cautions against relying solely or primarily on the firm's top managers. In view of the limited effect of changes in company performance on managers' personal wealth, these officers 'may decide that collusion and expropriation of security holder wealth are better than competition among themselves', thus removing senior executives' propensity to monitor and discipline their colleagues with a view to enhancing the overall success of the business enterprise.[91] According to Fama, this explains the tendency of public companies to appoint specialist 'outside' monitoring directors to fulfil this role, who are not intimately involved in management of the company on a full-time basis thereby guarding against the risk of them being 'captured' by the firm's executive.[92]

At the same time, though, these outside directors are disciplined by the market for their specialist supervisory services, 'which prices them according to their performance as referees'.[93] Thus the effect of the failure or underperformance of a company with which they are employed will impinge negatively on the directors' professional reputations as robust monitors. As a result, any short-term gains to be wrought by non-executive directors from colluding with a company's management are outweighed by the longer-term losses that will stem from the ensuing reduction in the value of their human capital as effective corporate 'referees'.

[90] Fama, 'Agency Problems', above n 22.
[91] Ibid.
[92] Ibid, 293–94.
[93] Ibid, 294.

That corporate boards should be composed primarily of non-executive monitoring directors does not mean that there should be no managerial representation on the board at all, though. On the contrary, the above logic suggests that senior corporate executives are normally the most influential members of the board given that they represent a crucial source of information on the business for the board's non-executive members. The key point, however, is that the company maintains a clear distinction between the respective functions of decision management and decision control.[94] Decision *management*, which entails the initiation and implementation of the company's strategic business decisions, should be the responsibility of the company's full-time executive officers led by the CEO. Decision *control*, involving the ex post facto ratification and monitoring of important managerial decisions together with the periodic appointment, removal and compensation of the executive office-holders, should be the exclusive preserve of the non-executive supervisory component of the board.[95]

While there may be some degree of overlap between the two functions, such as where ex-managerial outside directors provide advice to the executive team on corporate strategy, by and large these dual components of the company's governance structure should be exercised separately from one another. This ensures an effective system of 'checks and balances' at board level, precluding the concentration of decision-making power in the company's executive body and thus safeguarding securities holders against the risk of fraud or mismanagement.

Accordingly, through the above course of logic, contractarian scholars have succeeded in presenting arguably the most practically significant component of Anglo-American corporate governance at the micro level – namely the majority-independent board – as a fundamentally *endogenous* institution whose existence is derived at root from private contractual dynamics.[96]

[94] Fama and Jensen, 'Separation of Ownership and Control', above n 22, 308.

[95] On the essential nature of these two organisational decision functions, see Fama and Jensen, above n 22, ibid.

[96] On the historical evolution of the majority-independent board model within US and UK corporate governance – a development which provides cogent evidence in favour of the above endogeneity hypothesis – see below, respectively, ch 4 of this volume, pt VII and ch 5 of this volume, pt IV.

IV. LEGITIMATING RECIPROCAL POWER IMBALANCE WITHIN THE CONTRACTARIAN PARADIGM

A. Contractarianism and the Core Elements of Corporate Governance Enquiry

In the previous chapter, I highlighted what I regard to be the three core conceptual components of corporate governance as a subject of legal-academic enquiry: namely *power, accountability* and *legitimacy*. I emphasised that, in organisations (such as public corporations) where the discretionary administrative power of senior officeholders rests ultimately on the consent of the principal subjects of that power, it is essential that the former group be subject to a formal and conspicuous framework of accountability norms. This is to ensure that executive decision-making power is possessed and exercised on terms that can broadly be said to command the acquiescence of those principally affected by it, so as to legitimate – and hence sustain – the underlying reciprocal power imbalance between these two groups (which, in the corporate context, are constituted by management and shareholders respectively). I further explained in chapter one above that, although these basic elements of corporate governance debate are not always readily conspicuous, they are nonetheless intrinsic (whether explicitly or, in the more common case, *implicitly*) to all academic attempts to rationalise and justify the prevailing legal-institutional features of corporate governance as a system. This includes the dominant contractarian paradigm outlined in this chapter.

Therefore in this part of the chapter, I will pick up on the previous chapter's key themes by examining the principal *normative* dimensions of the contractarian paradigm. In essence, this entails querying how contractarians go about the crucial task of demonstrating the *legitimacy* of corporate-managerial power. Or, to put the issue another way: how – specifically – does the contractarian paradigm demonstrate that senior executive office-holders are being effectively held to account in the exercise of their discretionary administrative power, so as to ensure the continuing collective acquiescence of shareholders in the possession and exercise of such power within centralised managerial hands?

The principal normative dimensions of the contractarian paradigm, accordingly, are: (1) a common understanding of corporate-managerial power as a normatively *un*problematic phenomenon; (2) a general belief that investors are collectively (if not always individually) capable, whether directly or indirectly, of making rational and efficient private norm selection decisions on a systematic basis; (3) a general preference, on economic grounds, for micro-level private ordering over macro-level state ordering of corporate governance; and – finally – (4) a common perception that market-based criteria are superior to democratic considerations in justifying the prevailing legal-institutional features of corporate governance as a system. Each of these dimensions will now be critically examined.

B. The Principal Normative Dimensions of the Contractarian Paradigm

(i) Corporate-Managerial Power as a Normatively Unproblematic Phenomenon

From a contractarian standpoint, the broad sphere of discretionary decision-making power that is traditionally granted by law to the corporate board (and, indirectly, management) is generally regarded to be unproblematic. Rather, the existence of such power is both explained and – more significantly – *legitimated* within the contractarian paradigm in accordance with the theory's underpinning notional criteria of efficient institutional evolution and mutual (inter-shareholder) consent.

The contractarian frame of reference is built on the implicit understanding that market-driven pressures and rules are ultimately capable of constraining the decision-making power of corporate managers within generally acceptable bounds. Accordingly it becomes possible for contractarian theorists to interfuse the notion of corporate 'efficiency' – understood in the narrow sense of managerial responsiveness to capital market signals – with the dual tenets of 'accountability' and 'legitimacy' in the wider normative sense developed in chapter two above. In other words, managements that are compliant with the dictates of the capital markets are deemed to be *accountable*, with the effect that their possession and exercise of discretionary administrative power vis-à-vis shareholders (and other corporate participants) is implicitly rendered *legitimate*.[97]

Indeed, contrary to the dominant mid-twentieth-century perspective on corporate-managerial power as a threat to the individual liberty of citizens, contractarianism views the establishment of managerial authority or 'fiat' within the constitutional structure of the corporation, conversely, as a *product* of individual (principally shareholder) contractual free choice. It is said that corporate participants acquiesce in management's possession and exercise of such power voluntarily, in the interest of ensuring a more pragmatic and efficient form of productive organisation than would be possible via alternative decentralised or pluralist decision-making forms.[98]

It follows that the degree of decision-making power typically wielded by senior corporate officers is both economically and politically unproblematic

---

[97] See MT Moore and A Reberioux, 'Corporate Power in the Public Eye: Reassessing the Implications of Berle's Public Consensus Theory' (2010) 33 *Seattle University Law Review* 1109, 1136; Bowman, *The Modern Corporation*, above n 9, 137.
[98] See above nn 68–73.

insofar as shareholders, as metaphorical corporate 'citizens', have the ultimate collective power of appointment over the firm's supreme governing
body (ie its board of directors). Through this peculiar derivation of
Hobbesian social contract logic,[99] contractarianism significantly downplays
the extent of the legitimacy problem that is posed by reciprocal power
imbalance within the corporate structure, by perceiving managerial power
as something that is capable of being effectively eradicated (or, at least,
mitigated to a generally *un*problematic level) via privately formulated contractual bonding mechanisms.[100]

In the above way, contractarianism achieves the remarkable conceptual
feat of re-explaining the public corporation as a fundamentally private
and self-governing institution. Accordingly, corporate-managerial power
is presented as an inherently *self-correcting* problem when set within the
broader institutional context of a market-based governance system.[101] The
implication is that any extra-contractual regulatory responses by the state
to this perceived problem are both unnecessary and, moreover, bureau-
cratically illegitimate in the sense described in the previous chapter.

Consequently, from a contractarian perspective, state interventionism
in intra-firm governance matters is perceived as violating shareholders'
free choice with respect to legal-institutional design, by seeking to foreclose the opportunity that corporate contractors would otherwise have to
establish tailored and cost-effective managerial accountability norms
within individual firms. For this reason, public-regulatory design of corporate governance arguably risks severing the notional contractual 'mandate' that shareholders' capacity for micro-level institutional design is
perceived to provide in support of management's continuing hegemonic
rule over the firm and its economic resource base. In the absence of this
mandate, the normative foundation of corporate-managerial power
would be undermined.

(ii) Investors as Rational Private Norm Selectors

The above conception of corporate-managerial power as a phenomenon
that is, in the last place, contractually authorised and restrained (and
hence normatively *un*problematic), is necessarily dependent for its validity on a logically prior factor. That is the extent to which investors are able

[99] On the application of Hobbesian theory to the issue of corporate power generally, see
above ch 2 of this volume, fn 25.
[100] Atiyah explains that '[a] contractual relationship . . . is seen as deriving from agreement' and therefore 'is felt to be the creation of the parties, who give it life'. Accordingly,
'[f]ar from standing above, and beyond them, a contract is a thing *under the control of the
contracting parties* [in this case, shareholders] and *subordinate to their will*' (emphasis added).
See PS Atiyah, *The Rise and Fall of Freedom of Contract* (Oxford, Clarendon Press, 1979) 36.
[101] On this, see Ireland, *Property and Contract*, above n 11.

to mobilise appropriate legal-institutional mechanisms which have the effect of restraining unwarranted exercises of executive discretion within individual firms.

Moreover, in order to preserve the notional *private-contractual* basis of the board's – and, indirectly, management's – executive primacy, it must be established that investors (whether individually or collectively) have the *independent* capacity for micro-level institutional design, in the sense of being equipped to establish or engender effective managerial accountability norms in the absence of substantively significant state intervention. Otherwise, the aforementioned consent-based justification for managerial hegemony breaks down, thereby undermining the legitimacy of the reciprocal power imbalance in the equity relation.

At this point, though, contractarianism encounters a potential snag in its thread of logic. As explained above, within the contractarian paradigm shareholders' purported status as the exclusive collective beneficiary of managerial accountability norms is justified ultimately on the basis of their unique capacity for economy-wide diversification, and resultant propensity to bear firm-specific risk at a socially efficient level.[102] But shareholders' diversified status necessitates them remaining detached to a significant extent from the micro-level affairs of any individual firm in which they are invested. Therefore in order for contractarianism's private ordering model of norm selection to retain conceptual validity, the theory must be capable of explaining how firm-specific information impacts on investor choices in the substantial absence of direct shareholder monitoring activity at the micro level.

In particular, corporate equity investors must be sufficiently informed and discerning so as not only to be able to make informed securities selection choices based on historical and predicted corporate performance, but also to be able to determine whether the particular 'basket' of governance protections offered by any firm's management (whether via self-design or else by adoption of 'default' corporate law rules) offers sufficiently robust insurance against the risk of future loss or expropriation of shareholder wealth. This is a formidable dual task, especially in view of shareholders' acknowledged informational limitations within a widely-held ownership environment.

Thus the validity of the dual contractarian tenets of private ordering and shareholder exclusivity is necessarily contingent on the existence of a liquid and efficient stock market, whereby relevant information is incorporated quickly and comprehensively into the market clearing price of each issued corporate security. This state of affairs depends in turn on the presence of specialist securities market actors, who can be relied on to ensure the ongoing collation and subsequent dissemination to

---

[102] See above nn 59–64 and accompanying text.

investors of credible data on firms' relative performances and governance structures.[103]

Within the contractarian paradigm, the first group of actors who purportedly fulfil such a crucial informational role are informed professional traders such as institutional fund managers. In an efficient securities market, professional traders perform a function known as market arbitrage: that is to say, they strive to 'beat the market' by uncovering new information relevant to a particular firm or industry sector before it becomes more widely disseminated, thus gaining the financial benefits of first mover status. The rising demand and, in turn, price, of the relevant corporate securities represents a credible signal to which less-informed private investors will subsequently respond, up to the point where the potential gains to be made from purchasing the security are effectively cancelled out by its higher price.[104]

Secondly, contractarian theorists refer to the crucial information-processing function performed by investment banks in their capacity as professional underwriters of new corporate equity issues. Above all, investment banks are said to put their valuable institutional reputation on the line when establishing the correct price for newly-issued corporate securities on the basis of privately-acquired information about the relevant firm.[105] For this reason, the public offering price of a corporate equity can theoretically be relied on by investors as a credible indication of that firm's future performance prospects.[106]

Accordingly, both institutional investors and investment banks have a rational incentive to inform themselves about a particular firm's internal governance structure, and the consequent degree of protection that it affords to shareholders' equity investment, as a core component of their respective securities arbitrage and underwriting functions.

In addition, Easterbrook and Fischel have highlighted the important information-transfer function performed by private stock exchange operators, who themselves have rational incentives to offer the types of rules governing securities trades that investors – and, in turn, corporate issuers – are likely to value in order to encourage more public securities issues, and, correspondingly, higher fee income for the exchange operators. In

---

[103] MT Moore and A Reberioux, 'The Corporate Governance of the Firm as an Entity: Old Lessons for the New Debate' in Y Biondi, A Canziani and T Kirat (eds), *The Firm as an Entity: Implications for Economics, Accounting and the Law* (London, Routledge, 2007) 348, 351–52.

[104] On this, see Easterbrook and Fischel, *The Economic Structure of Corporate Law*, above n 12, 287, 293–94; RJ Gilson and R Kraakman, 'The Mechanisms of Market Efficiency Twenty Years Later: The Hindsight Bias' in J Armour and JA McCahery, *After Enron: Improving Corporate Law and Modernising Securities Regulation in Europe and the US*, 29, 40 (first published in (2003) 28 *Journal of Corporation Law* 715).

[105] Easterbrook and Fischel, *The Economic Structure of Corporate Law*, above n 12, 293.

[106] Professional securities analysts are alleged to fulfil a similar information-verification role when staking their reputations on recommendations made to uninformed investor clients.

particular, stock exchanges have an incentive to compete with one another in seeking to offer more effective rules to issuers with regard to disclosure of information on issues that are of concern to investors. These are likely to include especially controversial aspects of corporate governance such as board structures, external auditing procedures and anti-self-dealing rules.[107]

For the above reasons, contractarianism asserts that largely impersonal, market-induced mechanisms are likely to evolve so as to ensure the systematic inculcation of information on competing firms' internal governance structures into corporate securities prices, even in the absence of a mandatory state-imposed system of disclosure regulation to this effect.[108] Not only are these mechanisms believed to represent an adequate substitute for direct one-on-one supervision by investors of individual firms, but moreover they theoretically enhance the quality of corporate monitoring by substituting the cumulative allocative decisions of the securities market as a whole for the necessarily limited supervisory competences of both individual corporate 'owners' and professional securities market regulators (including the regulatory state itself).[109]

It is accordingly through the above course of logic that contractarianism succeeds in establishing the market-institutional preconditions for its private ordering model of corporate governance norm evolution. In doing so, it attempts to show that the principle of shareholder exclusivity in corporate governance is to a significant extent consistent with an informationally-efficient corporate securities market, notwithstanding the largely passive and uninformed status of the typical corporate equity investor with respect to micro-level firm affairs.

(iii) Economic Advantage of Micro-Level Private Ordering over Macro-Level State Ordering

The above discussion has demonstrated how – within the contractarian paradigm – the reciprocal power imbalance between management and shareholders is typically rationalised (and consequently legitimated) as the product of inter-investor free choice against the background of a robust market-based system of managerial accountability norms. It has

---

[107] Easterbrook and Fischel, *The Economic Structure of Corporate Law*, above n 12, 294–95.

[108] On this, see FH Easterbrook and DR Fischel, 'Mandatory Disclosure and Protection of Investors' (1984) 79 *Vanderbilt Law Review* 669.

[109] The logic behind this argument is premised on the Hayekian theory of informational dispersal, which denotes 'the fact that the knowledge of the circumstances of which we must make use never exists in concentrated or integrated form but solely as the dispersed bits of incomplete and frequently contradictory knowledge which all the separate individuals possess'. Accordingly, '[t]he economic problem of society is a problem of the utilization of knowledge *which is not given to anyone in its totality*' (emphasis added). See FA Hayek, 'The Use of Knowledge in Society' (1945) 4 *American Economic Review* 519, 519.

further been explained how such accountability norms are – ultimately – purportedly developed by management voluntarily at the micro level, consequent to managers' prudential interest in providing credible assurances to investors against future diminution of shareholder wealth. Meanwhile, the combined effect of the various informational intermediaries discussed above is to ensure the rapid dissemination of knowledge about competing firms' internal governance structures to potential buyers of corporate securities on public capital markets. Having outlined the key dynamics of the contractarian private ordering process, it remains to be asked what the proper role of the *law* – and, in particular, corporate law – should be within the above market-institutional framework.

In this regard, contractarians are typically inclined to assert the superiority of private and decentralised methods of ordering intra-firm governance affairs at the *micro* level. Correspondingly, contractarians tend to deny any significant role for the interventionist regulatory state as an active determinant of prevailing managerial accountability norms at the *macro* level. The basic argument is that, in view of the dynamic market environment within which corporations operate, competitive pressures will act as an effective proxy for coercive state regulation in compelling corporate managements to adopt governance norms and structures that are deemed generally acceptable by the investor community.

Moreover, on the Hayekian assumption that dispersed and self-interested market investors collectively have an informational advantage over central regulators in determining the most appropriate arrangements for governing any particular firm,[110] it purportedly makes sense to leave questions of internal corporate structure and power division to be resolved on a decentralised basis via ad hoc negotiation between shareholders and managers. The only alternative, as it is commonly perceived, is to subject nuanced issues of intra-firm organisation at the micro level to the clumsy and often misguided 'visible hand' of regulatory state design.

But such an approach arguably fails to respect the intricate governance needs of individual business entities by engendering a crude 'one-size-fits-all' approach, which in turn imperils the pluralism and diversity – in this case, of legal and organisational forms – that an autonomous (ie deregulated) corporate sector is likely to engender when left to keep its own proverbial house in order. More worryingly for contractarians, governmental 'grand design' of corporate law can be said to obfuscate the supposedly 'neutral', market-driven private ordering process by encouraging politically-motivated regulatory interventions that will inevitably reflect the partisan preferences of dominant social interest groups.[111]

---

[110] On this theory, see Hayek, 'The Use of Knowledge in Society', ibid.

[111] On these concerns, see SM Bainbridge, 'Is "Say on Pay" Justified', *Regulation* (Spring 2009) 42, 46–47.

It follows that the appropriate function of the regulatory state in the design of corporate governance norms is merely to replicate or 'mimic' the bargaining outcomes that key corporate participants (namely shareholders and managers) would be inclined to arrive at privately in the hypothetical scenario where they are able to negotiate both rationally and costlessly over their various terms of engagement with one another.[112] Consequently, corporate law – to the extent that it exists as a generally applicable phenomenon – should rightfully be regarded as nothing more than a surrogate form of contract law applicable to the internal governance affairs of incorporated business entities. As such, its sole and motivating purpose should be to provide, on an effective off-the-shelf basis, the terms that the majority of rational corporate contractors would be inclined to negotiate for individually in the hypothetical 'ideal bargaining scenario'.[113] This is the imagined situation where informational limitations and other transaction costs are non-existent, so that economically optimal outcomes are attainable by the negotiating parties.[114] It is argued that the state, by establishing these notionally optimal contractual terms within a default rule framework, in effect saves incorporators and pre-existing firms the extensive transaction costs that would otherwise be involved in establishing the same norms on an ad hoc contractual basis. It is further said that, at the same time, corporate laws should be designed in as flexible and informal a manner as is practicable under the circumstances, in order to afford significant space for firm-specific diversity and variability for those contractors that wish to deviate from the proverbial 'standard form' governance terms ascribed by law.[115]

Thus the contractarian paradigm avers that, by conforming as closely as possible to the above theoretical blueprint, corporate governance laws are best designed to achieve an effective equilibrium between the aforementioned conflicting concerns of: on the one hand, achieving a sufficient level of perceived managerial accountability to secure executive power-legitimacy; while, on the other, protecting against the converse risk of bureaucratic illegitimacy in cases where managerial accountability norms are deemed to be overall cost-*ineffective* at the micro level from a general investor perspective. It is asserted that, in this way, corporate law is best designed to facilitate – rather than usurp – the nuanced private ordering of intra-firm governance affairs at the micro level.

---

[112] Easterbrook and Fischel, *The Economic Structure of Corporate Law*, above n 12, 35.

[113] Easterbrook and Fischel, 'The Corporate Contract', above n 22, 1444; Bainbridge, 'Director Primacy', above n 54, 1744. For this reason, Bainbridge describes prevailing corporate law rules as establishing the 'majoritarian-default' position for contracting parties. See ibid.

[114] For a critical analysis of the hypothetical bargaining rationale for corporate law design, see below ch 7 of this volume, pt IV.

[115] See Easterbrook and Fischel, 'The Corporate Contract', above n 22, 1442.

(iv) Supremacy of Market over Democratic Factors in Justifying Prevailing Legal-Institutional Features of Corporate Governance

Most fundamentally of all, contractarians argue that regulatory state intervention in intra-firm governance affairs is not only economically inferior to private ordering, but is also highly problematic on a *political* level. By 'interfering' with the internal governance affairs of private enterprises via democratically-determined regulatory measures, the state is said to overstep the proper boundaries to its activities by seeking to effect intrusive public policy interventions in an area of human endeavour that *can* and therefore *should* rightfully be governed by the collective private preferences of individual citizens alone.

In re-conceptualising corporate governance evolution as an endogenous process determined ultimately by the prudential choices of notional contractors, contractarian theorists typically rely on the dual notions of individual rationality and internal agreement as a priori justification for the institutional status quo. In other words, rather than seeking to demonstrate on the basis of empirical enquiry and reasoned political debate whether prevailing corporate rules and structures are socially desirable, contractarian logic presumes their general acceptability by virtue of the fact of their continuing existence (by implicit agreement).[116]

This presumption derives from the Panglossian claim that current laws and institutions governing the internal power structure and functioning of corporations represent the best (or, on a more modest analysis, the *least worst*) of possible worlds by reflecting the unanimous preferences of all those individuals who choose to entrust their respective capital investments to any particular firm's controlling agents.[117] Accordingly, the primary question for academic corporate lawyers is that of *why* these notional 'agreements' are generally struck within firms, rather than whether the ensuing norms should exist in the first place. For this reason, contractarianism can justifiably be described as a *pathologically conservative* framework of analysis.[118]

---

[116] On this, see generally Ireland, *Property and Contract*, above n 11; Ireland, 'Recontractualising the Corporation', above n 48.

[117] A conspicuous example of the application of such logic is the normative justification that is typically advanced by contractarians in support of the prevailing majority-independent public company board structure, which essentially emphasises the board's alleged status as the endogenous product of implicit bargaining between corporate managers and equity investors. On this, see above pt III.B.(iii). In addition to inferring the survival value of the board and hence its efficiency on the basis of economic natural selection, the private ordering/endogeneity hypothesis also presents the existence and key structural features of the board as politically 'neutral' and hence untainted by the hand of arbitrary governmental design.

[118] In this regard, contractarianism's evolutionary logic could be said to bear certain parallels with 19th-century social-Darwinism as developed in the work of conservative Victorian political theorists such as Herbert Spencer. See, eg H Spencer, *Social Statics* (London, Chapman, 1851), as summarised in Duxbury, 'Modern American Jurisprudence', above n 2, 18.

From the point of view of establishing the social desirability of a corporate governance system as a whole, the contractarian conception of corporate law as a facilitative, politically neutral and freely derogable framework is crucial in imbuing prevailing governance rules and structures with the market-liberal characteristics of unanimity and non-coerciveness.[119] The politico-economic quality of 'unanimity', in the words of Milton Friedman, entails that '[i]n an ideal free market resting on private property, no individual can coerce any other, all cooperation is voluntary, all parties to such cooperation benefit or they need not participate'.[120] According to Friedman, '[t]he great advantage of the market [in contrast to political methods of consensus formation] is that it permits wide diversity', and therefore 'is, in political terms, a system of proportional representation' whereby '[e]ach man can vote, as it were, for the color of tie he wants and get it'.[121]

Transporting this logic into the context of corporate governance, since theoretically: (i) no individual firm need ever be subject to an internal corporate rule that its shareholders do not collectively signal their assent to; and (ii) no shareholder (or any other corporate participant for that matter) need ever remain invested in a firm whose internal governance structure they are unhappy with; it follows that corporate law is an intrinsically *non*-coercive institution, whereby no person need be compelled to abide by a state of affairs that they would not otherwise be inclined to accept on the basis of free contracting.

With the theoretical absence of violation of individual free will under corporate law, there is correspondingly no need for prevailing corporate rules and structures to derive legitimacy by recourse to the political-democratic principle which, according to Friedmanite market-liberal logic, comes into consideration within a social environment where 'conformity' is called for on the part of individuals. That is to say, where '[t]he individual must serve a more general social interest' with the consequence that it becomes 'appropriate for some to require others to contribute to a general social purpose whether they wish to or not'.[122]

In the latter type of situation, it is politically imperative within a democratic system for citizens to be able to reach collective agreement on the particular substantive outcomes that accord most fully with the majoritarian conception of the public interest. However, since – within the contractarian paradigm – corporate law already derives its legitimacy from the market-based unanimity principle, it is consequently unnecessary and,

---

[119] As Ireland explains: '[d]epicted in this [contractarian] way, corporations are deemed to be fundamentally "private" affairs, the non-coercive products of agreements voluntarily and consensually entered into by a range of private property owners'. See Ireland, *Property and Contract*, above n 11, 485.

[120] Friedman, 'The Social Responsibility of Business', above n 13.

[121] Friedman, *Capitalism and Freedom*, above n 8, 15.

[122] Friedman, 'The Social Responsibility of Business', above n 13. On this, see also *Capitalism and Freedom*, above n 8, 23.

moreover, politically *illegitimate* to engage in this wider democratic debate about the overall socio-economic objectives that the legal framework of corporate governance should be designed to achieve.

It follows that regulatory intervention in corporate governance risks blurring the divide between state and civil society by substituting the 'consensus' rationality of democratic politics for the 'unanimity' rationality of the marketplace. Within the latter system, *all* participants theoretically remain free to 'opt-out' of a particular relationship or arrangement that does not accord with their individual preferences, with the effect that no person can be compelled to submit to a state of affairs that they do not wish to be part of. However, public regulation by its nature entails the imposition of given obligations, limitations or structures onto citizens for the purpose of achieving some wider social objective that the affected individuals may or may not share.

When applied in respect of issues such as corporate governance that would otherwise fall to be determined by the collective prudential decisions of individual citizens (principally investors and corporate managers), such state interference with the supposed invisible hand of private ordering becomes highly problematic from a contractarian point of view. Largely for this reason, interventionist regulation of corporate governance affairs in the name of protecting the wider public interest is widely regarded by Anglo-American legal scholars today, whether in express or implied terms, as an intrusive constraint on private sector autonomy within a 'free' (ie market-liberal) political economy.

Accordingly, via the above course of reasoning, contractarianism seeks to legitimate the reciprocal power imbalance that is central to the corporate equity relation by reference to ideological criteria derived from market, as opposed to democratic, logic. The ultimate effect is to present existing corporate governance rules as being endogenous institutional phenomena that appropriately lie *outside of* the scope of democratic political debate. Against this background, existing managerial accountability norms can purportedly be defended and criticised only in a purely instrumental and politically 'neutral' manner, as effective practical solutions to the essentially *private* problem of efficient intra-firm resource coordination.

V. SUMMARY

In this chapter, I have outlined and examined the key aspects of the dominant contractarian paradigm of corporate governance, and indeed of corporate law generally. I have explained how the motivating objective of the contractarian rationalisation of this area is to present corporate law as an aspect of *private* law, which – like traditional such areas of law – is characteristically facilitative and *a*political in nature. Consequently, it can be said to lie outside of the appropriate scope of direct public-democratic control.

To clear up some potential confusion, this is *not* to say that all corporate and other allegedly market-facilitative laws are thus *undemocratic*, in the sense of being contrary to or unreflective of the general majoritarian will of citizens. The point – rather – is simply that, in a 'free' (ie liberal-democratic) political economy, such issues are generally perceived to be the appropriate remit of technically-minded Chancery courts and other specialist rule-making or interpretive bodies. The principal purpose of such actors is perceived to be that of making the relevant rules 'work' in a functional commercial sense, as opposed to seeking directly to bring about specific distributional or moral-political ends within economic society more generally. For this reason, corporate and other allegedly 'private' laws are widely perceived to be substantially 'beyond reach' of direct public policy determination. But this in itself can be regarded as a *reflection* – rather than abrogation of – the general public consensus with regard to how commercial and business activity is most effectively or appropriately kept in order by law.

On a more general conceptual level, meanwhile, the contractarian paradigm represents a coordinated intellectual attempt to 're-privatise' corporate governance as a subject of legal-academic enquiry, in particular by perceiving the most prominent legal-institutional features of Anglo-American corporate governance as being the outcome of implicit private bargaining processes. As such, the core structural elements of the Anglo-American corporation – most notably shareholder exclusivity, board primacy and majority-independent boards – are imbued with the quality of *endogeneity*. That is to say, they are perceived as essentially *organic* phenomena driven by a combination of capital market pressures and rational investor (and managerial) incentives, as opposed to being the notionally 'artificial' outcomes of regulatory state design.

Within the contractarian paradigm, the above assertion as to the endogenous and organic nature of corporate governance norms is not just a descriptive claim about the purportedly dominant characteristics of the laws in this area. It is also, more significantly, a normative claim about the supposedly ideal characteristics that corporate governance laws *should* embody. Consequently, contractarians tend in general to exhibit a preference for private prudential methods of institutional design within individual firms, as facilitated by a flexible and facilitative (as opposed to rigid and mandatory) legal framework that is conducive to widespread private ordering at the micro level.

Correspondingly, coercive or universalistic forms of legal-institutional design at the macro level – particularly when implemented by the regulatory state on social-distributional or other direct public policy grounds – are arguably inclined to be both economically sub-optimal (relative to private ordering outcomes) and politically problematic. This is because such forms of governmental engagement are allegedly likely at once to: (i) compel the incurrence of cost-ineffective levels of compliance and/or maladaptation costs at the micro level, thereby rendering them a source of bureaucratic illegitimacy in the aforementioned sense of the term; and also (ii) usurp the proper sphere of decentralised civil society ordering by inappropriately conflating the distinct public (state) and private (market) realms of political economy.

In summary, it can therefore be said that within the contractarian frame of reference, private ordering – rather than public policy – *is* and, moreover, *should be* the exclusive (or, at the very least, principal) determinant of prevailing managerial accountability norms, and also the main driver of future legal-institutional reforms to a corporate governance system. The focus of the next two chapters will accordingly be on how – in practice – the notionally ideal characteristics of law outlined in this chapter are actually manifested within the existing corporate governance frameworks of the United States and United Kingdom respectively. With this general aim in mind, we begin the following doctrinal study by looking at the key quasi-contractual characteristics of the former of these two systems.

4

The Contractual Dimensions of US Corporate Governance Law

I N THE FOLLOWING two chapters, I will assess the main respects in which the contractarian paradigm of corporate governance is actually manifested in the corporate governance systems of the United States and United Kingdom respectively. It will be shown that, whilst contractarianism is realised in markedly different ways within each of these countries' legal frameworks, its influence is nevertheless significant in establishing the unique doctrinal character of corporate governance law within both jurisdictions.

I will begin the comparative study in this chapter with a relatively brief and panoramic study of the US legal framework of corporate governance, with a view to highlighting its most significant quasi-contractual characteristics. From this analysis, I will seek to demonstrate that two broad and distinctive themes characterise much of US corporate governance as a system. The first such theme is the general doctrinal character of corporate law as a *quasi-commodity*: that is to say, as something that may in effect be 'purchased' by corporations and, indirectly, shareholders, in fundamentally the same way as one might purchase securities or other proprietary assets. Continuing the commodification theme, it will be shown that corporate law rules in the United States are to a significant extent also freely adaptable and malleable at the behest of key corporate participants (ie shareholders and managers) rather like any aspect of personal property.

As will be explained below, this dimension of US corporate law is manifested in the traditionally wide licence granted to corporate contractors to 'opt out' of statutory rules that are seemingly ill-fitted to a company's particular characteristics or circumstances. It is furthermore exemplified by the longstanding institution of competitive-federalism, permitting corporate contractors the extensive and legally uninhibited choice of corporate law jurisdiction both at the point of initial incorporation and thereafter. Finally, the doctrinal nature of corporate law as a quasi-commodity persists also at the federal level via the wide scope for private institutional design provided under the Securities and Exchange Commission's dynamic Rule 14a-8 shareholder proposal regime.

The second core theme of US corporate governance law is the deference that it affords to the internal contractual autonomy of the corporation. Thus corporate contractors are at liberty to determine the general objectives (or 'life plan') and key strategies of the firm, largely uninhibited by judicial interference. Moreover, the tradition of judicial deference and contractual flexibility in US corporate governance law today extends in significant part even to controversial managerial decisions concerning the proper response to threatened control changes in the firm. This is due to the pervasive influence of the business judgment rule at the heart of US (and particularly Delaware) corporate law jurisprudence at State level, as progressively expanded over recent decades into the realm of contests for corporate control. The theme of legal deference to internal contractual autonomy is also manifested at a fundamental level of US corporate governance in the very status of the board of directors itself, which persists as a substantially organic and *pre*-regulatory institution, whose basic existence and characteristics would appear historically to precede extraneous regulatory initiative.

In terms of the central themes of this book, the above two qualities of US corporate governance are crucial in sustaining the flexibility and responsiveness of laws to the specific circumstances and challenges of individual firms. Above all, the dual characteristics of contractual flexibility and judicial deference are – from a contractarian perspective – purportedly essential to preserving the capacity of firms to establish a framework of managerial accountability norms that is proximately 'optimal', in the sense of achieving the best available balance between the potentially conflicting criteria of power-legitimacy and bureaucratic legitimacy. For this reason, the above features of US corporate governance law can be regarded as important institutional means for securing the continuing acquiescence of investors in the reciprocal power imbalance underlying the corporate equity relation.

Accordingly, this chapter's analysis is structured as follows. In part I, I will examine the peculiar quasi-contractual tradition of 'opt-out', 'opt-in' and so-called 'reversible-default' rules in US corporate law. In part II, I will assess the practical and normative significance of competitive federalism to the overall fabric of US corporate governance as a system. In part III, I will highlight the extensive degree of judicial deference to private ordering that is compelled by the business judgment rule. In part IV, I will demonstrate the fundamentally contractual nature of hostile takeover defences in the US. I will also explain how the scope of business judgment protection has been progressively widened so as to permit significant judicial deference to such practices today. In part V, I will note how governmental deference to private ordering persists even at the federal level in the United States by virtue of the quasi-contractual shareholder proposal regime under SEC Rule 14a-8. Finally, in part VI, I will explain the contractual basis of the corporate board's existence in the United States, and the normative implications thereof.

I. 'OPT-OUT', 'OPT-IN', AND REVERSIBLE-DEFAULT RULES

In the United States, the pervasive influence of the private ordering para-digm inheres at least as much in the peculiar *form* that many core corporate law rules take, as in the substance of those doctrines themselves. Consistent with the general ideological impetus of the contractarian position, corpo-rate law scholars in the United States tend in general to show a preference for legal rules that are flexible and adaptable in their application.

From the contractarian assertion that there is no universally determinable 'right' way to structure a corporation's internal governance arrangements, there derives a commonly-held view in the United States that corporate law rules should be designed so as to allow ample space for deviation and diversity by contractors from the regulatory norm. Therefore in contrast to the orthodox 'command' conception of laws as a coercive means of engendering conformity by citizens with universally-applicable sovereign decrees,[1] US business entities law is commonly depicted by leading aca-demic texts in terms of an essentially *facilitative*, transaction-cost saving device or 'tool' that contracting parties are free to adopt or reject at their personal whim.[2]

Furthermore, since in the absence of state-promulgated corporate laws, shareholders and managers would be inclined to work out their own ad hoc contractual solutions to corporate governance problems in any event, the law in this context should – it is argued – rightfully be viewed as hav-ing no socially determinative value in its own right. Rather, the purpose of corporate law within the contractarian paradigm is simply to 'mimic' ex ante those contractual outcomes that hypothetical corporate parti-cipants would in general be inclined to favour if given the opportunity to bargain without cost over the internal division of power, rights and enti-tlements in respect of their mutual venture.[3]

From this understanding of law there derives a legislative preference (at least at State level) for providing generally – but not universally – accepted 'default' legal rules that are freely 'reversible' at the behest of key corporate participants.[4] Such reversibility is achieved by granting directors and/or shareholders the ad hoc licence to 'opt out' of any rule or

---

[1] On this, see J Austin, *The Province of Jurisprudence Determined* (edited by W Rumble) (Cambridge, Cambridge University Press, 1995) (first published 1832).

[2] See, eg C O'Kelley and R Thompson, *Corporations and Other Business Associations: Cases and Materials*, 6th edn (New York, Aspen, 2010) ch 1; F Easterbrook and D Fischel, *The Economic Structure of Corporate Law* (Cambridge, MA Harvard University Press, 1991) ch 1.

[3] On the concept of 'market-mimicking' rules in corporate law, see B Black, 'Is Corporate Law Trivial?: A Political and Economic Analysis' (1990) 84 *Northwestern University Law Review* 542, 552–55.

[4] On this, see SM Bainbridge, *The New Corporate Governance in Theory and Practice* (New York, Oxford University Press, 2008) 35–37.

doctrine that appears ill-fitted to their firm's peculiar characteristics or environment, by including a provision to this effect within a corporation's internal constitutional documents.[5] The longstanding global trail-blazer of the opting-out (and, conversely, opting-in) tradition in US corporate law is the State of Delaware, which has over the past century developed a highly flexible corporate law statute permitting individual firms significant leeway in their application of core governance norms.[6] This includes the freedom to limit or negate in respect of any one firm the effect of important statutory and common law rules concerning the balance of power, influence and accountability between shareholders and directors. Largely for this reason, Delaware has become the State domicile of choice for a majority of listed corporations in the United States, with the effect that Delaware State corporate law is commonly and justifiably regarded as a reliable proxy for US (public) company law in general.[7]

One of the most significant manifestations of US corporate law's opting-out tradition is section 141 of the Delaware General Corporation Law (DGCL) statute. As explained in chapter two above, section 141 is also the most fundamental doctrine of Delaware (and, by implication, US) corporate law insofar as it pertains to the basic allocation of decision-making power at the heart of the corporate structure by establishing the foundational legal principle of board primacy.[8] Whilst prima facie taking the form of a reversible rule, the flexibility of section 141(a) is in reality significantly limited by the fact that alterations to the certificate of incorporation after the initial formation of the company can only be initiated at the behest of the board itself.[9] This makes it effectively impossible for shareholders to diminish or remove the board's exclusive managerial prerogative. The implication is that – for all practical intents and purposes – the latter's decision-making supremacy within the corporation is inalienable.[10]

However, the adaptability of section 141 inheres not in the basic principle of board primacy itself, but rather in the main qualification to it. To this end, section 141(k) provides as a general default rule that '[a]ny director or the entire board of directors may be removed, with *or without cause,*

---

[5] On this, see LA Bebchuk, 'The Debate on Contractual Freedom in Corporate Law' (1989) 89 *Columbia Law Review* 1395, 1396–97.

[6] On this, see S Bowman, *The Modern Corporation and American Political Thought: Law, Power and Ideology* (PA, Penn State University Press, 1996) 60.

[7] For this reason, and in line with general legal academic custom, in the following discussion I will adopt Delaware as the exemplar system of State corporate law with respect to US public companies.

[8] See above ch 2 of this volume, pt I.D.

[9] Although shareholders have the collective power both to initiate and pass alterations to the corporation's constitutional bylaws independently of the wishes of the board, the bylaws are formally subordinate to the certificate (or 'charter') of incorporation and thus cannot be inconsistent with any provision in the corporation's charter or the general law, except where expressly provided otherwise by one of the latter documents. See DGCL § 109. On this, see above ch 2 of this volume, fn 52.

[10] On this, see above ch 2 of this volume, fn 53 and accompanying text.

by the holders of a majority of the shares then entitled to vote at an election of directors' (emphasis added). The express statutory authorisation of dismissal without cause is crucial from a corporate governance perspective insofar as, absent this provision, directors can legitimately be removed from office prior to the expiry of their tenure only in gross or extreme instances of misconduct or dereliction of duty.[11] Mere underperformance, even where it amounts to negligence, will in itself be insufficient to justify the corporation reneging on its continuing contractual commitments to the director(s) concerned.

Notwithstanding this default position, the shareholders' statutory power to dismiss the board without cause will automatically lapse if the relevant company's board is 'classified' (or 'staggered').[12] This term denotes a common governance practice whereby the board of directors is divided into three separate classes for the purposes of periodic retirement and reappointment, with the effect that each year only one-third of the board will automatically stand for re-election. The capacity of Delaware corporations to opt out of the removal-without-cause rule via board classification theoretically enables corporate contractors to weigh up, on an individual firm basis, the relative merits of: (i) increased directorial accountability to shareholders for ongoing firm performance (favouring a removable-*without*-cause board); and (ii) enhanced board stability, strategic continuity and autonomy from shareholder interference (arguably favouring a board that is removable *for* cause only).[13] In this way, section 141 provides a (limited) contractual framework for the effective balancing of power between the board and shareholders on a proactive, ex ante basis.[14]

Arguably the most controversial opt-out provision in the Delaware statute, however, concerns the separate issue of attributing liability within the firm ex post facto following an adverse business outcome. In such event, section 102(b)(7) permits a company to make provision in its certificate of incorporation for the exculpation (ie immunisation) of its directors – whether wholly or partially – from liability for any breach of duty that the latter might commit in the course of office. Although not expressly worded in terms of a reversible rule, section 102(b)(7) in effect enables a company's board to contract itself out of default liability at common law by

---

[11] For an indication of the circumstances where for-cause removal of a director will (and, likewise, will *not*) be valid under Delaware law, see *Alderstein v Wertheimer* 2002 WL 205684 (Del 2002). In any event, the director(s) whose dismissal is proposed must be given advance notice of the meeting at which the question of their dismissal will be determined, and must also be given the prior opportunity to 'put their case' to shareholders by circulating a proxy statement at the company's expense.

[12] DGCL § 141(k).

[13] See ibid, § 141(b).

[14] On the further practical benefit of classification in providing insulation for boards against potential control changes, see below nn 52–54 and accompanying text.

obtaining the approval of a majority of shareholders to the requisite constitutional amendment.

This widely-invoked provision was introduced into the Delaware statute in the mid-1980s in response to the Delaware Supreme Court's landmark decision in *Smith v Van Gorkom*.[15] In this frequently-cited case,
members of a public corporation's board of directors (a majority of whom
were independent non-executives) were each held personally liable for
breach of their fiduciary duty of care on the ground that they collectively
approved the terms of a leveraged buyout merger, without sufficiently
informing themselves beforehand of the potential premium that could be
achieved for shareholders in the underlying control transaction. Although
the case against the directors was eventually settled for US$23,500,000
prior to the court's ruling on damages, the overall estimated losses to the
company's shareholders (for which the directors were potentially liable)
were far in excess of the US$100 million mark. The somewhat surprising
ruling of the Supreme Court in *Van Gorkom* arguably went against the
grain of the Delaware judiciary's traditionally liberal and deferential
approach to determining the propriety of business decisions, especially
those – like the board's approval decision in *Van Gorkom* – that are reached
in good faith and without the taint of improper motive.

The perceived diminution by *Van Gorkom* of the judicial protection
formerly afforded to boards triggered an outcry within the US business
community and a retrenchment response by insurers, who consequently
took steps to increase the cost to companies of obtaining directors' and
officers' (D&O) liability coverage. Within this adverse market climate,
section 102(b)(7) was designed to enable companies to mitigate – on a
firm-specific basis – both: (i) the apparent 'chilling' effect of *Van Gorkom*
on the incentives for high-quality personnel to serve on Delaware company boards and approve risky managerial decisions therein; and (ii) the
increased cost to companies of compensating and insuring directors
against liability risk in the post-*Van Gorkom* era.

The statutory exculpation provision is expressly and logically limited in
scope, insofar as directors cannot obtain liability waiver under section
102(b)(7) in respect of conduct that is disloyal (to the company and its
shareholders), improperly self-benefiting, or in bad faith (including know-
ing violations of law). Moreover, the immunising effect of the provision
extends only to the money liability consequences of a director being found
in breach of duty, and does not 'undo' the underlying breach itself.[16] This

---

[15] *Smith and Gosselin v Van Gorkom and others* 488 A 2d 858 (Del 1985).

[16] Furthermore, statutory exculpation does not cover the legal fees and court costs incurred
by a director in defending himself against an alleged breach of duty. However, section 145 of
the DGCL empowers a corporation to indemnify any of its directors or officers for such additional defence costs and also any damages awards, fines and compensation amounts personally incurred in the course of office. It is standard commercial practice for a public corporation
to cover the cost of providing such indemnities by maintaining directors' and officers' (D&O)

is significant in that directors remain subject to the adverse reputational and educative effects of publicised breaches of duty, independently of the personal financial consequences (or lack of) for wrongdoers. From a private ordering perspective, one might regard this outcome as an optimal contractual equilibrium between the dual functional concerns of preserving effective board accountability whilst minimising the aforementioned costs to companies (and, in turn, shareholders) of directors' liability exposure. Notwithstanding this, the phenomenon of contractual exculpation remains a cause of justifiable unease for those who regard directors' fiduciary duties – and the sanctions for breach thereof – as embodying certain public standards or expectations of professional conduct that transcend the private prudential preferences of boards and shareholders alone.

In addition to giving companies the licence to opt out of default governance norms in the above ways, the Delaware statute also makes some less widely accepted provisions available on an 'opt-in' basis, meaning that firms can choose to adopt them proactively via appropriate amendment to their constitutional bylaws. Two of the most noteworthy and also recent examples of such a rule are sections 112 and 113 of the DGCL, which were introduced into the statute in 2009. The former of these provisions permits the voluntary initiation of shareholder access to the corporate ballot,[17] so as to enable any shareholder satisfying specified minimum ownership, holding and/or other requirements or conditions to nominate their own candidate(s) for election to the company's board of directors. Additionally or alternatively to this, the latter rule allows a company's bylaws to provide for reimbursement by it of a shareholder for the expenses incurred in launching a proxy contest. Such reimbursement can be permitted where the contestant shareholder uses the company's own proxy form to nominate directorial candidates consequent to an installed section 112 procedure, and

---

liability insurance coverage in respect of each officer as part of his compensation package. Exercise by the corporation of its statutory indemnity power is subject to the express condition that the defendant director(s) acted in good faith and in a manner reasonably believed to be in the company's best interests. Where a director is unsuccessful on the merits in defence of his action, indemnity of defence costs is not guaranteed but rather will be at the discretion of the corporation (meaning in effect its board). Therefore, whilst the statutory indemnity power is a helpful complement to an exculpation provision, it is not a substitute for it in terms of providing reliable assurance to directors against liability exposure.

[17] Immediately following its enactment, the practical effectiveness of section 112 was significantly restricted by the fact that, under the then-applicable SEC Rule 14a-8(i)(a) (discussed below in pt IV), shareholders were prohibited from including proposals relating to board elections on the company's proxy card. This meant that, in order to adopt a section 112 (or section 113) bylaw amendment without the prior cooperation of the board, the proponent shareholder had to initiate an independent proxy contest against the board at his own expense. However, following a recent significant amendment to SEC Rule 14a-8, shareholder proposals for the reform of corporate election procedures may now permissibly be included on a company's proxy card. It is therefore now possible for section 112 and 113 bylaw amendments to be proposed by shareholders of public corporations at minimal personal cost. On this, see below nn 120–24 and accompanying text. For a further discussion of Rule 14a-8 generally, see below pt V.

also in the traditional case where a shareholder self-solicits proxies in opposition to the board's nominees independently of the company's formal proxy communications.[18]

Despite their limited non-default status, these provisions are nonetheless highly significant within the wider normative fabric of Delaware corporate law, which has traditionally regarded the board's exclusive control over directorial nominations as a legitimate and intrinsic part of its managerial prerogative under section 141. Insofar as sections 112 and 113 provide for the lawful variation of this formerly blanket position on a firm-specific basis at the initiative of shareholders, they can be said to represent an important extension of contractual rationality over core US corporate governance processes.

II. COMPETITIVE FEDERALISM

The tradition of adaptability and opting-out in US corporate law is reinforced by the country's unique competitive-federalist law-making system. Ingrained into the jurisprudential fabric of US corporate law is the long-standing 'internal affairs' doctrine, which dictates that the State of incorporation – as the formal source of a corporation's legal existence – has exclusive law-making prerogative over intra-firm affairs involving the rights and powers of shareholders, directors and managers.[19]

Thus, incorporators – both 'start up' first-time incorporators and 'midstream' reincorporating firms[20] – enjoy a legally uninhibited choice of 51 intra-national jurisdictions[21] as the formal legal domicile for their company. Moreover, applicable rules of US corporate law – in contrast to other aspects of civil or criminal law – are to be determined purely by a corporation's State of registration irrespective of whereabouts in the country (or

---

[18] Absent section 113, any attempt by a shareholder to propose such a bylaw amendment via the standard route of an SEC Rule 14a-8 proposal could lawfully be thwarted by the board via exclusion of the proposal from the company's proxy card. This would be on the ground that such a bylaw provision effectively fetters the board's legitimate discretion under §141 to refuse to facilitate the nomination of any candidate whose appointment would, in the opinion of the board, be against the company's best interests. On this, see *CA Inc v AFSCME Employees Pension Plan* 953 A 2d 227 (Del 2008).

[19] On this, see D DeMott, 'Perspectives on Choice of Law for Corporate Internal Affairs' (1985) 48 *Law & Contemporary Problems* 161; F Tung, 'Before Competition: Origins of the Internal Affairs Doctrine' (2006) 32 *Journal of Corporation Law* 33.

[20] 'Straight' re-incorporation in another State is impracticable in that it would necessarily entail winding up the company in its original State of incorporation and re-constituting it entirely in its new domicile. However, in practice, the same basic migration effect is achieved by incorporating a shell corporation in the new State, and then effecting a merger between the original corporation and the new entity whereby the latter becomes the original firm's holding company, and the shareholders of the first company are able to exchange their stock for corresponding shares in the new entity.

[21] This figure includes all 50 US States plus the District of Columbia, which operates its own incorporations regime.

world) its physical activities and transactions are subsequently carried out.[22] This means that, with respect to corporate law at least, the choice of State of incorporation in effect amounts to a choice *of law*, thereby creating a quasi-consumerist tendency to view each individual State's corporate law system as an effective 'menu' of choices that can be weighed up against those competing regulatory 'products' offered by other States.[23]

Unsurprisingly, many of the most emphatic academic supporters of the competitive-federalist model are situated within the contractarian school of thought.[24] In rationalising and defending the United States' devolved corporate law-making framework, contractarian scholars essentially extend the basic neo-classical tenet of competitive self-interest-seeking from the micro level of internal corporate contractors to the macro level of the regulatory State itself. Accordingly, States can each be regarded (admittedly to varying extents[25]) as having a compelling prudential interest in attracting both newly incorporating and mid-stream firms to incorporate within their jurisdiction.

Of course, as mentioned above, the fact that a firm has chosen to incorporate within a particular State is of no significance to the entirely independent questions of whether and to what extent that company will carry on its physical operations within the same State. Therefore the attractiveness of a State as a forum for incorporation should not be overplayed, as it is largely non-determinative of a State's ability to attract wealth-creating productive activity and resultant employment and corporation tax revenues within its borders. At the same time, though, the economic benefits to a State of establishing itself as an incorporation regime of choice should not be underestimated either, as States have the capacity to raise a not-insignificant amount of public revenue via the incorporations system itself. Such revenues typically take the form of administrative fees levied

---

[22] R Romano, *The Genius of American Corporate Law* (Washington DC, AEI Press, 1993) 1.

[23] See, eg FH Easterbrook and DR Fischel, *The Economic Structure of Corporate Law* (Cambridge MA, Harvard University Press, 1991) 5: 'The fifty states offer different menus of devices (from voting by shareholders to fiduciary rules to derivative litigation) for the protection of investors'.

[24] See, eg Easterbrook and Fischel, ibid, ch 8; FH Easterbrook, 'Managers' Discretion and Investors' Welfare: Theories and Evidence' (1984) 9 *Delaware Journal of Corporate Law* 540; DR Fischel, 'The "Race to the Bottom" Revisited: Reflections on Recent Developments in Delaware's Corporation Law' (1982) 76 *Northwestern University Law Review* 913; SM Bainbridge, 'Director Primacy and Shareholder Disempowerment' (2006) 119 *Harvard Law Review* 1735, 1741–44.

[25] It can be surmised that certain States, because of their inherent characteristics, will have a stronger motivation than others to appeal to potential incorporators. For instance, small States with a relatively low population base and limited other sources of public revenue will likely be inclined to place a heavier reliance on incorporations as a revenue source than their larger and more economically eclectic (in terms of other potential interests and sources of comparative advantage) counterparts. On this, see Romano, *The Genius of American Corporate Law*, above n 22, 721–22; LA Bebchuk, 'Federalism and the Corporation: The Desirable Limits on State Competition in Corporate Law' (1992) 105 *Harvard Law Review* 1435, 1451–52.

during the initial incorporation process, and also a continuing franchise tax payable by domiciled corporations periodically thereafter.[26]

Furthermore, since formation of a company within any State entails subjection to its framework of corporate laws, it follows that the legislative and judicial systems of a popular State of incorporation will be a source of correspondingly high interest amongst litigants and legal professionals. This enables that State to develop a specialised legal infrastructure geared to advising the directors, managers and shareholders of the companies incorporated within its boundaries. Consequently, that State is likely to enjoy the direct[27] and indirect[28] economic benefits that ordinarily flow from hosting a vibrant professional services sector in its geographic locality.[29]

Adopting the aforementioned logic of competitive self-interest-seeking, it can accordingly be deduced that – just as corporations compete with each other to offer the securities and governance systems that appeal to investors – at a higher level States can also be seen as competing with one another to offer the legal 'terms' that corporations themselves are likely to find attractive.[30] Whereas the imputed motivating force for a corporation in offering attractive terms to investors is reduction of its cost of capital and, ultimately, profit maximisation, for States the corresponding imperative is perceived to be maximisation of incorporation revenues and attendant benefits.[31] In this way, the same competitive and maximising logic is used in effect to 'marketise' the mentality of the hypothetical regulatory State, so that prudential and wealth-maximising considerations are perceived to trump distributive or other public policy concerns in the notional law-maker's mindset. Accordingly, the orthodox chain of regulatory cause and effect is reversed in the sense that regulatees, as notional 'consumers' of legal rules, dictate the decisions of regulators as notional 'producers' on the corporate law marketplace.

[26] See Bebchuk, ibid, 1447.

[27] Direct economic benefits for States include tax revenues from the profits of law firms and associated professional organisations, plus the employment opportunities available for residents of the State within the sector. Of course, to the extent that law firms located outside of the State are capable of generating in-house expertise on the laws of that State (such as where New York-based firms develop a specialism in Delaware corporate law), these benefits will predictably be diminished.

[28] Indirect benefits include the 'network effect' of a dynamic legal services sector in stimulating the provision of contingent professional and other services in a locality, plus the macro effect of greater opportunity and prosperity in bringing about increased consumer demand and general economic activity.

[29] See Bebchuk, 'Federalism and the Corporation', above n 25, 1447.

[30] As Stephen Bainbridge surmises: 'Because investors will demand the governance terms they prefer and managers have strong incentives to meet that demand, it follows that states have incentives to adopt corporate laws providing such terms off the rack. The more charters the state grants, the more franchise and other taxes it collects. States thus compete in granting corporate charters. This process of competitive federalism tends to produce those laws preferred by investors'. Bainbridge, 'Director Primacy', above n 24, 1742.

[31] Bebchuk, 'Federalism and the Corporation', above n 25, 1451.

Such a portrayal of the rule-making process, moreover, aligns logically with the aforementioned opting-out tradition in corporate law. On a private ordering analysis it could be said that an incorporator, having chosen to 'purchase' a particular set of rules by incorporating her firm within a chosen jurisdiction, should thereafter be free as the notional 'owner' of those rules to adapt them to her personal preference, just as one might wish to make perceived improvements to a house or car following its purchase. Although the issue of legal sovereignty in the constitutional law sense is usually elided in corporate contractarian discussion, the implication would appear to be that – just as effective 'sovereignty' on a competitive product marketplace rests with the consumer – likewise in a competitive laws marketplace regulatory sovereignty can be perceived as residing ultimately in the corporation and its shareholders. In moral-political terms, the end result is to externalise the evolutionary dynamic of corporate law entirely from its political-democratic source, with the result that general public policy or citizenry concerns become relevant considerations for corporate law only when translated into the governing discourse of rational choice and quasi-private wealth maximisation.

From this ideological perspective, the uniquely pluralist quality of the American corporate law-making tradition has frequently been lauded for both positive and negative reasons: positively for engendering a number of dynamic (State) 'laboratories' of diverse and efficient solutions to evolving business needs;[32] and in negative terms for providing corporations with a crucial and ready escape route from seemingly tyrannous or badly designed laws – an option which, moreover, would likely be lacking or at least significantly constrained within a unitary (ie one State) law-making system.[33]

In respect of publicly traded corporations at least, the clear and much-lauded winner in the inter-jurisdictional 'contest' for incorporations is the aforementioned State of Delaware, which has undoubtedly developed a world-leading judicial infrastructure in terms of substantive specialisation, jurisprudential sophistication, and receptiveness to the complexities and practical exigencies of governance and control disputes in widely held corporations. In view of the above factors, Delaware's experience in the United States is commonly advanced within contractarian circles as hard evidence that multi-partite private ordering of corporate law 'works';

---

[32] The term 'laboratory' as used in this context is descended from Justice Louis Brandeis of the US Supreme Court, who coined the phrase in his dissenting judgment in the classic 1932 case of *New State Ice Co v Liebmann*, 285 US 262 (1932). Although this case was not directly concerned with inter-State incorporations (but rather with State restraint of trade), Justice Brandeis's term has since been taken up in the context of the incorporations debate. See, eg SM Bainbridge, 'Is "Say on Pay" Justified?', *Regulation* (Spring 2009) 42, 46.

[33] Bainbridge, ibid.

or, at the very least, that it provides more economically and politically[34] desirable outcomes than the alternative option of concentrating law-making responsibility within a centralised and dominant governmental authority such as a federal regulator.[35]

Whilst the precise source and extent of Delaware's alleged superiority as a jurisdiction of choice is an uncertain and contentious issue,[36] its continuing position as the preferred State of incorporation amongst the US public corporate elite is almost[37] entirely beyond question. Meanwhile, for those corporations that opt to incorporate in a jurisdiction other than Delaware, the Model Business Corporation Act (MBCA) is designed to fulfil a fundamentally similar function to the Delaware statute as a purported manual of national corporate law best practice. Promulgated and updated by the American Bar Association, the MBCA has no formal statutory status in itself but nonetheless represents a highly influential summation and amalgamation of legal doctrines developed within different States (including Delaware). The MBCA is, vice versa, adopted in significant part by many individual States as an effective blueprint for their own corporate law codes, thus ensuring substantial uniformity and the rapid cross-importation of generally desirable corporate governance norms.

The MBCA can accordingly be regarded in contractarian terms as an 'off-the-shelf' selection of legal doctrines that States themselves are readily able to adopt and/or adapt in designing their respective corporate law

---

[34] The political desirability of competitive federalism in the US derives principally from its 'pluralising' quality, in that by eradicating (via multi-level market pressures) any semblance of socially determinative authority in the system, it theoretically conforms to the republican governmental ideal of widespread power decentralisation. This longstanding ideological predisposition, which is arguably endemic to the American constitution, political system and general national psyche, is expressed most eloquently in the following observation of De Tocqueville: 'Nothing is more striking to a European traveller in the United States, than the absence of what we term the Government, or the Administration. Written laws exist in America, and one sees the daily execution of them; but although everything moves regularly, the mover can nowhere be discovered. The hand which directs the social machine is invisible'. A De Tocqueville, *Democracy in America* (R Heffner (ed)) (New York, Mentor, 1956) 62.

[35] However, on the conspicuous expansion of federal governmental involvement in US corporate governance over recent years, see below ch 6 of this volume, pt I.A.

[36] Advocates of the 'race-to-the-top' theory of competitive-federalism such as Easterbrook, Fischel and Bainbridge have attributed Delaware's competitive supremacy to the success of its substantive corporate law rules in ensuring wealth-maximising outcomes for shareholders. However, less sanguine accounts of Delaware's dominance, such as Roberta Romano's classic study, have identified the jurisdiction's comparative advantage as residing principally in the formal predictability and stability of outcomes that its legislative and judicial infrastructure offers to corporate participants, in distinction from the substantive content of the law itself. On this debate, see Bebchuk, 'Federalism and the Corporation', above n 25, 1445–48.

[37] For a recent empirical study suggesting that Delaware's jurisdictional pre-eminence is being threatened by a sharp drop in the State's popularity as a forum for corporate litigation, see J Armour, B Black and B Cheffins, 'Delaware's Balancing Act' (2012) 87 *Indiana Law Journal* 1345, available at: ssrn.com/abstract=1677400.

statutes, in a manner not-dissimilar to how investors and managers use the resultant State statutes. This arguably adds an additional third layer to the quasi-private rule selection process in US corporate law, at least for the significant minority of large public corporations that are incorporated outside of Delaware.

III. JUDICIAL DEFERENCE TO PRIVATE ORDERING: THE BUSINESS JUDGMENT RULE

A defining feature of the contractarian theory of the firm, as I explained in the previous chapter, is its understanding that the internal mechanics of corporations – like those of all business entities and other lawful private associations – lie beyond the acceptable bounds of public governmental direction.[38] This position is arguably a logical consequence of respecting the independent legal personhood of the corporation which, as an autonomous private entity, is entitled to form (or, more accurately, *have* formed) its own associational goals and relationships reflective of the mutual wishes of its incorporators and appointed agents.

Accordingly, whereas the external regulatory (ie *non*-corporate law) environment in which companies operate is rightfully open to democratic scrutiny and political reform, the internal contractual (ie corporate law) domain of a company is by contrast a legal-institutional 'closed space'. One notable practical consequence of this – as discussed above – is the characteristic flexibility and indeterminacy of statutory decrees relevant to corporate governance matters.[39] A further and equally significant implication, though, is the traditionally liberal and non-interventionist approach adopted by US State judiciaries to assessing the propriety of managerial decisions concerning corporate objectives and strategy. Such judicial reluctance to second-guess or otherwise pass opinion on the merits of internal corporate decisions has moreover been formalised doctrinally in the form of the business judgment rule, which pervades the application of directors' fiduciary duties by US and particularly Delaware courts.

On the issue firstly of the rightful objectives of a business corporation, it is a well-accepted implication of the business judgment rule that a court will defer to the good faith decisions of management (as affirmed formally by the board) so long as there is 'some rationally related benefit' to shareholders – however indirect or tangential – from a proposed corporate plan of action.[40] Within the wide ambit of this judicial policy, a range of prima facie philanthropic or otherwise non-commercial corporate activities have historically been upheld as valid and proper uses

---

[38] On this, see above ch 3 of this volume, fns 13–20 and accompanying text.
[39] See above pt II.A.
[40] *Revlon Inc v MacAndrews & Forbes Holdings Inc* 506 A 2d 173 (Del 1986).

of a business corporation's assets, including political and charitable donations, and profit-sacrificing measures aimed at enhancing the welfare of workers and local communities.[41]

The only real limitation on management's freedom to determine the broad goals of the enterprise, besides the general fiduciary requirements of loyalty and good faith (denoting honest commitment to the company and an absence of fraud or self-dealing), is that directors must be able to point to some plausible potential benefit that the corporation stands to gain from the conduct in question, notwithstanding how improbable or far-fathomed it may be. Such projected consideration could be in the form of improved customer goodwill (in the case of charitable donations), increased employee loyalty and productivity (in the case of profit-sacrificing workforce or community programmes), a more business-friendly regulatory environment (in the case of political donations) or otherwise.[42] The notion of corporate goal-

[41] The classic example of US judicial liberalism in assessing the legitimacy of corporate objectives is the ruling of the Illinois Appellate Court in *Shlensky v Wrigley* 237 NE 2d 776 (Ill 1968). In this case, the court upheld the refusal by Philip K Wrigley as President of the (Delaware-incorporated) Chicago Cubs baseball corporation to permit the installation of floodlights at the Cubs' stadium, Wrigley Field, which would have enabled matches to be played at night so as to generate greater ticket revenues. In approving Wrigley's stance on this matter (as approved by the corporation's board under Wrigley's dominance), Judge Sullivan pointed to the likely long-term effect of the no-lighting policy in maintaining the quality of life and attractiveness of the local neighbourhood around the stadium. In the court's opinion, this could conceivably prevent the neighbourhood from 'deteriorating', with potentially adverse effects on the value of local properties (including Wrigley Field itself) and also the general affluence of the local community as a prospective customer base for the baseball club. Through this creative application of what later become known (in *Revlon*, above n 40) as the 'rationally related benefit' test, the Illinois court effectively sanctioned a prima facie anti-commercial corporate policy as a legitimate exercise of the board's discretion in fulfilment of its fiduciary duties to the corporation and its shareholders.

[42] The most well-known example of a case where a corporation's management stepped over the line between enlightened corporate self-interest and fully-fledged social beneficence is *Dodge v Ford Motor Co* 170 NW 668 (Mich 1919). In this case, the Michigan Supreme Court approved a lower court order enjoining (ie prohibiting) the company under the leadership of its founder and dominant officer, Henry Ford, from refusing to pay dividends to shareholders, on the ground that retention of distributable profits in the circumstances was an illegitimate use of corporate funds. In an oft-quoted passage, Chief Justice Ostrander emphasised (684) that '[a] business corporation is organized and carried on primarily for the profit of the stockholders', and therefore that '[t]he discretion of directors is to be exercised in the choice of means to attain that end and does not extend to a change in the end itself, to the reduction of profits or to the non-distribution of profits among stockholders in order to devote them to other purposes'. The element of impropriety in Ford's decision stemmed not from the non-payment of dividends in itself (which was permissible), nor from the decision to retain the profits for reinvestment in the business (which was potentially susceptible to commercial justification). Rather the problematic element of Ford's non-payment policy was the way in which it was justified to shareholders and subsequently the court, namely that it was for the express purposes of: first, expanding the company's industrial operations so as to provide for increased employment opportunities in the city of Detroit; and, secondly, enabling the company's output to be sold at a below-market price in order to expand automobile ownership amongst the general citizenry. In the court's view, Ford's plan in effect constituted a proposal 'to continue the corporation henceforth as a semi-eleemosynary institution and not as a business institution', this being a breach of shareholders' basic legitimate expectations as to the use of their equity funds (ibid, 683).

setting as a strictly private internal affair, subject only to a base level of judicial scrutiny to prevent wasteful or manifestly irrational uses of corporate funds, is entirely consistent with the contractarian understanding of the board's role and powers: that is to say, the idea that the board – and, in turn, management – is entitled to exercise the wide executive discretion placed in it by shareholders so long as some foundational and logically implicit contractual expectations are honoured regarding the use of the latter's equity.[43]

The same basic 'hands off' judicial attitude extends also to questions as to the propriety of individual strategic decisions, such as whether to enter into a particular venture or market, whether to postpone or limit profit distributions to shareholders for the purpose of funding longer-term business expansion, or whether to proceed with a so-called 'game-ending'[44] event such as a major asset restructuring or proposed merger with another firm.[45] In approving managerial decisions on such matters, the board will be subject to its usual fiduciary duty of care. According to this standard, liability will only be triggered by a finding of gross negligence in the sense of egregious conduct falling far below what can reasonably be expected in such circumstances. The express judicial rationale is to limit any disparity between the potential upside and downside 'payoffs' for public company directors of approving risky and uncertain decisions, so as to guard against the aforementioned 'chilling' effect on directors of (economically) excessive liability exposure.[46]

Additionally, the business judgment rule dictates that the board's conclusions and ensuing actions will be beyond judicial reproach on the ground of absence of due care, subject to its members satisfying certain basic standards of procedural propriety.[47] These require that directors act: (i) honestly for the benefit of the company, (ii) absent any personal conflicts of interest and (iii) on an informed basis. By virtue of the rule, a

---

[43] For an excellent academic rationalisation and defence of this position, see SM Bainbridge, 'Director Primacy: The Means and Ends of Corporate Governance' (2003) 97 *Northwestern University Law Review* 547.

[44] This term is attributable to LA Bebchuk, 'The Case for Increasing Shareholder Power' (2005) 118 *Harvard Law Review* 833.

[45] The exception to this basic position is questions concerning changes in control over the firm, which will be discussed separately below at pt II.C.

[46] See *Gagliardi v Trifoods International Inc* 683 A 2d 1049 (Del Ch 1996) 1052 (Chancellor Allen): 'Corporate directors of public companies . . . enjoy (as residual owners) only a very small proportion of any "upside" gains earned by the corporation on risky investment projects. If, however, corporate directors were to be found liable for a corporate loss from a risky project on the ground that the investment was too risky . . . their liability would be joint and several for the whole loss . . . Given the scale of operation of modern public corporations, this stupefying disjunction between risk and reward for corporate directors threatens undesirable effects'.

[47] The business judgment rule has been described as an 'abstention doctrine', in that where applicable it has the effect of precluding judicial examination of the merits of directors' decisions entirely in duty of care actions. See S Bainbridge, 'The Business Judgment Rule as Abstention Doctrine' (2004) 57 *Vanderbilt Law Review* 83.

director will furthermore be *presumed* to be acting in a loyal, bona fide and reasonably well-informed manner unless affirmatively proven otherwise.[48] The only exception is in the extraordinary instance where one or more of the above three facets of the presumption can be rebutted by a plaintiff establishing concrete evidence to the contrary,[49] or else by showing that a given transaction is so devoid of effective consideration or rationality as to constitute a waste of corporate assets (in which latter case it cannot by definition be regarded as a rational business judgment deserving of the benefit of the presumption).[50]

Like the aforementioned judicial approach to the issue of determining overall corporate objectives, the application of the business judgment presumption to managerial strategy formation decisions can be said to respect the integrity of the company's internal governance arrangements and the authority of its appointed agents. This is subject only to the board satisfying certain basic contractual expectations underpinning the continuing integrity of its relationship with the corporation and its shareholders, to the effect that its members have exhibited honesty, fidelity and basic fitness for office in scrutinising and approving high-level management decisions.[51]

---

[48] *Aronson v Lewis* 473 A 2d 805 (Del 1984) 812.

[49] However, even where a plaintiff successfully rebuts one or more facets of the presumption, this will not in itself guarantee an outcome in their favour. Rather, the effect of rebutting the presumption is to trigger an 'entire fairness' examination whereby the court will scrutinise the questionable decision and any relevant evidence pertaining to it. At this latter stage of proceedings, the onus will lie contrarily on the defendant directors to establish that their conduct on the whole was intrinsically fair to the corporation and its shareholders, both *procedurally*, in that the relevant decision was properly approved, and *substantively*, in the sense that the corporation and its shareholders received a 'fair' or sufficient (as opposed to just rationally plausible or conceivable) price as part of the transaction or initiative in question. On the contours and application of this doctrine (in the factual context of a 'cash-out' merger), see *Weinberger v UOP Inc* 457 A 2d 701 (Del 1983).

[50] Two of the most noteworthy examples of Delaware cases where plaintiffs attempted (unsuccessfully) to rebut the business judgment presumption on the ground that the defendant board's conduct (in approving a purportedly exorbitant executive compensation package) amounted to a waste of corporate assets are *Aronson v Lewis*, above n 48; and *Brehm v Eisner* 746 A 2d 244 (Del 2000) (which concerned the extensive compensation and termination payments due to Michael Ovitz following his short and ill-fated spell as President of the Walt Disney Company).

[51] For the sake of simplicity, the foregoing discussion of the business judgment rule mentions only its application to boards of directors who collectively approve questionable executive decisions in arguable breach of their fiduciary duties. However, it is now a well-established tenet of Delaware law that fiduciary duties are owed not just by directors but also by senior managerial officers below board level, who should by implication be entitled to an analogous level of judicial protection under the aforementioned presumption. See *Gantler v Stephens* 965 A 2d 695 (Del 2009) 708–9.

IV. ANTI-TAKEOVER MEASURES

A. The Contractual Nature of Staggered Boards and Poison Pills

In addition to its aforementioned indirect effect under Delaware law in securing the opt-out of a company from the removal-without-cause rule,[52] board classification has the additional and direct outcome of ensuring that the directors' respective periods of tenure are not co-terminous. It therefore provides a crucial layer of insulation for boards (and, in turn, managers) against potential forced changes of control, by significantly increasing the cost to an outsider of launching a proxy contest to displace the incumbent management team from office. Where a staggered board is in place, a prospective acquirer of corporate control (or 'raider') must instigate two successful proxy contests in consecutive years in order to secure a majority of board seats for their nominees. Insofar as the resultant expense and time delay acts as a disincentive to potential acquirers of control, a staggered board can be said to represent an effective 'shark repellent'[53] defence to hostile takeovers in the United States.[54]

A related and highly controversial phenomenon in the United States is the widespread use by listed corporations of shareholder rights plans or 'poison pills' as an additional pre-emptive response to the threat of hostile takeover. Whereas staggered boards are designed principally to thwart proxy contests by outsiders aimed at wresting control over the company's voting franchise in their favour, poison pills are geared to preclude contests for control that are instigated by the alternative route of outright share acquisition via a tender offer to shareholders.

Although contractarian opinion is split on the overall merit of such devices from a corporate governance point of view,[55] their inherently contractual quality is beyond dispute. Poison pills, like other inventive takeover defences in the United States,[56] are a professional rather than regulatory

---

[52] See above nn 12–14 and accompanying text.

[53] A 'shark repellent' defence is an anti-takeover measure that is typically put in place prior to the company attracting attention from any particular bidder. As such, it is designed to act as a general deterrent to any prospective control-acquirers. Other examples of such pre-emptive defences are shareholders rights plans (or 'poison pills') and super-majority merger approval provisions. On the former of these, see below nn 55–57 and accompanying text. On the latter, see below n 58.

[54] It has traditionally been common commercial practice for listed US corporations to classify or stagger their boards. However, over the past decade the number of staggered boards within the largest US listed corporations has diminished rapidly in response to growing institutional shareholder activism on corporate governance issues. On this, see M Kahan and E Rock, 'Embattled CEOs' (2010) 88 *Texas Law Review* 987, 1007–9.

[55] On this, see below pt IV.B.(i)–(ii).

[56] A notable exception to this position is the 'business combination' defence to a hostile takeover, which is established on a default legislative basis by section 203 of the DGCL. This reversible rule forbids a corporation from engaging in any business combination (eg a

creation. As such, they can embody a number of diverse and continually evolving forms, depending on the circumstances of the relevant company and the creativity of the law firm that is employed to design its anti-takeover rearguard. In the most common case, a poison pill takes the form of a constitutional provision in a corporation's charter or bylaws, vesting each of its shareholders – excluding a potential acquirer of control – with the option to subscribe for a large quantity of newly-issued shares at a heavily discounted price relative to the market value of the company's equity. The right is typically not absolute but rather is conditional on the occurrence of a specified event. Normally, the triggering event will be a potential control-acquirer reaching a prescribed ownership threshold such as 15 per cent of the target company's voting equity capital.[57]

The value of a poison pill to a target company and its management resides not in the pill's actual use (which is never seriously envisaged), but rather in its preventive effect in discouraging raiders from proceeding with tender offers without the formal authorisation of the target's board of directors. This is because, if the pill is triggered or 'swallowed' by the raider, his holding will be diluted to such an extent by the discounted share issue as effectively to obliterate any realistic hope of completing the planned acquisition. At the very least, creation of the pill compels a potential control-acquirer to negotiate the terms of his bid directly with the board as a necessary precondition to the latter removing the pill so as to enable any planned tender offer to proceed. Moreover, where a corporation has put in place both a poison pill and staggered board in conjunction with one another, that firm is generally regarded to be 'takeover-proof': that is to say, it will in most cases be infeasible (or at least cost-ineffective) for any would-be raider to acquire effective majority voting control over the target by way of either tender offer or proxy contest.[58]

merger) with an 'interested stockholder' – defined as one holding 15 per cent or more of a company's voting equity capital – for a period of 3 years following the time at which that person became an interested stockholder within the meaning of the section. Where triggered, the prohibition can only be disabled with the approval of an 85 per cent super-majority vote of shareholders. Alternatively, it can be disapplied ex ante with the prior approval of the board of directors (before the triggering threshold is reached by the bidder). The practical effect of this rule is to prevent, or at least significantly delay, the completion of a tender offer that is instigated without the cooperation of the target company's board.

[57] The general validity of the poison pill as a hostile takeover defence was first recognised by the Delaware Supreme Court in the 1985 case of *Moran v Household International, Inc* 490 A 2d 1059 (Del 1985). However, the propriety of the pill's use in particular factual scenarios has frequently been a matter of intense judicial scrutiny. On this, see below part IV.B.(iii).

[58] A common additional anti-takeover measure is the inclusion of a super-majority merger approval provision in a company's bylaws. Such provision is designed to take effect when a prospective control-acquirer crosses a specified voting threshold (typically 20 per cent of the target's voting equity capital). When triggered, it has the effect of increasing the requisite shareholder approval threshold (typically from 50 per cent to 67 per cent) for effecting a 'close-out' merger between the acquirer and acquired entities. This is the standard legal process in the US – as prescribed in Delaware by section 251 of the DGCL – whereby an offeror gains full voting control over a target company following a successful tender offer to acquire

B. The Legitimacy of Anti-Takeover Measures Within the Contractarian Paradigm

(i) The Contractual Flexibility Thesis

The scholarly debate on the relative merits of anti-takeover devices such as staggered boards and poison pills is voluminous and inconclusive.[59] Furthermore, as mentioned above, the permissibility of hostile takeover defences is one of the few areas of corporate governance that tends to engender a sharp division of views within the contractarian school of thought as to the proper approach of the law in apportioning decision-making power between shareholders and managers. There are two general normative positions on this matter within the contractarian paradigm.

Proponents of what is most appropriately termed the contractual flexibility thesis argue that, in responding to an unsolicited tender offer, a target company's board of directors should be entitled to the same degree of business judgment protection as would be applicable to a non-control-related decision. Indeed, from this point of view, the importance of showing deference to the board's professional insight and bona fide judgment is arguably paramount in a takeover scenario, given the extraordinary significance of a change of control in determining the future direction and fortunes of a company's business. It follows that a decision by a target company's management to retain the pill, or to deploy an alternative defensive strategy, would in effect be exempt from substantive evaluation by a court except where a plaintiff was successful in overturning the business judgment presumption.[60]

The attractiveness of the contractual flexibility thesis from a contractarian perspective inheres principally in the leeway that it affords corporate managements to devise their own responses to tender offers on an ad hoc

---

a majority stake. For an example of a scenario where a target company's board was permitted to retain a three-fold rear-guard of staggered board, poison pill and super-majority merger approval provision in the face of a hostile bid, see *Air Products and Chemicals v Airgas* 16 A 3d 48 (Del Ch 2011) (*Airgas*), discussed below nn 95–96 and accompanying text.

[59] Amongst the leading contributions to this debate are: FH Easterbrook and DR Fischel, 'The Proper Role of a Target's Management in Responding to a Tender Offer' (1981) 94 *Harvard Law Review* 1161; LA Bebchuk, 'The Case Against Board Veto in Corporate Takeovers' (2002) 69 *University of Chicago Law Review* 973; R Gilson, 'The Case Against Shark Repellent Amendments: Structural Limitations on the Enabling Concept' (1982) 34 *Stanford Law Review* 775; R Gilson, 'Unocal Fifteen Years Later (and What We Can Do About It) (2001) 26 *Delaware Journal of Corporate Law* 491; M Lipton and P Rowe, 'Pills, Polls and Professors: A Reply to Professor Gilson' (2002) 27 *Delaware Journal of Corporate Law* 1; L Stout, 'Do Antitakeover Defenses Decrease Shareholder Wealth? The Ex Post/Ex Ante Valuation Problem' (2002) 55 *Stanford Law Review* 845.

[60] That is, by affirmatively establishing that the defensive response was approved by the company's board in bad faith, on an uninformed basis, or for a motivating purpose other than the best interests of the corporation and its shareholders.

basis depending on the identity of the bidder and the terms (and especially price) of the offer that is put to shareholders. Accordingly the law, by affording the cloak of business judgment protection to a board that refuses to remove the pill (or that deploys a defensive strategy of similar effect) when faced with an unsolicited bid, would in effect empower the target company's directors to have the ultimate say on the merits or otherwise of any offer proceeding: in other words, to 'just say no'[61] if it so chooses. The substantially unrestrained power to say 'no' would entitle the board to reject advances from bidders that are intrinsically undesirable notwithstanding the attractiveness of the tender offer price that is put to shareholders. In the case of less obviously objectionable bids, meanwhile, it would indirectly afford management the bargaining leverage to extract an optimal[62] control premium for shareholders, whether via one-on-one negotiation or else by inviting a competing 'friendly' third party bidder to initiate a control auction.[63]

For the above reasons, the contractual flexibility thesis infers that the vesting of authority in a target company's board to 'just say no' to hostile takeover bids is the legal norm that the majority of hypothetical corporate contractors would, on balance, ultimately be inclined to agree to if given the opportunity to apportion decision-making rights over unsolicited tender offers ex ante.[64] Similarly to the contractarian justification for general managerial hegemony,[65] the assertion here is that the material gains for shareholders of entrusting control-related decisions exclusively to the board's business judgment will more than justify the corresponding surrender of governance power that this entails.

(ii) The Shareholder Protectionism Thesis

The shareholder protectionism thesis, by contrast, emphasises the peculiar conflict of interest that unsolicited tender offers present for a target

---

[61] This term is attributable to JN Gordon, 'Corporations, Markets, and Courts' (1991) 91 *Columbia Law Review* 1931.

[62] The purported optimality of the resulting control premium is attributable to the (assumed) fact that the original bidder, if successful, would be compelled to share the prospective gains from the takeover with the target company's current shareholders a priori, up to the point where any further increase in the bid price would render the acquisition economically unviable (and therefore not worthwhile) for the bidder.

[63] In any event, the 'just say no' defence would not be entirely preclusive of future changes in control insofar as a 'rejected' bidder retains the option of initiating a proxy contest to gain control over the board. Whilst, as explained above, the deployment of a staggered board may render such an option prohibitively expensive in many cases, there is nevertheless at least a theoretical possibility of a hostile takeover being achieved by proxy contest notwithstanding a target board's unwieldy stance in refusing to cooperate with the bidder under any circumstances.

[64] For an argument to this effect, see SM Bainbridge, *The New Corporate Governance in Theory and Practice*, above n 4, 141–53.

[65] On this, see above ch 3 of this volume, pt III.B.(ii).

company's management and board. On the one hand, directors (and senior executive officers) are required by their fiduciary position to give honest and reasonably diligent consideration to any bid for control, and – where appropriate – to cooperate with the bidder by removing any structural barriers (eg a poison pill) impeding an acquisition attempt. On the other hand, a hostile takeover is – next to business failure – typically one of the most destabilising corporate governance events for an incumbent management team and board. Where an unsolicited tender offer is successfully executed, it will almost certainly be followed by wide-scale reorganisation of senior corporate personnel as the new owner-controller seeks to impose her own strategic vision and influence on the firm. This is especially likely in cases where a hostile acquisition is motivated by the objective of correcting perceived corporate underperformance or mismanagement.[66] Against this somewhat unappealing backdrop, it is unsurprising that incumbent corporate officers are often prone to regard the option of cooperating with a bidder as tantamount to 'turkeys voting for Christmas'. The result is that managerial resistance to outside tender offers tends to persist notwithstanding the objective desirability of a proposed control change for the corporation and its shareholders as a whole.

Given the purported importance of the hostile takeover threat to the overall functioning of corporate governance as a managerial-disciplinary system, the shareholder protectionism thesis rejects the assertion of the contractual flexibility school that control-related questions should be left to the (inherently conflicted) judgement of target company boards. On the contrary, advocates of the former position stress that an active and structurally unimpeded market for corporate control is a core and essential component of an efficient and well-functioning corporate governance system. It is claimed that a credible and ongoing hostile takeover threat makes diversification of equity cost-effective by precluding the need for direct monitoring by shareholders of managerial performance. At the same time, the ready possibility of wholesale share acquisition via tender offer preserves the value of the shareholder franchise within public corporations by providing an outlet for the amalgamation of otherwise powerless minority equity stakes en masse. This in turn stimulates the self-selection by managers, under shareholder pressure, of efficient corporate governance norms in other respects.[67]

---

[66] At the very least, the consequent transition from widely-held to concentrated corporate ownership that a tender offer entails (whether under entrepreneurial, private equity or holding company control) is likely to reduce many of the private benefits of control that a public company's management team enjoys. These include full control over corporate strategy and cash flows, and relatively limited external scrutiny by equity holders.

[67] The most influential academic articulation of this general position is provided by Easterbrook and Fischel. See 'The Proper Role of a Target's Management in Responding to a Tender Offer', above n 59; *The Economic Structure of Corporate Law*, above n 2, 171–74. See also Bebchuk, 'The Case Against Board Veto in Corporate Takeovers', above n 59.

Largely for these reasons, the shareholder protectionism thesis avers that most rational corporate contractors would be inclined to agree ex ante to disapply the business judgment presumption in the hostile take-over scenario, and also to allocate decision-making power over control-related issues to shareholders. This is by way of exception to the general contractual governance norm of managerial hegemony in other (*non-control-related*) decision-making contexts. Empowerment of shareholders in the takeover context can be achieved in practice via a general rule of board passivity, requiring that management and the board remain inactive when faced with a tender offer, except for taking any necessary steps to remove pre-existing structural obstacles to the successful execution of the bid. The result would be to allow shareholders to dictate the outcome of the bid with regard to the sole consideration of whether the price on offer represented adequate value, both for their equity stake in the business and the added premium benefit of control.[68]

C. The Legitimacy of Anti-Takeover Measures under Delaware Corporate Law

Over the past three decades, questions as to the legitimacy of managerial takeover defences have posed galling intellectual challenges for the Delaware judiciary. In providing jurisprudential answers to these questions the courts have, as mentioned earlier, demonstrated an unparalleled acumen in analysing the nuances of some of the most complex business and financial transactions.[69]

The Delaware courts have essentially developed something of a compromise approach that takes into account normative considerations from both of the above schools of thought, but without wholeheartedly adopting the prescriptive recommendations of either one. Consistent with the shareholder protectionism thesis, hostile takeover defences have been regarded as lying outside of the remit of normal business judgment protection. This is because, in the courts' opinion, the unique conflict of interest that an

---

[68] Whilst, as explained above, the converse rule of board primacy in the takeover context would arguably benefit shareholders by giving managers the power to negotiate bids on shareholders' behalf, there is the obvious risk that this power will be abused by managers as a licence to reject all bids outright for self-protectionist reasons. Furthermore, even where directors and managers can be trusted to use their powers properly for the purpose of extracting optimal value for shareholders from a potential bidder, the adverse indirect effect of this would be to remove entirely the incentives for ongoing monitoring by shareholders of managerial performance in non-takeover scenarios, in the knowledge that any ensuing underperformance can be 'corrected' in the form of a compensating takeover premium. For the above reasons, therefore, it may be surmised that – contrary to the assertions of the contractual flexibility thesis – the vesting of decision-making power in the board in control-related scenarios is not an outcome that rational shareholders would be inclined to agree to in their notional governance 'contract' with management.

[69] On this point generally, see above nn 34–37 and accompanying text.

unsolicited tender offer presents makes it near-impossible for management to make a genuinely impartial assessment of its merits. At the same time, and in line with the contractual flexibility position, the courts have been reluctant to overlook the cognitive benefits that independent and well-informed boards can bring to bear on important control-related decisions. Therefore Delaware law has stopped considerably short of advocating outright board passivity as an appropriate tender offer response.

Delaware's doctrinal compromise between the above two academic extremes is a system of conditional business judgment protection for hostile takeover defences. Accordingly, a target company's board – in order to avoid judicial invalidation of an anti-takeover measure – must justify its actions by showing that it had reasonable grounds to believe 'a danger to corporate policy and effectiveness' was posed by an unsolicited tender offer.[70] Significantly, the existence of reasonable grounds in this regard can be established by showing that the target company's directors acted in good faith and on the basis of reasonable investigation of the bid and its likely consequences.[71] Proof of reasonable investigation will be materially enhanced by the presence of a majority-independent board to approve management's conclusions on the matter,[72] although it will remain necessary for the board in all events to articulate some discernible corporate threat that their defensive action was geared in response to.[73] Furthermore, the defensive measure adopted must not be unreasonable or disproportionate to the particular threat that the bid poses to the corporation and its shareholders.[74]

With the progressive development of Delaware takeover jurisprudence from the 1980s onwards, there has occurred a notable expansion in the range of factors that are expressly capable of constituting a corporate 'danger' or threat in the judicially defined sense. In the leading early case law of the era, the courts were vigilant about policing the boundaries of management's permissible discretion in responding to unsolicited tender offers, so as to mitigate the scope for 'Trojan horse' managerial protectionism disguised as concern for long-term corporate interest.[75] Hence in its

---

[70] See *Cheff v Mathes* 199 A 2d 548 (Del 1964) 554–55 (Carey J); *Unocal Corp v Mesa Petroleum Co* 493 A 2d 946 (Del 1985) 955 (Moore J).

[71] *Cheff v Mathes*, ibid, 555; *Unocal*, ibid, 955.

[72] *Unocal*, above n 70.

[73] *Airgas*, above n 58, 16 A 3d 48 (Del Ch 2011) 94 (Chancellor Chandler).

[74] *Unocal*, above n 70, 493 A 2d 946 (Del 1985) 955–56. This position was subsequently developed by the Delaware Supreme Court in *Unitrin v American General Corp*, 651 A 2d 1361 (Del 1995) 1386–88, Holland J, so as to render legitimate any defensive tactics falling within a broad 'range of reasonableness' as determined by the court on an ex post facto basis. On this, see below nn 93–94 and accompanying text.

[75] Furthermore, as noted in one influential early decision, 'human nature may incline *even one acting in subjective good faith* to rationalize as right that which is merely personally beneficial' (emphasis added). See *City Capital Associates v Interco* 551 A 2d 787 (Del Ch 1988) (*Interco*) 796 (Chancellor Allen).

landmark *Unocal* decision in 1985,[76] the Delaware Supreme Court – despite granting business judgment protection to a board in respect of an anti-takeover measure – nonetheless took considerable care to avoid establishing a carte blanche licence for boards to adopt similar such measures in future cases. The decision therefore focused primarily on its relatively narrow factual context, which concerned immediate threats to shareholder welfare resulting from the manipulative or coercive structure of certain bids.[77] This fairly cautious judicial approach seemed to suggest that wider managerial concerns such as the perceived adequacy of the bid price and the implications of a proposed control change for the long-term health of the company's business were secondary factors at best, and on their own insufficient to justify a defensive response.[78]

The zenith of shareholder protectionism in US corporate takeover law, however, was the Delaware Supreme Court's influential *Revlon* decision one year later.[79] In addition to prohibiting a target company's directors from citing non-shareholder (eg creditor- or worker-related) concerns as the basis for a defensive stance except where a rationally related benefit for shareholders is involved, the *Revlon* decision also featured the clearest judicial affirmation in US corporate law to date of the so-called 'shareholder wealth maximisation' norm: that is, the notion that directors are required to maximise wealth or 'value' for shareholders as a consequence of their fiduciary duties.[80] The specific *Revlon* duty to maximise shareholder wealth in the corporate sale process is only invoked in the relatively narrow (and, it may be said, somewhat arbitrary) circumstances where directors either encourage a bidding war for the company under conditions that make its eventual 'break up' inevitable,[81] or else actively facilitate the transfer of majority voting control over the company to a non-publicly-held entity.[82] Notwithstanding its fairly limited factual application, though, the *Revlon* doctrine was normatively significant in establishing the apparent centrality of shareholder welfare as a determin-

[76] See above n 70.

[77] Such questionable practices included bids designed mainly to elicit 'greenmail' payoffs from target corporations as the effective price for abandoning a threatened hostile bid, and also 'two-tier front-loaded' tender offers structured so as to compel shareholders to sell to the bidder regardless of the overall merit of the bid.

[78] As examples of additional concerns that may potentially constitute a relevant corporate threat, the court in *Unocal* cited (inter alia) the (in)adequacy of the bid price and the impact of the proposed acquisition on non-shareholder constituencies. See above n 70, 493 A 2d 946 (Del 1985) 955. However, the non-centrality of these observations to the court's ruling in *Unocal* rendered them of merely peripheral authoritative value at the time, a position that was indeed confirmed by the Supreme Court's further marginalisation of concerns unrelated to shareholder welfare in its *Revlon* decision the following year. On the latter decision, see below nn 79–84 and accompanying text.

[79] See *Revlon v MacAndrews & Forbes Holdings* 506 A 2d 173 (Del 1986).

[80] On this notion, see above ch 3 of this volume, fns 14–15 and accompanying text.

[81] This was the scenario in the *Revlon* case itself.

[82] See, eg *Paramount Communications v QVC Network* 637 A 2d 34 (Del 1994).

ant of what constitutes a cognisable corporate threat under the *Unocal* test. Above all, *Revlon* emphasised the legal duty of a target company's board, in specified circumstances, to obtain the highest possible price for the company as its effective 'auctioneers'.[83] From a contractarian perspective, *Revlon* consequently represented (for better or worse[84]) a conspicuous curtailment of managerial discretion and contractual flexibility in favour of shareholder protectionism, at least with respect to the determination of certain corporate control changes.

Since then, however, the general judicial trend has seemingly been to recognise an increasing number of fact situations as capable of giving rise to a relevant *Unocal* threat. This has in turn enabled the Delaware courts to grant a progressively greater scope of business judgment leeway to target company boards that opt to defend their firms against unwanted bids.[85] Most notable in this regard was the Delaware Supreme Court's watershed 1990 decision in *Paramount Communications v Time*,[86] where it was recognised that a *Unocal* threat to the corporation and its shareholders can be posed even by a structurally non-coercive 'all-cash' tender offer, simply by the combination of: first, an inadequate (as determined by the target company's board) tender offer price that fails to reflect the long-term earnings potential of the company's business; and, secondly, the threat that shareholders will mistakenly be led to tender their shares to the bidder at that price.[87] The capacity of target boards post-*Time* to defend against non-coercive offers purely on grounds of price is arguably the clearest and most controversial manifestation of directors' prerogative under Delaware law to decide vicariously what is in shareholders' best

---

[83] See *Revlon*, above n 79 (Moore J), 506 A 2d 173 (Del 1986) 182.

[84] Within the contractarian paradigm, one's particular normative perspective on the merits of the *Revlon* doctrine presumably depends on whether a contractual flexibility or shareholder protectionism perspective is adopted. From the former perspective, the ensuing reduction in managerial discretion is both unwarranted and illegitimate. From the latter perspective it is, conversely, prerequisite to the board's (and, in turn, management's) contractual flexibility in other respects. On the distinction between these two academic positions, see above pt IV.B.

[85] For a critical assessment of this trend (viewed from a shareholder protectionist standpoint), see Gilson, 'Unocal Fifteen Years Later', above n 59.

[86] *Paramount Communications Inc v Time Inc* 571 A 2d 1140 (Del 1989).

[87] See ibid, 1153–54 (Horsey J). It would appear that, in reaching this conclusion, the Delaware Supreme Court was influenced by the then-recent decision of the Delaware Chancery Court in *Interco*, where Chancellor Allen set out the reasoning behind this position in the following succinct terms: 'Even where an offer is non-coercive, it may represent a "threat" to shareholder interests in the special sense that an active negotiator with power, in effect, to refuse the proposal may be able to extract a higher or otherwise more valuable proposal, or may be able to arrange an alternative transaction or a modified business plan that will present a more valuable option to shareholders'. See above n 75, 551 A 2d 787 (Del Ch 1988) 798. The 'threat' to shareholders inherent in a structurally non-coercive but underpriced tender offer is commonly described as a 'substantively' coercive offer. This term was coined by Ronald Gilson and Reinier Kraakman in their article 'Delaware's Intermediate Standard for Defensive Tactics: Is There Substance to Proportionality Review?' (1989) 44 *Business Lawyer* 247, 258.

interests.[88] This is because, *Revlon*-type cases aside, boards are thereby in effect permitted to foreclose (via anti-takeover measures) the opportunity that shareholders would otherwise have to decide for themselves whether a given offer price represents adequate value for their securities as an aspect of their personal property.[89]

Moreover, the Supreme Court in *Time* held that long-term enterprise considerations not directly related to immediate shareholder welfare were capable of constituting a relevant *Unocal*-type danger, even in situations where a target board's defence resulted in the loss of a significant immediate premium for shareholders.[90] Although the Court stopped short of sanctioning a 'just say no' defence,[91] its decision in *Time* nevertheless demonstrated judicial willingness to adopt a considerably less paternalistic stance towards the protection of shareholder interests in a change of control scenario than had previously appeared to be the case. Accordingly (and with the exception of limited *Revlon*-type cases), independent and informed boards could within wide bounds be entrusted to act as honest and effective guardians of the general corporate and shareholder interest in a hostile takeover situation, in preference to pursuing a self-protectionist or otherwise improper defensive agenda. For this reason, *Time* represented a significant victory for contractual flexibility over judicial protectionism in determining the legitimacy of anti-takeover measures.

In continuation of this general trend, the mid-1990s witnessed two important Delaware Supreme Court decisions that considerably enhanced the potential range of structural weaponry available to target company boards in defending against unsolicited approaches from raiders. In

[88] Furthermore, the Delaware Chancery Court has recently indicated in its controversial *Airgas* decision that the autonomy of the board to speak for the best interests of shareholders in a takeover scenario is especially valuable in the common situation where merger arbitrageurs have purchased shares with a specific view to making a short-term return on the prospective bid control premium. Chancellor Chandler indicated that, in such circumstances, the risk of a majority of shareholders tendering into an inadequate offer based on 'ignorance or mistaken belief' would be exacerbated. See above n 58, 16 A 3d 48 (Del Ch 2011) 57, borrowing from the dictum of Holland J in *Unitrin*, above n 74, 651 A 2d 1361 (Del 1995) 1385.

[89] In its later *Unitrin* decision in 1995, the Supreme Court reaffirmed this position by explaining that 'the directors of a Delaware corporation have the prerogative to determine that the market undervalues its stock and to protect its stockholders from offers that do not reflect the long-term value of the corporation under its present management plan'. See *Unitrin*, above n 74, 1376 (Holland J).

[90] In setting out the Supreme Court's position in *Paramount Communications Inc v Time Inc*, Judge Horsey provided the following broad and emphatic endorsement of the validity of the contractual flexibility thesis in the takeover context: 'Delaware law imposes on a board of directors the duty to manage the business and affairs of the corporation. This broad mandate includes a conferred authority to set a corporate course of action, including time frame, designed to enhance corporate profitability'. Above n 86, 571 A 2d 1140 (Del 1989) 1150.

[91] In particular, the ruling in *Time* required boards to demonstrate a pre-existing strategic plan that would be imperilled by a proposed change of control, so as to render the prospective hostile bid a 'danger' to the incumbent board's furtherance of that policy in the *Unocal* sense. On this requirement, see also *TW Services Inc v SWT Acquisition Corp*, A 2d, 1989 WL 20290 (Del Ch 1989).

QVC[92] and *Unitrin*[93] it was held that particularly 'heavy-handed' managerial anti-takeover measures, such as poison pills and large-scale corporate share repurchases, are not susceptible to invalidation merely because their effect goes above and beyond what is strictly necessary to protect against a threat to corporate or shareholder welfare. Rather, so long as the collective set of defences deployed is not coercive or preclusive – in that the defences do not foreclose entirely the realistic possibility of a control change (whether by tender offer or proxy contest) – they will be permissible subject only to passing *Unitrin*'s fairly broad and liberal 'range of reasonableness' test.[94]

At the time of writing, there has recently occurred a further noteworthy judicial step in the direction of re-enforcing target boards' defensive discretion under Delaware law. In two recent decisions of the Delaware Supreme Court and Court of Chancery in 2010 and 2011 respectively, it has been determined that a target board's dual adoption of a staggered board and poison pill will not be regarded as constituting a 'preclusive' defence to unwanted changes of control for purposes of the above *Unitrin* test.[95] The courts reached this conclusion despite recognising that the likely combined effect of these measures is to foreclose any realistic possibility of a hostile takeover except by the significantly costly, uncertain and prolonged process of instigating two successful proxy contests in consecutive years.[96]

Assessing the above developments as a whole, the following general observations can be made. The Delaware judiciary, after initially wavering roughly midway between the apparently conflicting poles of shareholder protectionism and contractual flexibility in developing its jurisprudence on contests for corporate control, has over recent years pitched its doctrinal tent firmly – but not entirely – towards the latter end of that scale. It would of course be erroneous to conclude that standard business judgment protection now applies to target boards in the takeover context as a matter of course. It would likewise be a crude oversimplification to suggest that target boards have the legal flexibility today

---

[92] *Paramount Communications Inc v QVC Network* 637 A 2d 34 (Del 1994).

[93] *Unitrin v American General Corp*, above n 74.

[94] On this, see *Unitrin*, above n 74, 1386–88.

[95] See *Versata Enterprises Inc v Selectica Inc* 5 A 3d 586 (Del 2010); *Airgas*, above n 58.

[96] The purpose of this course of action by a raider would be to secure control over a majority of board seats, enabling the raider to effect the removal of the pill so that the planned tender offer can finally proceed. The rationale for the courts' permissive stance in this regard was apparently twofold: first, since a combined staggered board and poison pill is a common and longstanding governance practice in Delaware corporations, invalidation of this practice on preclusivity grounds would be practically problematic; and, secondly, upholding the validity of a combined staggered board and poison pill in this scenario would necessarily result only in the *delay* of the eventual transfer of control, but crucially would not preclude the possibility of a change in control occurring 'at some point in the future' (to quote Chancellor Chandler in *Airgas*, above n 58, 115). See *Selectica*, above n 95, 604 (Holland J); *Airgas*, above n 58, 115–16 (Chancellor Chandler).

simply to say 'no' to a hostile bid that they honestly perceive to be against the company's best interests.

Nonetheless, it is undeniable that the distinction between the respective levels of deference traditionally afforded by courts to control- and non-control-related board decisions has been considerably attenuated over the past three decades. This in turn demonstrates a growing judicial willingness to leave managers and shareholders, via the medium of informed and independent boards, to make their own internal structural arrangements as to how best to respond to unexpected challenges to the former group's incumbency. By adopting such a 'back seat' regulatory role, the Delaware courts have progressively restricted their perceived function to that of establishing broad procedural and substantive boundaries to the private ordering of anti-takeover measures, whilst steadfastly avoiding substituting their own decisions in place of those reached in the proper manner by informed and independent boards.

V. FEDERAL DEFERENCE TO PRIVATE ORDERING: THE RULE 14A-8 PROPOSAL

In part II.B above, I highlighted the general contractarian preference for decentralised development of US corporate law rules at an individual State level. I also noted the corresponding aversion by proponents of private ordering towards federal regulation of internal firm affairs, which is typically regarded as an (economically) inefficient and (politically) illegitimate constraint on institutional flexibility and variety. At this juncture, though, it should be noted that in one very important respect, the federal regulation of corporate governance in the United States – far from being preclusive of contractual processes – paradoxically serves to *stimulate* the private selection of efficient rules on a firm-specific basis. Indeed, one of the most dynamic and effective forms of private ordering in US-listed companies is actually made possible by mandatory federal rules.[97]

As a natural adjunct to its regulatory sovereignty over matters relating to financial disclosure by public securities issuers,[98] the federal Securities and Exchange Commission is responsible for determining the rules of the proxy solicitation process accompanying the annual shareholders' meetings of US-listed companies. This is the legally-prescribed system whereby public corporations engage in formal communications with their investor community, for the dual purpose of disseminating important information

---

[97] As I will show below and also in the following two chapters, this is one of many respects in which the contractual and regulatory dynamics of rule-making intertwine with one another, making the neat delineation of corporate law's notionally 'private' and 'public' dimensions impossible.

[98] On this topic generally, see below ch 6 of this volume, pt II.

on specified issues and also facilitating the use by shareholders of their voting rights in upcoming meetings. As a consequence of its general managerial prerogative under state law, an issuer corporation's board (and, indirectly, senior management) is ordinarily in control of the corporate proxy machinery. Management is thus able to determine what proposals are inserted into the company's 'proxy card' to be subsequently voted on by shareholders, and also to formulate supporting statements for the purpose of encouraging shareholders to back management-sponsored proposals and initiatives.[99]

The process for soliciting proxies from shareholders is regulated by SEC Regulation 14A. Whilst the bulk of the Regulation covers the standard case of management proxy solicitations, Rule 14a-8 governs the limited circumstances in which a shareholder will be entitled to have her own proposal included on a company's proxy card alongside and in opposition to management's proposals.[100] In essence, the Rule requires a company to include a shareholder proposal in its annual proxy card and supporting statement in specified circumstances and subject to certain conditions. In order to be entitled to submit a proposal to the company under Rule 14a-8, a shareholder must have continuously held at least US$2,000 in market value, or one per cent, of the company's voting equity

---

[99] In a proxy solicitation, each shareholder will be sent a proxy card in advance of an upcoming meeting. This is a form containing a list of all the resolutions proposed to be voted on by shareholders, including those mandated by law (eg as to the (re)appointment of the company's directors and auditor) and also any additional proposals that management chooses to add. Each proposal will normally be followed by three tick-boxes giving the shareholder the option of instructing her proxy to vote either for or against that resolution, or alternatively to abstain from voting on the matter. The exception is the resolution pertaining to (re)appointment of directors, with respect to which a shareholder will ordinarily be given the choice of either giving or withholding authority to her proxy to vote for the nomination of each listed nominee. Significantly, by filling in and submitting her proxy card, a shareholder is not personally casting her vote on these issues but is rather instructing her proxy (who will typically be an appointee of management) to vote on her behalf and in accordance with her instructions. The proxy card will usually be accompanied by management's proxy statement, in which it will seek to influence the way that shareholders vote on each resolution by way of authoritative recommendations. The proxy solicitation process is a crucial aspect of corporate governance, especially within widely-held ownership systems such as those of the US and UK, in that it enables effective voting notwithstanding the tradition of widespread non-attendance by shareholders at annual meetings. However, the control wielded by management over the proxy card – particularly with respect to nominating the 'slate' of new or continuing directors each year – has led many observers to doubt the overall efficacy of the process. For instance Berle and Means, writing in 1932, claimed that the nature of the proxy nomination process resulted in boards being under the control of autocratic and self-perpetuating managers, rather than shareholders. See AA Berle and G Means, *The Modern Corporation and Private Property*, 4th edn (New York, Harcourt, Brace & World, 1968) (first published 1932) 81–83. As the following discussion in this part will show, however, the increased influence of activist institutional shareholders and professional corporate governance advisors over recent decades would appear to have reversed this trend to a considerable extent.

[100] SEC Rule 14a-8 was adopted in its initial form by the Commission in 1942 under delegated rule-making powers introduced by section 14 of the Securities Exchange Act of 1934.

capital for at least one year prior to the date of submission of the proposal. Furthermore, that person (or institution) must continue to hold her quali- fying shareholding up until the date of the meeting at which her proposal is due to be voted on.[101]

Consistent with the longstanding internal affairs doctrine in US corpo- rate law,[102] the SEC has traditionally perceived its regulatory remit in this context as extending only to *procedural* aspects of the proxy solicitation process, with a view to engendering the effective flow of self-generated information, proposals and opinions between managers and shareholders of public corporations. As regards: (i) the substance of management and shareholder proxy solicitations, and (ii) the extent to which a corpora- tion's management may legitimately refuse either to circulate or to act upon a proposal put to them collectively by shareholders, the SEC has consistently deferred to the realm of individual contractor choice and applicable State corporate law. To this end, Rule 14a-8(i) has traditionally allowed management to exclude a shareholder proposal from a compa- ny's proxy card on the ground that the proposal is not a proper subject for action by shareholders under the law of that company's State of incorpora- tion. By adopting such a deferential stance, the agency has historically been able to achieve an appreciable measure of public investor protection within the communication process surrounding the corporate sharehold- ers' meeting, but without effecting any material federal intrusion into the private and state ordering of intra-firm affairs.

In acknowledging the primacy of State law on the above matters, the SEC has moreover provided space for the Delaware courts[103] to strike what has traditionally been regarded as an appropriate balance within public corporations between the dual considerations of: on the one hand, affording a material degree of practical influence to shareholders over the determination of high-level strategic and governance issues; and, on the other, protecting the board's managerial prerogative and formal auto- nomy from 'outside' shareholder interference in core business affairs. This has been achieved via the Delaware judicial convention of recognising as valid only those shareholder proposals under Rule 14a-8 that take the

---

[101] Rule 14a-8(b).

[102] On this, see above n 19 and accompanying text.

[103] Since, as explained above, Rule 14a-8 permits exclusion of a shareholder proposal on the basis of its inconsistency with State law, it has become customary for the SEC to refer questions of a proposal's conformance with applicable State law for resolution by the rele- vant State (normally Delaware) courts. The SEC will typically make such a referral in response to a request by a company's management for issuance of a 'no action' letter, which specifies that the agency will not take proceedings against a company on account of its exclusion of a particular shareholder proposal. This explains the somewhat paradoxical arrangement whereby – notwithstanding Rule 14a-8's federal status – the appropriateness of proposed 14a-8 resolutions by shareholders often falls to be determined at State level. For an example of an influential opinion by the Delaware Supreme Court on such a matter, see *CA Inc v AFSCME Employees Pension Plan* 953 A 2d 227 (Del 2008).

form of 'precatory' or advisory recommendations,[104] which the board may rightfully decline to follow where it determines that doing so would not be in the company's best interests.[105]

In spite of its prima facie limited effectiveness as a weapon of shareholder empowerment, the 14a-8 precatory proposal has – in the past decade at least – proved to be a useful catalyst to private ordering of corporate governance at the individual firm level.[106] Where a 14a-8 proposal for corporate governance reform (eg board de-staggering) gains the support of a majority of votes cast in a shareholders' meeting, the board itself will be called upon to give due consideration to the proposal.[107] And, whilst implementation of the proposed amendment is not formally obligatory, the board must consider it against the background of their fiduciary duties and also the threat of a potentially adverse market reaction in the event of a passive response.[108]

For the above reasons, informed institutional investors satisfying the Rule's relatively liberal ownership and holding requirements have succeeded over recent years in generating a rich 'test bed' of proposed corporate governance reforms for consideration by the wider shareholder community. In turn, this relatively informal and substantially

---

[104] Precatory proposals can be contrasted with legally-binding orders that seek compulsory to effect a given strategic or governance outcome within a company irrespective of the board's view on the matter. As will be discussed below in ch 6 of this volume (pt III.B), the latter type of shareholder communication is legally provided for in the UK, albeit seldom used within a public company setting.

[105] A legally-binding proposal would be in clear violation of State law by undercutting the board's – and, indirectly, management's – exclusive executive prerogative as provided for under section 141 of the DGCL. Such a coercive proposition would also constitute an attempted fettering of the board's discretion to act freely at all times in a manner best calculated to advance the company's interests, and as such would be contradictory to the director's duty of loyalty at (State) common law. On this general principle, see *CA v AFSCME*, above n 103; *Quickturn Design Systems, Inc v Shapiro* 721 A 2d 1281 (Del 1998).

[106] Kahan and Rock report that the number of corporate-governance-related 14a-8 proposals in S&P 1500 companies that gained the majority approval of shareholders rose from 25 in 2001 to 86 in 2008. Meanwhile, those that were ultimately implemented by boards rose from a figure of 3 in 2001 to 43 in 2008, representing a 'success rate' rise of 12 per cent to 50 per cent over this period. See Kahan and Rock, 'Embattled CEOs', above n 54, documenting findings by the proxy solicitation firm Georgeson in its annual *Corporate Governance Review*.

[107] Furthermore, where a board anticipates that a corporate-governance-related 14a-8 proposal will be approved at a forthcoming shareholders' meeting, it may opt to introduce the requested reform voluntarily so as to pre-empt a shareholder vote on the matter and thus avoid potential acrimony and adverse publicity. See Kahan and Rock, 'Embattled CEOs', above n 54, 1035.

[108] The ultimate form of 'market sanction' against directors for disregard of a shareholder-approved governance proposal is outright loss of office, which may follow in the (not inconceivable) event of the dissatisfied proponent subsequently engaging in a proxy contest against the incumbent board. The term 'persuasive communication with punch' has been used to describe the now common activist shareholder practice in the US of coupling 14a-8 proposals on specific corporate governance issues with the (express or implicit) threat of an ensuing independent proxy contest against the board in the event of a successful proposal's non-adoption. See O'Kelley and Thompson, *Corporations and Other Business Associations*, above n 2, 230–32.

market-driven process of shareholder influence has made possible a number of significant and likely lasting improvements in formal shareholder empowerment within US public corporations.[109] These include the de-staggering of many boards,[110] the rapid and widespread introduction of majority (over orthodox plurality) voting[111] in board elections,[112] the voluntary implementation (at the individual company level[113]) of advisory 'say on pay' votes on executive compensation,[114] the growing popularity of divided CEO/chairman board leadership structures,[115] and

[109] On this generally, see Kahan and Rock, 'Embattled CEOs', above n 54; R Thomas and J Cotter, 'Shareholder Proposals in the New Millennium: Shareholder Support, Board Response, and Market Reaction' (2007) 13 *Journal of Corporate Finance* 368.

[110] The last decade has seen a marked drop in the number of large-scale public companies opting for staggered boards, amidst growing shareholder and public concerns about standards of board accountability. Consequently almost all S&P 100 company boards and the majority of S&P 500 boards are now 'de-staggered'. On this, see Kahan and Rock, 'Embattled CEOs', above n 54, 1007–9. This development can arguably be viewed as cogent empirical evidence in support of the contractarian explanation for the organic evolution of efficient (or, at least, generally acceptable) corporate governance norms.

[111] Where a corporation operates a system of *plurality* voting, the candidate who receives the most votes for each vacant seat on the board will be elected. Therefore in the almost universal case where only one candidate is nominated for each vacant seat, those individuals will be (re-)appointed into office regardless of the percentage of votes that are expressly withheld for each, so long as each nominee receives at least one 'for' vote (since the option of expressly voting 'against' a nominee's appointment is customarily not available on proxy forms where plurality voting is deployed). Under the most common forms of *majority* voting in the US, by contrast, any incumbent director who receives more 'withheld' or 'against' votes than 'for' votes will automatically not be re-elected, or alternatively will be required to tender his resignation for subsequent consideration by the board (in conformance with its members' fiduciary duties). A majority voting system of this nature can be implemented in a formal manner via a constitutional bylaw amendment (as is the most common practice today), or else informally by way of a non-binding corporate governance principle. A popular type of informal principle on majority voting today is the so-called 'Pfizer plan', named after the well-known pharmaceutical company where the first such provision was introduced. Under this system, a director who fails to secure majority support in an election must automatically tender his resignation, which will thereafter be considered by a specialist corporate governance committee composed of independent directors. The committee will then make a recommendation to the full board on whether the latter should accept the director's recommendation on the matter, with the board retaining the final decision on the matter.

[112] Kahan and Rock observe that, over the period from 2003 to 2009, the number of S&P 100 companies applying majority voting increased from 10 (out of 100) to 90. Between 2005 and 2007 alone, this number increased by a factor of nine. The authors describe the rise of majority voting in the US as 'meteoric'. See 'Embattled CEOs', above n 54, 1010–11. The sharpness and significance of this trend has led one leading commentator to the confident conclusion that 'majority voting will become universal'. See M Lipton, 'Some Thoughts for Boards of Directors in 2008', *Briefly* (January 2008) 1, cited in Kahan and Rock, ibid, 1011.

[113] The practical significance of such firm-specific initiatives has since been undermined by the universal introduction of 'say on pay' within US-listed companies under the federal Dodd-Frank Act, on which see below ch 6 of this volume, pt I.A.

[114] This development was relatively recent, and followed the SEC's ruling in 2007 to the effect that 14a-8 recommendations for the adoption of precatory 'say on pay' procedures cannot be excluded by boards from company proxy cards. On this, see Kahan and Rock, 'Embattled CEOs', above n 54, 1034–36.

[115] Kahan and Rock report a notable rise between 2003 and 2006 in the proportion of S&P 100 companies that had split the CEO and chairman positions, from 18 per cent to 26 per cent. See 'Embattled CEOs', above n 54, 1030.

in some cases even the removal by boards of anti-takeover poison pill mechanisms.[116]

Such empowerment measures, moreover, tend to be promoted in the first place not by shareholders themselves, but rather by specialist corporate governance advisory firms contracted to provide influential voting recommendations on behalf of major institutional investors.[117] This remarkable market development[118] has enabled shareholders to transcend to a large extent the most significant traditional barrier to the effective private ordering of corporate laws: that is, the general lack of awareness of (not to mention interest in) investee companies' internal governance features and the relative merits thereof.[119]

For fear of undermining the corporation's state-determined internal authority structure, Rule 14a-8(i)(8) has traditionally prohibited the making of shareholder proposals relating to directorial election issues, whether these take the form of actual director nominations or proposed structural reforms to the firm's election procedure. This important proviso to Rule 14a-8 has historically enabled the SEC to prevent shareholders from using the rule to undercut the board's traditional control over the directorial nomination process under State law.[120] Consequently, an insurgent shareholder's only practicable means of challenging the board's slate of candidates has been the costly and uncertain one of instigating an independent proxy contest outside of the 14a-8 procedure to solicit outright control of the board election vote from her peers.[121] However, under a significant

---

[116] See Thomas and Cotter, 'Shareholder Proposals in the New Millennium', above n 109, 389–90. The authors recorded 149 proposals from the 2002–2004 proxy seasons requesting either outright pill redemption or adoption of a vote on redemption. They also noted a 'particularly marked' trend of increasing shareholder support and board responsiveness on this issue over the relevant time period.

[117] The market-leading corporate governance advisory firms in the US are Institutional Shareholder Services or ISS (now a subsidiary of MSCI) and Glass, Lewis & Co.

[118] On this development generally, see Kahan and Rock, 'Embattled CEOs', above n 54, 1005–7; MT Moore, '"Whispering Sweet Nothings": The Limitations of Informal Conformance in UK Corporate Governance' (2009) 9 *Journal of Corporate Law Studies* 95, 122–23.

[119] Kahan and Rock explain that corporate governance advisory firms 'may function as central coordinating and information agents who help create a unified front of institutional investors, and thereby increase collective institutional shareholder influence': Kahan and Rock, 'Embattled CEOs', above n 54, 1007.

[120] The SEC's longstanding (pre-2009) stance on this matter is set out in its release *Shareholder Proposals Relating to the Election of Directors*, Release No 34–56914; IC–28075; File No S7–17–07 (11 December, 2007), available at: www.sec.gov/rules/final/2007/34-56914fr. pdf . The Commission's 2007 release followed a prior contrary interpretation of Rule 14a-8 (as permitting shareholder proposals relating to the reform of board election procedures) by the US Court of Appeals for the Second Circuit in *American Federation of State, County & Municipal Employees (AFSCME) v American International Group (AIG) Inc* 462 F 3d 121 (2d Cir 2006).

[121] Where an insurgent opts to solicit proxies outside of the 14a-8 process, they must communicate directly with the other shareholders and provide their own alternative proxy card and supporting statement to shareholders at personal expense. In this regard, section 219 of

recent reform to Rule 14a-8(i)(8), the SEC has for the first time expressly permitted shareholders to use the 14a-8 procedure in order to propose the introduction of shareholder access to the ballot within individual companies.[122] In the case of Delaware corporations, the reformed Rule 14a-8 can be expected to work in tandem with the aforementioned recent reforms to the DGCL permitting the initiation by shareholders of corporate bylaw amendments to the same effect.[123] The intention is to enable particularly activist shareholders to make formal provision for contested election proceedings in individual cases, where board accountability concerns render unopposed directorial elections unsustainable from a general investor perspective.[124]

On the whole, the above developments arguably substantiate the contractarian claim that capital market pressures can act as an effective surrogate for mandatory regulation in driving widespread conformance with generally accepted corporate governance norms, at least in the presence of an informed and activist institutional shareholder community. They could furthermore be said to demonstrate the potential market-facilitative role of procedural law – even at the federal level – in providing an institutional forum for the private selection of efficient (or at least generally desirable) rules and structures for the protection of shareholders.

---

the DGCL aids an insurgent shareholder by requiring the company to prepare a complete list of shareholders entitled to vote at an upcoming meeting at least 10 days prior to the meeting date, which any shareholder will be entitled to inspect for a proper purpose related to the business of the meeting (which includes preparation of a proxy contest). The advantage of initiating an independent proxy contest in this way is that the proponent shareholder will not be bound by the aforementioned limitations of Rule 14a-8. This means – in particular – that they will potentially be able to obtain the authorisation of shareholders to vote the latter's shares for the express purpose of opposing the reappointment of the company's incumbent board and/or proposing an alternative slate of nominees to fill any vacancies arising on the board.

[122] See Securities and Exchange Commission, *Facilitating Shareholder Director Nominations: Proposed Rule*, Release Nos 33-9046; 34-60089; IC-28765; File No S7-10-09 (2009) 120–23. Available at: www.sec.gov/rules/proposed/2009/33-9046.pdf . As a more controversial element of the same proposed set of reforms, the SEC furthermore proposed introducing a mandatory shareholder right to nominate new directors under proposed new Rule 14a-11(the so-called 'proxy access' reform). However, this latter aspect of the reforms has since been enjoined by the DC Circuit Court of Appeals on Administrative Procedure Act Grounds, and consequently has been scrapped. On this, see below ch 6 of this volume, fns 45–46 and accompanying text. This has not affected the separate reform to existing Rule 14a-8 discussed above, though.

[123] On this, see above nn 12–14 and accompanying text.

[124] At the time of writing, it remains uncertain to what extent the reformed 14a-8 will be used by activist shareholders for the purpose of proposing shareholder access to the corporate ballot. However, the level of interest that this general topic has attracted over recent years suggests that the take-up rate will likely be significant. Moreover, the adverse publicity that a so-called 'proxy access' proposal risks attracting for incumbent directors, even where it fails to command majority support in a shareholders' vote, suggests that many boards may be inclined voluntarily to adopt bylaw amendments to this effect so as to preclude such an outcome. On this general practice, see above n 107.

VI. THE US CORPORATE BOARD AS A
PRE-REGULATORY INSTITUTION

A final important manifestation of contractarianism in US corporate governance law is the status of the most central and arguably fundamental corporate governance institution – namely the independent board of directors – as an endogenous and *pre*-regulatory phenomenon.

In view of the longstanding and axiomatic importance of board governance to the functioning of the US corporate system as a whole,[125] it is remarkable that the institution of the corporate board has traditionally lacked any entrenched legal form. Indeed, Delaware law provides no formal legal explication of the desired size or structure of corporate boards besides the basic requirement that a corporation *should have* directors.[126] Moreover, regulatory and judicial efforts to specify the expected composition and characteristics of public company boards have in general been relatively recent and limited.[127]

Therefore the fact that organisational boards – both within and outside of the corporate business environment – have historically tended to adopt roughly similar characteristics;[128] and, more fundamentally, that they exist *at all* in the absence of any formal legal template to define their basic structure and functions, arguably provides cogent empirical support for the validity of the private ordering hypothesis in this context. Furthermore, the market-evolutionary understanding of the corporate board within contractarian thought[129] is arguably reinforced by the organic and piecemeal manner in which directors' duties have been developed judicially. In the case of the Delaware courts, the jurisprudential outcome of this process has been the establishment of broad substantive standards and judicial 'smell tests' based on the equitable fiduciary doctrine,[130] which have

---

[125] The most noted study of corporate boards in the United States remains Myles Mace's classic 1971 work, *Directors: Myth and Reality*, revised edn (Cambridge MA, Harvard Business School Press, 1986) (first published 1971).

[126] Section 141 of the DGCL specifies only that '[t]he business and affairs of every corporation organized under this chapter shall be managed by or under the direction of a board of directors', which 'shall consist of 1 or more members [as determined by the bylaws or certificate of incorporation]' and who 'need not be stockholders unless so required by the certificate of incorporation or the bylaws'.

[127] On this, see below ch 6 of this volume, fns 20–23 and accompanying text.

[128] On the pre-industrial origins of the board governance model, see F Gevurtz, 'The Historical and Political Origins of the Corporate Board of Directors' (2004) 33 *Hofstra Law Review* 89. On the cognitive advantage of board (relative to individual) decision-making as a general social phenomenon (albeit with particular regard to the corporate-business context), see SM Bainbridge, 'Why a Board? Group Decisionmaking in Corporate Governance' (2002) 55 *Vanderbilt Law Review* 1, 12–41.

[129] On this, see above ch 3 of this volume, pt III.B.(iii).

[130] As La Porta et al explain: 'Legal rules in the common law system are usually made by judges, based on precedents and inspired by general principles such as fiduciary duty or fairness. Judges are expected to rule on new situations by applying these general principles

permitted factually-tailored judgements characterised by high sensitivity to business and especially managerial exigencies.[131]

If indeed empirically validated by the above factors, the principal normative implication of the contractarian understanding of the corporate board is that prevailing legal and structural characteristics of US boards – particularly directors' fiduciary duties and the independent directorial function – can be said to represent effective and desirable market-inspired solutions to managerial accountability concerns.[132] It arguably follows from this position that any wholesale regulatory reform of the board's composition or responsibilities in the purported 'public interest' is thus both unnecessary and undesirable.

VII. SUMMARY

In the preceding discussion, I have highlighted the key practical manifestations of the contractarian paradigm of corporate governance within US legal doctrine. Overall, the core purpose of the analysis has been to highlight how, to a significant extent and in varying ways, US corporate governance would appear to conform to its contractarian prototype as a legal-institutional system that is designed to support – *but not supplant* – the privately-constituted arrangements of individual corporate contractors.

It may accordingly be said that, in the various respects outlined in this chapter, US corporate governance law seeks to provide the institutional conditions for the effective formulation and enforcement by investors of a proximately optimal framework of managerial accountability norms at the micro level. As such, it arguably contributes to securing the legitimacy – and, in turn, sustainability – of the reciprocal power imbalance that is intrinsic to the corporation's core and characteristic decision-making structure. Additionally, the above features would appear to provide empirical support for the common contractarian characterisation of corporate law (including corporate governance law) as a phenomenon that is purely market-facilitative and thus politically 'colourless' in nature. The purported normative implication of this perspective is that the laws in this area should remain blind to social-distributional concerns that are

---

even when specific conduct has not yet been described or prohibited in the statutes'. See R La Porta, F Lopez-de-Silanes, A Shleifer and R Vishny, 'Investor Protection and Corporate Governance' (2000) 58 *Journal of Financial Economics* 3, 9.

[131] On this generally, see above pts III and IV.C.

[132] For a modern argument to this effect, which posits independent directors as an investor-impelled informational conduit between corporate managers and outside capital market actors (particularly securities analysts), see JN Gordon, 'The Rise of Independent Directors in the United States, 1950–2005: Of Shareholder Value and Stock Market Prices' (2007) 59 *Stanford Law Review* 1465, 1510–40.

extraneous to the prudential preferences of key corporate participants (namely shareholders and managers).

In chapter six, I will challenge the above portrayal of US corporate governance law to an extent, by highlighting its significant and growing *mandatory* or *regulatory* components. I will seek to demonstrate here that such aspects of corporate governance law contrarily seek to *displace* contractually-determined outcomes via extraneous (mainly federal) regulatory interventions. Before doing so, though, I will attempt in the next chapter to survey the key quasi-contractual contours of the United Kingdom's system of corporate governance law, as a prelude to its subsequent counter-critique in chapter six along essentially similar lines.

5

The Contractual Dimensions of UK Corporate Governance Law

I N CONTRAST TO the US model of corporate law-making outlined in the previous chapter, the corresponding British system is for most practical intents and purposes *unitary* in nature.[1] Furthermore, in respect of the majority of significant corporate governance matters the United Kingdom's principal corporate law statute, the Companies Act 2006, operates on a mandatory and thus irreversible basis.[2] More generally, the use of mandatory and irreversible statutory rules to afford protection to shareholders of UK corporations has been widely accepted and thus seldom questioned either academically or judicially.[3]

Nonetheless, as I will seek to demonstrate in this chapter, the dual contractual qualities of flexibility and reversibility of laws are maintained within the English company law tradition in other important respects. The influence of contractarian rationality within British corporate law is manifested most notably in the greater significance that UK law-makers – by comparison with their US counterparts – afford to the privately-ordered corporate constitution vis-à-vis statutory rules as a source of core

---

[1] This is notwithstanding the effects of (internal) devolution and legal pluralism, and (external) European Union membership, on the UK's national law-making dynamics. On this, see below ch 7 of this volume, fns 11–13 and accompanying text.

[2] On the longstanding and continuing *non*-derogability of Companies Act provisions pertaining to the liability of directors for breach of duties in particular, see below nn 79–81 and accompanying text.

[3] Amongst the likely explanations for this tendency is the greater political lobbying power of institutional shareholders and other influential groups sympathetic to shareholder interests in the UK, which has arguably operated against the development of a Delaware-style 'opt-out' culture in respect of core shareholder rights in Britain. On this, see J Armour and D Skeel, 'Who Writes the Rules for Hostile Takeovers, and Why? The Peculiar Divergence of US and UK Takeover Regulation' (2007) 95 *Georgetown Law Journal* 1727, 1771; B Black and J Coffee, 'Hail Britannia?: Institutional Investor Behavior Under Limited Regulation' (1994) 92 *Michigan Law Review* 1997, 2034–55. A further notable factor in this regard is the absence in the UK of a dedicated judicial specialisation in corporate law in the vein of the Delaware Court of Chancery. It can thus be surmised that English and Scottish courts – and, in turn, legal academics – have been correspondingly less inclined than their Delaware counterparts to regard corporate law as a qualitatively distinctive field of jurisprudential analysis. This has, in turn, largely prevented the peculiar contractual logic of agreement and adaptation from supplanting the orthodox statutory characteristics of command and conformity within dominant legal-theoretical understandings of British companies legislation.

governance norms. UK corporate law is comparatively unique, moreover, in providing express quasi-contractual status and effect to a company's constitutional articles of association, which consequently are both enforceable and alterable by 'members' (ie shareholders) at will. Indeed, the basic contractarian notion of private ordering lies at the very heart of UK corporate law by virtue of the 'contractual principle' that has traditionally underpinned the corporate constitution. This doctrine in general gives binding legal force to the stipulations in a company's articles of association concerning the firm's internal governance affairs, including – in particular – the division of decision-making power between its shareholders and board of directors.[4]

Allied to and reinforcing the contractual principle at the heart of the English company law model is the common law internal management doctrine, which in effect affirms the essential privity of the firm's corporate governance arrangements by treating questions concerning the authority and liability of managerial officers as matters that should appropriately be determined on a micro level by a company's supreme governance organ, and correspondingly *not* on a macro level by courts. It will be shown that, although the United Kingdom lacks both a business judgment rule and statutory exculpation system in the US sense, the English internal management rule has had a similar normative effect to the abovementioned Delaware provisions by putting questions as to the propriety of corporate objectives or managerial conduct almost wholly beyond the acceptable realm of judicial macro-analysis.

Whilst the longstanding statutory facility of retrospective judicial liability relief has simultaneously (and somewhat curiously) *extended* the reach of the English courts in passing ex post facto judgement on directorial decisions and behaviour, its overall effect has been to imbue the jurisprudence on directorial negligence with a highly functional and circumstantially-sensitive slant. In this way, as will be highlighted below, the availability of retrospective liability relief in the United Kingdom has compensated to a significant extent for the corresponding unavailability of Delaware-esque ex ante exculpation in British companies.

Moreover, as the previous chapter observed with respect to the US system, in the United Kingdom the basic issue of the structure and composition of corporate boards has likewise elided legislative or judicial formalisation except to a marginal extent, thereby arguably confirming the commonly-held contractarian view of the board as an endogenous and market-driven institution. And, whilst recent decades have seen significant regulatory incursions into core corporate governance issues (including board structure and composition) in the form of the UK Corporate Governance Code and Takeover Code, both sets of norms – in spite of their

---

[4] See Companies Act 2006, s 33.

pivotal force in determining the balance of power and influence within UK listed companies today – are nevertheless attributable to the initiative of rule-making bodies that operate substantially outside of the public state framework. As such, these bodies owe their existence and political legitimacy principally to (private) market-based rather than (public) democratic criteria.

Accordingly, in the above respects, it can be said that – just as the US system of corporate law is designed to render intra-firm governance affairs contractually determinable at the micro level, and thus beyond the acceptable bounds of regulatory-state determination – the UK corporate law framework has also been developed in such a way as apparently to put the majority of core corporate governance issues substantially 'out of public reach' on a normative level.

Furthermore, in the United Kingdom, as in the United States, an important theme underpinning the rationality of many corporate law rules is the conceptual reversal of the traditional 'command-style' regulatory relationship, so that prevailing doctrines and institutions are deemed generally acceptable on the basis that they appear to be *privately selected by* – as opposed to publicly imposed on – the company and its constituent members. In other words, the contractarian qualities of rational choice and unanimity[5] in effect usurp the orthodox democratic criteria of consensus and conformity as the principal ideological criteria for determining the defensibility of established governance norms and practices.

To this end, the ensuing analysis is structured as follows. In part I, I will examine the aforementioned contractual principle as set out in section 33 of the Companies Act 2006. Here I will explain how this doctrine animates the basic (private) legal character of the British corporate constitution, and also provides an institutional basis for determining and enforcing the division of corporate decision-making power at the micro level.

In part II, I will highlight the most significant aspects of judicial deference to private ordering within the UK corporate law system, including the longstanding internal management rule, the consequent tradition of judicial *non*-interventionism in questions concerning the propriety of business objectives and decisions, and the supporting framework of retrospective judicial liability relief under successive British Companies Acts over the course of the twentieth century.

In part III, I will briefly discuss – from a historical perspective – the endogenous and largely *pre*-regulatory nature of the board governance model in UK corporations. In part IV, I will survey the peculiarly British legal phenomenon of non-statist, 'market-invoking' regulation as exemplified most notably in the UK Corporate Governance Code and Takeover

---

[5] On the concept of 'unanimity' within neo-liberal political theory, as applied to the design of corporate law rules, see above ch 3 of this volume, fns 119–22 and accompanying text.

Code. I will demonstrate how these influential sets of norms – by virtue of their formally private and extra-governmental character – have brought about far-reaching regulatory change in dominant corporate governance practices in the United Kingdom, while largely eliding the formal public scrutiny and consultation to which state-ordered reforms are ordinarily subject. Finally, I will summarise by linking this chapter's perspectives to the corresponding observations on the US corporate law system documented in the previous chapter.

I. THE CONTRACTUAL PRINCIPLE

A. Section 33 of the Companies Act 2006: The Articles as a Contract

The contractual principle is – on a normative level at least – the most fundamental legal principle of UK corporate governance law insofar as it establishes the quintessentially private and self-ordered nature of a company's 'indoor' management affairs.[6] As such, it provides the ideological bedrock for an associational conception of the firm based upon the logic of membership and association, which in turn legitimates the exclusive entitlement of shareholders to hold and exercise formal governance power over the board (and, indirectly, management).

This longstanding doctrine, which today takes the form of section 33 of the Companies Act 2006, gives express quasi-contractual effect to a company's articles by providing that the provisions therein 'bind the company and its members to the same extent as if there were covenants on the part of the company and of each member to observe those provisions'.[7] Furthermore, the terms of the multi-partite agreement between the company and each of its individual members embodied in the articles of association are, rather like those of a partnership agreement, freely alterable by the members at will. Whereas in a partnership the unanimous consent of partners is required to effect an alteration to the terms of the agreement, UK company law permits alteration of the articles subject to approval by a special majority (ie 75 per cent or more) of votes cast by the members

---

[6] On the significance of this principle of UK (or English) company law generally, see RC Nolan, 'The Continuing Evolution of Shareholder Governance' (2006) 65 *Cambridge Law Journal* 92.

[7] Of course, as any English company lawyer will readily testify, enforcement of the articles by an aggrieved member is by no means as straightforward as enforcement of a standard multilateral contractual agreement, and – in particular – is encumbered by some longstanding doctrinal obstacles (including the well-known 'qua member' and 'personal rights' requirements). However, the existence of such obstacles would appear to be attributable principally to practical considerations concerning the potential multi-partite enforcement of the articles, as opposed to any judicial denial of the validity of the contractual metaphor in the corporate context. On this, see KW Wedderburn, 'Shareholders' Rights and the Rule in *Foss v Harbottle*' (1957) 15 *The Cambridge Law Journal* 194.

collectively in General Meeting.[8] The basic contractarian qualities of flexibility and private ordering are accordingly rendered common constitutional features of both types of firm.

The centrality and normative significance of the contractual doctrine within the fabric of UK corporate law as a whole is emphasised by Richard Nolan, who explains that:

> English law has at its core a simple – but very flexible – empowering, facilitative principle, through which shareholders can establish in a company's articles of association . . . how they will interact with each other, and with other participants in the company. This principle . . . giving enduring legal effect to shareholders' bargains as to how their company is to be run – is vital, flexible and powerful.[9]

The somewhat peculiar contractual nature of the corporate constitution stems from the historical origins of English joint-stock company law in the mid-nineteenth century as a derivation of partnership law. Under the latter system, formally internal issues of firm governance procedures and partners' rights and obligations are embodied literally in the form of an inter-personal private agreement between partners. On the introduction of free incorporation upon registration, however, this associational logic was in effect carried over to the developing field of company law where it likewise became the doctrinal basis for regulating internal disputes between 'members' (ie shareholders) of incorporated firms.[10]

---

[8] Companies Act 2006, ss 21 and 283(1). It may be protested that the operation of the principle of majority rule within the company removes the contractual dimension to inter-member relations, at least insofar as disempowered minorities are concerned. In respect of this point, however, Atiyah has noted a prevalent early judicial attitude to the effect that, 'so long as the rules [embodied in a company's articles] were altered in accordance with the statutory procedures, no member could complain that he was being deprived of his contractual rights'. This was on the understanding that '[h]is rights . . . must be read subject to the statutory powers of alteration'. See PS Atiyah, *The Rise and Fall of Freedom of Contract* (Oxford, Clarendon Press, 1979) 740–41. In any event, English company law has for a long time provided (limited) equitable protection for minority shareholders who are adversely affected by alterations to articles carried out on a mala fides basis, and the modern unfair prejudice remedy further protects any quasi-contractual fundamental understandings of the harmed parties that may have been breached in such a scenario (at least within relatively small, closely-held firms where such understandings can feasibly be discerned). On the former, see *Allen v Gold Reefs of West Africa Ltd* [1900] 1 Ch 656 (CA); *Greenhalgh v Arderne Cinemas Ltd* [1951] Ch 286 (CA); *Citco Banking Corporation NV v Pusser's Ltd* [2007] BCC 205 (Privy Council). On the latter, see Companies Act 2006, s 994; *Re Saul D Harrison & Sons plc* [1995] 1 BCLC 14; *O'Neill and Another v Phillips and Others* [1999] UKHL 24. All in all, then, it may be said that the rationality of contract pervades this particular area of the law in the UK.

[9] Nolan, 'Shareholder Governance', above n 6, 95.

[10] Moreover, in view of the limited spread of widely-held ownership in the majority of UK industries until the later part of the twentieth century, and the widespread preservation of entrepreneurial and family ownership during this time, it could be argued that on a *functional* (as well as a formal) level such a sense of shareholders as quasi-partners persisted even within many of the largest British business organisations until the relatively recent past. On this issue generally, see BR Cheffins, *Ownership and Control: British Business Transformed* (Oxford, Oxford University Press, 2009).

In the case of incorporated firms, however, there was the key difference that the company itself – as an autonomous legal entity (and, indirectly, its controlling board) – became recognised for internal purposes as a central party to the notional contractual agreement embodied in the articles. This enabled members' constitutional rights, notably including their basic voting and dividend entitlements, to be enforced directly against the company itself in the form of a quasi-contractual action. The major normative effect of the contractual principle was to engender a doctrinal understanding of companies in terms of the logic of inter-personal association. Indeed, even the literal terms 'company' and 'members' are evocative of this fact, connoting the fundamentally humanistic and quasi-partnership quality of the incorporated firm, and the private associational basis of shareholders' status therein. That is to say, irrespective of its formally autonomous personality from the perspective of creditors and other third parties, when distilled down internally the company, in effect, ultimately *is* its collective body of members (ie shareholders) and owes its existence to their common endeavour.[11]

From a negative perspective, meanwhile, the logic of membership and association by definition carries implications of privilege and selectivity, in the sense that those *not* entitled to membership status within the company's contractual order are correspondingly excluded from the enclosed realm of internal firm affairs. Thus from the initial phase of its development British company law had, largely by virtue of its own doctrinal path dependence, developed a somewhat curious ideological perspective on corporate entities whereby shareholders are positioned 'inside' the company from a governance perspective, and, correspondingly, non-shareholder constituents such as creditors and employees deal *with* the company–member contractual nexus 'from the outside' only.[12]

---

[11] In the US, by comparison, the term 'corporation' is conventionally used to refer to widely-held incorporated firms, thereby emphasising their corporeal/organisational dimension rather than their inter-personal/associational quality. The Americanesque term is arguably allied more to a traditionally state-centric or 'concession' theory of the firm, which emphasises first and foremost the essential *distinctiveness* of companies from unincorporated firms, as opposed to the common characteristics that these respective entities share. On this distinction, see LCB Gower, 'Some Contrasts Between British and American Corporation Law' (1956) 69 *Harvard Law Review* 1369, 1371–72. On the influence of competing theoretical conceptions of the firm on the early development of corporate/company law and economic thinking in the US and UK respectively, see WW Bratton, 'The New Economic Theory of the Firm: Critical Perspectives from History' (1989) 41 *Stanford Law Review* 1471, 1483–85. See also above ch 2 of this volume, fns 46–48 and accompanying text.

[12] This may partly explain the largely insular development of British company law over subsequent decades, which up until the 1970s and 1980s occurred largely independently from substantively overlapping areas of law concerning the protection of non-shareholder interests, such as labour and insolvency law.

B. The Contractual Basis of the Board's Authority

The contractual principle's dual themes of private ordering and shareholder exclusivity have been particularly influential in establishing the contours of the United Kingdom's characteristic approach to resolving what is arguably the core structural dilemma in respect of public corporations: that is, determining the appropriate division of decision-making power between the company's shareholders and board of directors. In contrast to the United States where the powers of the board are generally established under State legislation,[13] UK corporate law has traditionally left the crucial issue of the board's authority to be determined privately in the articles of association. The standard rule to this effect, namely the decision-making primacy of the board in respect of management affairs,[14] is conventionally applied to newly incorporating companies by default when they implicitly adopt, on an 'off-the-shelf' basis, the relevant set of Model Articles provided by the government under secondary legislation.[15] However, Model Article 3 makes clear that the board's executive authority is not an absolute prerogative, but rather is held subject to the ultimate entitlement of the shareholders collectively to revoke any or all management powers by means of an appropriate constitutional amendment to this effect.[16] The Model Articles additionally permit shareholders, by way of special resolution, to make specific positive or negative orders to the board concerning the latter's running of the business, thus further affirming the former group's sovereign status within the corporate constitutional structure.[17]

The essentially private, quasi-contractual basis of the board's authority in the United Kingdom is likewise explicated within early English judicial rationalisations of the company's decision-making power structure. Unlike in the United States, where (as explained in chapter two above) directors' powers were recognised by courts from an early stage as being

---

[13] For example, § 141(a) of the Delaware General Corporation Law states that: 'The business and affairs of every corporation organized under this chapter shall be managed by or under the direction of a board of directors, except as may be provided in this chapter or in its certificate of incorporation'.

[14] On this doctrine generally, see above ch 2 of this volume, fns 42–45 and accompanying text.

[15] The board's decision-making authority is established as a default constitutional principle under the Model Articles provided by the government to newly incorporating firms. Article 3 thereof provides that: 'Subject to the articles, the directors are responsible for the management of the company's business, for which purpose they may exercise all the powers of the company'. See The Companies (Model Articles) Regulations 2008 (SI 2008/3229) art 3, discussed above ch 2 of this volume, fn 44 and accompanying text.

[16] This is made clear by the words 'Subject to the articles' at the beginning of the relevant provision (see ibid).

[17] See SI 2008/3229, art 4(1).

'original and undelegated',[18] the corresponding English tradition has been to regard the board's authority as a thoroughly contingent phenomenon.[19] Dignam and Lowry have noted that, from a judicial point of view, 'the role and position of directors within the corporate management matrix is coloured by the fact that company law is rooted in the law of partnership which is based upon agency principles'.[20] Accordingly, 'each partner is an agent of his fellow partners'.[21] However, whereas in a partnership each member of the firm herself represents the collective body of partners in management affairs,[22] in companies this collective representational role is vested by mutual agreement in the board of directors, which consequently has power to bind the totality of members indirectly via the medium of the corporate entity. It follows logically from this that a company's shareholders are prohibited from attempting to give ad hoc orders to directors or otherwise interfering with the board's management discretion except in the specific ways provided for in the company's articles.[23] To do otherwise would amount to a usurpation of the members' collective constitutional agreement as to the centralisation of corporate decision-making authority, which would be contrary to the contractual principle underpinning the legitimacy of the company's governance framework.[24]

In summary, consistent with the contractarian paradigm in corporate theory, UK law adopts the view that a company's board of directors holds its decision-making powers at the ultimate behest of the general body of shareholders. It furthermore affirms the general contractarian belief that shareholders alone – as the sole signatories to the notional corporate

---

[18] *Hoyt v Thompson's Executor*, 19 NY 207, 216 (1859) (Court of Appeals of New York) (Comstock J). On this, see above ch 2 of this volume, fns 46–50 and accompanying text.

[19] See, eg *Automatic Self-Cleansing Filter Syndicate Co Ltd v Cunninghame* [1906] 2 Ch 34 (CA) 45 (Cozens-Hardy LJ): '[Directors] are in the position of managing partners appointed to fill that post by a mutual arrangement between all the shareholders'.

[20] A Dignam and J Lowry, *Company Law*, 6th edn (Oxford, Oxford University Press, 2010) 271.

[21] Ibid. Wedderburn has observed more generally that '[t]he [English] registered company was in origin "a hybrid growth . . . a partnership which has been invested with the character of incorporation"; and it is not, therefore, surprising that the "rules which are applicable are partly referable to both characters"'. See Wedderburn, 'Shareholders' Rights', above n 7, 53, quoting *Australian Coal & Shale Employers' Federation v Smith* (1938) 38 SR (NSW) 48.

[22] In the UK, this longstanding rule is established by section 5 of the Partnership Act 1890.

[23] On the formal defensibility of the board's powers from outside interference (in particular vis-à-vis shareholders), see (in a UK context) *Automatic Self-Cleansing Filter Syndicate*, above n 19; *Gramophone and Typewriter Co v Stanley* [1908] 2 KB 89 (CA); *John Shaw & Sons (Salford) Ltd v Shaw* [1935] 2 KB 113 (CA).

[24] As explained by Cozens-Hardy LJ in *Automatic Self-Cleansing Filter Syndicate*: 'You are dealing here, as in the case of a partnership, with parties [ie members] having individual rights to which there are mutual stipulations for their common benefit, and when once you get that, it seems to me that there is no ground for saying that the mere majority can put to an end the express stipulations contained in the bargain which they have made'. See [1906] 2 Ch 34 (CA) 45. For an academic analysis of this longstanding common law principle, see D Kershaw, *Company Law in Context: Text and Materials* (Oxford, Oxford University Press, 2009) 191–94.

contract embodied in the articles of association – are entitled to determine the shape of the company's internal governance structure in exclusion from other 'non-member' constituents in the firm such as its workforce. On a fundamental doctrinal level at least, therefore, the core features of UK corporate governance law can with justification be characterised as significantly contractarian in nature.

II. JUDICIAL DEFERENCE TO PRIVATE ORDERING

A. The Internal Management Doctrine

By means of this comparatively longstanding doctrine, English courts have traditionally taken the position that the internal governance affairs of the company are a purely private matter unbefitting of ex post facto judicial scrutiny.[25] Initially an aspect of pre-corporate partnership law,[26] the doctrine's core theme of judicial non-interventionism in business affairs was subsequently carried forward into the developing field of joint-stock company law on the introduction of free incorporation by registration.[27] In the words of Lord Davey: 'It is an elementary principle of the law relating to joint stock companies that the Court will not interfere with the internal management of companies acting within their powers, and in fact has no jurisdiction to do so'.[28] The same rule furthermore dictates that ongoing irregularities committed by officers in the course of running the company, including breaches of duty and constitutional powers, are 'excusable' by majority ratification.[29] This is on the understanding

---

[25] As Scrutton LJ remarked in *Shuttleworth v Cox Bros & Co (Maidenhead) Ltd* [1927] 2 KB 9, 23: 'It is not the business of the court to manage the affairs of the company. That is for the shareholders and the directors'.

[26] In this context, Lord Eldon had famously remarked in 1812 that '[t]his Court is not to be required on every Occasion to take the Management of every Playhouse and Brewhouse in the Kingdom'. See *Carlen v Drury* (1812) 1 Ves & B 154, 158.

[27] On this, see Wedderburn, 'Shareholders' Rights', above n 7, 196–98.

[28] *Burland v Earle* [1902] AC 83 (PC) 93. Or, as one academic commentator has succinctly put it: 'in the final analysis it is necessary to draw a line beyond which the courts and indeed lawyers should not venture in the determination of what are essentially managerial decisions'. See B Rider, 'Amiable Lunatics and the Rule in Foss v Harbottle' (1978) 37 *Cambridge Law Journal* 270, 287.

[29] The principal exceptions to this general rule are directorial conduct involving either self-enrichment at the company's expense or direct deprivation of members' personal property rights, which is deemed to be incapable of ratification and thus outside the remit of the internal management doctrine. See, respectively, *Daniels v Daniels* [1978] Ch 406, 414 (Templeman J); *Pender v Lushington* (1877) LR 6 Ch D 70, 80–81 (Jessel MR). By contrast, gross negligence (absent directorial self-enrichment) is ratifiable at common law on the basis that it is a mere managerial 'irregularity', which is consequently 'correctable' by the majority regardless of the wider public interest in ensuring that directors are held to account legally for serious corporate mismanagement. See, eg *Pavlides v Jensen* [1956] Ch 565. As against this today, section 260(3) of the Companies Act 2006 for the first time makes it expressly possible for derivative claims to be brought in respect of 'pure' (ie non-self-benefiting) negligence.

that only the company itself, and no individual member, has suffered harm as a result of the conduct in question.[30]

Interpreted in its most general sense, the internal management doctrine essentially dictates that where the corporate contract vests sovereignty (in the sense of supreme governance power) in a particular organ, that organ consequently has the power to determine – in the last place – what conduct does and does not constitute a legally cognisable harm to the company. In particular, the company's sovereign organ has the power to decide that technical irregularities or improprieties committed by managerial personnel in the course of running the business are excusable on the basis that they occasion no subjective damage to the company's interests.[31] It follows logically from this that courts should refrain from questioning any such legal abnormality that the company itself has the capacity to uphold via ratification.[32] To do otherwise would arguably amount to a paternalistic usurpation of the corporate ratification or 'forgiveness' function, and thus would be averse to the doctrine's core contractarian rationality of intra-firm autonomy.[33]

In the same way that the US business judgment rule has permitted a broad and permissive interpretation of the acceptable bounds of the board's discretion, the English internal management doctrine has – over the course of the past century – enabled courts to adopt a liberal and non-interventionist stance with respect to a progressively wider range of arguably questionable corporate activities. Whilst the basic practical impetus of both principles is therefore similar, there is however a notable

---

However, the express continuing status of pure negligence (under section 239(1) of the Act) as a ratifiable wrong, coupled with the ongoing treatment of ratification (under s 263(2)(c)(ii)) as a mandatory bar to the continuation of a minority shareholder's derivative claim against a directorial wrongdoer, makes it likely that many instances of corporate mismanagement will still merit immunity under the traditional internal management doctrine even in the context of the new statutory derivative claims procedure.

[30] See *Foss v Harbottle* (1843) 2 Hare 461, 490 (Sir James Wigram VC): 'the conduct with which the Defendants are charged in this suit is an injury not to the Plaintiffs exclusively; it is an injury to the whole corporation by individuals whom the corporation entrusted with powers to be exercised only for the good of the corporation . . . [and i]n law the corporation and the aggregate members of the corporation are not the same thing for purposes like this'.

[31] As explained by Jenkins LJ: 'where the alleged wrong is a transaction which might be made binding on the company or association and on all its members by a simple majority of the members, no individual member of the company is allowed to maintain an action in respect of that matter for the simple reason that, *if a mere majority of the members of the company or association is in favour of what has been done, then cadit quaestio. No wrong had been done to the company or association and there is nothing in respect of which anyone can sue'* (emphasis added). See *Edwards v Halliwell* [1950] 2 All ER 1064 (CA) 1066.

[32] See *Macdougall v Gardiner* (1875) LR 1 Ch D 13 (CA) 22–23 (James LJ): 'putting aside all illegality on the part of the majority, it is for the company to determine whether it is for the good of the company that the thing should be done, or should not be done, or left unnoticed'.

[33] As Wedderburn explains: 'the judges have for long been reluctant to interfere in the internal affairs of companies and similar associations', and therefore 'have usually abdicated their jurisdiction in favour of the obvious alternative authority – the majority of the members'. See Wedderburn, 'Shareholders' Rights', above n 7, 194.

difference in their respective underpinning rationalities. The US business judgment rule, as originally formulated, rests on the basis that the board enjoys formal decision-making primacy within the corporate constitutional framework. Accordingly, a company's directors are 'an elected body of officers constituting the executive agents of the corporation', who 'hold such office charged with the duty to act for the corporation according to their best judgment [and therefore] cannot be controlled in the reasonable exercise and performance of such duty'.[34]

The English internal management doctrine, by contrast, is premised at root on protecting the constitutionally-guaranteed prerogative of the 'company', in the sense of the firm's collective body of members acting on a majoritarian basis in General Meeting.[35] Consistent with the general quasi-partnership impetus of English company law jurisprudence, the internal management doctrine protects the privity of the members' internal governance 'contract' by both reflecting and affirming a general judicial reluctance to upset the company's self-determined balance of decision-making power. As such, the principle operates in the vast majority of instances so as to legitimate majority initiative against perceived 'interference' by dissident minority shareholders, particularly in decisions concerning the merits of bringing litigation against directors who act in breach of duty or in excess of their constitutional authority.[36]

---

[34] *People ex rel Manice v Powell* 201 NY 194, 201 (1911) (Court of Appeals of New York) (Chase J) (previously cited above, ch 2 of this volume, fn 47).

[35] It should be noted that when the internal management doctrine was judicially established over the mid-to-late 1800s, the General Meeting was unqualifiedly recognised as the supreme governance organ in the company, to which the board of directors was directly accountable in a principal-agent capacity. An important implication of this was that a majority of shareholders could make formal orders binding upon the board, as recognised for example in *Isle of Wight Railway Co v Tahourdin* (1884) LR 25 Ch D 320 (CA). However, in the early decades of the twentieth century, this position was revised so that directors were regarded not as agents of shareholders, but rather as contractually appointed 'managing partners' empowered to represent the shareholders (majority and minority) as a whole, even where this entailed usurping the immediate preferences of the majority (see *Automatic Self-Cleansing Filter Syndicate*, [1906] 2 Ch 34 (CA) 45). However, the internal management doctrine was not itself revised to take account of this new judicial rationalisation of the board's status, so that the majoritarian principle continued to govern the ex post facto ratification process, even though the General Meeting in itself – acting by bare majority consensus – no longer had determinative ex ante power over the board. This curious conceptual mismatch between the contractual principle and internal management doctrine remains to this day, even though both rules remain fundamentally contractarian in nature, in that they each embody the implicit agreement of members as to the appropriate allocation of, respectively, corporate decision-*making* and decision-*review* powers.

[36] As Mellish LJ eloquently put it in *Macdougall v Gardiner*: 'In my opinion, if the thing complained of is a thing which in substance the majority of the company are entitled to do, or if something has been done irregularly which the majority of the company are entitled to do regularly, or if something has been done illegally which the majority of the company are entitled to do legally, there can be no use in having a litigation about it, the ultimate end of which is only that a meeting has to be called, and then ultimately the majority gets its wishes'. (1875) LR 1 Ch D 13 (CA) 25.

Prima facie, the internal management doctrine would appear to be relevant exclusively to private or closely-held companies, where majority shareholders typically act in a dual director-member capacity or at least have determinative voting control over the board, so that proprietary dominance translates directly into governance influence. In the public company context, by contrast, it may be surmised that majority prerogative has little practical value given the general lack of concentrated ownership interests within widely-held listed entities. As an empirical matter, however, shareholders in public companies will typically defer to the judgement of the board or, where serious mismanagement or impropriety occurs, seek an alternative non-litigation-based remedy.[37] Consequently, the indirect effect of the internal management doctrine in this context has been to afford substantial protection to the decisions of the board, as the authorised vicarious voice of the shareholder collective,[38] unless and until the majority take affirmative steps to displace the incumbent directors from their corporate representative capacity via exercise of their voting rights.[39]

Moreover, in cases where a suspected directorial wrongdoing occurs, and a majority of independent shareholders adopt the general view – whether expressly or 'by silence' – that the costs to the company (both financial and non-financial) of initiating litigation against the director in question exceed the likely benefits, the majority's view (or, rather, *lack of*) will likely be determinative of the matter.[40] This is regardless of whether

[37] The most obvious and straightforward remedies available to shareholders vis-à-vis perceived corporate mismanagement or underperformance in the public company setting are either to exercise their 'exit' option via disposal of their holding on a liquid market, or else to seek to use 'voice' by collectively effecting the removal or, at the very least, non-reappointment of the officer(s) concerned. On this generally, see A Keay, 'Company Directors Behaving Poorly: Disciplinary Options for Shareholders' [2007] *Journal of Business Law* 656. On shareholders' statutory power to remove the board without cause under section 168 of the Companies Act 2006, see below ch 6 of this volume, pt III.C.

[38] As Wedderburn observed (writing in 1957): 'whether [the internal management doctrine] is a wholly adequate basis for judicial policy in the area of modern company law is open to doubt', given that 'the "majority" in the modern public company is usually under the effective control of a small body of managers'. See 'Shareholders' Rights', above n 7, 194.

[39] Indeed, as emphasised by the Court of Appeal in assessing the (notoriously costly) attempted minority shareholder litigation in *Prudential Assurance v Newman Industries*: '[w]hen the shareholder acquires a share he accepts the fact that the value of his investment follows the fortunes of the company and that he can only exercise his influence over the fortunes of the company by the exercise of his voting rights in general meeting'. See *Prudential Assurance Co v Newman Industries (No 2)* [1982] Ch 204, 224.

[40] This is the essence of the 'independent majority' principle advanced by Knox J in *Smith v Croft (No 3)*, whereby a claimant shareholder can be lawfully prevented from bringing a derivative claim in respect of a suspected breach of directorial duty where 'it is an expression of the corporate will of the company by an appropriate independent organ' that such action should not proceed. The definition of 'independence' for this purpose is such as to exclude from the relevant majority any shareholders who cast (or risk casting) their votes 'with a view to supporting the defendants rather than securing benefit to the company'. See *Smith v Croft (No 3)* (1987) 3 BCC 218, 255. Following the introduction of the new discretionary derivative claims procedure under Part 11 of the Companies Act 2006, the absence of wrongdoer control

the majority's decision on the matter is swayed by mere passivity or lack of interest as opposed to calculated judgement,[41] and likewise irrespective of whether prosecution of the action by a disgruntled minority share-holder might serve the wider interests of justice or achieve effective accountability of the wrongdoer in the public interest.[42]

In the above way, the internal management doctrine ensures that in public companies, the private convenience of contractors in attaining cost-effective governance outcomes in effect 'trumps' any broader socio-economic considerations that might justify more rigorous judicial scrutiny of managerial decision-making or conduct within large-scale business enterprises. As such, the principle could be said to function as a form of retrospective corporate 'opt-out' (via ratification) from enforcing impro-prieties including breaches of directorial duty, which retains validity not-withstanding the blanket prohibition of Delaware-style exculpation provisions under successive UK Companies Acts in the modern era.[43]

The effect of the internal management doctrine in maintaining the for-mal privity of a company's internal governance arrangements, and the consequent insulation of its managerial decisions and authority relations from external (non-contractual) determination, is intrinsic to the prin-ciple's very jurisprudential foundations. In the landmark nineteenth-century case of *Foss v Harbottle*, where the doctrinal parameters of the doctrine were first sketched, Sir James Wigram VC made this important normative point in the following dictum:

over the corporate ratification process is no longer a formal bar to prosecution of an action by a minority shareholder, as was the traditional position at common law. However, the continu-ing centrality of the independent majority test in determining the court's willingness (or unwillingness) to permit continuation of a minority derivative claim is emphasised in section 263(4) of the Act, which states that '[i]n considering whether to give permission (or leave) the court shall have particular regard to any evidence before it as to the views of members of the company who have no personal interest, direct or indirect, in the matter'.

[41] This would appear to be implicit in the Court of Appeal's obiter dictum in *Prudential* to the effect that an appropriate independent organ of the company can legitimately prevent the bringing of minority shareholder litigation where it concludes that such action is likely to occasion 'more harm than good' to the company's interests, regardless of whether that assessment be 'sound or unsound'. See above n 39, [1982] Ch 204, 221.

[42] Indeed, in the following passage, the Court in *Prudential* expressly rejected the pur-ported notion that shareholder derivative claims were a form of vicarious public regulation of corporate affairs: 'We were invited to give judicial approval to the public spirit of the plaintiffs who, it was said, are pioneering a method of controlling companies in the public interest without involving regulation by a statutory body. In our view the voluntary regula-tion of companies is a matter for the City. The compulsory regulation of companies is a mat-ter for Parliament'. Ibid, 224.

[43] It has been observed that '[w]hile the United States law has permitted a corporation to amend its articles to eliminate its directors' liability even for gross negligence, English law has strictly prohibited any elimination of liability'. See MR Pasban, C Campbell and J Birds, 'Section 727 and the Business Judgment Rule: A Comparative Analysis of Company Directors' Duties and Liabilities in England and United States Law' (1997) 6 *Journal of Transnational Law and Policy* 201, 221. On the relationship between ratification and exculpation, see below nn 82, 97–98 and accompanying text.

Corporations like this, of a private nature, are in truth little more than private partner-ships; and in cases which may easily be suggested it would be too much to hold that a society of private persons associated together in under-takings, which, though certainly beneficial to the public, are nevertheless matters of private property, are to be deprived of their civil rights (emphasis added).[44]

Adopting the same quasi-partnership logic, his Lordship furthermore provided a contractual basis for majority rule – and, correspondingly, minority disempowerment – by imputing to a company's members the following implicit mutual understanding:

the majority of the proprietors at a special general meeting assembled, independently of any general rules of law upon the subject, by the very terms of the incorporation in the present case, has power to bind the whole body, and *every individual incorporator must be taken to have come into the corporation upon the terms of being liable to be so bound* (emphasis added).[45]

In conclusion, it can thus be said that the internal management doctrine, as understood in the above sense, functions in coordination with the aforementioned contractual principle. Whereas the contractual principle enables corporate contractors to determine ex ante how governance power will be divided without material regulatory constraint, the internal management doctrine further permits corporate contractors to preclude – via subjective ratification – the ex post facto external (judicial) scrutiny of managerial decisions that are made by the company's elected executive representatives. Accordingly, these two doctrines jointly affirm the inherently private character of the corporate decision-making framework, and the corresponding immunity of most intra-firm arrangements and decisions from extra-contractual public control or oversight (whether regulatorily or judicially).[46]

---

[44] *Foss v Harbottle* (1843) 2 Hare 461, 491–92.

[45] Ibid, 494.

[46] An arguable exception to this general position is the statutory unfair prejudice doctrine as currently enshrined in section 994 of the Companies Act 2006, which (theoretically at least) provides English and Scottish courts with the express licence to intervene in arrangements and decisions that have a detrimental effect on the interests of any individual – particularly minority – shareholders. As against this, however, it should be noted that the unfair prejudice doctrine has been interpreted by the courts so as to apply almost exclusively to private companies, thus in practice precluding shareholders of public companies (which are the exclusive focus of concern in this book) from obtaining judicial relief under this statutory head. See J Armour, B Black, B Cheffins and R Nolan, 'Private Enforcement of Corporate Law: An Empirical Comparison of the United Kingdom and the United States' (2009) 6 *Journal of Empirical Legal Studies* 687, 695–96. Moreover, the narrow manner in which the doctrine has been developed jurisprudentially – as a means of protecting the quasi-contractual 'legitimate expectations' of members rather than substantive standards of justice writ large – has resulted in the unfair prejudice rule *reinforcing*, as opposed to detracting from, the traditional contractarian logic underpinning the inter-shareholder relation under English law. See *O'Neill and Another v Phillips and Others* [1999] 1 WLR 1092 (HL) 1098–99 (Lord Hoffman): 'a member of a company will not ordinarily be entitled to complain of unfairness unless there has been some breach of the terms on which he agreed that the affairs

B. Judicial Non-Interventionism in Business Objectives and Decisions

UK corporate law has traditionally lacked a business judgment rule in the Delaware sense:[47] that is to say, a formal and rebuttable presumption to the effect that any non-wasteful directorial decision has been reached on a loyal, informed and unconflicted basis.[48] However, a similarly deferential and 'arm's length' judicial approach to determining the propriety of business judgments – in respect of both the broad objectives of the company and specific managerial decisions – has been achieved via extension of the internal management doctrine's non-interventionist logic into the realm of directorial decisions on corporate objectives and strategy. In assessing the propriety of a company's objectives, English courts have increasingly been inclined to apply the doctrine's aforementioned quasi-contractual rationality. Accordingly, all members are bound by bona fide decisions of the majority of shareholders – which, in public companies, are typically made on a vicarious basis by the board – concerning the range and type of activities that the firm's wealth is used in the pursuit of.

This is subject to the logical precondition (in an ordinary commercial company at least) that those activities are reasonably incidental to advancement of the company's core business affairs, in which case it can be surmised that members have implicitly assented to the company's deployment of their capital in this regard.[49] However, within these wide

---

of the company should be conducted'. On this, see also P Davies, *Gower and Davies' Principles of Modern Company Law*, 8th edn (London, Sweet & Maxwell, 2008) 691–96. Finally, in a recent decision the Court of Appeal further expanded the contractual character of the unfair prejudice remedy in establishing that the right of a petitioner to seek relief under section 994 is not an unalienable prerogative, but rather can in effect be 'opted out of' via a preceding agreement to submit an inter-shareholder dispute to arbitration as a privately-ordered alternative to invoking the statutory scheme. On this, see *Fulham Football Club (1987) v Richards & Another* [2011] EWCA Civ 855 (CA), critically analysed in H McVea, 'Section 994, Companies Act 2006 and the Primacy of Contract' (2012, currently unpublished article, forthcoming).

[47] In its wide-reaching review of British corporate law that preceded the promulgation of the Companies Act 2006, the UK government's *Company Law Review Steering Group* briefly considered the idea of introducing a statutory business judgment rule along Australian lines. However, the Committee swiftly rejected this notion on the ground that 'there are major difficulties in drafting such a provision which would add complexity and is likely to be inflexible and unfair, being too harsh in some cases and allowing too much leeway in others'. The Committee also believed that the newly codified duty of care and skill, as set out today in section 174 of the 2006 Act, 'as drafted leaves room for the courts to develop this approach'. See *Modern Company Law for a Competitive Economy: Developing the Framework* (London, Department for Trade and Industry, 2000) para 3.70. On the introduction of a statutory business judgment rule in Australia, see JH Farrar, 'Towards a Statutory Business Judgment Rule in Australia' [1998] *Australian Journal of Corporate Law* 302.

[48] For a description of the US business judgment rule's key doctrinal features, see above ch 4 of this volume, pt IV.

[49] See *Hutton v West Cork Railway Co* (1883) LR 23 Ch D 654 (CA) 678, 671 (Bowen LJ): 'I think a willing majority has no right to bind a dissentient minority by any resolution so conceived . . . [The majority] can only spend money which is not theirs but the company's, if

doctrinal boundaries, majorities – and, in turn, boards – have for long been vested with substantially unrestrained discretion in allocating the company's (including minority's) resources in the service of ends of the former's own choosing; including charitable, gratuitous, political and educational causes linked tangentially at best to the company's commercial interests.[50] In one of the earliest and most influential affirmations of this position, Bowen LJ explained – in typically functional terms – the rationale for courts adopting a permissive approach to assessing the propriety of corporate activities falling outside the strict bounds of the company's constitutional objects:

> It seems to me you cannot say the company has only got power to spend the money which it is bound to pay according to law, otherwise the wheels of business would stop, nor can you say that directors . . . are always to be limited to the strictest possible view of what the obligations of the company are. They are not to keep their pockets buttoned up and defy the world unless they are liable in a way which could be enforced at law or in equity. Most businesses require liberal dealings.[51]

The above dictum of 1883 represents one (early) part of a progressive shift away from regulatory rigidity towards contractual flexibility in establishing the permissible scope of a company's objects and powers. Traditionally, the ultra vires doctrine – an institutional remnant of the pre-industrial public chartered corporation – operated so as to constrain a company's freedom to determine the breadth of its own (business and non-business) activities on a continuing basis. This was with a view to protecting the expectations of investors and the general public to the effect that the company would conform to its pre-determined objects clause as set out in the memorandum of association. However, the ensuing century saw a steady judicial – and, in turn, legislative – diminution of the ultra vires rule. This ongoing process of doctrinal erosion occurred largely in response to the evolving ingenuity of legal professionals, who succeeded in drafting ever-wider constitutional qualifications to the rule so as to ease corporate clients' access to external capital for the purpose of pursuing diverse entrepreneurial ventures.

---

they are spending it for the purposes which are *reasonably incidental to* the carrying on of the business of the company. That is the general doctrine. *Bona fides* cannot be the sole test, otherwise you might have a lunatic conducting the affairs of the company, and paying away its money with both hands in a manner perfectly *bona fide* yet perfectly irrational. The test must be what is reasonably incidental to, and within the reasonable scope of carrying on, the business of the company' (emphasis added).

[50] See, eg *Evans v Brunner, Mond & Co Ltd* [1921] 1 Ch 359; *Charterbridge Corp Ltd v Lloyds Bank Ltd* [1970] Ch 62; *Re Horsley & Weight Ltd* [1982] Ch 442 (CA); *Simmonds v Heffer* [1983] BCLC 298. For an excellent academic analysis of this general line of case law, see JE Parkinson, *Corporate Power and Responsibility: Issues in the Theory of Company Law* (Oxford, Oxford University Press, 1993) 271–77.

[51] See *Hutton v West Cork Railway Co*, above n 49, 672.

In spite of an initial judicial backlash to such sharp practices, the courts eventually succumbed to the dictates of commercial exigency. In what may be regarded as the classic example of the market-mimicking type of legal development revered by contractarians, English courts over the latter decades of the twentieth century adopted increasingly more liberal interpretations of objects clauses, with a view to upholding the validity of corporate transactions in favour of bona fide third parties.[52] Meanwhile, Parliament followed suit with a series of progressively more permissive legislative measures to the same end, partly in response to initiatives at European Community level.[53] This trend culminated in (i) the outright abolition of objects clauses for newly incorporating companies under the Companies Act 2006 (unless incorporators expressly elect to include such a clause in the articles); and (ii), insofar as pre-existing companies are concerned, the downgrading of the formal status of the ultra vires doctrine – for the first time in history – from a mandatory to a reversible-default rule.[54]

One important normative implication of the ultra vires rule's substantial dismantlement is the greater degree of regulatory deference thus afforded to intra-firm governance and authority relations. Whereas the ultra vires doctrine previously had the intended effect of imposing limitations on the scope of a company's (internal and external) contractual autonomy in the interest of protecting the wider public; the effect of the aforementioned series of reforms to the rule has been to 'carve out' a wider ambit of extra-regulatory space within which a company's pre-existing transactions will be afforded primacy over the interests of any relevant parties (eg future investors or the public generally) situated *outside of* the immediate corporate-contractual nexus.

In determining the propriety of specific managerial decisions taken by or under the authority of a company's board, meanwhile, English courts have traditionally been guided to a significant extent by the same basic logic of judicial non-interventionism in internal firm affairs.[55] Thus judges have historically tended to show respect for a company's internal man-

---

[52] See, eg *Charterbridge Corp Ltd v Lloyds Bank Ltd*, above n 50; *Rolled Steel Products (Holdings) Ltd v British Steel Corp* [1985] Ch 246 (CA).

[53] See, eg the default 'general commercial company' objects clause introduced by the Companies Act 1989, and previously set out in section 3A of the Companies Act 1985; and the statutory 'whitewash' provisions introduced over the 1980s in conformance with the UK's obligations under the European Communities Act 1972 (and today contained in sections 39 and 40 of the Companies Act 2006), which uphold the validity of ultra vires transactions and transactions with bona fide third parties entered into in excess of directors' constitutional powers.

[54] Both of these revisions are effected by section 31 of the Companies Act 2006, which provides: first, that unless a company's articles specifically restrict the objects of the company, its objects are unrestricted; and, secondly, that a company may add, alter or remove its objects clause by giving appropriate notice to the registrar of companies.

[55] On this point generally, see Parkinson, *Corporate Power and Responsibility*, above n 50, 92–96.

agement command chain and the authority of its appointed representative officers, to the extent of sanctioning – or, at the very least, excusing – managerial decisions or omissions of prima facie questionable rationality or professional competence.

Underpinning and characterising the orthodox judicial approach to business judgment evaluation in England (as in Delaware) is a vehemently *anti*-paternalistic stance with respect to internal corporate affairs and authority relations. That is to say, English courts have demonstrated a long-held reluctance to transplant externally or retrospectively determined standards of managerial conduct in place of those governance norms and arrangements that are determined by private contractors (ie members and directors) ex ante on a firm-specific basis. Accordingly, the orthodox tests at common law for assessing the propriety of directorial conduct – from both a loyalty and prudence perspective – are highly subjective in nature. As such, they have operated so as to preclude courts from second-guessing or otherwise interfering in bona fide entrepreneurial decisions made under 'real world' business conditions, except to the bare minimum extent required to uphold members' implicit contractual expectations as to the honesty and basic rationality of the company's appointed managerial agents. In this way, English courts have re-affirmed and extended the core normative rationality of company law as a mechanism for *upholding* – rather than displacing – notional contractual outcomes with respect to corporate governance matters. With respect to broader *public* considerations that might justify more exacting standards of conduct for directors (at least in larger business enterprises),[56] meanwhile, English courts have traditionally been dismissive – the apparent judicial assumption being that beneficial social outcomes can be expected to follow indirectly from allowing the private ordering of managerial affairs (including occasional errors and omissions) to 'run its course' in the natural way of things.

Thus in determining whether a particular managerial decision is in conformance with a director's fiduciary duty of loyalty, English courts have habitually resorted to the well-established position that '[t]he duty imposed on directors to act bona fide in the interests of the company is a subjective one',[57] requiring that directors 'exercise their discretion *in what they consider – not what a court may consider* – is in the interests of the company' (emphasis added).[58] As explained by Jonathan Parker J:

---

[56] In this regard, it has notably been argued that '[w]here a company is negligently operated the potential for economic and social harm is tremendous', in that '[b]ad and incompetent management places shareholders, creditors, employees, suppliers and consumers at risk'. See Rider, 'Amiable Lunatics', above n 28, 286–87.

[57] *Regentcrest plc (in liquidation) v Cohen* [2001] BCC 494, 513 (Jonathan Parker J).

[58] *Re Smith & Fawcett Ltd* [1942] Ch 304, 306 (Lord Greene MR).

The question is not whether, viewed objectively by the court, the particular act or omission which is challenged was in fact in the interests of the company; still less is the question whether the court, had it been in the position of the director at the relevant time, might have acted differently. Rather, the question is whether the director honestly believed that his act or omission was in the interests of the company. *The issue is as to the director's state of mind* (emphasis added).[59]

Moreover, the inherent subjectivity of the traditional judicial test for determining conformance with the duty of loyalty has since been carried over into the contemporary statutory statement of the duty. In this regard – and largely echoing the basic tenor of these earlier authorities – section 172 of the Companies Act 2006 provides that '[a] director of a company must act in the way *he considers, in good faith*, would be most likely to promote the success of the company for the benefit of its members as a whole' (emphasis added).[60]

Given the principal focus of the above bona fides test on the state of mind of the relevant director, rather than the nature of his conduct or wider economic circumstances thereto, the logical limit of the court's deference to managerial discretion consequently lies at the extreme point of the psychological spectrum: that is, where an act or decision is inherently incapable *by its very nature* of being in the interests of the company, such that – to coin a notorious lawyerly phrase – only an 'amiable lunatic',[61] devoid of ordinary rationality, could have concluded that such conduct was in the company's interests.[62] Since such extraordinary instances lie outside of the reasonable bounds of members' expectations in subscribing to the corporate contract, there is arguably no inconsistency at all with the contractual principle in holding directors' decisions in these cases to be an improper and thus unauthorised exercise of their constitutional authority as agents of the company.

---

[59] *Regentcrest v Cohen*, above n 57, 513–14.

[60] Companies Act 2006, s 172(1).

[61] This oft-used term was first cited in argument in *Pavlides v Jensen*, as denoting the situation where a director commits an act that is – viewed objectively – inherently incapable by its very nature of being in the interests of the company. The hypothetical example suggested in argument in this case was the selling off of a company's products by a controlling majority at greatly below cost price. See above n 29, [1956] Ch 565, 570 (*Charles Russell QC* and *Kenneth Mackinnon*). Put another way, the same test can be phrased in Pennycuick J's terms as posing the question of 'whether an intelligent and honest man in the position of a director of the company concerned, could, in the whole of the existing circumstances, have reasonably believed that the transactions were for the benefit of the company'. See *Charterbridge Corp Ltd v Lloyds Bank Ltd*, above n 50, 74.

[62] It can be reasoned that, in such instances, the presumption of bona fides is necessarily overridden on the facts, on the basis that 'what no reasonable board could have believed to be beneficial to the company, the actual board could not have believed either, or in other words, that where the means adopted could not on any reasonable view lead to the end of benefiting the company, the directors could not have been motivated by a desire to achieve that end'. See Parkinson, *Corporate Power and Responsibility*, above n 50, 96.

Where the issue in question is not the suspected disloyalty of a director, but rather his professional competence for office, the basic approach at common law is not dissimilar from that outlined above. A uniting theme of the traditional case law on the director's duty of care is the general view that, if members put corporate representatives in office, they implicitly agree to abide by the consequences of that decision, while retaining ultimate power to determine the continuation and terms of the latter's official tenure.[63] Moreover, English Chancery judges have – like their Delaware counterparts – for a long time been expressly appreciative of the fact that competitive business enterprise by nature entails making speculative decisions based on necessarily limited information, foresight and objective guidance in the context of unique and largely incomparable factual contexts: something that members could be said to have constructive awareness of as part of their notional governance pact with the board.[64] From this there derived the common belief that a court should not seek itself to determine the proper terms of what is essentially a private (agency) relationship between a director and his employer company, by formulating or applying any general or objective standard of reasonableness that is insensitive to the peculiar circumstances and challenges of the business scenario in question.[65] Furthermore, in deference to the company's self-determined internal command chain, it has traditionally been established that, in the absence of grounds for suspicion, directors are formally at liberty to rely upon the judgement, information and advice of

---

[63] See, eg *Lagunas Nitrate Company v Lagunas Syndicate* [1899] 2 Ch 392 (CA) 465–66 (Rigby LJ): 'These are the directors by whose acts the company and every member thereof have agreed to be bound'.

[64] See, eg *The Overend & Gurney Co v Gibb* (1872) LR 5 HL 480, 495 (Lord Hatherley LC): 'I think it extremely likely that many a judge, or many a person versed by long experience in the affairs of mankind, as conducted in the mercantile world, will know that *there is a great deal more trust, a great deal more speculation, and a great deal more readiness to confide in the probabilities of things, with regard to success in mercantile transactions, than there is on the part of those whose habits of life are entirely of a different character.* It would be extremely wrong to import into the consideration of the case of a person acting as a mercantile agent in the purchase of a business concern, those principles of extreme caution which might dictate the course of one who is not at all inclined to invest his property in any ventures of such a hazardous character' (emphasis added).

[65] In the words of Lord Hatherley, 'it would be a very fatal error in the verdict of any Court of justice to attempt to measure . . . the amount of prudence that ought to be exercised by the amount of prudence which the judge himself might think, under similar circumstances, he should have exercised'. See *Overend & Gurney Co v Gibb*, ibid, 494–95. This view was reiterated by Neville J in *In Re Brazilian Rubber Plantations and Estates* [1911] 1 Ch 425, 437–38: 'whether the directors acted without reasonable prudence . . . must not be tested by considering what the Court itself would think reasonable'. See, likewise, *Dovey v Cory* [1901] AC 477 (HL) 488 (Lord Macnaghten): 'I do not think it desirable for any tribunal to do that which Parliament has abstained from doing – that is, to formulate precise rules for the guidance or embarrassment of business men in the conduct of business affairs. There never has been, and I think there never will be, much difficulty in dealing with any particular case on its own facts and circumstances; and, speaking for myself, I rather doubt the wisdom of attempting to do more'.

managerial colleagues,[66] and to delegate functions to subordinates in the expectation that such tasks will be honestly fulfilled.[67]

The only exception to the above is the truly outlying case where directorial negligence is so egregious as to offend ordinary personal standards of prudence, in which case it would arguably undermine members' legitimate quasi-contractual expectations were a court *not* to so intervene. For this purpose, the courts have traditionally applied the *de minimis* standard of *crassa negligentia*, whereby imprudent directorial conduct will give rise to negligence liability only where the directors concerned 'were cognisant of circumstances of such a character, so plain, so manifest, and so simple of appreciation, that *no men with any ordinary degree of prudence*, acting on their own behalf, would have entered into such a transaction as they entered into' (emphasis added).[68]

This principle can be rationalised contractually on the ground that a director who exhibits *crassa negligentia* is acting (or, alternatively, *in*acting) in a manner manifestly outside of his agent's mandate to benefit the company as his effective principal,[69] and thereby contravening the fundamental basis of his governance relationship with the company and, in turn, the legitimate expectations of its members.[70] Since the concept of *crassa negligentia* is underpinned by the logic of implied agency, it requires from a director only the degree of care that would ordinarily be expected within

---

[66] Traditionally, such reliance was permitted even in the situation where a director consequently refrained from examining entries in the company's financial records that were laid before him on the boardroom table for reference. See *Dovey v Cory*, [1901] AC 477, 492–93 (Lord Davey).

[67] On this, see Romer J's well-known dictum in *Re City Equitable Fire Insurance Co Ltd* [1925] Ch 407 (CA) 429, to the effect that '[i]n respect of all duties that, having regard to the exigencies of business, and the articles of association, may properly be left to some other official, a director is, in the absence of grounds for suspicion, justified in trusting that official to perform such duties honestly'.

[68] *Overend & Gurney Co v Gibb*, (1872) LR 5 HL 480, 493 (Lord Hatherley LC).

[69] See ibid, 494.

[70] The classic *crassa negligentia* test was elaborated on in the frequently-cited 1925 judgment of Romer J in *Re City Equitable Fire Insurance Co Ltd*, where it was noted that '[a] director need not exhibit in the performance of his duties a greater degree of skill *than may reasonably be expected from a person of his knowledge and experience*' (emphasis added) (above n 67, [1925] Ch 407, 428). This dictum is often presented as suggesting a more demanding standard of competence than the basic 'ordinary prudent man' threshold of the *crassa negligentia* doctrine in that, under the *City Equitable* test, the particular competencies of individual directors arguably merit a case-by-case raising of the negligence bar. However, it is submitted that Romer J's comments are more accurately interpreted principally as a simple re-affirmation of the pre-existing position that a director who lacks any professional qualifications or competencies will not be rendered vulnerable to potential liability by virtue of this fact. Indeed, this much seems clear in Romer J's subsequent statement that '[a] director of a life insurance company, for instance, does not guarantee that he has the skill of an actuary or of a physician' (ibid, 428). Even if one adopts the former, more demanding interpretation of the directorial standard of care, this would not appear to signal any material development on the basic *crassa negligentia* doctrine, insofar as an ordinary person would naturally be expected to use any personal skills, experience or knowledge at his disposal in tending to his own personal affairs in a prudent manner.

a principal-agent relationship: that is, 'all the *ordinary* prudence that can be properly and legitimately expected from any person in the conduct of the affairs of the world' (emphasis added).[71] But in the absence of any formally public or bureaucratic dimension to the company director's function at common law, it follows logically that a director is 'not bound to bring any special qualifications to his office' nor to 'take any definite part in the conduct of the company's business'.[72] Rather, as long as a director exercises 'the same amount of prudence which, in the same circumstances, he would exercise *on his own behalf*, he will be deemed to have acted in conformance with his traditional quasi-contractual standard of care at common law (emphasis added).[73] The separate question as to whether the relevant director is fit for office from a wider public interest perspective is, under the above rationality, entirely *superfluous* to the appropriate scope of judicial enquiry.[74]

C. Retrospective Judicial Liability Relief for Negligent Directors

One of the most noteworthy developments in US corporate law in the modern era, as documented in the previous chapter,[75] has been the statutory legitimation and subsequent proliferation of exculpation provisions designed to immunise directors from liability for bona fide breaches of duty including gross negligence. It was highlighted how such clauses are both

---

[71] *In Re Brazilian Rubber Plantations and Estates*, above n 65, [1911] 1 Ch 425, 437 (Neville J).

[72] Ibid.

[73] Ibid. An examination of the law in relation to directors' negligence in the UK is far from complete, though, without considering the impact of modern (post-1980s) judicial developments in the field as recently codified under section 174 of the Companies Act 2006. This has established a test that – prima facie at least – is materially more objective and demanding in nature than the preceding *crassa negligentia* standard. On this, see below ch 6 of this volume, pt I.B.(ii). Since the purpose of the present discussion is to highlight the general (and largely continuing) English judicial tradition of non-interventionism in intra-firm governance affairs (rather than directors' negligence liability specifically), consideration of these more recent developments is not called for at this point in the discussion.

[74] Note, however, the modern development of directors' disqualification legislation and the publicly-oriented concept of 'unfitness' that is central thereto. See Company Directors' Disqualification Act 1986, s 6 and Sch 1. As a regulatory means of protecting the public interest by ensuring generally responsible standards of corporate management in the UK, the directors' disqualification regime is in practice significantly limited by the fact that it only applies to directors of companies whose mismanagement is so serious as to result in the eventual insolvency of the firm. Moreover, the Act's substantive definition of 'unfitness' adds little over and above the existing grounds for private (shareholder) action under directors' general duties, whilst the capacity of the Secretary of State for Business to initiate public enforcement proceedings under the Act is in reality limited by obvious considerations of public resource constraint. For these reasons, the significance of the directors' disqualification regime within the broader framework of UK corporate governance should not be overestimated. On this procedure generally, see: R Williams, 'Disqualifying Directors: A remedy Worse than the Disease?' (2007) 7 *Journal of Corporate Law Studies* 213.

[75] See above ch 4 of this volume, fns 15–16 and accompanying text.

motivated and justified by the overtly functional rationale of mitigating liability risk for directors, and the resultant transaction costs for corporations, in the post-*Van Gorkom* era. From a private ordering perspective, moreover, encouragement of a priori exculpation on an 'opt in' basis can be regarded as a laudable legislative position insofar as it enables corporate contractors to provide optimal incentives for managerial risk-taking at the individual firm level.

Interestingly, the traditional judicial view in England on the legitimacy of directorial liability relief was comparatively liberal to the contemporary Delaware position: that is to say, money damages liability for gross negligence – absent fraud or bad faith on the relevant director's part – was freely excludable by means of an appropriate term in a company's articles. This position derived from the explicitly contractualist reasoning of Lord Justice Cozens-Hardy in an early-twentieth-century decision of the Court of Appeal, to the effect that:

> [t]he articles, though not themselves a contract between the company and the director, must be regarded as shewing the terms upon which on the one hand he agrees to act as director, and on the other hand the company agree to pay him remuneration for his services.[76]

Relying on this earlier authority, Neville J posited in the 1911 case of *Re Brazilian Rubber Plantations and Estates* that the directorial duty of care could in effect be trumped by a countervailing provision of the corporate constitution, on the basis that 'this immunity was one of the terms upon which the directors held office in this company', it being 'not . . . illegal for a company to engage its directors upon such terms'.[77] Additionally, directors who were made defendant to any legal action in consequence of their office could seek indemnification from the company for any resulting expenses incurred, including damages for negligence, in a broadly similar manner to directors of Delaware corporations today. This was on the orthodox contractual basis that 'as agents and trustees [they] were entitled to be indemnified by companies against losses and expenses bona fide sustained by them in managing the company's business'.[78]

In 1926, however, the government-commissioned Greene Committee on company law reform responded to concern about the perceived exploitation by directors and promoters of increasingly broad-reaching exculpation and indemnification provisions, which shareholders moreover were deemed in general to have little de facto influence over.[79] The Committee's

---

[76] *Molineaux v London, Birmingham and Manchester Insurance Co Ltd* [1902] 2 KB 589 (CA), 596.

[77] Above n 65, [1911] 1 Ch 425, 440.

[78] R Cranston, 'Limiting Directors' Liability: Ratification, Exemption and Indemnification' [1992] *Journal of Business Law* 197, 204.

[79] See *Company Law Amendment Committee, 1925-26, Report* (Cmd 2657, 1926) (The Greene Report) 20, discussed in Cranston, ibid, 205.

recommendations led, inter alia, to the statutory invalidation of both types of clause whether contained in a company's articles or in any external contract with a director, with the limited exception of provisions empowering companies to indemnify directors for costs incurred in defending successful civil or criminal legal proceedings.[80] The basic position of UK law in this regard has since remained substantially unchanged, notwithstanding the legitimation of company-maintained D&O insurance for directors under a reform introduced at the end of the 1980s.[81] It is today embodied in section 232 of the Companies Act 2006, subsection (1) of which states that:

> Any provision that purports to exempt a director of a company (to any extent) from any liability that would otherwise attach to him in connection with any negligence, default, breach of duty or breach of trust in relation to the company is void.

Subsection (2) furthermore states that any provision by which a company directly or indirectly provides an indemnity for a director against any liability attaching to him in connection with (inter alia) negligence or breach of duty is void, with the notable exception of D&O insurance coverage for directors that is maintained at the company's expense.

It should be pointed out that, in spite of the general anti-exculpatory thrust of section 232(1), ratification nevertheless remains legally permissible on the generally-accepted ground that a ratifying resolution does not constitute a provision seeking to exempt a director from liability for a breach of duty entirely. Rather, ratification represents merely the formal ad hoc declaration of the majority that it will not authorise the company to take action against the relevant director in respect of the wrong in question, notwithstanding his continuing liability for breach.[82] In spite of its limitations, the continuing availability of ratification for breaches of duty short of manifest impropriety has historically been crucial in mitigating the liability risk to which directors would otherwise be left exposed by the unavailability of ex ante exculpation.

[80] The relevant statutory provision in this regard was section 152 of the Companies Act 1929.

[81] This amendment was effected by a revision to section 310 of the (then-applicable) Companies Act 1985, implemented under the Companies Act 1989. The applicable provision to this effect today is section 233 of the Companies Act 2006.

[82] See Rider, 'Amiable Lunatics', above n 28, 279. There has been much academic debate over whether ratification is sufficient to immunise a wrongdoing director from potential liability for a particular breach *in perpetuity*, or whether – notwithstanding the fact of prior ratification – it is possible for a future action to be initiated against the director following a change of control over the company (such as in a takeover or, alternatively, liquidation scenario). The latter of the above views would appear to be the preferred one, leading to the practical conclusion that a director, in order to obtain outright liability relief effective in all future eventualities, should seek a further shareholder resolution providing formal liability release subsequent to the initial ratification resolution. On this, see Cranston, 'Limiting Directors' Liability', above n 78, 200.

At the same time, the 'sting' to directors from the enforced absence of exculpatory protections in the United Kingdom over the past century has been further alleviated by an important countervailing statutory provision introduced two decades prior to the aforementioned prohibition. In 1906 the Company Law Amendment Committee of the time, cognisant of an apparent reluctance on the part of many qualified persons to serve as directors, perceived the need to provide an extra layer of protection against directors' increased liability risk at the time (especially with respect to prospectus contents on the public issue of corporate securities).[83] To this end, the Committee – inspired by a pre-existing provision applicable to trustees[84] – formulated the concept of retrospective judicial liability relief for directors, which was introduced in its original form by statute the following year.[85]

The corresponding rule today, which remains largely similar in effect to its early precursors, is set out in section 1157 of the Companies Act 2006. This provision vests a court with discretion to relieve a director or other corporate officer who is a defendant to an action for (inter alia) negligence or breach of duty, either wholly or in part, from liability on such terms as it thinks fit. Furthermore, an officer is entitled to apply to the court for pre-emptive liability relief where he has reason to apprehend that such a claim will or might be made against him, with a view to preventing any future action from proceeding.[86] The court is empowered to relieve the relevant officer from liability where it is apparent from all the circumstances of the case that, notwithstanding that person's actual or potential liability, he has nonetheless acted *honestly and reasonably* and therefore ought *fairly* to be relieved from any ensuing money damages liability.[87]

The availability of retrospective judicial liability relief under section 1157 is the most conspicuous formal endorsement of judicial deference to business exigencies within the British corporate law framework.[88] At its core lies what may prima facie be perceived as an intrinsic logical inconsistency: as Hoffman LJ considered in *Re D'Jan of London*, '[i]t may seem

---

[83] See 'Company Law Amendment Committee 1906' (Cd 3052, 1906), cl 24; discussed in R Edmunds and J Lowry, 'The Continuing Value of Relief for Directors' Breach of Duty' (2003) 66 *Modern Law Review* 195, 195, fn 2.

[84] The relevant provision was section 3 of the Judicial Trustees Act 1896. See MR Pasban, C Campbell and J Birds, 'Section 727 and the Business Judgment Rule: A Comparative Analysis of Company Directors' Duties and Liabilities in England and United States Law' (1997) 6 *Journal of Transnational Law and Policy* 201, 204.

[85] The inaugural version of the provision was section 32 of the Companies Act 1907, although this was reproduced and also extended one year later in the form of section 279 of the Companies (Consolidation) Act 1908. See Edmunds and Lowry, 'Relief for Directors' Breach of Duty', above n 83, 195, fn 2.

[86] Companies Act 2006, s 1157(2).

[87] Ibid, s 1157(1).

[88] Indeed, the provision has previously been described as 'the principal protection for directors under English company law'. See Pasban, Campbell and Birds, 'Section 727 and the Business Judgment Rule', above n 84, 202.

odd that a person found to have been guilty of negligence, which involves failing to take reasonable care, can ever satisfy the court that he acted reasonably'.[89] Courts have resolved this apparent paradox in practice by exploiting the wide discretion with which they are vested in determining the eligibility of applications for relief on a case-by-case basis.[90] This has in turn enabled the provision to be applied in a highly subjective manner, with courts exhibiting an acute receptiveness to the peculiar fact patterns[91] and 'economic realities'[92] surrounding individual instances of actual or alleged mismanagement. The essential logic of the rule is that, whilst a director may have acted in what is formally considered to be a grossly negligent manner, his behaviour can nevertheless be 'pardoned' judicially on the basis that the impropriety was either of a 'purely technical'[93] rather than morally opprobrious nature; or, at the very least, that his actions (or, alternatively, *in*action) were reasonably understandable under the given circumstances.[94] In this way, an application for judicial liability relief can be regarded as a traditional second line of defence for directors faced with a negligence action,[95] which moreover is characterised by an even greater

---

[89] *Re D'Jan of London Ltd* [1993] BCC 646, 649.

[90] Section 1157(1) expressly provides that a court '*may*' (rather than 'shall' or 'will') grant relief where satisfied that all the requirements of the section have been satisfied, so that it retains ultimate discretion on the matter in all cases. On this, see Pasban, Campbell and Birds, 'Section 727 and the Business Judgment Rule', above n 84 at 205, 212.

[91] In particular, section 1157(1) provides that the court should make a decision on an application for relief only after 'having regard to all the circumstances of the case'. It has been noted that this 'appears to permit the judges to examine *all or any of the aspects of the company's business and the directors' conduct* in weighing the evidence for and against granting the relief' (emphasis added). Pasban, Campbell and Birds, above n 84, 212.

[92] This sub-criterion was expressly considered by Hoffman LJ in *Re D'Jan*, above n 89, [1993] BCC 646, 649: 'I think that the economic realities of the case can be taken into account in exercising the discretion under [section 1157]'.

[93] See *Re Gilt Edge Safety Glass Ltd* [1940] Ch 495, 503 (Crossman J); cited and analysed in Edmunds and Lowry, 'Relief for Directors' Breach of Duty', above n 83, 208.

[94] For example, in the aforementioned *Re D'Jan* case, a director was successful in attaining liability relief despite being deemed by the same court to have acted negligently. This was on account of him having failed to read an insurance policy document before signing it, with the result that the company was unable to claim on the policy for subsequent fire damage to its property. Hoffman LJ took the view that the director's omission, whilst putting him in breach of his duty of care, was nevertheless 'the kind of thing which could happen to any busy man'. Largely for this reason, his Lordship felt justified in holding the defendant's conduct to be excusable under what is now section 1157 of the Companies Act 2006. See above, n 89, [1993] BCC 646, 649. Observing this decision and also other cases decided along similar lines, Edmunds and Lowry submit that 'the determination of relief is necessarily a fact intensive exercise', whereby '[c]haracteristics such as the technicality of the breach, the absence of loss and acting on expert advice figure prominently in allowing relief from prospective liability'. See 'Relief for Directors' Breach of Duty' above n 83, 214.

[95] Indeed, Edmunds and Lowry have attributed the low number of successful claims based on (what is today) section 1157 to the fact that statutory liability relief is commonly advanced as a secondary argument in defence to a breach of duty action, with many such cases falling to be determined on the basis of the first (existence of breach) argument alone. This arguably further explains why the provision has attracted relatively little direct judicial consideration throughout its history. The authors stress that, for this reason, the lack of attention afforded to

degree of factual sensitivity (in favour of the defendant) than the classical *crassa negligentia* test for determining initial breach of duty itself.[96]

Critics of judicial non-interventionism in corporate law are likely to regard retrospective judicial liability relief as a further protective cushion for negligent directors – alongside ratification and employer-maintained liability insurance – against the obligation to internalise, in money terms, the adverse implications of their mismanagement for shareholders and others. From a private ordering perspective, though, the principle can be said to exhibit a clear functional rationale insofar as it 'fills the gaps' in directors' liability risk coverage that the other available protections necessarily leave open. In particular, judicial relief from liability due to bona fide technicalities or one-off lapses is important in situations where ratification is either impossible or rendered practically redundant, such as where a company is brought under new majority shareholder(s) following a subsequent change of control,[97] or where a misfeasance action is brought against wrongdoers by the liquidator upon the company's winding up.[98] It can furthermore be regarded as an important institutional re-enforcement to D&O liability insurance, insofar as directors and officers inevitably lack full a priori assurance that all aspects of mismanagement will be covered under the terms of their protection policy.

In conclusion, it can thus be said that, in the above ways, the dual institutions of: (i) a liberal shareholder ratification power in respect of bona fide managerial irregularities and improprieties; and (ii) a residual system of discretionary judicial liability relief on a retrospective basis, together fulfil a comparable role in the United Kingdom to that played by exculpation provisions in the US corporate law environment.[99] The notable difference, of course, is that the British form of exculpation operates on an ex

---

the provision should *not* be regarded as an indication of its lack of importance within the wider fabric of UK corporate law. See 'Relief for Directors' Breach of Duty' above n 83, 221.

[96] In considering the more recent (post-1980s) case law on judicial liability relief, a significant factor to take into account is the progressive reformulation of the traditional directorial duty of care that has taken place in the UK over the past two decades, both judicially and under the Companies Act 2006. As a result, the duty has become significantly more objective and rigorous in nature than the traditional *crassa negligentia* threshold, especially as applied to directors of large public companies. On this, see below ch 6 of this volume, pt I.B.(ii).

[97] On the limitations of ratification as a method of directorial liability relief, especially in companies that undergo a subsequent change of control, see above n 82.

[98] Section 212 of the Insolvency Act 1986 expressly empowers a liquidator to pursue suspected directorial wrongdoers on an insolvent company's behalf as part of the winding up proceedings, with a view to recouping funds for the benefit of unsecured creditors.

[99] Notwithstanding, from an empirical point of view there remains understandable cause for uncertainty about the actual extent of the wider economic benefits that are likely to ensue from a system of judicial liability relief. In this regard, Edmunds and Lowry argue that '[b]roadly speaking, it does not seem credible that the availability of relief for breach of duty influences the choice of business form for the owner-manager. Nor is it likely to figure significantly in decisions about accepting directorships in large companies'. See Edmunds and Lowry, 'Relief for Directors' Breach of Duty, above n 83, 199.

post facto rather than ex ante basis. However the basic 'immunising' function of the rules is the same in both legal environments, as is the irrelevance of wider third-party or public concerns to the determination of directorial liability relief within both the US and UK systems. Thus exculpation stands out as a prime example of one of the key themes that this book seeks to highlight: that is, the traditional and intrinsic *privity* of Anglo-American corporate governance law, in the sense of its purported autonomy (within the contractarian paradigm at least) from public policy concerns extraneous to the quasi-contractual interests of core corporate participants (namely shareholders, directors and managers).[100]

III. THE ENDOGENEITY OF THE BRITISH CORPORATE BOARD

In the United Kingdom as elsewhere, it is trite that at the heart of every business corporation sits a board of directors, which is formally appointed by equity holders and bears collective responsibility as a group for the success or failure of the company's business. Moreover, the concept of delegated management in a board – like the doctrines of corporate personality and limited liability – is one of those fundamental legal institutions which not only transcend the peculiarities of different jurisdictions,[101] but also precede the birth of the modern registered company itself. Indeed, over two centuries prior to the enactment of the first British Companies Act, centralised corporate governance by an appointed board was a common institutional feature of state chartered companies and private joint-stock merchant guilds alike.[102]

Whilst the importance of the specialised 'monitoring board' model has increased significantly within the UK listed company sector following recent financial scandals, it remains the case that the basic composition of the *corporate* board is not radically out of keeping with that of other types of complex organisation in Britain. Indeed, boards of directors, governors or trustees are typically regarded as a practical exigency in a variety of contexts including charities, schools, private associations, and – in the form of the 'Cabinet' system – even British government itself.[103] On this

[100] On this, see above ch 3 of this volume, pt I.

[101] See J Armour, H Hansmann and R Kraakman, 'What is Corporate Law?' in Kraakman et al, *The Anatomy of Corporate Law: A Comparative and Functional Approach*, 2nd edn (Oxford, Oxford University Press, 2009) 1, 13.

[102] F Gevurtz, 'The Historical and Political Origins of the Corporate Board of Directors' (2004) 33 *Hofstra Law Review* 89.

[103] Under the British system of Cabinet government, the Prime Minister formally represents 'first amongst equals' rather than a presidential source of authority in the US sense. It is furthermore customary for ministers to maintain something akin to an 'arm's length' or fleeting relationship with the top executives of departments that they are put in charge of, so as to preserve a sufficient level of objectivity to enable the identification of necessary macro-level policy changes unencumbered by the inertia and minutiae of managerial bureaucracy. On this, see S James, *British Cabinet Government*, 2nd edn (London, Routledge, 1999) esp ch 3.

wider institutional level, the essential characteristic of governance by way of a board – aside from its obvious feature of collective decision-making[104] – is the subjection of full-time professionals or specialist administrators to the collective oversight and control of a part-time (and often lay) non-executive panel, which, in theory at least, offers a broader base of expertise and perspectives than that available to narrow-focused technocratic 'insiders'.[105]

In the specific corporate context, not only has the formative development of boards in the United Kingdom occurred largely outside of the institutional strictures of companies legislation, but – more fundamentally – the British board governance model has never been formally entrenched in law. Certainly, all UK-registered companies *must have* directors,[106] and any person appointed as a company director must comply with a multitude of legal responsibilities including the long list of directors' general statutory duties set out in Part 10 of the Companies Act 2006.[107] There are also certain provisions of companies legislation that presuppose the existence of a functioning board, such as the requirements for board approval of self-interested directorial transactions.[108] But at no place in British companies legislation, nor in the recorded English common law, is there any affirmative requirement regarding the creation, structure or composition of corporate boards.[109] Likewise, the formal law has tradi-

---

[104] On this, see SM Bainbridge, 'Why a Board? Group Decisionmaking in Corporate Governance' (2002) 55 *Vanderbilt Law Review* 1, 12–41, previously referred to above ch 4 of this volume, fn 128.

[105] On the capacity of boards to broaden the range and variety of perspectives considered within organisational (particularly corporate) decisions, see A Cadbury, *Corporate Governance and Chairmanship: A Personal View* (Oxford, Oxford University Press, 2002) ch 4; M Mace, *Directors: Myth and Reality*, revised edn (Cambridge MA, Harvard Business School Press, 1986) (first published 1971); R Morck, 'Behavioral Finance in Corporate Governance – Independent Directors and Nonexecutive Chairs', Harvard Institute of Economic Research Discussion Paper No 2037 (April 2007); D Langevoort, 'The Human Nature of Corporate Boards: Law, Norms, and the Unintended Consequences of Independence and Accountability' (2001) 89 *Georgia Law Journal* 797.

[106] Section 154 of the Companies Act 2006 requires that every private company have at least one director, and every public company at least two. Besides the statutory minimum age requirement of 16, however, no further requirements are specified with regard to desired characteristics or qualifications of candidates.

[107] See, in particular, ss 171–77 of the Companies Act.

[108] See, eg Companies Act 2006, ss 175(4)(b), 177(2) and 182(1).

[109] However, on the significant influence of the non-statutory UK Corporate Governance Code in this regard, at least over the past two decades, see below pt V. Main Principle A.1 of the Code provides in particular that '[e]very company should be headed by an effective board which is collectively responsible for the long-term success of the company', thus reaffirming the collective nature of the board's responsibility at common law. On this, see *Re Westmid Packing Services Ltd (No 3)* [1998] BCC 836 (CA) 842 (Lord Woolf MR): 'the collegiate or collective responsibility of the board of directors of a company is of fundamental importance to corporate governance under English company law'.

tionally remained largely silent on the question of how boards should function.[110]

In this regard, UK corporate law is comparatively peculiar. In European civil law jurisdictions such as Germany and The Netherlands, larger companies are subject to mandatory statutory provisions prescribing relatively complex two-tier board structures, which must comprise a 'lower' executive and 'upper' supervisory arm, the latter of which should be structured so as to ensure dual shareholder and employee representation. Even in the United States, whose relatively flexible, common law-based corporate governance system is regarded to be closely analogous to that of the United Kingdom, the tendency nevertheless is for State legislatures to provide a specific statutory basis for the board's existence and powers.[111]

In the United Kingdom, by contrast, such issues formally remain a matter for private ordering under each individual company's articles, although in reality the governmentally-provided Model Articles set an almost universally-adopted default rule in this regard.[112] The principally *facilitative* (and, by implication, substantively *non*-determinative) nature of the legal mechanisms for apportioning power and responsibility at the intra-board and sub-board levels was both recognised and preserved by the government's Company Law Review Steering Group in its far-reaching review of UK company law at the turn of the twenty-first century. In particular, the Steering Group recorded how 'the legal definitions of the role and functions of directors are partly designed to serve the

---

[110] Granted, in respect of large public companies at least, it is the accepted legal position today that where board meetings are duly convened, all directors should actively play their part in the proceedings both by sufficiently informing themselves – within reason – of any necessary particulars in advance of a meeting, and by asking pertinent questions of the company's senior managers during the course of the boardroom discussion. Non-executive directors, in particular, are expected to bring an independent perspective to the board's deliberations and therefore should not rely blindly on the information and opinions provided to them by managerial officers. See *Re Barings Plc (No 5), Secretary of State for Trade and Industry v Baker (No 5)* [1999] 1 BCLC 433; *Equitable Life Assurance Society v Bowley and Others* [2004] 1 BCLC 180; and, in an Australian context, *Daniels v Anderson (1995) 16 ACSR 607 (New South Wales Court of Appeal); Australian Securities and Investments Commission v Healey* [2011] FCA 717, analysed in J Lowry, 'The Irreducible Core of the Duty of Care, Skill and Diligence of Company Directors' (2012) 75 *Modern Law Review* 249. Beyond this, however, the common law is largely unhelpful as an authoritative guide to the proper functions of a corporate board. A much more illuminating – albeit largely *informal* – regulatory statement of the board's core functions is set out today in the UK Corporate Governance Code (see below n 126), Principle A.1 of which expressly sets out the role of the board in the following terms: 'The board's role is to provide entrepreneurial leadership of the company within a framework of prudent and effective controls which enables risk to be assessed and managed. The board should set the company's strategic aims, ensure that the necessary financial and human resources are in place for the company to meet its objectives and review management performance. The board should set the company's values and standards and ensure that its obligations to its shareholders and others are understood and met'. On the UK Corporate Governance Code generally, see below pt IV.

[111] See, eg § 141(a) of the Delaware General Corporation Law, quoted above n 13.

[112] See above nn 15–16.

public interest but are *mainly set by private and contractual arrangement'* (emphasis added).[113] Far from seeing this as a usurpation of the government's policy-making prerogative in the field of corporate governance, the Steering Group regarded such regulatory deference to private ordering to be a source of 'contractual freedom',[114] such 'flexibility [being] a great strength which enables the law to continue to adapt to developing commercial, technological and market demands'.[115]

Against this quasi-contractual institutional backdrop, the fact that British corporate boards have historically tended to adopt roughly similar characteristics – and, more fundamentally, that they exist *at all* in the absence of any formal legal basis for their creation – has lent strong empirical support to proponents of the contractarian paradigm. From this ideological perspective, it can accordingly be surmised that the very existence of a dominant board model in the United Kingdom represents a priori evidence of its economic efficiency and, in turn, its normative acceptability. Thus the functional prevalence of a one-tier, shareholder-oriented and outsider-dominated board model in British public companies today suggests that this particular structure, above all else, has withstood the notional contractarian 'survival of the fittest' contest.[116] Similarly to the aforementioned case of its US counterpart,[117] therefore, the historical development of corporate boards in the United Kingdom would appear fundamentally to affirm the validity of the contractarian board endogeneity hypothesis.[118]

---

[113] Company Law Review Steering Group, *Modern Company Law for a Competitive Economy: Developing the Framework* (March 2000) para 3.3.

[114] Ibid.

[115] Ibid, para 3.10.

[116] In this 'contest', firms are continually driven by the need to raise funds on increasingly competitive international equity and debt markets, forcing the evolution of common corporate governance structures (including an effective monitoring board) which offer credible assurances or 'bonds' to small-scale investors that their capital will not be expropriated or otherwise diminished via mismanagement of the business. For an influential – albeit much criticised – argument asserting the global superiority of the [Anglo-]American corporate board (and general governance) model on this basis, see H Hansmann and R Kraakman, 'The End of History for Corporate Law' (2001) 89 *Georgetown Law Journal* 439. That this particular structure is recommended today by the influential UK Corporate Governance Code, with which all premium-listed companies in the UK are required to comply at the cost of having to account publicly to investors for non-compliance, is arguably of little normative relevance from the above perspective given that the Code expressly purports to represent the consolidation of investor-demanded best practice on governance. On the UK Corporate Governance Code and its underpinning concept of 'comply or explain' generally, see below pt IV.

[117] On this, see above ch 4 of this volume, pt VI.

[118] On this generally, see above ch 3 of this volume, pt III.B.(iii).

IV. MARKET-INVOKING REGULATION

A further distinctive dimension of UK corporate law's rich private order-ing heritage is its extensive resort to non-statist 'soft law' techniques that lie *beyond* the orthodox realm of statutory and common law, and which (theoretically at least) provide scope for flexibility, diversity or opt-out at the point of firm-specific norm application.[119] This comparatively peculiar aspect of UK corporate law can be attributed to the cultural path depend-encies underlying the so-called 'London approach' to financial market regulation,[120] a central characteristic of which is the implicit devolution – by government – of far-reaching regulatory responsibilities to individuals or groups directly affected by the ensuing rules.[121]

In the United Kingdom's financial services sector especially, there is a long history of governmental deference to private rule-making.[122] Indeed, up until 1986, London's securities markets were regulated by a confluence of private bodies representative of the various main classes of professional market participant, who operated without formal statutory powers and independently of the control of any government department or officials.[123] Accordingly, the Listing Rules of the London Stock Exchange traditionally had the status of a private contract between each company listed on the Exchange and the Exchange itself,[124] and thus operated in a manner not fundamentally dissimilar to the rules of a private members' club.[125]

---

[119] The UK Financial Reporting Council has recounted that the City of London 'has a his-tory of encouraging free trade and good corporate governance, based on the application of simple principles to the individual and distinct circumstances of each entity'. See Financial Reporting Council (FRC), *The UK Approach to Corporate Governance* (November 2006).

[120] On this notion generally, see FRC, ibid.

[121] As Cheffins explains, 'the theory is that an institution which acts as a front-line regula-tor will be operated and run primarily by the same class of market practitioner which it supervises'. See B Cheffins, *Company Law: Theory, Structure and Operation* (Oxford, Oxford University Press, 1997) 366.

[122] On this generally, see M Moran, *The Politics of the Financial Services Revolution: The USA, UK and Japan* (London, Macmillan, 1991) 61–68.

[123] On this, see Cheffins, *Company Law*, above n 121, 365.

[124] Cheffins, *Company Law*, above n 121, 368.

[125] This traditional self-regulatory system was curtailed first by the Financial Services Act 1986, which vested the governmental Department of Trade and Industry (and, later, the Treasury) with ultimate regulatory powers with respect to the UK financial services sector (albeit that this power was delegated to the non-governmental Securities and Investment Board (SIB)); and subsequently by the Financial Services and Markets Act 2000, which vested the then-newly-established (non-governmental) Financial Services Authority with directly-exercisable statutory powers in this regard, thereby creating a unitary (as opposed to plural-ist) regulatory regime for the first time. The statutory basis of the SIB and – subsequently – FSA's powers from 1986 onwards means that the modern (post-1986) regulatory regime is more appropriately regarded as 'co-regulatory' (dual public-private) rather than self-regulatory in nature, although the formally *non*-governmental status of the key rule-making bodies therein has persisted. On the concept of co-regulation both in the UK financial services con-text and more generally, see, respectively, Cheffins, *Company Law*, above n 121, 367; I Ayres and J Braithwaite, *Responsive Regulation: Transcending the Deregulation Debate* (Oxford, Oxford

In the field of corporate governance, meanwhile, the so-called 'soft law' phenomenon has manifested itself in two main forms. The first of these is the aforementioned system for regulation of listed company board structures and risk oversight practices under the UK Corporate Governance Code:[126] an informal body of norms promulgated by the non-governmental Financial Reporting Council, and whose enforcement is characterised by the dynamic and (theoretically) investor-driven practice of 'comply or explain'.[127] The second of such forms is the United Kingdom's so-called 'privatised' system of corporate takeover regulation under the remit of the Panel on Takeovers and Mergers: a non-statist rule-making and executive body comprising mainly appointees from financial institutions that are broadly representative of the City of London's institutional shareholder (and associated professional) community. The Panel administers and adjudicates on the application of its influential Takeover Code,[128] and also publishes regular updates to the Code in response to developing market practices.

A common misapprehension that is made about the UK Corporate Governance and Takeover Codes is that they are examples of self-regulation, insofar as each of these sets of norms is promulgated and administered by a regulatory body whose members operate at the proverbial 'coal face' of the operations that they seek to control.[129] Whilst the latter of the above claims is largely true, it does not follow that the ensuing rule systems are thereby vested with a self-regulatory character. Rather, both of the aforementioned Codes – whilst formally classifiable as *non-governmental* in nature – nevertheless operate within the substantial shadow of the regulatory state, insofar as they are expressly sanctioned by

---

University Press, 1992) 102. By contrast, the US securities law regime has for the best part of the past century exhibited a strongly statist, public-regulatory hue, by virtue of the fundamentality to the overall system of the Securities Act 1933 and the Securities Exchange Act 1934, the latter of which establishes the Securities and Exchange Commission (SEC) as a federal governmental agency vested directly with rule-making and enforcement powers.

[126] See Financial Reporting Council (FRC), UK Corporate Governance Code (June 2010), available at: www.frc.org.uk/corporate/ukcgcode.cfm .

[127] On the concept of 'comply or explain' generally, see ibid, 4–5; for a brief historical account of the development of the 'comply or explain' principle in the UK, see MT Moore, '"Whispering Sweet Nothings": The Limitations of Informal Conformance in UK Corporate Governance' (2009) 9 *Journal of Corporate Law Studies* 95, 104–7.

[128] See The Panel on Takeovers and Mergers, The Takeover Code (September 2011), available at: www.thetakeoverpanel.org.uk/wp-content/uploads/2008/11/code.pdf.

[129] The governmental practice of deferring regulatory responsibilities to individuals who are active participants in the field of activity that is to be regulated, is arguably justified in certain contexts on the basis that 'the more complicated and fast-moving the commercial and financial operations that are being regulated, the more difficult it is to create a satisfactory governmental supervisory body. The governmental body may not be close enough to the operations to know what is happening and it may not move quickly enough'. See A Johnston, *The City Take-over Code* (Oxford, Oxford University Press, 1980) 4.

government[130] and also enforced in accordance with powers that are ultimately attributable to formal legislative initiative.[131]

[130] The UK Corporate Governance Code's sponsoring body, namely the FRC, is constituted on a private sector basis in the form of a limited company. However, it operates under indirect government influence insofar as its Chair and Deputy Chair are appointed by the Secretary of State for Business Innovation and Skills. The Chair and Deputy Chair in turn appoint the Council's other board members, who are typically from an institutional investment, industry, accounting or legal-professional background (on this, see below n 137). Furthermore as Brian Cheffins has pointed out, the promulgation of the inaugural version of the Code – by the Cadbury Committee in 1992 – 'was carried out under the shadow of possible government intervention' following a spate of widely-documented financial scandals involving corporate governance lapses in major British companies. See B Cheffins, *Company Law*, above n 121, 375. Whilst the government has no such power of appointment over any member(s) of the Takeover Panel, it would be erroneous to describe the Takeover Code regime as operating entirely independently of governmental interference or influence. The early development of the Code in its inaugural guise in the late 1950s and early 1960s took place amidst growing public and political unease about corporate takeover practices, such that the government-commissioned Jenkins Committee on company law reform was given an explicit mandate to consider the issue (see Report of the Committee (Cmd 1749, 1962)). Furthermore, the establishment of the Takeover Panel in 1968 was effected under significant influence from the Governor of the Bank of England, which also provided the Panel with significant secretarial support and – in the Bank's former Deputy Governor Sir Humphrey Minors – even its first chairman. On this, see Johnston, *The City Take-over Code*, above n 129, chs 3–4. Since then, the Takeover Panel and governmental Department of Trade and Industry (now the Department for Business Innovation and Skills) have coordinated loosely with one another on important issues relating to takeover policy and regulation, against the persisting backdrop of potential statutory intervention by government in the event that the non-statist regulatory framework fails to command continuing market and general public acceptance. This was exemplified most recently in the two bodies' contemporaneous public consultations on reform of takeover regulation in 2010, in light of the widespread criticism of the circumstances surrounding Kraft plc's takeover of Cadbury plc at the beginning of that year. See The Takeover Panel, *Review of Certain Aspects of the Regulation of Takeover Bids* (June 2010), available at: www.thetakeoverpanel.org.uk/wp-content/uploads/2008/11/PCP201002.pdf; House of Commons Business, Innovation and Skills Committee, *Mergers, Acquisitions and Takeovers: The Takeover of Cadbury by Kraft* (HC 234, April 2010), available at: www.publications.parliament.uk/pa/cm200910/cmselect/cmbis/234/234.pdf; Department for Business Innovation and Skills, *A Long-Term Focus for Corporate Britain: A Call for Evidence* (October 2010) ch 6, available at: www.bis.gov.uk/assets/biscore/business-law/docs/l/10-1225-long-term-focus-corporate-britain.pdf.

[131] Although the 'comply or explain' principle underpinning the Code's enforcement means that compliance with its requirements is essentially voluntary, the Code nevertheless cannot be regarded as self-regulatory in form. This is because the Code's application is underpinned by a mandatory disclosure obligation contained in the UK Listing Rules, requiring a company's board to make a dual statement within their statutory annual directors' report as to: (a) how they apply the Main Principles of the Code, detailing the particular governance policies that the board has adopted in order to implement those Principles within the specific and current circumstances of the company's business; and (b) whether the company complies with all of the more specific lower-level Provisions of the Code, together with supporting reasons in the event of non-compliance with any one or more of those Provisions (see UK Listing Rule 9.8.6(5)–(6)). This demonstrates that, on a formal level, the foundation of the Code's coerciveness lies in the UK Listing Authority's delegated statutory powers to enforce the underlying conformance-disclosure obligation, without which the Code's practical impact would almost certainly be nullified. At the time of the Code's inception in its inaugural guise (as the Cadbury Code of Best Practice) in 1992, the UK Listing Authority was the London Stock Exchange. However, contemporaneously with the inception of the first Combined Code on Corporate Governance in 2000, the LSE was replaced in this role by the then-newly formed Financial Services Authority (FSA), whose enforcement powers were considerably stronger than those of its predecessor. It is expected

At the same time, though, successive UK governments have consistently been unwilling to displace the perceived prerogatives of the FRC and Takeover Panel to determine the substantive content of the Codes, or to transplant any core Code provisions onto a legally-binding statutory basis. An important political consequence of this is that the Codes' respective rule systems – in spite of bringing about significant and far-reaching innovations to UK corporate governance practices over recent decades[132] – have nevertheless slipped under the proverbial public policy radar by largely eluding formal democratic scrutiny. Instead, they have derived their general social acceptability from two alternative – albeit overlapping – normative sources.

The first of these is the Codes' reputed quasi-contractual status as relatively flexible[133] and investor-determinable norms, which purport only to consolidate pre-existing 'best practice' rather than having any socially determinative effect in their own right.[134] Accordingly, the Codes could be said to derive their widely-perceived political legitimacy from the Friedmanite notion of market unanimity outlined in chapter three above,

that from 2013, the FSA's responsibilities in this regard – along with further 'stepped-up' enforcement powers – will be reallocated to the proposed new Financial Conduct Authority (FCA) as part of the current coalition government's planned restructuring of the UK's financial regulatory regime. Regarding the Takeover Code, meanwhile, whilst the Code was originally administered on an entirely extra-legal basis, this is no longer the case today. Further to the UK's implementation of the EU Takeover Directive, the existence and functions of the Takeover Panel are now statutorily formalised under sections 942–56 of the Companies Act 2006. As a consequence, the Code's enforcement is today underpinned by a residual avenue of recourse to the formal courts system, which may be invoked on the application of the Panel (under section 955 of the 2006 Act) in the event of a failure to comply with any of its rules or rulings. On this, see below ch 6 of this volume, pt I.B.(iii). A further notable nexus between the Takeover Code and the English courts derives from the Court of Appeal's ruling in *R v Panel on Takeovers and Mergers, ex parte Datafin Ltd* [1987] QB 815, where it was held that the public function performed by the Panel (in spite of its non-statist and financially independent status) rendered its decisions potentially susceptible to judicial review, albeit on a historical rather than contemporaneous basis so as to preclude scope for tactical litigation aimed at stalling the course of a bid in progress.

[132] On this, see below nn 139–42 and accompanying text.

[133] Compliance with the Takeover Code is policed flexibly by means of informal 'real time' communication between the Panel executive and professional intermediaries to tender offers, and the Code's application is reinforced by the threat of mainly reputational sanctions for non-compliance with only very limited available recourse to the formal courts system (on which, see above n 131). By contrast, the US system of takeover regulation is significantly formalised under both federal legislation and State common law, with the result that courts are often heavily involved in determining the outcome of tender offer bids, especially those that are carried out on a hostile or contested basis. On the relative flexibility of the UK system in this regard, see Cheffins, *Company Law*, above n 121, 370; Armour and Skeel, 'Who Writes the Rules?', above n 3, 1729.

[134] As the Cadbury Committee explained in the preface to its inaugural 1992 Code of Best Practice on corporate governance: 'The basic system of corporate governance in Britain is sound. The principles are well known and widely followed. Indeed the Code closely reflects existing best practice. This sets the standard which all listed companies need to match'. See *Report of the Committee on the Financial Aspects of Corporate Governance* (December 1992), para 1.7, available at: www.ecgi.org/codes/documents/cadbury.pdf.

insofar as they commonly seek to reflect rather than displace the collective rational choices of the principal rule 'users' (ie investors).[135]

And, secondly, there is the apparently 'neutral-technocratic'[136] system by which the respective Codes are formulated, whereby leading financial and legal intermediaries devise rules in an apparently practical and politically colourless forum,[137] guided by a prevailing professional sense of what regulatory outcomes are functionally 'correct' – in the sense of optimally efficient – from the perspective of industry and financial market participants generally. According to this view, the purported 'neutrality' – and, by implication, public defensibility – of the Codes inheres in the fact that the members of the relevant rule-making bodies (that is, the FRC and Takeover Panel) are elected exclusively on the basis of their perceived practical expertise in the relevant fields, and correspondingly *not* on account of any particular political or ideological predisposition that they seek to bring to bear on their respective regulatory and supervisory tasks.[138]

---

[135] On this, see above ch 3 of this volume, pt IV.B.(iv).

[136] On this, see M Stokes, 'Company Law and Legal Theory' in W Twining (ed), *Legal Theory and the Common Law* (Oxford, Blackwell, 1986) 155, 177. For an influential sociological exposition of the concept of technocracy, with particular regard to its operation within large-scale business organisations, see JK Galbraith, *Economics and the Public Purpose* (London, Andre Deutsch, 1973) ch 9. In this chapter, I use the term in a different context from the above writers, to explain how the concept of technocracy supports the perceived apolitical neutrality of key corporate governance regulators in the UK, which in turn justifies the public trust that is placed in them to exercise their significant rule-making powers on a non-arbitrary basis outside of the normal checks and balances of the democratic state framework.

[137] By way of illustration, at the time of writing the FRC's board (including its chairman and deputy chair) – from a total number of 16 members – comprises five members from a predominantly investment management background, four from a financial accounting background, two from a legal-professional background, 3.5 from a governmental background and 1.5 from an (non-financial) industry background. The 0.5 figures are attributable to the inclusion within the data sample of the FRC's current chairman Baroness Hogg, whose professional background has spanned both business and government in comparable measures. It should be pointed out that board members from a governmental background participate in the FRC's activities in an entirely non-governmental capacity. Out of the 25 listed members of the Takeover Panel at the time of writing (including the Panel's chairman and two deputy chairmen), meanwhile, nine are from a predominantly institutional investment / investment management background, eight from an investment banking background, three (including Baroness Hogg, who also currently sits on the Takeover Panel) are from a (non-financial) industry background, two are from a legal-professional background (including the current Panel chairman Sir Gordon Langley, a former High Court judge), and there is also one member each from, respectively, a financial accounting, Bank of England and trade union background.

[138] The logic of this approach to establishing regulatory legitimacy is explained by Tony Prosser as follows: '[I]t has been argued that regulation can ideally be accomplished by the application of economic reasoning designed to achieve the single goal of maximising economic efficiency, mainly allocative efficiency. This provides the legitimacy of the regulator through his or her economic expertise; what should be avoided, it is argued, is sullying this with social goals which are for elected governments, not unelected regulators'. T Prosser, 'Theorising Utility Regulation' (1999) 62 *Modern Law Review* 196, 197. Prosser further highlights how, against this normative backdrop, 'avoiding giving social responsibilities to [democratically *un*elected] regulators appears to be supported by a powerful argument from democracy', which is 'that, whilst economic matters can be resolved through the regulators' expertise, social concerns involve matters of policy which can only be determined by Parliament through its democratic mandate'. Ibid, 199.

Therefore, whereas neither the UK Corporate Governance Code nor the Takeover Code can correctly be termed self-regulatory or even market-dependent in nature, both institutions can certainly be referred to as examples of market-*invoking* regulation insofar as the effectiveness of each is predicated on the expected investor reaction to perceived compliance or non-compliance therewith. At the same time, the continuing normative acceptability of each is based principally on private (prudential and professional) rather than public (democratic or policy-based) criteria. On a substantive level, this important institutional characteristic of the Codes is exemplified in their common investor-protectionist ethos, and corresponding disregard for public policy concerns extraneous to considerations of shareholder welfare.

Thus successive corporate governance committees, charged with devising and revising the UK Corporate Governance Code and its predecessors over the past two decades, have maintained a deliberate and consistent disregard for questions as to the rightful beneficiaries of managerial accountability mechanisms. As such, Code reform agendas throughout this period have focused exclusively on the (functional) *means* rather than (normative) ends of purportedly efficient boardroom practice. The main legacy of the UK Corporate Governance Code (and former Combined Code on Corporate Governance), besides the 'comply or explain' enforcement method itself, has been its exaltation of directorial 'independence' – denoting the absence of professional, proprietary, trading or familial links with an employer company – as the principal touchstone of boardroom accountability and effectiveness.[139]

The basic position of the Code in this regard has been manifested in a number of specific ways over recent years, including the near-universalisation of US-style majority-independent boards within large-cap listed companies[140] and also the de facto (albeit not de jure) entrenchment of independent sub-board committees on nominations, audit and remuneration matters as an integral feature of the typical corporate organisational structure.[141] However the FRC, by formally promoting the mantra of directorial independence under the apparent guise of *a*political functionality, has been able to elide grappling with the wider social-distributional implications of the independent board paradigm.

[139] The directorial independence requirement in respect of UK listed companies is contained in Provisions B.1.1–B.1.2 of the UK Corporate Governance Code (above n 126). Provision B.1.2 states that in the case of FTSE 350 companies at least half the board, excluding the chairman, should comprise non-executive directors determined by the board to be independent. Provision B.1.1 establishes a relatively detailed definition of 'independence' for this purpose.

[140] The fact that, under Provision A.2.1 of the Code (above n 126), the chairman should also be an independent non-executive officer means that in effect the Code establishes majority-independent boards as a general norm for FTSE 350 companies in the UK.

[141] See UK Corporate Governance Code, above n 126, Provisions B.2.1, C.3.1 and D.2.1 (respectively).

These include the arguable behavioural effect of independent directors in accentuating within the board's collective mind-set the criterion of shareholder wealth maximisation – reflected in the company's external stock market valuation – as the foremost determinant of corporate effectiveness, vis-à-vis alternative organisational goals such as long-term enterprise sustainability or wider stakeholder welfare.[142]

Likewise, the Takeover Code, with very limited exceptions,[143] is focused exclusively on ensuring the procedural fairness and efficiency of takeover bids from the perspective of a target company's shareholders.[144] The principal doctrinal means established by the Code towards this end are: first, the board passivity or 'no frustration' principle, whereby a target company's directors are prohibited (absent prior shareholder authorisation) from denying shareholders – via the use of preclusive defensive tactics – the opportunity to consider directly any tender offer that is made to them;[145] and, secondly, the effective prohibition – by means of minimum ownership and time thresholds to any tender offer (including the much-lauded mandatory bid rule[146]) – of coercive bids that reduce shareholders' practical capacity to evaluate the offer freely and with exclusive regard to its price and other objective merits.

However, the Code has for the most part remained silent or 'neutral' when it comes to questions concerning the substantive outcomes of takeovers, in terms of the long-term health of a target corporation's business or the wider social implications of corporate control changes including their impact on workers' welfare.[147] At the same time, though, the Code has lent

---

[142] For an influential academic argument to this effect (albeit written in a US context), see J Gordon, 'The Rise of Independent Directors in the US, 1950–2005: Of Shareholder Value and Stock Market Prices' (2007) 59 *Stanford Law Review* 1465. However, on the purported negative correlation between directorial independence and firm-specific expertise (and the arguably adverse economic implications thereof), see Y Biondi, P Giannoccolo and A Reberioux, 'Financial Disclosure and the Board: A Case for Non-independent Directors', Bologna University Department of Economics Working Paper No 689 (20 January 2010), available at: papers.ssrn.com/sol3/papers.cfm?abstract_id=1540027 .

[143] See, eg the (somewhat outlying) labour-centric requirement in Rule 24.2 of the Takeover Code to the effect that the offeror 'state its intentions with regard to the future business of the offeree company and explain the long-term commercial justification for the offer', detailing (inter alia) 'its intentions with regard to the continued employment of the employees and management of the offeree company and of its subsidiaries, including any material change in the conditions of employment'; and also 'its strategic plans for the offeree company, and their likely repercussions on employment and the locations of the offeree company's places of business'. See The Takeover Code, above n 128, p J3.

[144] As emphasised in a leading historical account of the Code regime by one of the original Panel members, 'the Code is concerned with the procedures by which take-over bids are conducted. It deals with ways and means. The Code is not concerned with whether take-overs generally or individually are good or bad'. Johnston, *The City Take-over Code*, above n 129, 'Preface'.

[145] See The Takeover Code, above n 128, General Principle 3 (p B1) and Rule 21 (p I13).

[146] See The Takeover Code, above n 128, Rule 9 (p F1).

[147] The traditional view of the Takeover Panel on such issues – as explained by Sir Alexander Johnston – is that '[w]hether mergers and take-overs should be encouraged or

significant *implicit* ideological support to the takeover mechanism, and the ensuing market for corporate control, by formally and consistently hallmarking unimpeded 'outside' control challenges as a legitimate mechanism of shareholder protection and business efficiency in the United Kingdom for over half a century.[148]

In the above respects, therefore, the British phenomenon of market-invoking regulation has progressively extended the reach of contractarian rationality – and its associated notion of legal privity[149] – into further central aspects of UK corporate governance. In the process it has had the tacit political effect of implementing, on a far-reaching scale, some core institutional preconditions of effective managerial accountability to shareholders – including majority-independent boards and unrestrained corporate control contests.[150] Insofar as such regulatory developments have taken place outside of the orthodox democratic-legal process, however, they have for the most part been *unaccompanied* by surrounding public policy debate as to the desirability or otherwise of their overall social effect.

V. SUMMARY

From the comparative analysis of the last two chapters it can be observed that: whereas the US legal qualities of competitive-federalism and 'opt-out' permit significant scope for private ordering *within* the interstices of the formal (statutory and common) law itself; the apparently flexible and

discouraged is a matter of public policy to be considered by the Government and ultimately by Parliament', whereas the appropriate jurisdiction of the Panel extends only to 'the methods by which take-over bids [are] effected'. See *The City Take-over Code*, above n 129, 8. That this basic position persists today is clear from the introduction to the current version of the Code, which states that: 'The Code is not concerned with the financial or commercial advantages or disadvantages of a takeover. These are matters for the offeree company and its shareholders. In addition, it is not the purpose of the Code either to facilitate or to impede takeovers. Nor is the Code concerned with those issues, such as competition policy, which are the responsibility of government and other bodies'. See The Takeover Code, above n 128, Introduction, section 2(a) (p A.1).

[148] Indeed, in the introduction to the inaugural version of what is today the Takeover Code, namely the Notes on Amalgamations of British Businesses, formulated by a group of leading City representative bodies in 1959, is was stated – in strikingly normative terms – that '[t]he [takeover] process is a natural one and, since it is generally based on the best utilisation of physical capacity, managerial experience and available labour, it has almost always proved to be in the national interest' such that 'it is . . . important that it should continue and should not be artificially impeded'. See The Issuing Houses Association, 'Notes on Amalgamations of British Businesses' (1959), cited in Johnston, *The City Take-over Code*, above n 129, 20.

[149] For an explanation of this concept, see above ch 3 of this volume, pt I.

[150] On the effect of hostile takeovers in magnifying the relative significance of shareholder welfare vis-à-vis that of other corporate constituents (most notably workers), see A Schleifer and L Summers, 'Breach of Trust in Hostile Takeovers' in A Auerbach (ed), *Corporate Takeovers: Causes and Consequences* (Chicago, University of Chicago Press, 1991) (first published 1988) ch 2; S Deakin and G Slinger, 'Hostile Takeovers, Corporate Law, and the Theory of the Firm' (1997) 24 *Journal of Law and Society* 124, 144.

'tailor-made' quality of UK corporate governance law derives instead from the governmental propensity to devolve much rule-making responsibility to substitute non-state actors, whether to a company's shareholders via the corporate constitution, or else to investor-representative regulatory agencies such as the FRC or Takeover Panel situated outside of the formal public realm. An important quasi-contractual feature of both systems, meanwhile, is their common tradition of judicial deference to privately-determined firm arrangements and decisions: a position achieved under Delaware law by means of the business judgment rule, and in the United Kingdom via the comparatively permissive[151] internal management doctrine.

As the above discussion in this chapter has illustrated, the British legal phenomena of contractual flexibility, judicial non-interventionism, board endogeneity and market-invoking regulation together have had the remarkable – albeit implicit – normative effect of presenting existing UK corporate governance rules and institutions as the outcome of decentralised and fundamentally consensual private ordering processes. Similarly to the case with the corresponding features of US law analysed in the previous chapter, the ultimate outcome of this has been to portray core concerns pertaining to the allocation of corporate power and influence between managers and shareholders as issues that are readily resolvable via market-driven private ordering methods alone.

With respect to the task of establishing effective managerial accountability norms, the legal doctrines documented above appear designed to play, at best, a 'back seat' facilitative role – by providing a broad procedural structure to the decentralised determination of such matters at a micro level, without seeking to usurp the substantive outcomes established contractually on a firm-specific basis. Furthermore, the fact that many important managerial accountability norms in the United Kingdom are embodied in the form of non-statist, market-invoking forms of regulation infers that such issues appropriately lie beyond the reach of direct governmental ordering, except where the motivation for such intervention is the *a*political facilitation of efficient rule selection and design by private actors. In short, then, the UK system of corporate governance law has, like its US counterpart, evolved along a trajectory that – to a significant extent – is appropriate to an area of *contractually* determinable and market-*facilitative* private law, as opposed to an aspect of *democratically* determinable and market-*controlling* public or regulatory law.

As I will seek to demonstrate in the following chapter, however, the contractarian paradigm ultimately provides only a limited rationalisation of Anglo-American corporate governance law as a whole. This is because

---

[151] That is to say, permissive in favour of corporate directors and managers' executive discretion.

many crucial aspects of corporate governance in the United States and United Kingdom are governed by mandatory rules whose characteristics are more regulatory than contractual in nature, thus rendering them prima facie more consistent with a public-statist – rather than private-contractarian – understanding of the corporate rule-making function. Moreover, as I will also show in chapter six, even those dimensions of Anglo-American corporate governance law that can properly be termed 'contractual' in nature are – to a significant extent – *themselves* dependent for their effective functioning on an underpinning body of mandatory rules and institutions whose continuing existence necessarily lies *beyond* the permissible boundaries of private ordering. The significant analytical implications of these observations, in reshaping common scholarly under-standings of how and why many important corporate governance laws develop within the Anglo-American environment, will subsequently be the focus of chapter seven.

6

The (Expanding) Regulatory Dimensions of Anglo-American Corporate Governance Law

T HE PREVIOUS CHAPTERS have demonstrated that, within the contractarian paradigm of corporate governance, legal rules in respect of the structure and operation of business firms derive their perceived effectiveness largely from their inherent qualities of flexibility and practical instrumentality. Therefore, from a functional or economic perspective, it is commonly argued that corporate governance norms should be readily adaptable and reversible so as to be responsive to the individual preferences of key corporate participants (principally shareholders and managers) as expressed in the market-determined 'bargains' that they are notionally inclined to strike with one another.[1] From a political point of view, meanwhile, flexible and reversible rules could be said to resonate with the basic pluralist values of liberal civil society, on account of their apparent status as the product of decentralised private ordering as distinct from governmental imposition or 'grand design'.[2]

In this chapter, however, I will identify fundamental aspects of Anglo-American corporate governance law that are – at least at first sight – *inconsistent* with the contractarian paradigm due to their inherently mandatory or regulatory character. I will seek to demonstrate that the widespread and expanding presence of mandatory rules within both the US and UK corporate governance frameworks represents a major empirical aberration to the contractarian depiction of legal-institutional evolution as an essentially organic and decentralised process of private norm selection.

I should point out that this chapter's analysis will not be concerned with mandatory aspects of corporate law that directly concern the interests of third parties extraneous to the 'core' shareholder-management relation. This category includes the (limited) creditor-protective dimension of the director's duty of loyalty,[3] and also wider 'public interest' protections such

---

[1] On this, see above ch 4 of this volume, pt I.
[2] On this, see above ch 3 of this volume, pt IV.B.
[3] On this, see above ch 2 of this volume, fns 9–10 and accompanying text.

as the statutory directors' disqualification procedure[4] and Companies Act 1985 investigation procedure[5] in the United Kingdom. Since these types of regulatory protection are focused on the interests of parties who ordinarily are not entitled to influence intra-firm governance affairs, they are generally uncontroversial from a contractarian perspective,[6] and hence do not merit detailed evaluation in the context of the present discussion.

My focus in this chapter, rather, is on the extent to which mandatory regulation is determinative of the key legal-institutional features of the equity relation that lies at the heart of the corporate decision-making structure. To the extent that important aspects of this relation are attributable to public-regulatory rather than private-contractual dynamics, it can be argued that corporate governance law is fulfilling a fundamentally *paternalistic* function in displacing or pre-empting otherwise self-determinable contractual outcomes pertaining to intra-firm governance issues. Furthermore, the necessarily universalistic nature of mandatory rules in corporate governance puts into question the common contractarian claim that the task of designing effective intra-firm managerial accountability norms is most appropriately fulfilled on a micro-prudential basis in response to capital market signals at the individual firm level.

Notwithstanding the significant contractual dimensions of US and UK corporate governance law as detailed in the preceding two chapters, it is nonetheless a somewhat inconvenient truth for contractarian theorists that a number of important corporate governance concerns in these two systems are resolved in a manner that, on initial reflection at least, is *antithetical to* private ordering logic. Indeed, UK corporate governance law has for a long time exhibited significant mandatory components, and recent developments in the US system would suggest that it is likewise coming to embrace mandatory rules to an appreciable extent, at least with respect to major governance issues arising in the listed company sector. These mandatory rules, it will be shown, are instrumental in shaping the contours of the corporation's internal decision-making structure under both national legal frameworks. On a more fundamental level, meanwhile, it can justifiably be said that the very institutional foundations of private ordering in the US and UK systems are, paradoxically, *themselves* ultimately the product of public-regulatory intervention.

The observations of this chapter have major implications for the core themes of this book. In particular, they represent an empirical challenge to

---

[4] On this, see above ch 5 of this volume, fn 74.

[5] On this, see Companies Act 1985, Part XIV; E Walker-Arnott, 'Company Law, Corporate Governance and the Banking Crisis' (2010) *International Corporate Rescue – Special Edition* 3, esp 9–10.

[6] But this is only insofar as their function is restricted to that of mitigating the occasional externalities that result from managerial (and, indirectly, shareholder) pursuit of private wealth-maximising outcomes, as opposed to altering or obfuscating the ultimate (shareholder) inclination of managerial accountability norms in corporate law.

the implicit contractarian assertion that effective managerial accountability norms can be elicited at the micro level via legally-facilitated private ordering practices alone. The significant extent to which mandatory rules are determinative of intra-firm governance norms and practices in the United States and United Kingdom suggests that regulatory-state interventionism at the broader, macro level has in fact *superseded* private ordering as the principal institutional driver of many characteristic features of the law in this area. Consequently, this chapter's findings lay down a challenge for defenders of the contractarian paradigm of corporate governance to provide a convincing theoretical explanation for the prima facie outlying empirical aspects of their subject-matter.

The discussion in this chapter is thus structured as follows. In part I, I will highlight the most noteworthy recent developments in Anglo-American corporate governance law that arguably are indicative of a 'de-privatisation' trend: that is to say, the removal of a partial but significant body of norms and practices from the realm of firm-specific private ordering, and their replacement with mandatory publicly-determined rules as entrenched in legislative or regulatory form.

Throughout the remainder of the chapter, I will examine more generally those aspects of Anglo-American corporate governance law concerning the protection of shareholders' interests vis-à-vis managers that arguably challenge the contractarian claim as to corporate law's privity. Such provisions – by virtue of their inherently regulatory character – imply the displacement of contractual private ordering in favour of state-promulgated public policy as the principal determinant of corporate governance rules and institutions.

To this end, in part II, I will highlight the mandatory nature of corporate disclosure regulation – a fact which, moreover, is widely accepted by many scholars who otherwise espouse the benefits of flexibility and private ordering in corporate governance. I will demonstrate the normative significance for contractarians of conceptually distinguishing (private) corporate law from (public) securities law, which allows for the convenient compartmentalisation of regulatory disclosure requirements, so that they do not appear to threaten the characteristically contractual nature of notionally 'internal' corporate governance laws. Ultimately, though – as I will show – the distinction between the purportedly distinct fields of corporate and securities law is both empirically and logically unsustainable, with the outcome that contractarians are compelled to accept the fact of mandatory disclosure regulation as a core and unavoidable component of modern corporate governance law.

In part III, I will analyse what is arguably the most noteworthy factor distinguishing the 'Anglo' in the Anglo-American descriptor. That is, the significant degree to which the structural division of power between shareholders and the board at the heart of UK corporations is attributable to mandatory regulatory rules, as enshrined most recently in the Companies Act 2006. Here I will demonstrate, moreover, that the very notion of private ordering in UK corporate governance law is fundamentally paradoxical, in that it is contingent on the operation of certain underlying constitutive rules, which are mandatory in nature and together establish – on a centralised, macro basis – the institutional parameters of the decentralised norm selection process to the extent that it operates at the micro level.

Finally, in part IV, I will study the most fundamental and longstanding aspect of shareholder empowerment in the Anglo-American legal environment, which is the equitable fiduciary principle as originally established by the English Chancery courts in the pre-industrial (and, indeed, pre-*corporate*) era. As I will show, in spite of influential contractarian protestations to the contrary, the fiduciary doctrine is – by its very intrinsic nature – *not* a contractually removable or determinable phenomenon. On the contrary, it is a central and underpinning structural precondition of the extensive discretionary administrative power that is habitually vested by law in corporate directors (and, indirectly, managers), in the various ways documented in earlier chapters. Consequently, far from being a removable obstacle to the free possession and exercise of discretionary decision-making power by corporate managers vis-à-vis shareholders, the mandatory existence of the fiduciary principle is logically necessary to the continuing legitimacy – and sustainability – of the equity relation's reciprocal power imbalance.

Discussion of the principal ways in which defenders of the contractarian paradigm have responded to the above revelations, together with the empirical and logical limitations of these responses, will be reserved for the next chapter.

I. THE 'DE-PRIVATISATION' OF ANGLO-AMERICAN CORPORATE GOVERNANCE LAW?

A. Developments in the United States

(i) Sarbanes-Oxley

Academic concern about a perceived 'de-privatisation' trend in corporate governance law has been expressed most vehemently in the United States, which over recent years has witnessed increasing federal government involvement in the traditionally State-dominated realm of internal corporate governance affairs. Regulatory limitations on the permissible scope of private ordering in US corporate governance have tended to derive from the expanding involvement of federal government in corporate governance, a process which has been described (in somewhat pejorative terms) as one of federal regulatory 'creep'.[7]

A major consequence of the longstanding internal affairs doctrine in US corporate law – which regards the regulation of intra-corporate decision-making processes as being the exclusive preserve of individual States[8] – is that federal interventions in this area have historically tended to take the form of securities market measures aimed principally at enhancing the public transparency of corporate performance and dealings.[9] With limited exceptions (such as the federally-prescribed system of proxy solicitation under SEC Rule 14[10]), these interventions have tended to affect US corporate governance practices only in an *indirect* and largely uncontroversial way, insofar as informationally efficient securities markets are widely regarded as an institutional pre-requisite of effective managerial monitoring and private rule selection within widely-held corporations.[11]

In a notable recent break from this trend, however, the corporate governance components of the 2002 Sarbanes-Oxley[12] and 2010 Dodd-Frank[13] Acts have sought – respectively – to increase directly the formal accountability of listed company boards to shareholders, and to empower shareholders to influence matters formerly subject to the exclusive prerogative of the board under State law.[14] Both Acts take the form of wide-reaching legislative or regulatory measures that, whilst formally billed as *extra*-corporate financial reforms, have nevertheless had a considerable 'overspill' impact on *intra*-corporate governance norms and practices. From an orthodox contractarian point of view, these developments are doubly controversial insofar as they represent a limited erosion of the traditional division of law-making functions between federal and

---

[7] See, eg SM Bainbridge, 'Is "Say on Pay" Justified?', *Regulation* (Spring 2009) 42, 44, who claims that '[w]e live in an era of creeping federalization of corporate law'.

[8] On this doctrine generally, see above ch 4 of this volume, fns 19–23 and accompanying text.

[9] The dual legislative basis of the federal government's securities law-making function in the US is the Securities Act of 1933 and the Securities Exchange Act of 1934, together with regulations promulgated thereunder by the US securities market regulator (itself established under the latter Act), the Securities and Exchange Commission (SEC).

[10] On this generally, see above ch 4 of this volume, fns 97–99 and accompanying text.

[11] On this, see above ch 3 of this volume, fn 103 and accompanying text.

[12] See The Public Company Accounting Reform and Investor Protection Act of 2002 (Pub L 107-204) (SOX). The shorthand title of the Act is derived from the surnames of Senators Paul Sarbanes (Democrat) and Michael G Oxley (Republican), who were the Act's co-sponsors.

[13] See The Dodd-Frank Wall Street Reform and Consumer Protection Act of 2010 (Pub L 111-203) (Dodd-Frank). The Act was named after Chris Dodd, chairman of the US Senate Banking Committee; and Barney Frank, chairman of the US House of Representatives' Financial Services Committee.

[14] For a comprehensive and detailed evaluation of these two extensive legislative initiatives, see, respectively: SM Bainbridge, *The Complete Guide to Sarbanes-Oxley* (Avon, Adams Media, 2007); D Skeel, *The New Financial Deal: Understanding the Dodd-Frank Act and its (Unintended) Consequences* (Hoboken NJ, Wiley, 2011).

State level, and also a regulatory concretisation of formerly flexible governance practices.[15]

The first such prima facie financial reform measure with a corporate law 'sting in the tail' was the Sarbanes-Oxley (or SOX) Act of 2002,[16] which was enacted in the immediate wake of the Enron and WorldCom scandals at the turn of the century. SOX was presented as a comprehensive regulatory response to the extensive accounting fraud and financial audit failures exposed in the aftermath of these and other high-profile corporate collapses of the time.

From a private ordering perspective, arguably the most controversial implication of SOX for US corporate governance was its 'top-down' implementation of compulsory intra-firm accountability processes that, in terms of procedural rigour, went significantly above and beyond previously accepted norms of self-regulatory best practice. Most notable in this regard are the oft-criticised internal control requirements laid down by sections 302 and 404 of SOX. Taken together, these provisions have the effect of vesting a corporation's senior managerial officers – and, in particular the Chief Executive Officer and Chief Finance Officer – with responsibility to act as ultimate guardians of the firm's internal system of financial information flows by formally certifying the reliability and integrity thereof.[17]

Prior to 2002, the offices of CEO and especially CFO had been regarded as contractually contingent organisational functions. Accordingly, the existence and contours of these offices were determinable privately by boards in exercise of their inherent right to delegate and sub-divide executive powers on a flexible and discretionary basis, and to structure a firm's managerial hierarchy accordingly.[18] However, a largely unwelcome by-product of SOX has been its effect in affording express statutory recognition to the formerly endogenous CEO and CFO positions, thereby establishing these phenomena as formal legal role definitions.[19]

Other post-Enron regulatory measures in the United States took the (comparatively less controversial) approach of concretising previously informal and self-regulatory norms of best practice on a mandatory and

---

[15] On this, see A Barden, 'US Corporate Law Reform Post-Enron: A Significant Imposition on Private Ordering of Corporate Governance?' (2005) 5 *Journal of Corporate Law Studies* 167; Bainbridge, 'Is "Say on Pay" Justified?', above n 7, 44–46.

[16] See above n 12.

[17] In essence, section 404 of SOX imposes a mandatory requirement on US listed corporations to document and disclose their enterprise-wide system of internal financial information flows. Section 301, meanwhile, requires the CEO and CFO each to certify personally the reliability and integrity of the annual financial statements that result therefrom.

[18] Under Delaware law, such organisational freedom is expressly permitted under § 141(c)(2) of the DGCL, which provides boards with the licence to delegate managerial powers within the firm however they see fit.

[19] I am indebted to Professor Charles O'Kelley for first highlighting this development to me in personal conversation.

legally-prescribed basis. The most notable such reforms were the introduction in US stock exchange listing rules of express requirements for
majority-independent boards[20] and fully-independent sub-board nominating and compensation committees,[21] together with a detailed supporting definition of directorial 'independence' for these purposes.[22] Also
noteworthy in this regard was the more demanding definition of independence established under section 301 of SOX for application to audit
committees.[23] Whilst these latter types of reform – unlike the former – did
not in general seek to elicit fundamental change in established practices,
they were nevertheless problematic from a contractarian perspective in
that they both universalised and formalised certain corporate governance
norms that had previously been susceptible to inter-firm variation or
occasional exception.

(ii) Dodd-Frank

More recently, the Obama administration's principal legislative response
to the financial crisis of 2007 and 2008, namely the Dodd-Frank Wall Street
Reform and Consumer Protection Act of 2010,[24] has continued in the trend
of SOX by introducing significant federal amendments to US corporate
governance under the apparent head of financial regulatory reform.
However, in contrast to SOX's focus on reforming the internal monitoring
function of corporate boards, the corporate governance aspect of Dodd-
Frank was concerned primarily with increasing the direct external influence of shareholders within the corporate decision-making process.

In particular, Dodd-Frank sought (inter alia) to recalibrate the traditional State law division of power between boards and shareholders in the
latter group's favour with a view to ensuring greater managerial accountability and improved standards of shareholder risk oversight. The two
principal regulatory innovations that Dodd-Frank sought to introduce in
purported fulfilment of this objective were: (i) shareholder access to the
corporate election ballot; and (ii) the introduction of precatory 'say on
pay' procedures within US listed firms.

Under the first of these reforms, the Securities and Exchange Commission
was vested with delegated statutory authority to formulate rules permitting shareholders of US listed corporations to nominate their own candidates for election to the board of directors.[25] This so-called 'proxy access'
provision was designed so as to permit significant change to be made to the

---

[20] See New York Stock Exchange Listed Company Manual, § 303A.01.
[21] See ibid, § 303A.04–303A.05.
[22] See ibid, § 303A.02.
[23] See SOX, above n 12, § 301(3).
[24] See above n 13.
[25] See Dodd-Frank, above n13, § 971.

long-established traditional process for electing directors in US corporations, whereby the board of directors (and, indirectly, management) itself is
vested with the exclusive right to determine the particular 'slate' of candidates that will be proposed to shareholders for election or re-election to the
board each year.[26]

In exercise of its rule-making authority in this regard, the SEC in 2010
promulgated the highly controversial Exchange Act Rule 14a-11. Proposed
SEC Rule 14a-11 purported to allow any 'significant, long-term'[27] shareholder satisfying certain minimum ownership and holding requirements[28]
to have their directorial nominee or nominees[29] included in the proxy voting card that is circulated by the corporation in advance of its annual
shareholders' meeting,[30] alongside and in opposition to those candidates
nominated by the board.

By virtue of the second of the above reforms, shareholders of US-listed
corporations were statutorily vested with the collective right to pass a
periodic precatory[31] (ie advisory) vote on the compensation arrangements
for executive officers.[32] This is an amended version of the so-called 'say on
pay' procedures that have been a fixture of UK public company Annual
General Meetings since 2002.[33] Under Dodd-Frank, the shareholder 'say
on pay' vote, whilst compulsory, is nevertheless not legally binding on the
board. It therefore does not interfere with the latter's ultimate formal
authority over the determination of employee compensation.[34] The
intended purpose of requiring corporations to convene a special compen-

---

[26] Accordingly, shareholders' traditional role in the corporate election process is, in the
ordinary course of things, restricted to that of giving or withholding approval in respect of
the board's nominations on an ex post facto basis. On this, see LA Bebchuk, 'The Case for
Shareholder Access to the Ballot' (2003) 59 *The Business Lawyer* 43.

[27] See US Securities and Exchange Commission, 'SEC Adopts New Measures to Facilitate
Director Nominations by Shareholders', Press Release, 25 August 2010, available at: www.
sec.gov/news/press/2010/2010-155.htm.

[28] Specifically, the Rule would have required a shareholder to have held at least three per
cent of the company's voting equity capital on a continuous basis for at least three years,
before being entitled to invoke the directorial nomination procedure.

[29] Under the proposed Rule, a qualifying shareholder would have been entitled to nominate one director, or a number of directors together constituting no more than 25 per cent of
the seats on the company's board of directors (whichever is greater).

[30] On the corporate proxy procedure generally, see above ch 4 of this volume, fn 99.

[31] On precatory resolutions generally, see above ch 4 of this volume, fns 104–5 and accompanying text.

[32] See Dodd-Frank, above n 13, § 951.

[33] See Companies Act 2006, ss 420–22; Large and Medium-sized Companies and Groups
(Accounts and Reports) Regulations 2008 (SI 2008/410) Sch 8. On the UK experience of 'say
on pay', see JN Gordon, '"Say on Pay": Cautionary Notes on the UK Experience and the
Case for Shareholder Opt-In' (2009) 46 *Harvard Journal on Legislation* 323. On the recent (2012)
UK government proposal to vest statutory 'say on pay' votes with legally-binding effect, see
Department for Business Innovation and Skills, 'Directors' Pay: Consultation on Revised
Remuneration Reporting Regulations' (June 2012) 10.

[34] Such authority is a consequence of the board's general constitutional primacy over
managerial affairs under § 141(a) of the DGCL. On this, see above ch 2 of this volume, pt I.D.

sation approval vote is rather to improve the board's de facto external accountability to shareholders on executive pay issues, by increasing the transparency of its contractual dealings on these matters. In this way, the threat of investor and public opprobrium is relied on as an effective disincentive to the setting of egregiously large, cost-ineffective or excessively risk-inducing compensation awards.

In a clear rejection of the contractarian paradigm, the SEC resolutely adopted the position that the proposed Rule 14a-11 proxy access requirement should supersede any conflicting rules of State law, and also that its effect should be incapable of reversal or reduction by means of any corporate constitutional 'opt out' provision.[35] Likewise, whilst the SEC proposed to grant a degree of leeway to firms in respect of the frequency of 'say on pay' resolutions,[36] the rule's basic position was nevertheless that such votes *must* be held at least once every three years, regardless of whether there is material investor demand to this effect.[37]

In spite of the considerable procedural and substantive limitations on the above regulatory provisions,[38] both the proxy access and 'say on pay' reforms attracted widespread criticism within the business and academic communities for a number of reasons.[39] A prominent cause of concern has been the common perception of these rules as a further sharp lurch in the direction of widespread federalisation of 'core' US corporate law, and the concomitant threat that this poses to corporate law's traditional private ordering dynamic.[40] A further source of unease has been the fact that,

---

[35] See Securities and Exchange Commission, 'Facilitating Shareholder Director Nominations (Final Rule)', 15 November 2010, where the Commission emphasised in avowedly *anti*-contractarian terms that: 'corporate governance is not merely a matter of private ordering. Rights, including shareholder rights, are artifacts of law, and in the realm of corporate governance some rights cannot be bargained away but rather are imposed by statute. There is nothing novel about mandated limitations on private ordering in corporate governance'. Ibid, 17. To exemplify this proposition, the Commission referred to the widely-acknowledged fact that '[n]o provision of the federal securities laws can be waived by referendum'. Ibid, 19.

[36] Specifically, the SEC proposed that 'say on pay' votes be permitted either on a yearly, two-yearly or three-yearly basis, as determined by a company's shareholders via a separate resolution on 'say on pay' vote frequency, itself to be held at least once every six years. Furthermore, in addition to being able to pass an informed vote on a company's executive compensation arrangements generally, shareholders must also be afforded the contemporaneous opportunity (whether yearly, two-yearly or three-yearly) to approve (or, alternatively, reject) any 'golden parachute' agreements whereby the firm's executive officers are due additional compensation in the event of the acquisition, merger, consolidation, sale, or other disposition of all, or substantially all, of its assets. See Dodd-Frank, above n 13, § 951(b).

[37] On the arguable rigidity and over-inclusiveness of this requirement, see Gordon, 'Say on Pay', above n 33.

[38] See above nn 28–31 and accompanying text.

[39] See, eg Gordon, 'Say on Pay', above n 33; Bainbridge, 'Is "Say on Pay" Justified?', above n 7; BS Sharfman, 'Why Proxy Access is Harmful to Corporate Governance' (2012) 37 *Journal of Corporation Law* 387; M Kahan and E Rock, 'The Insignificance of Proxy Access' (2011) 97 *Virginia Law Review* 1347; JE Fisch, 'The Destructive Ambiguity of Federal Proxy Access' (2012) 61 *Emory Law Journal* 435; WW Bratton and ML Wachter, 'The Case Against Shareholder Empowerment' (2010) 158 *University of Pennsylvania Law Review* 653.

[40] See, eg Bainbridge, 'Is "Say on Pay" Justified?', above n 7, 44.

since the relevant rules' mandatory status renders them unsusceptible to bargaining and market 'pricing' by those persons whose interests are directly affected by them (ie investors and managers), they are correspondingly more likely to exhibit inefficiencies and, consequently, to have an overall wealth-*reducing* effect on the US corporate sector as a whole.[41]

On a substantive level, meanwhile, both provisions were attacked as unwarranted intrusions into the deeply entrenched prerogative of boards under US State law to exercise supreme and untrammelled decision-making authority over all aspects of corporate management, which extends to questions concerning the proposed composition and financial compensation of a firm's top executive team.[42] It was feared that uninformed investors – when empowered in either of the above ways – would be liable to impede the intricate prudential determination by management of complex and firm-specific personnel issues.[43] Moreover, insofar as the corporation's characteristic central command structure is regarded as a contractually-determined phenomenon at root,[44] the implication follows that any regulatory attempt to subvert this position – even for the express purpose of shareholder empowerment – is an unwarranted public usurpation of shareholders' rationally expressed preferences as to the proper delegation of executive authority within the firm.

In respect of the proxy access issue at least, the above debate has since been rendered largely academic (in the pejorative sense) in light of the July 2011 decision of the DC Circuit Court of Appeals in *Business Roundtable v Securities Exchange Commission*,[45] which struck down proposed SEC Rule 14a-11 on Administrative Procedure Act grounds.[46] Notwithstanding the invalidation of Rule 14a-11, the SEC nevertheless proceeded with the introduction of proxy access on a non-mandatory 'opt-in' basis by removing the former restriction in Rule 14a-8 on the tabling of shareholder resolutions relating to the reform of directorial election procedures.[47] The effect has been to slant the private ordering process considerably more in shareholders' favour while leaving companies ultimately free to deter-

[41] See, eg Sharfman, 'Why Proxy Access is Harmful to Corporate Governance', above n 39. However, for a counter-perspective alleging the substantial *immateriality* of the SEC's proposed proxy access reforms, see Kahan and Rock, 'The Insignificance of Proxy Access', above n 39.

[42] See Sharfman, ibid, 399–401; Bainbridge, 'Is "Say on Pay" Justified?', above n 7, 46–47.

[43] See, eg Sharfman, above n 41, 402–6; Bratton and Wachter, 'The Case Against Shareholder Empowerment', above n 39, 696–705.

[44] On this, see above ch 3 of this volume, pt III.B.(ii).

[45] *Business Roundtable v Securities Exchange Commission* 647 F 3d 1144 (DC Cir 2011).

[46] An analysis of the specific (mainly administrative law) grounds for the Court's decision in this case is beyond the scope of the present study. However, for a critical examination of the decision, see JR Brown, 'Shareholder Access and Uneconomic Economic Analysis: Business Roundtable v SEC' (2011) 88 *Denver University Law Review Online*, available at: ssrn.com/abstract=1917451; JE Fisch, 'The Long Road Back: Business Roundtable and the Implications for Future SEC Rule-Making' (2012) 97 *Seattle University Law Review* (forthcoming).

[47] On this, see above ch 4 of this volume, fns 120–24 and accompanying text.

mine their own procedures for nomination of directors, as opposed to supplanting private ordering altogether with a regulatorily-determined election procedure.

In any event, the equally controversial 'say on pay' reform has successfully been brought into effect, and – even though the proxy access issue is now off the policy agenda (at least for the foreseeable future) – the Rule 14a-11 experience as a whole stands as evidence of the federal government's political resolve to attempt to override US (State) corporate law's traditional private ordering dynamic where political circumstances apparently necessitate a more interventionist regulatory stance.[48]

B. Developments in the United Kingdom

(i) The Comparatively Uncontroversial Nature of Shareholder Empowerment in the United Kingdom

In the markedly different legal culture and political climate of the United Kingdom, there is evidence to indicate a corresponding de-privatisation trend in corporate governance law over recent years. Just as the US reforms recounted above have proved controversial within that country's peculiar federalist and market-liberal law-making environment, some recent developments in the United Kingdom have created challenges that are in large part specific to Britain's own path-dependent corporate governance system.

Notably, however, the thorny American concern of empowering shareholders vis-à-vis boards and managers within corporate governance has traditionally been an uncontroversial issue in Britain, and UK corporate law has in general been more effective than its US counterpart at providing formal protection and influence to shareholders within the corporate decision-making framework.[49] A number of possible explanations can

---

[48] While some may regard the proxy access issue, and indeed the Dodd-Frank reforms in general, as the peculiar product of a particularly interventionist Democrat (Obama) administration, such party-political attribution is rendered largely redundant when one considers that the comparatively market-interventionist Sarbanes-Oxley reforms were implemented in 2002 by a Republican (GW Bush) administration. On the effect of extraordinary crises in motivating systematic federal-regulatory reform of corporate and financial activities in the US, see DA Skeel, *Icarus in the Boardroom: The Fundamental Flaws in Corporate America and Where They Came From* (New York, Oxford University Press, 2005) esp ch 6; JC Coffee, 'The Political Economy of Dodd-Frank: Why Financial Reform Tends to be Frustrated and Systemic Risk Perpetuated' (2012) 97 *Cornell Law Review* 1020, available at: ssrn.com/abstract=1982128.

[49] On this, see below pt III. Indeed, the apparently more shareholder protectionist stance of UK corporate law relative to its US counterpart has been a source of considerable interest to academics over recent years. See, eg C Bruner, 'Power and Purpose in the "Anglo-American" Corporation' (2010) 50 *Virginia Journal of International Law* 579; LA Bebchuk, 'The Case for Increasing Shareholder Power' (2005) 118 *Harvard Law Review* 833, 847–50; J Armour and

been advanced for this conspicuous fault line between the two national systems, including: (i) the historically greater political enfranchisement of UK shareholders relative to their less institutionalised and coordinated US counterparts;[50] (ii) the natural shareholder-protectionist slant of the market-facilitative 'London approach' to corporate governance regulation;[51] and (iii) the arguably lower propensity for pro-directorial – and, correspondingly, anti-shareholder – judicial doctrines within the United Kingdom's largely unitary law-making system, where the impediments to potential 'backlash' re-incorporations in response to unattractive laws (from managers' perspective) are far greater than they would be in an American-esque federalist environment.[52]

Hence, in the United Kingdom, mandatory shareholder access to the corporate election process has been available for over half a century via an overall less restrictive (from shareholders' perspective) statutory variant of the now-defunct US 14a-11 procedure.[53] And, whilst compulsory 'say on pay' is a relatively recent phenomenon in Britain, its introduction at the beginning of the twenty-first century – in a notably more demanding form than the recently-implemented US version[54] – was a source of considerably less public and academic criticism than the later American reform. In fact, the establishment of 'say on pay' in the United Kingdom was, on the whole, warmly welcomed in 2002 as a positive addition to the British corporate governance framework at a time of widespread public unease about managerial and board accountability issues within UK listed companies.[55]

In respect of internal matters of board structure and function, the UK regulatory response to Enron and other corporate failures at the turn of the century was, comparatively to the aforementioned US reforms, extensive in terms of its impact on established national corporate governance practices.

DA Skeel, 'Who Writes the Rules for Hostile Takeovers, and Why? – The Peculiar Divergence of US and UK Takeover Regulation' (2007) 95 *Georgetown Law Journal* 1727, 1734–38.

    [50] On this, see Armour and Skeel, ibid, 1751–64.

    [51] On this, see Financial Reporting Council, *The UK Approach to Corporate Governance* (November 2006).

    [52] It is interesting to note that the idea of a unitary incorporation statute was considered by Progressive Era thinkers and policy-makers in the United States, as a potential response to the widely perceived inadequacy of State laws to regulate effectively the growing power of modern corporate enterprises. Ultimately, however, antitrust law was promoted in the US as the principal federal regulatory check on amalgamated corporate power, whilst corporate law has traditionally remained almost exclusively the province of individual States. On this, see SR Bowman, *The Modern Corporation and American Political Thought: Law, Power and Ideology* (PA, Penn State University Press, 1996) 131.

    [53] On this procedure, see below, nn 141–47 and accompanying text.

    [54] See above n 33. In UK quoted companies, 'say on pay' votes must be held on an annual basis, and companies have no flexibility (like their US counterparts) to reduce the frequency of the vote.

    [55] Although, for a notable exception to this general trend of the time, see BR Cheffins and RS Thomas, 'Should Shareholders Have a Greater Say Over Executive Pay?: Learning from the US Experience' (2001) 1 *Journal of Corporate Law Studies* 277.

Ensuing British reforms came in the form of the Financial Reporting Council's significant revisions to the United Kingdom's (then-called) Combined Code on Corporate Governance in 2003, following the influential recommendations in 2002 of the Higgs and Smith Committees.[56] These changes included the introduction of a requirement for US-style majority-independent boards within UK FTSE 350 companies, which represented a significant change to the executive-dominated, 'majority-insider' board model that had previously been customary within the British listed company sector.[57] Also affirmatively required for the first time by the 2003 version of the Code were fully independent and financially skilled audit committees,[58] independent non-executive chairmen,[59] and senior independent directors.[60] These requirements were reinforced moreover by a rigorous regulatory definition of directorial independence that established an effective presumption against long periods of office-holding.[61]

The 2003 Code reforms were by no means free from controversy in the United Kingdom.[62] Nevertheless, they largely escaped many of the criticisms levelled against the contemporaneous regulatory reforms in the United States on account of the Code's officially 'soft' presumptive status as a set of non-statutory 'best practice' norms, underpinned by the market-invoking principle of 'comply or explain'[63] rather than the binding and absolute force of state sanction. This feature of the Code makes it difficult for critics of corporate governance reforms in the United Kingdom to raise SOX-esque concerns of 'ill-fit' with pre-existing norms, given the continuing flexibility afforded to British boards to opt for reasoned non-compliance in cases where maladaptation concerns apparently render full Code compliance cost-ineffective at the micro level.[64]

The UK Corporate Governance Code (as it is called today) has thus been able to maintain its self-claimed status as a fundamentally facilitative and non-coercive institution, in spite of the typically limited degree of deviation

---

[56] See The Higgs Report: Review of the Role and Effectiveness of Non-Executive Directors (London, Department of Trade and Industry, 2003) (The Higgs Report); Audit Committees: Combined Code Guidance (London, Department of Trade and Industry, 2003) (The Smith Report).

[57] The Combined Code on Corporate Governance (July 2003), Provision A.3.2.

[58] Ibid, Provision C.3.1.

[59] Ibid, Provisions A.2.1 and A.2.2.

[60] Ibid, Provision A.3.3.

[61] Ibid, Provision A.3.1. In particular, any director who had served on the board for more than nine years from the date of first election was in effect subject to a rebuttable Code presumption of *non*-independence.

[62] See, eg A Alcock, 'Higgs – the wrong answer?' (2003) 24 *The Company Lawyer* 161.

[63] On this, see above ch 5 of this volume, pt IV.

[64] However, on the practical limitations of the 'comply or explain' principle in achieving such conformance-flexibility in the UK, see MT Moore, '"Whispering Sweet Nothings: The Limitations of Informal Conformance in UK Corporate Governance' (2009) 9 *Journal of Corporate Law Studies* 95, esp 117–29.

from its core norms that tends to occur in practice.[65] As such, the Code can be said merely to embody, in a responsive and instrumental manner, the purportedly efficient governance arrangements that boards and investors would be inclined to agree upon with one another privately if possessed with full awareness of the contractual choices available to them. I explained in chapter five that the Code's purported quasi-contractual 'neutrality' in the above regard has been crucial for maintaining its continuing legitimacy as a private ordering mechanism, and also the legitimacy of its promulgator – the Financial Reporting Council – as a non-statist rule-making body.[66] This is in spite of the deep and sweeping reforms to British boardroom norms and practices that the Code is widely acknowledged to have brought about over the past two decades, within a national political climate generally favourable to the increased regulation of corporate activities in the public interest.

(ii) The 'Juridification'[67] of Directors' General Duties under the Companies Act 2006

Notwithstanding the general resilience of UK corporate law's underpinning normative fabric to the regulatory developments described above, the characteristic privity of the UK corporate governance system has by no means been immune from challenge over recent years. Most notably in this regard, the United Kingdom has witnessed a growing trend of statutory 'spread' in corporate law, which would appear to evoke fundamentally similar concerns to those that have arisen with respect to the aforementioned US regulatory reforms.

The principal factor in this trend was the UK Labour government's promulgation and implementation of the Companies Act 2006 which, at over 1300 sections long, constitutes the longest piece of legislation in British history. The most controversial aspect of the new Act has been its perceived 'juridifying' effect. Accordingly, an increased number of core corporate governance concerns in the United Kingdom, the most notable of which being the formulation and content of directors' general duties, have been displaced from their traditional common law or equitable realm into the arguably more rigid[68] and politically reactive[69] territory of statute law.

---

[65] On this, see Moore, ibid.

[66] See, in particular, ch 5 of this volume, fns 133–38 and accompanying text.

[67] I have borrowed this term from Chris Riley, who first adopted it in this context in his paper 'The Juridification of Corporate Governance', in J de Lacy, *The Reform of United Kingdom Company Law* (London, Cavendish, 2002) 179.

[68] In this regard, it has been inferred by one prominent US corporate law scholar that, whereas 'the common law . . . permits contractual flexibility', in contrast 'statutory regulation . . . mandates obligations'. See R Romano, 'Comment on Easterbrook and Fischel, "Contract and Fiduciary Duty"' (1993) 36 *Journal of Law & Economics* 447, 449.

[69] Such a conception of statute law would appear to underlie Richard Posner's juxtaposition of: on the one hand, 'the common law system of privately enforced rights'; and, on the

The most conspicuous and controversial example of this phenomenon is the director's statutory duty of loyalty under section 172 of the 2006 Act.[70] This provision constitutes an attempted codification of the formerly nebulous judicial construct of the 'interest of the company', which lies at the heart of the test for determining the propriety of directorial conduct under the equitable fiduciary doctrine. Traditionally, Anglo-American courts have been reluctant to articulate exactly what the pursuit of a company's 'interest' entails, preferring instead to reserve such matters for ex ante resolution by corporate contractors themselves.[71] To this end, courts have tended to show deference to the conclusions reached by boards – in exercise of the latter's contractually delegated managerial powers and resulting ambit of business judgment discretion – as to what was best calculated to serve a company's overall welfare in any given instance.[72] Moreover, with the progressive diminution of the common law ultra vires doctrine, such judicial deference to private ordering has been inclined to extend even to directorial decisions that prima facie appear to achieve no direct or obvious commercial benefit to the corporation or its shareholders.[73]

In the limited range of cases where courts have attempted to give some doctrinal meaning to the company's interests, they have tended to adopt an individualistic or 'aggregate' perspective: that is, an approach focused on the contractually-expressed preferences of the firm's individual incorporators (and, indirectly, their collective directorial representatives) rather than any autonomous or super-contractual understanding of the greater

---

other, 'the administrative system of direct public control'. See RA Posner, *Economic Analysis of Law* (Boston MA, Little, Brown, 1972) 156. From a similar perspective, it has been posited that civil law jurisdictions, which – at the level of fundamental legal principles at least – are much more heavily reliant than their common law counterparts on codified statutory laws, are correspondingly more likely to engender 'greater government intervention in economic activity and weaker protection of [investors'] private property than in common law ones'. See R La Porta, F Lopez-de-Silanes, A Shleifer and R Vishny, 'Investor Protection and Corporate Governance' (2000) 58 *Journal of Financial Economics* 3, 12.

[70] Section 172(1) of the UK Companies Act 2006 provides that: '[a] director of a company must act in the way he considers, in good faith, would be most likely to promote the success of the company for the benefit of its members as a whole, and in doing so have regard (amongst other matters) to – (a) the likely consequences of any decision in the long term, (b) the interests of the company's employees, (c) the need to foster the company's business relationships with suppliers, customers and others, (d) the impact of the company's operations on the community and the environment, (e) the desirability of the company maintaining a reputation for high standards of business conduct, and (f) the need to act fairly between members of the company'.

[71] On this, see (in a US context) CM Bruner, 'The Enduring Ambivalence of Corporate Law' (2008) 59 *Alabama Law Review* 1385; (and, in a UK context) JE Parkinson, *Corporate Power and Responsibility: Issues in the Theory of Company Law* (Oxford, Oxford University Press, 1993) 76–96.

[72] On this, see (in a US context) above ch 4 of this volume, fns 38–43 and accompanying text; (and, in a UK context) above ch 5 of this volume, fns 47–51 and accompanying text.

[73] On this, see above ch 5 of this volume, fns 52–54 and accompanying text.

corporate 'good'.[74] Anglo-American courts have therefore steadfastly resisted the temptation to impute judicially-determined interests or goals to the corporation over and above those that are determined by its incorporators and management privately, the implicit assumption being that a company can have no cognisable 'interest' other than what its participants collectively determine amongst themselves.[75]

However, section 172 challenges this orthodox doctrinal logic in three significant respects. First, it juridifies and therefore concretises the 'interests of the company', by defining the corporate objective explicitly in terms of the success of the company for the benefit of its shareholders as a whole.[76] Whilst it had previously been conventional for English lawyers to equate the interests of the company with those of the general body of shareholders for the purpose of interpreting the scope of the director's duty of loyalty,[77] there was a scarcity of direct judicial authority on this point. At the same time, relevant statutory provisions prior to 2006 – most notably sections 309 and 719 of the Companies Act 1985 – if anything, served to *detract from*, rather than reaffirm, the assumed primacy of shareholders as a corporate beneficiary (at least vis-à-vis employees).[78] As

---

[74] See, eg *Greenhalgh v Arderne Cinemas* [1951] Ch 286 (CA) (Evershed MR): 'the phrase "the company as a whole" does not . . . mean the company as a commercial entity, distinct from the corporators: it means *the corporators as a general body*. That is to say, the case may be taken of an individual hypothetical member and it may be asked whether what is proposed is, in the honest opinion of those voted in its favour, for that person's benefit' (emphasis added).

[75] On this, see KW Wedderburn, *The Future of Company Law: Corporate Governance, Fat Cats and Workers* (Liverpool, Institute of Employment Rights, 2004) 25–26.

[76] That is, at least insofar as ordinary commercial companies are concerned. With respect to companies that are formed for the pursuit of express objects *other than* the benefit of their shareholders, section 172(2) provides that subsection (1) thereof (on which, see above n 70) 'has effect as if the reference to promoting the success of the company for the benefit of its members were to achieving those purposes'.

[77] See above n 74; D Attenborough, 'How Directors Should Act When Owing Duties to the Company's Shareholders: Why We Need to Stop Applying Greenhalgh' (2009) 20 *International Company and Commerical Law Review* 339. In John Parkinson's view: 'The correct position [under English law] is thus that the corporate entity is a vehicle for benefitting the interests of a specified group of groups. These interests the law has traditionally defined as the interests of the shareholders. The duty of management can accordingly be stated as a duty to promote the success of the business venture, *in order* to benefit the members'. See Parkinson, *Corporate Power and Responsibility*, above n 71, 77.

[78] Section 309(1) of the Companies Act 1985 provided that '[t]he matters to which the directors of a company are to have regard in the performance of their functions include the interests of the company's employees in general, as well as the interests of its members'. Section 719(1) of the same Act, meanwhile, provided that '[t]he powers of a company include (if they would not otherwise do so apart from this section) power to make . . . provision for the benefit of persons employed or formerly employed by the company or any of its subsidiaries . . . in connection with the cessation or the transfer to any person of the whole or part of the undertaking of the company or that subsidiary', and 'notwithstanding that [this power's] exercise is not in the best interests of the company'. Section 309 was repealed on implementation of the Companies Act 2006, and in effect replaced by the principle of 'enlightened shareholder value' under section 172 of the 2006 Act (see above n 70). Section 719 has been retained today, with minor variations, in the form of section 247 of the 2006 Act.

against this, section 172 represents an important normative bastion of the shareholder protectionism agenda in that it puts the lexical primacy of shareholders on an entrenched legislative footing (at least insofar as commercial companies are concerned) for the first time, thereby arguably immunising UK corporate law from the charge of 'enduring ambivalence'[79] when it comes to ascertaining the proper objective of the company.[80]

The second respect in which section 172 challenges English judicial orthodoxy is by adopting an arguably paternalistic approach to specifying the proper scope of considerations that a board should take into account in determining what courses of action are conducive to a commercial company's success. Prior to section 172's implementation, this question fell to be answered almost entirely on a firm-specific basis by liberal recourse to the board's internal management prerogative.[81] By contrast, section 172 apparently establishes a procedural mandate[82] to consider a non-exhaustive list of socio-economic factors within the calculus of any major strategic decision, including the long-term consequences of the decision, the interests of the company's employees, business relationships with suppliers and customers, and the preservation of the company's reputational capital.[83]

Thirdly and most fundamentally, section 172 involves going beyond the traditionally aggregate and anthropocentric understanding of the corporation that contractarian logic instils, by attributing both non-individualistic and non-humanistic dimensions to the interests of the company.[84] This is true insofar as section 172(1)(d) lists both 'the community' and, more remarkably, 'the environment' (however defined) as prescribed criteria in the directorial 'success' calculus. Admittedly, the dual status of shareholders both as the exclusive ultimate beneficiary of the duty, and the sole

On the former provision, see Parkinson, ibid, 82–87; C Villiers, 'Section 309 of the Companies Act 1985: Is it Time for a Reappraisal?' in H Collins, P Davies and P Rideout (eds), *Legal Regulation of the Employment Relation* (The Hague, Kluwer, 2000). On the latter provision, see Parkinson, above n 71, 86–87.

[79] See Bruner, 'The Enduring Ambivalence of Corporate Law', above n 71.

[80] Although, on the continuing ambiguity of section 172's application, see A Keay, 'Good Faith and Director's Duty to Promote the Success of their Company' (2011) 32 *The Company Lawyer* 138.

[81] See above nn 71–72 and accompanying text.

[82] On the notion of section 172 of the Companies Act 2006 – in conjunction with the complementary corporate disclosure regime under section 417 of the same Act – as part of a framework of mechanisms for enhancing the quality of directorial decision-making *procedures*, see J Lowry, 'The Duty of Loyalty of Company Directors: Bridging the Accountability Gap Through Efficient Disclosure' (2009) 68 *Cambridge Law Journal* 607.

[83] Even the core directorial mandate under section 172 to 'promote the success of the company for the benefit of its members as a whole' arguably represents a paternalistic statutory pre-emption of private ordering, notwithstanding the non-shareholder aspects of the provision (which are arguably capable of being considered, in any event, under the old judicial formulation of the director's duty of loyalty). See above nn 70–73 and accompanying text.

[84] I am indebted to Carrie Bradshaw for first alerting me to the social-scientific concept of anthropocentrism, and its implications within the present context.

permissible derivative claimant group in respect of it,[85] might suggest that such concerns are overplayed.[86] Notwithstanding this fact, though, the provision at the very least calls upon lawyers and, in turn, directors to grapple with concepts and terminology that previously have had no logical place within the individual-rights-based discourse of common law reasoning.

A further noteworthy respect in which the 2006 Act's codification of directors' general duties has effected a juridification of corporate governance norms concerns the applicable standard of care for the purpose of directors' negligence liability. As I explained in chapter five, the traditional *crassa negligentia* standard at common law – as revised incrementally in *City Equitable Fire Insurance* – was consistent with the contractarian paradigm insofar as it permitted shareholders to determine for themselves the acceptability of managerial error or omission, short of impropriety or gross incompetence.[87]

By contrast, section 174 of the Act establishes beyond doubt that the 'duty of care, skill and diligence' in its modern guise incorporates a firmly objective standard of conduct for directors, which is linked at root to the implicit requirements of the director's official functions and responsibilities.[88] The effect of this statutory innovation has been to consolidate and regularise a modern trend of increasing judicial interventionism with respect to questions of directorial competence, especially in large and socially significant corporations.[89]

---

[85] Section 260(1) of the Companies Act 2006 expressly provides that the statutory derivative claims machinery in part 11 of the Act applies only to 'proceedings ... *by a member* of the company', echoing the previous common law position in this regard (emphasis added).

[86] On the fundamental economic-individualistic emphasis of section 172, and its resultant limitations as a mechanism for affording meaningful protection to environmental interests, see C Bradshaw, 'The Environmental Business Case and Unenlightened Shareholder Value' (2013) 33 *Legal Studies* (forthcoming).

[87] See above ch 5 of this volume, fns 63–74 and accompanying text.

[88] Specifically, section 174 of the Companies Act 2006 requires that '[a] director of a company exercise ... the care, skill and diligence that would be exercised by a reasonably diligent person with – (a) the general knowledge, skill and experience *that may reasonably be expected of a person carrying out the functions carried out by the director in relation to the company*, and (b) the general knowledge, skill and experience that the director has' (emphasis added).

[89] See, eg *Norman v Theodore Goddard* [1992] BCLC 1028, where Lord Hoffman accepted the ambitious but undisputed counsel submission that the established common law standard of care and skill was accurately stated by the (seemingly more onerous) test of diligence for wrongful trading set out in s 214(4) of the Insolvency Act 1986, which – in particular – requires a director to exhibit 'the general knowledge, skill and experience that may reasonably be expected of a person carrying out *the same functions* as are carried out by that director in relation to the company' (emphasis added). See also *Re D'Jan of London* [1994] 1 BCLC 561, where his Lordship reaffirmed the validity of this (seemingly new) approach at common law. See, further, *Daniels v Anderson* (1995) 16 ACSR 607 (New South Wales Supreme Court), where Chief Justice Rogers emphasised that '[a] person who accepts the office of director of a particular company undertakes the responsibility of ensuring that he or she *understands* the nature of the duty a director is called upon to perform', a duty that, moreover, 'will vary according to the size and business of the company and the experience or skills that the director held himself or herself out to have in support of appointment to office' (emphasis added). Similarly, see Jonathan Parker J's dictum in *Re Barings Plc (No 5), Secretary of State for Trade*

De-Privatisation of Anglo-US Law   195

There is evidence to suggest, moreover, that this trend has impacted most significantly on the positions of non-executive directors in public companies, whose monitoring and risk oversight responsibilities are arguably more susceptible to objective judicial determination than the entrepreneurial functions of executives.[90] Indeed, it would appear to be the accepted legal position today that NEDs in any industry sector provide an independent and informed judgement on high-level policy issues, whilst also constructively challenging management proposals and identifying key risk factors therein.[91] Consequently, the traditional deference shown by courts to the internal corporate command chain as the exclusive institutional stop on managerial incompetence is widely regarded today as a remnant of a bygone era, especially in the context of the British public company sector.

(iii) The Juridifying Impact of EU Harmonisation Measures: The Experience of the Takeover Directive

Any discussion of the phenomenon of juridification in UK corporate governance law would be incomplete without considering the influence of EU harmonisation measures in this area.[92] Indeed, the notion of inter-jurisdictional harmonisation in the European sense is arguably antithetical

and Industry v Baker (No 5) [1999] 1 BCLC 433, to the effect that '[d]irectors have, both collectively and individually, a continuing duty to acquire and maintain a sufficient knowledge and understanding of the company's business to enable them properly to discharge their duties as directors', whilst 'the higher the office within an organisation that is held by an individual, the greater the responsibilities that fall upon him' (emphasis added). Finally, see Gregson v HAE Trustees Ltd [2008] EWHC 1006 (Ch), where the court confirmed (at first instance) that section 174 codifies the pre-existing common law with respect to directorial negligence.

[90] See, eg Equitable Life Assurance Society v Bowley and Others [2004] 1 BCLC 180, where Langley J asserted that '[i]t is plainly arguable . . . that a company may reasonably at least look to non-executive directors for independence of judgment and supervision of the executive management' (emphasis added). See also Australian Securities and Investments Commission v Healey [2011] FCA 717, analysed in J Lowry, 'The Irreducible Core of the Duty of Care, Skill and Diligence of Company Directors' (2012) 75 Modern Law Review 249.

[91] In this regard, the most recent (2010) edition of the UK Corporate Governance Code stipulates that, '[a]s part of their role as members of a unitary board, non-executive directors should constructively challenge and help develop proposals on strategy'. In particular, it recommends that all non-executive directors: (i) scrutinise the performance of management in meeting agreed goals and objectives and monitor the reporting of performance, (ii) satisfy themselves on the integrity of financial information and that financial controls and systems of risk management are robust and defensible, (iii) determine appropriate levels of remuneration of executive directors, and (iv) take a prime role in appointing and, where necessary, removing executive directors, and in succession planning. See Financial Reporting Council, UK Corporate Governance Code (June 2010), Principle A.4, available at: www.frc.org.uk/corporate/ukcgcode.cfm .

[92] The most noteworthy corporate governance initiatives at the pan-European level over recent years have been the Takeover Directive (Directive 2004/25/EC), the Shareholders' Rights Directive (Directive 2007/36/EC), and the recent post-crisis EU Green Paper on Corporate Governance. See 'Green Paper: The EU Corporate Governance Framework' (2011), available at: ec.europa.eu/internal_market/company/docs/modern/com2011-164_en.pdf.

to the rationality of private ordering. Whereas US-style competitive federal-ism operates on an endogenous 'bottom-up' basis, with any inter-State 'harmonising' initiatives (eg the Model Business Corporation Act) merely reflective of pre-established regulatory best practice,[93] EU-style harmonisa-tion by contrast works in an exogenous 'top-down' manner, and for the express purpose of driving substantive convergence between different legal systems where it would not otherwise be inclined to exist.[94]

Therefore, in spite of what may be connoted by the notion of 'harmony', harmonisation of laws is in reality a process that entails varying degrees of mandated regulatory conformity at the individual state level, at least insofar as the subject state wishes to remain part of the relevant inter-state order. These characteristics contradict the basic tenets of voluntariness and unanimity that underpin the contractarian concept of the 'prudential state' as an individually rational rule-selector. Furthermore, harmonisa-tion measures require formal implementation within a Member State's legal system in order for the relevant state to be deemed compliant with its treaty obligations. The effect is that statutory entrenchment of practices and institutions becomes the regulatory norm, in some cases at the expense of institutional flexibility or diversity.

In UK corporate governance law, the most conspicuous and contro-versial example of EU-compelled juridification has occurred in the area of takeover regulation. As I explained in chapter five, the regulation of public company takeovers in the United Kingdom is administered on a 'privatised' basis by the non-governmental Panel on Takeovers and Mergers, which promulgates and enforces the non-statutory UK Takeover Code.[95] In light of the Panel and Code's widely acknowledged success in this regard, the EU Takeover Directive – which came into force in 2004 – was designed with a view to extending long-established features of the UK's flexible and market-liberal system of takeover regulation (including, inter alia, the mandatory bid requirement and prohibitions on frustrative tactics) across EU Member States as a whole. The ultimate policy objective was to afford heightened protection to cross-border investors in respect of control-related issues, and, in turn,

---

[93] On this, see above ch 4 of this volume, pt II.

[94] As against this, however, the general principle of subsidiarity – coupled with the ten-dency of the European Commission to make significant concessions to individual Member States on contentious issues – has meant that in practice such convergence has tended to be relatively limited in this field. See, eg the experience of the Draft Fifth Directive on the European Company, which – in spite of its lofty initial ambition in the 1970s to establish a uni-form corporate structure for business entities operating across the Community as a whole – was significantly diluted over the succeeding three decades, so as to be rendered a mere shadow of the original draft insofar as its unifying effect was concerned. On this, see J Dine and J-J Du Plessis, 'The Fate of the Draft Fifth Directive on Company Law: Accommodation instead of Harmonisation' [1997] *Journal of Business Law* 23.

[95] See above ch 5 of this volume, pt IV.

facilitate the free movement of corporate capital on a Community-wide basis.[96]

However, whilst the content of the Directive has been heavily influenced by pre-existing UK takeover norms,[97] the subsequent trans-European harmonisation of these rules has necessarily entailed that the United Kingdom *itself* formally implement the provisions of the Directive, thereby reducing to an extent the previous informality of the relevant norms at domestic level. Thus a curious side-effect of the Directive has been to require the United Kingdom to give statutory authorisation to the Takeover Panel in formal support of its rule-making, executive and adjudicative functions, notwithstanding the fact that the Panel has been carrying out these functions for the past four decades. More fundamentally, Part 28 of the UK Companies Act 2006 – in addition to formally establishing the Panel's powers[98] and its new right of judicial recourse for enforcement of sanctions[99] – also gives express statutory recognition to the Panel for the first time in its history.[100] As a result, the Panel has – somewhat inadvertently – become entrenched as an indirect part of the British government apparatus,[101] thereby transforming it from a private sector institution into a quasi-public regulatory agency.[102]

C. Summary of this Part

The above analysis does not purport to be a comprehensive survey of the US and UK corporate governance systems by any means. Rather, the purpose of the foregoing discussion is simply to highlight an arguable trend towards greater mandatory regulatory intervention in core aspects of Anglo-American corporate governance, as manifested in a number of conspicuous key respects. From a contractarian perspective, it could be said that this trend – if it continues – potentially threatens the characteristic privity of Anglo-American corporate governance law, by undermining

[96] See Directive 2004/25/EC of the European Parliament and of the Council of 21 April 2004 on takeover bids [2004] OJ L142/12 (preamble).

[97] See, in particular, the General Principles of the Directive (ibid), listed in Article 3 thereof.

[98] See Companies Act 2006, ss 942(2), 945–47, 952 and 954.

[99] See Companies Act 2006, s 955.

[100] See section 942(1) of the Companies Act 2006, which expressly states that '[t]he body known as the Panel on Takeovers and Mergers ("the Panel") is to have the functions conferred on it by or under this Chapter'.

[101] It could be argued that this development had already occurred to a material extent following the landmark decision of the Court of Appeal in *Re Datafin plc* [1987] QB 815, where the Panel's decisions were rendered susceptible to judicial review on account of the fact that the Panel – whilst formally a private body – could nonetheless be regarded as exercising functions that were public in nature.

[102] At the same time, both the Code and Panel remain largely unchanged in terms of substantive content and day-to-day administration.

its traditionally perceived nature as a facilitative body of rules reflective of prudential contractual choices only.

As I will demonstrate in the following part, however, on closer examination the above regulatory reforms and initiatives are not particularly unusual within the broader institutional framework of Anglo-American corporate governance as a whole. In fact, both US and UK corporate governance law have for a long time exhibited significant mandatory components that, prima facie at least, take the form of public-interventionist regulation rather than quasi-contractual norms. Moreover, as I will further show below, the very institutional foundations of private ordering in US and UK corporate governance are themselves attributable – in the last place – to mandatory regulatory initiative. This suggests that the quasi-contractual protection of shareholders within the corporate decision-making framework – far from being an inert or pre-ordained feature of the Anglo-American corporate governance system – is, on the contrary, a politically-determined and legally-contingent phenomenon in its own right.

II. THE MANDATORY NATURE OF CORPORATE DISCLOSURE REGULATION IN THE UNITED STATES AND UNITED KINGDOM

A. Is Corporate Information-Production a Contractual or Regulatory Phenomenon?

In chapter three, I observed how – within the contractarian paradigm – the capacity of investors to make efficient private selections with respect to both corporate securities and governance norms is dependent on the existence of continuous flows of accurate and reliable data about relative firm performance.[103] Prima facie, this represents a challenge to the contractarian position insofar as effective private ordering cannot be assumed a priori, but rather is contingent on an underpinning informational infrastructure.[104]

As I further explained in chapter three, this difficulty is conceptually resolvable within contractarian logic by recourse to the various informational intermediaries – mainly professional arbitrageurs, investment underwriters, securities analysts and private stock exchange operators – who (theoretically) act together so as to ensure, via the sum of their respective self-interested initiatives, that prevailing securities prices are reflective of all relevant available information including an awareness of intra-firm governance norms.[105] The prescriptive implication is that mandatory regulation of securities markets – and, in particular, the regulatory compulsion of corporate information disclosure – is both unnecessary and, moreover,

---

[103] See above ch 3 of this volume, pt IV.B (ii).
[104] See above ch 3 of this volume, fns 102–03 and accompanying text.
[105] See above ch 3 of this volume, fns 104–07 and accompanying text.

economically sub-optimal (relative to decentralised private methods of data-finding)[106] from a general investor and social perspective.[107]

As elegant as the above course of logic is, however, it is out of keeping with the reality of how corporate securities markets operate today. Admittedly, there was once considerable empirical truth in the notion of securities markets as a self-governing and pre-regulatory domain in the contractarian sense. Prior to the initiation of the modern federal framework of SEC regulation in the 1930s, securities markets in the United States could with some justification be regarded as private and self-determining phenomena, which were subject (albeit with some degree of modification) only to the ordinary rules of State-level civil and criminal law applicable to all commercial transactions.[108] Moreover, as I explained in chapter five, until as late as 1986 the protection of investors in capital markets in the United Kingdom was administered within an entirely private and self-regulatory framework, whereby rule-making responsibilities were vested in various self-regulatory organisations (SROs) representative of the City of London's main financial-professional sectors. Accordingly, the London Stock Exchange had the effective status of a 'club' whose listing rules constituted a private agreement between the exchange itself and each member company.[109] In consequence, until relatively recently capital markets remained largely outside of the purview of determinative state control in the United Kingdom, during which time the country's securities law system conformed much more closely to the status of a private-contractual rather than public-regulatory law field.[110]

Therefore, the contractarian notion that functioning corporate securities markets *can* exist in the substantial absence of regulatory state support would appear to be unquestionable. However, similarly beyond question today – even amongst many advocates of private ordering in corporate law generally – is the claim that efficient and investor-protective securities markets require significant public-regulatory underpinnings as a necessary supplement to the aforementioned private informational conduits. Accordingly, even within the parameters of the contractarian paradigm of corporate governance, it is increasingly accepted today by scholars that

[106] See above ch 3 of this volume, fns 108–09 and accompanying text.

[107] Coffee has observed that '[t]he beneficiaries of increased allocative efficiency include virtually all members of society, not just investors'. See JC Coffee, 'Market Failure and the Economic Case for a Mandatory Disclosure System' (1984) 70 *Virginia Law Review* 717, 736.

[108] See FH Easterbrook and DR Fischel, *The Economic Structure of Corporate Law* (Cambridge MA, Harvard University Press, 1991) 285.

[109] On this, see above ch 5 of this volume, fns 122–26 and accompanying text.

[110] As Lowry and Reisberg have found, moreover, even with the enactment of the Financial Services Act 1986, the government retained the general view that 'the UK's first general system of investor protection was to be characterised as a feature of the private sector rather than state regulation', so that 'investor protection was to remain company law, rather than become securities regulation'. See J Lowry and A Reisberg (eds), *Pettet's Company Law: Company and Capital Markets* Law, 3rd edn (Harlow, Longman, 2009) 349.

the mandatory state regulation of securities markets – in particular for the purpose of ensuring universal disclosure and verification of inter-company data – is structurally essential to the overall functioning of corporate law as a system.

B. Information as a 'Public Good'

An arguable paradox at the heart of this 'progressive' contractarian perspective is the claim that a publicly-mandated system of disclosure and verification of company information at the macro (economy-wide) level is a necessary institutional precursor to the effective private selection of corporate laws at the micro (intra-firm) level. This is due to the commonly-accepted fact that in any market environment (but especially in complex financial securities markets) information has the special status of a 'public good': that is to say, it is both *non-excludable* and *non-divisible*. The former quality denotes that those who expend the costs involved in producing and verifying information cannot exclude those who have not paid for it from benefiting from it, insofar as information is by nature capable of (and also prone to) being circulated beyond its immediate recipients. The latter quality indicates that information – unlike most other commodities – is not exhausted or diminished in utility by being used, with the effect that those who pay to receive information will continue to derive significant use value from it even in the presence of a number of 'free riders' who also stand to benefit from it indirectly.[111]

Against this background, where information is generated and verified by private actors alone, those paying for the information will – due to the inevitability of free riders – be incapable of appropriating all of the benefits of their search efforts.[112] As a result, such persons will be disinclined to invest in acquiring information to the 'optimal' extent that they would if they could exclusively exploit the full economic benefits thereof. It follows that company information will be systematically under-produced; or, more likely, over-produced in certain isolated respects (that paying investors value most) whilst under-produced in others.[113]

This is one of the classic economic scenarios where the pursuit (by investors) of individual rationality en masse leads not to overall allocative efficiency, but rather to the 'collective folly' of a socially sub-optimal outcome (specifically, informational incompleteness and imbalance in corporate securities markets). Accordingly, since private actors (ie investors) will not be inclined to generate individually the quantity and quality of

---

[111] See FH Easterbrook and DR Fischel, 'Mandatory Disclosure and the Protection of Investors' (1984) 70 *Virginia Law Review* 669, 681.

[112] See Coffee, 'Market Failure', above n 107, 726–27.

[113] On this, see Easterbrook and Fischel, 'Mandatory Disclosure and the Protection of Investors', above n 111, 681–82.

company data that they would ideally wish for as a general group, a mandated universal system of disclosure is necessary in order to 'correct' this innate disparity between individual and collective rationality, so as to produce an optimal level of information from the perspective of investors (and, in turn, society) as a whole.

C. The Normative Significance of Distinguishing Corporate and Securities Law

On a normative level, the accommodation of mandatory disclosure regulation within an institutional paradigm otherwise hostile to regulatory interference in private ordering is achieved by drawing a (frequently grey) conceptual 'dividing line' between the purportedly distinct spheres of corporate/company and securities/capital markets law. The former is presented as an aspect of facilitative private law, and the latter – contrarily – as a sub-set of public-regulatory law. Accordingly, securities law is purportedly dedicated to the mandatory and pre-contractual 'correction' of structural market failures that would otherwise inhibit the efficient operation of private ordering processes within corporate law. On this basis, federal legislative and administrative control over corporate disclosure regulation has been widely accepted in the United States as both functionally necessary and politically legitimate, in spite of the internal affairs doctrine's formal hostility to supra-State intervention in other areas of corporate governance.[114]

Given the irrelevance of such intra-national federalist concerns to UK corporate governance, the importance of ensuring a distinct division between company and capital markets law has been of lesser normative importance within the British regulatory environment. Here the principal legal rules pertaining to the disclosure and verification of information in respect of public companies are situated in a somewhat disorderly and seemingly illogical domain, spanning parts of orthodox company law,[115] financial markets legislation,[116] and also the listing requirements of the London Stock Exchange.[117]

[114] On the internal affairs doctrine in US corporate law generally, see above ch 4 of this volume, fns 19–25 and accompanying text.

[115] See, eg Part 15 (Accounts and Reports) and Part 16 (Audit) of the Companies Act 2006. See also *Percival v Wright* [1902] 2 Ch 421; *Allen v Hyatt* (1914) 30 TLR 444 (PC); *Coleman v Myers* [1977] 2 NZLR 225 (New Zealand Court of Appeal), concerning the (limited) requirement at common law for a company's directors to disclose price-relevant information as counterparties to transactions for the purchase or sale of the firm's securities.

[116] See, eg Part VIII of the Financial Services and Markets Act 2000, which establishes the wide-reaching administrative offence of market abuse.

[117] See, eg the United Kingdom Listing Authority Disclosure Rules and Transparency Rules (DTR) applicable to UK listed companies, which cover (inter alia) audit committees (DTR 7.1), corporate governance statements (DTR 7.2), and vote holder and issuer notification rules (DTR 5).

Irrespective of the specific national institutional environment, though, understanding corporate disclosure regulation as a *non*-corporate law field is – for a variety of reasons – highly convenient both doctrinally and politically. On a policy level, it legitimates federal interventions in the United States (such as the SOX and Dodd-Frank reforms discussed above[118]) that, whilst formerly billed as aspects of securities law, nevertheless carry a significant internal corporate governance 'sting in the tail'. In the UK and wider European context, meanwhile, the normative effect of branding a particular EU regulatory innovation in corporate governance (eg the Takeover Directive or Shareholder Rights Directive) as an aspect of capital markets rather than company law is to legitimate it on common market grounds as a facilitator of cross-border free movement of financial capital. In such instance, the political impediments to successful transnational importation of the provision in question are likely to be less severe (although by no means absent) than if the relevant innovation purported to be concerned exclusively with the so-called 'social dimension' of European integration as it applies to intra-company governance relations and the distribution of power and wealth between corporate participants.[119]

From the viewpoint of teaching and understanding the law, moreover, the separate categorisation of corporate and securities law makes it easier for students and scholars of corporate governance (broadly defined) to handle and rationalise a highly complex body of primary and secondary materials that, in terms of substantive volume, considerably exceeds the normal size of a typical law course or textbook. The tendency of legal scholars to divide – and, indeed, further sub-divide – these two areas of study is exemplified by the prolific array of specialist academic course and literary offerings (arguably including the present work!) that purport to deal exclusively with one of these two specific fields.

Finally and most fundamentally, regarding corporate and securities law in distinction from one another matters a great deal on a conceptual level, insofar as it enables the validity of the private ordering paradigm in corporate law to be continually asserted notwithstanding the arguable incongruity between the theoretical ideal and empirical reality. This is because aspects of corporate governance – such as mandatory disclosure regulation – that fail to 'fit' the facilitative contractarian blueprint can effectively be 'carved out' of the conceptual picture leaving only those features of the law that support the prevailing theoretical characterisation of the subject-matter.

---

[118] See above pt I.A.

[119] On the conflict between the economic (single market) and social dimensions of EU integration generally (viewed from a constitutional perspective), see D Schiek, U Liebert and H Schneider, *European Economic and Social Constitutionalism after the Treaty of Lisbon* (Cambridge, Cambridge University Press, 2011).

D. The Definitional Grey Area: Corporate Governance Norms in Securities Law Clothing

An outstanding definitional difficulty with the above distinction, though, is that some commonly accepted elements of so-called 'securities' or 'capital markets' law affect corporate governance in ways beyond merely mandating ongoing corporate transparency. Some such regulatory provisions, rather, go directly to the division of power and influence at the heart of the corporate structure, thereby challenging the artificial internal/external dichotomy that has traditionally separated corporate and securities law respectively. Reference has already been made above to the new federal 'say on pay' and (now defunct) proxy access rules in the United States, which undeniably are of this ilk. However, some much more longstanding – and, correspondingly, less controversial – securities law provisions in the United States and United Kingdom also fall into this category.

For instance, the 14a-8 shareholder resolution procedure described in chapter four, despite being a product of an SEC rule promulgated under the Securities and Exchange Act of 1934, is nonetheless of central importance to US corporate governance in that it embodies the only guaranteed right that shareholders have actually to initiate issues for consideration by management, as opposed to just responding retrospectively to management initiatives already in existence. And whilst, as I explained in chapter four, the necessarily precatory status of 14a-8 proposals gives them a quasi-contractual rather than mandatory form,[120] this does not detract from the fact that the shareholder proposal – and proxy solicitation process surrounding the annual shareholders' meeting generally – are determined in the last place by mandatory federal regulation rather than decentralised private ordering or State law.

Of comparable significance to internal governance affairs of US listed companies is the wide-reaching anti-fraud protection contained in SEC Rule 10b-5, which notably provides a right of action both to harmed investors in secondary markets and the SEC itself, on account of any statements by (inter alia) corporate officers that are intentionally either untrue or misleadingly incomplete.[121] In cases where a manager makes a *public*

---

[120] On this, see above ch 4 of this volume, fns 104–08 and accompanying text.

[121] Specifically, SEC Rule 10b-5(b) provides that '[i]t shall be unlawful for any person, directly or indirectly ... [t]o make any untrue statement of a material fact or to omit to state a material fact necessary in order to make the statements made, in light of the circumstances under which they were made, not misleading'. Furthermore, the US Supreme Court has interpreted an omitted fact as being 'material' in the above sense 'if there is a substantial likelihood that a reasonable shareholder would consider it important in deciding how to vote'. See *TSC Industries v Northway* 426 US 438 (1976) (Burger CJ). On the significance of this provision generally (viewed from a comparative Anglo/American perspective), see J Armour, B Black, B Cheffins and R Nolan, 'Private Enforcement of Corporate Law: An Empirical Comparison of the United Kingdom and the United States' (2009) 6 *Journal of*

statement of the above nature, moreover, he risks being found liable for the extensive 'fraud on the market' wrong, entitling *every* affected investor to sue for any resulting personal loss.[122]

As well as being an important regulatory precondition of capital market efficiency, and consequently of indirect importance to corporate governance, this provision is also of direct significance thereto in two crucial respects. First, it compels caution by management in making predictions of future firm performance to shareholders, thereby improving market monitoring of managerial performance and investor-management communications generally. And secondly, Rule 10b-5 represents a powerful managerial-disciplinary mechanism in its own right where there is a danger of it being invoked on account of a management failure to disclose material risk factors causing subsequent loss of shareholder wealth. The ex ante disciplinary effect of the rule is manifested to the extent that managers are driven to improve intra-firm monitoring systems in an attempt to prevent economically harmful events potentially giving rise to such litigation in future.

The mandatory 'market abuse' provision in the UK Financial Services and Markets Act 2000,[123] whilst not privately actionable by affected investors or as substantively far-reaching as its US counterpart, includes a fundamentally similar general prohibition on the provision of false or misleading information to participants in secondary trading markets.[124] As such, it could be said to likewise sit uneasily across the artificial conceptual divide between the securities and corporate law domains.

The same could be said for other nominally market-oriented protections that in substance affect the core distribution of decision-making power within UK public companies. These include the important mandatory rights vested collectively in the shareholders of a UK premium-listed company to approve or veto significant asset transactions and related party transactions involving managerial officers.[125] Also included in this category are the compulsory vote-holder notification rules contained in the UK Disclosure and Transparency Rules (DTR), which permit the public 'tracking' of large-scale share acquisition patterns with a view to identifying the formation of major corporate ownership stakes that could be indicative of a future takeover or other major control-related event.[126]

Empirical Legal Studies 687, 712.

[122] See *Basic v Levinson* 485 US 224 (1988).

[123] See Financial Services and Markets Act 2000 (FSMA), s 118.

[124] In particular, s 118(7) of FSMA defines market abuse as encapsulating (inter alia) 'the dissemination of information by any means which gives, or is likely to give, a false or misleading impression as to a qualifying investment by a person who knew or could reasonably be expected to have known that the information was false or misleading'.

[125] See United Kingdom Listing Authority Listing Rules (LR), LR 10 (Significant Transactions: Premium Listing) and LR 11 (Related Party Transactions).

[126] See DTR, above n 117, DTR 5.

Lastly and perhaps most significantly of all, the basic 'comply or explain' requirement underpinning the UK's characteristic system of market-invoking corporate governance norms is itself a public-regulatory phenomenon. In spite of the flexible and quasi-contractual nature of the UK Corporate Governance Code as discussed in chapter five, the Code's driving conformance-disclosure obligation is set out in the UK Listing Rules promulgated by the FSA in exercise of its statutorily delegated authority.[127] In consequence, this requirement is mandatory for both UK-incorporated and overseas premium-listed companies on the London Stock Exchange,[128] and also attributable in the last place to government itself as the formal determinant of the FSA's rule-making powers[129] (as illustrated by the coalition government's recent decision to abolish the FSA in its current form, and reallocate its former market-regulatory responsibilities to a new and more specialised Financial Conduct Authority [FCA], effective from 2013 onwards[130]).

E. The Inherent Arbitrariness of the Corporate/Securities Law Conceptual Dichotomy

However, even in situations where compulsory corporate disclosure regulation does little more than render corporate affairs and performance more conspicuous to the investor community, it cannot be said that this outcome is either extraneous to, or formally separable from, so-called 'core' corporate governance processes and norms (as the US internal affairs doctrine would seem to imply). Mandated corporate transparency, even in the most basic form of requiring periodic disclosures on ongoing financial performance, entails the regulatory state going considerably above and beyond its limited neo-liberal remit of enforcing contracts, property rights and surrounding 'rules-of-the-game'.[131]

---

[127] On this, see above ch 5 of this volume, fn 131.

[128] As of 2010, companies (both UK- and overseas-incorporated) listing on the Main Market of the London Stock Exchange are given the opportunity to opt for either a Standard or Premium Listing. The latter scheme entails a higher regulatory burden, but is expected correspondingly to elicit a lower cost of capital for listing companies. Under the UK Listing Rules, all listed UK-incorporated companies, plus all overseas companies with a Premium Listing, are mandatorily subject to the UK Corporate Governance Code's underpinning conformance-disclosure obligation. On this, see ch 5 above, ibid.

[129] The FSA's general rule-making power is established under section 138 of FSMA 2000. A range of more specific rule-making powers, meanwhile, are constituted under the other provisions of pt X, ch I of the Act.

[130] On this, see above ch 5 of this volume, fn 131; Lowry and Reisberg (eds), *Pettet's Company Law*, above n 110, ch 15.4.C.

[131] This term denotes labour, tort, environmental and other *non*-corporate-laws that seek to 'correct', by way of civil and criminal pecuniary penalties, the socially undesirable outcomes of corporate activities for third parties. On this, see above ch 3 of this volume, fns 16–18 and accompanying text.

Rather, a publicly-administered disclosure regime for the benefit of investors constitutes direct governmental action aimed at mitigating the informational disparity between managers and shareholders, so as to recalibrate – by means of interventionist regulation – the prevailing balance of governance power in the latter constituency's favour. This is arguably at least as much an aspect of direct investor protectionism inspired by political-distributional considerations, as it is a technical means of correcting failures in securities market pricing mechanisms.

Consequently, mandatory securities laws are not as readily susceptible to conceptual expulsion from the realm of 'internal' corporate to 'external' regulatory law as contractarian theorists have sought to infer. This important finding has the normative effect of 'blurring' the conventionally-perceived boundaries of corporate law as a subject and, in turn, undermining the purported privity of Anglo-American corporate governance as asserted within the dominant contractarian frame of reference.

III. THE REGULATORY DIVISION OF CORPORATE DECISION-MAKING POWER IN THE UNITED KINGDOM

A. The Distinctiveness of the 'Anglo' in the Anglo-American Descriptor

The above discussion has illustrated that, if mandatory corporate disclosure regulation is understood in its rightful sense as a core aspect of the law relating to internal corporate governance, then the basic character of corporate governance law as a subject of enquiry takes on a less contractually facilitative and, correspondingly, more public-regulatory hue. In the context of the US legal environment, this observation demonstrates the significant direct influence of federal transparency requirements in determining the formal contours of the shareholder-management relation within listed companies. As such, it challenges the significance of the internal affairs doctrine as a normative buffer between the federal and individual State law-making domains.

In the substantially unitary system of the United Kingdom,[132] by comparison, such concerns about the appropriate jurisdictional domain of corporate laws have not been relevant, although – as noted above – the influence of capital market regulation over corporate governance norms

---

[132] This is not to underestimate the influence of EU harmonisation measures over the modern development of UK corporate law, particularly in governance-related fields such as takeovers and shareholders' rights. A further significant dimension of the UK system is the effect of non-statutory 'soft' law measures in determining important corporate governance norms outside of direct legislative or judicial control, on which see above ch 5 of this volume, pt IV. I accordingly use the term 'unitary' merely to denote the *non*-federalist nature of the UK system, without meaning to undermine the importance of its uniquely pluralist character.

and processes has been no less significant within the British and wider European context. However, to focus only on the influence of corporate disclosure requirements within the British framework would be to elide the most significant public-regulatory dimension of UK corporate governance over the past century; and, indeed, the one legal trend that – arguably more than any other – marks out the distinctiveness of the 'Anglo' component within the Anglo-American corporate governance descriptor. This is the significant influence of successive post-war UK Companies Acts – the most recent of which being the Companies Act 2006 – in directly and mandatorily determining the structural division of decision-making power between directors and shareholders within the corporate-constitutional framework.[133]

Whilst – as I explained in chapter five – the powers of corporate boards in the United Kingdom are expressly stated to rest on a quasi-contractual basis,[134] other features of UK company law pertaining to the internal corporate power dynamic are, however, less readily reconcilable with the contractarian paradigm. In fact, some of the most crucial and comparatively distinctive shareholder rights in the United Kingdom are mandatory and irreversible in form. This means that their legal effect in respect of any individual company cannot be 'undone' by insertion of an appropriate offsetting provision in that firm's articles of association. In terms of the core themes of this book, the significant presence of mandatory corporate laws in the United Kingdom represents a potential challenge to the proposition that the British legal framework of corporate governance can be validly rationalised in accordance with contractarianism's private ordering ethos.

As will be discussed below, an especially difficult conceptual dilemma is thrown up by the fact that those provisions of UK company law which together represent the basis of the aforementioned contractual principle are *themselves* enshrined largely in the form of mandatory rules. At least at first sight, this appears fundamentally contradictory to the purpose that those provisions are designed to serve, which is to imbue corporate laws and structures with the perpetual qualities of flexibility and malleability. I will subsequently examine in chapter seven whether and to what extent this curious paradox underlying the United Kingdom's corporate law system represents an issue of concern for defenders of the contractarian paradigm.

---

[133] The initial and arguably most noteworthy such legislative initiative in the UK was the Companies Act 1948, which implemented the recommendations of the 1945 Cohen Committee Report on enhancing the influence of shareholders over core corporate decisions and affairs. With respect to reform of the internal balance of corporate decision-making power, the effect of subsequent post-1948 UK Companies Acts – including the current 2006 version – has by comparison been fairly limited. On this, see RC Nolan, 'The Continuing Evolution of Shareholder Governance' (2006) 65 *Cambridge Law Journal* 92, 103–09.

[134] See above ch 5 of this volume, pt III.

B. The (Paradoxical) Mandatory Basis of the Contractual Principle

Like any effective institutional feature of a supposed 'free' and 'deregulatory' market system, the contractual principle in UK corporate law – despite outward appearances – does not arise spontaneously out of thin air but rather is underpinned by a sophisticated and pre-ordained public-regulatory infrastructure. For this reason, the whole conceptual notion of 'private ordering' in UK corporate law can be regarded as a classic example of Orwellian 'double speak'.

Most fundamentally – as acknowledged in the previous chapter – the very formal status of the corporate constitution as a supposedly 'private' contractual document itself rests paradoxically on a *public* statutory basis: that is, section 33 of the Companies Act 2006 (and its previous statutory incarnations).[135] Moreover, this has been the case since the inception of the modern registered company in Great Britain.[136] Likewise, the corporate constitution's quasi-contractual characteristic of free alterability is also traditionally a creation of statute, and continues in this form today in the guise of section 21 of the Companies Act 2006, which provides for alteration of a company's articles by special resolution of its members.[137]

Of particular interest from the point of view of the current discussion is that both of the above Companies Act provisions are also rendered mandatory in form.[138] Therefore, with the exception of the very limited prescribed circumstances in which entrenchment of the articles is permitted today under statute,[139] the above provisions are generally incapable of

[135] On this, see above ch 5 of this volume, fns 6–7 and accompanying text.

[136] Furthermore, as Stephen Bottomley has observed, the early statutory versions of the present-day 'articles as contract' provision were concerned principally with simplifying the formal practicalities of the company registration process. Accordingly, the articles were deemed by statute to have legal effect vis-à-vis each member *as if* – or, in other words, *irrespective of* – whether they had in fact been signed and sealed by that person in accordance with standard contractual custom. Therefore it is arguably the case that the purported significance of this particular provision in establishing the fundamentally quasi-contractual nature of the corporate constitution has merely been assumed by academic and judicial observers ex post facto. See S Bottomley, *The Constitutional Corporation: Rethinking Corporate Governance* (Aldershot, Ashgate, 2007) 24–25.

[137] See above ch 5 of this volume, fn 8 and accompanying text.

[138] This is because of the default mandatory status of the provisions of the Companies Act 2006, which are incapable of constitutional ouster or amendment in respect of any individual firm unless expressly stated otherwise in the relevant sections of the Act itself. On this, see D Kershaw, *Company Law in Context: Text and Materials* (Oxford, Oxford University Press, 2009) 212.

[139] Section 22(1) of the Companies Act 2006 admittedly introduces for the first time into UK corporate law a limited constitutional entrenchment provision whereby '[a] company's articles may contain provision ("provision for entrenchment") to the effect that specified provisions of the articles may be amended or repealed only if conditions are met, or procedures are complied with, that are *more restrictive* than those applicable in the case of a special resolution' (emphasis added). However, the permissible scope for entrenchment of a company's articles under this provision is significantly limited, being possible only on the initial

being reversed or otherwise amended by constitutional provision regard-less of the level of shareholder support to this effect.[140]

In addition to having the aforementioned collective right formally to pass proposed changes to the articles, shareholders of UK companies are also empowered proactively to initiate proposals for constitutional amendment, which will subsequently be voted on by the company in General Meeting. Partly to this end, section 338 of the Companies Act 2006 permits one or more shareholders representing at least five per cent of the company's total voting rights, or alternatively 100 or more shareholders each holding at least £100 of voting shares, to propose special members' resolutions to be added to the agenda for a forthcoming General Meeting. In a public com-pany, any proposed members' resolutions must also be added to the proxy card[141] that is conventionally sent out by the company to its shareholders in advance of a General Meeting.[142] Significantly, under UK corporate law members' resolution – where successfully carried by the requisite majority of votes in General Meetings – are legally binding on the board, which ren-ders them a potentially more coercive governance tool for shareholders than precatory 14a-8 proposals in US public companies.[143]

The relevant shareholders may additionally request circulation, at the company's expense, of a written statement (of 1,000 words or less) in sup-port of their proposed resolution to be voted on at the meeting.[144] And, in urgent instances, shareholders representing at least five per cent of the total value of the company's voting shares may even request the board to con-vene an Extraordinary General Meeting outside of the normal annual meet-ing cycle, so as to enable any particularly pressing members' resolutions to be voted on.[145] Similarly to the aforementioned provisions, moreover, these

formation of the company or else by the unanimous resolution of members. In view of the practical near-impossibility of gaining unanimous support for a proposed resolution in a public company, coupled with the likelihood of strong investor hostility to proposed entrenchment provisions in respect of listed firms' constitutions, it can be confidently sur-mised that this innovation to UK corporate law will have a negligible impact outside of the closely-held private company sector (although its significance in this latter context is not disputed).

[140] The logical rationale for this was explained by Lord Lindley MR in *Allen v Gold Reefs of West Africa Ltd* [1900] 1 Ch 656 (CA) 671, on the overt public policy basis that '[b]e its nature what it may, the company is empowered by statute to alter the regulations contained in its articles from time to time by special resolutions; and any regulation or article purporting to deprive the company of this power is invalid on the ground that it is contrary to statute'.

[141] On the proxy card, and proxy voting process generally within public companies, see above ch 4 of this volume, fn 99.

[142] The company is furthermore obliged to pay the expenses incurred by the members in preparing the statement if sufficient requests for a resolution are received by the company before the end of the previous financial year.

[143] On the latter mechanism, see above ch 4 of this volume, pt IV.

[144] Companies Act 2006, ss 314–16.

[145] Companies Act 2006, s 303; as amended by The Companies (Shareholders' Rights) Regulations 2009 (SI 2009/1632) (which reduced the relevant threshold requirement from ten per cent to five per cent).

powers of shareholders are established on a mandatory and irreversible footing.

Although rarely used within UK public companies,[146] shareholders' statutory initiation rights are a crucial component of the contractual principle in UK corporate law insofar as they have the effect of re-balancing the constitutional amendment process in shareholders' favour vis-à-vis the company's board and senior managers. If shareholders of public companies did not possess the power of initiation in respect of constitutional amendments, their role would in effect be restricted to that of either approving or vetoing proposals made by management to this effect on an ex post facto basis.[147]

Accordingly, the above provisions as a whole together establish the important normative position that, in UK companies, directors' executive authority is subject to the inalienable collective prerogative of the shareholders to limit or even revoke entirely the board's managerial powers under the corporate constitution at any given moment in time. However, somewhat curiously from a contractarian perspective, the set of corporate law rules that make up this fundamental norm take the form of mandatory statutory pronouncements and thus, as a matter of legal form at least, are prima facie antithetical to the rationality of private ordering.

C. Shareholders' Statutory 'Shotgun' Right

Allied to and reinforcing shareholders' sovereign status within the corporate-constitutional structure is the most coercive of their rights vis-à-vis a company's board and senior management. This is the collective power that a company's members enjoy under section 168 of the Companies Act 2006 to dismiss (or 'fire') any or all of the firm's directors, even without due contractual cause, by passing an ordinary (ie majority) resolution to this effect in General Meeting. This important corporate governance provision – which may be referred to for want of a better term as the shareholders' 'shotgun' power – is superimposed by statute onto the standard constitutional procedure for rotational retirement and reappointment of directors of public companies at three-year intervals.[148]

---

[146] Certainly, s 338 proposals in the UK are used considerably less frequently than 14a-8 proposals in the US, even accounting for the UK's much smaller public company population.

[147] With the (limited) exception of those issues in respect of which shareholders have been permitted to make 14a-8 proposals (on which, see above ch 4 of this volume, pt IV), this has traditionally been the accepted dynamic of shareholder-management relations within US public companies. On this, see above ch 2 of this volume, fns 51–52 and accompanying text.

[148] Model Articles for Public Companies, arts 20–21. In the case of those public companies that: (a) have a Premium Listing on the Main Market of the London Stock Exchange; and (b) are in the FTSE 350 group of companies; the most recent (June 2010) version of the UK Corporate Governance Code further recommends that all directors of the firm subject themselves to re-appointment by shareholders on an annual basis. See UK Corporate Governance Code, above n 91, Provision B.7.1.

Under UK corporate law, the shareholders' shotgun power is mandatory and irreversible,[149] which marks a crucial point of distinction between the UK corporate governance system and its US (Delaware) counterpart.[150] In UK companies, shareholders' mandatory shotgun power allied to their aforementioned rights of access to the company's proxy card (if necessary, by means of a specially-convened EGM) gives them the capacity to propose the dismissal of any or all of the board, and their replacement with nominated substitutes, at any time.

Admittedly, as a practical matter, the exercise of shareholders' power in this regard is significantly constrained by a number of factors. Section 168 does not deprive a director who is fired without cause of any compensation or damages due to him on account of his premature termination, which in the case of highly remunerated directors can make the use of this provision cost-ineffective from the company's perspective.[151] Further factors discouraging the ready use of this power are the likelihood of causing disturbance to the company's business and/or generating negative publicity (especially where the intended target of the proverbial shotgun is the board as a whole), the difficulties of finding superior replacements for the sacked directors, and also the immense challenge of mobilising sufficient shareholder support within a public company both to propose and carry a dismissal resolution in the first place.[152]

But although the above impediments invariably restrict the actual exercise of shareholders' aforementioned rights of intervention to the most exceptional or manifest cases of corporate mismanagement, from a private ordering perspective the shotgun power can potentially have a significant indirect effect. Through a contractarian lens, the shotgun power can be depicted metaphorically in terms of a legal 'nuclear deterrent': in that whilst its direct use can inflict considerable collateral costs on all parties involved, the mere prospect of it being mobilised as a last resort influences in shareholders' favour the terms of their notional 'bargaining game' with management concerning the ultimate objectives of the firm. In turn, it can help to

---

[149] Admittedly, the controversial House of Lords decision in *Bushell v Faith* [1970] AC 1099 rendered it permissible for directors indirectly to entrench themselves in office by virtue of weighted voting rights exercisable in their capacity as a shareholder, which could be used in order to defeat any dismissal resolution proposed against them. However, similarly to the statutory constitutional entrenchment provision referred to in note 139 above, the likelihood of strong investor hostility to so-called *Bushell v Faith* clauses in widely-held public companies is likewise liable to restrict the use of such provisions almost exclusively to the closely-held private company sector (in which latter context they can fulfil a highly valuable regulating function in respect of inter-personal membership disputes). On this, see Kershaw, *Company Law in Context*, above n 138, 215–16.

[150] On the latter system's approach to this issue, see above ch 4 of this volume, fns 11–14 and accompanying text.

[151] See Companies Act 2006, s 168(5).

[152] On this, see A Keay, 'Company Directors Behaving Poorly: Disciplinary Options for Shareholders' [2007] *Journal of Business Law* 656, 673–75.

engender the reflexive development of powerful extra-legal substantive norms that exert an ongoing low-level influence on managers independently of the company's formal governance mechanisms.

Indeed, the statutory shotgun provision is for the above reasons arguably the most significant legal-institutional factor underlying the centrality of the so-called 'shareholder wealth-maximisation norm'[153] within UK corporate governance today, notwithstanding the absence of any explicit judicial or legislative decree to this effect in the annals of British corporate law.[154] As such, it is a crucial component of shareholders' privileged quasi-contractual status within the UK corporate governance model. However, like shareholders' other statutory rights of intervention in corporate decision-making discussed above, the shotgun right rests on a mandatory statutory basis. Prima facie, this renders it thoroughly *anti*-contractual in form, and consequently puts into further question the validity of private ordering as a normative rationalisation of the UK corporate governance system's prevailing characteristics.

D. Shareholders' Statutory Anti-Dilution Rights

In the preceding examination of shareholders' statutory rights of intervention or 'voice' in corporate decision-making, it was emphasised that such rights remain highly significant within the broader framework of UK corporate governance notwithstanding the relative rarity of instances where they are actually invoked. However, a further distinctive characteristic of the equity relation in UK companies (at least in relation to their US counterparts) is the role of mandatory corporate finance regulation – and, in particular, shareholders' statutory anti-dilution rights – in protecting the prevailing distribution of equity interests and resulting voting power within the corporate-constitutional structure. Insofar as shareholders' anti-dilution rights (unlike their aforementioned 'voice' rights) are in fact frequently invoked in British public companies, they can consequently be said to be of foremost practical influence in mitigating management's scope for exploitation or unilateral disempowerment of investors within the UK environment.

The key statutory provisions in this regard – both of which are today contained within the Companies Act 2006 – are: first, the prohibition on unauthorised share allotments;[155] and, secondly, the phenomenon of shareholders'

---

[153] On this phenomenon generally, see above ch 3 of this volume, fn 14.

[154] As one leading commentator has pointed out, '[h]istorically there has been in most jurisdictions no legislative proclamation or unequivocal judicial statement which provides directors with a clear answer to what is the corporate objective'. See A Keay, 'Ascertaining The Corporate Objective: An Entity Maximisation and Sustainability Model' (2008) 71 *Modern Law Review* 663, 666.

[155] See Companies Act 2006, ss 549–51.

pre-emption rights.[156] By virtue of the former provision, the directors of a public company (or private company with one more than one class of shares) may only exercise the company's power to issue new shares with the approval of the shareholders in General Meeting.[157] Consequent to the latter provision, meanwhile, a company's existing shareholders must be granted a 14-day or more period of 'first refusal' over any new ordinary shares that that company proposes to allot, in proportion to their respective existing equity stakes in the company.[158] Although neither of these rights can properly be regarded as an aspect of authorised shareholder 'voice' in the sense of the other rights described above, they are nonetheless both crucial aspects of the division of corporate decision-making power in the United Kingdom, insofar as their joint effect is to restrict the discretionary leeway that management would otherwise enjoy in making decisions with respect to the firm's capital structure.[159]

From an investor protection perspective, the above provisions are crucial in safeguarding shareholders against unauthorised dilution of their equity interest, and also against uncompensated transfers of wealth from existing to new shareholders following a share issue at below the prevailing market price of a company's equity.[160] The same rules can also be regarded as fulfilling an important managerial-disciplinary function by preventing a company's controlling officers from allotting new equity on a covert and/or selective basis in response to capitalisation or cash flow shortfalls. As a result, managers are compelled to 'return to the market' to raise new capital, whereby they will be expected in effect to 'submit' both their past performance record and future capital allocation plans for collective investor scrutiny, as a precondition to the firm being able to continue to raise external (ie non-internally-retained) capital or funds on relatively advantageous terms.[161]

---

[156] See Companies Act 2006, ss 561–63, as reinforced by the additional (and longer standing) pre-emption rights requirement applicable to UK listed companies under Listing Rule 9.3.11.

[157] Companies Act 2006, ss 549(1) and 551(1).

[158] Companies Act 2006, ss 561(1) and 562(5), as amended by Reg 2 of the The Companies (Share Capital and Acquisition by Company of its Own Shares) Regulations 2009 (SI 2009/2022), which reduced the former 21-day statutory minimum period for acceptances from existing shareholders to 14 days. In the case of the corresponding Listing Rules requirement, the relevant minimum offer period is stated as 10 *business* days (excluding weekends and bank holidays), although the effect is by and large equivalent (see Listing Rule 9.5.6).

[159] On this, see PL Davies, 'Shareholder Value, Company Law and Securities Markets Law – A British View' (2003), available at: ssrn.com/abstract=250324, 20. Although my textual references here are to the online (SSRN) version of the paper, it has latterly been published in KJ Hopt and E Wymeersch (eds), *Capital Markets and Company Law* (Oxford, Oxford University Press, 2003) 261.

[160] See ibid.

[161] On the corporate external capital-raising process as a managerial disciplinary mechanism generally, see FH Easterbrook, 'Two Agency Cost Explanations of Dividends' (1984) 74 *American Economic Review* 650.

Most significantly of all from a corporate governance perspective, both of the above provisions also provide shareholders with legally guaranteed control over the corporate voting franchise. This is crucial in the context of contests for corporate control because, in the absence of legal protection against equity dilution, poison pills and other selective stock issue schemes can be implemented by managers in response to an unwanted bid for the company.[162]

From the perspective of the argument at hand, the above provisions would on first inspection appear to *support*, rather than undermine, the empirical validity of the contractarian paradigm within the UK context. This is for two main reasons. First of all, both the statutory prohibition on unauthorised share allotments and statutory pre-emption rights doctrine are expressly rendered susceptible to disapplication at the collective behest of shareholders.[163] Consequently, investors retain the capacity to permit the board in future to effect share allotments generally without specific shareholder approval, and also to allot new equity to any specific investor(s) on a selective and *non*-pre-emptive basis.[164] Therefore, in circumstances where the bureaucratic costs to a company of allotting equity on an authorised and pre-emptive basis are deemed to outweigh the corresponding benefits to investors in the form of enhanced managerial accountability, such procedural requirements can lawfully be overridden by corporate participants in the interest of administrative cost-effectiveness. Prima facie at least, this seems like an archetypical example of the contractarian paradigm of corporate governance 'in action'.

A second reason as to why the structure of shareholders' statutory anti-dilution rights in the United Kingdom could be regarded as consistent with contractarian rationality is the fact that, to a significant extent, these provisions are arguable examples of regulatory 'gold-plating'. That is to

[162] As Parkinson explains: 'The intended framework of shareholder decision-making and management accountability would . . . be undermined if the board were free to alter the composition of the majority in order to neutralize shareholder power', and '[t]he most obvious form of manipulation is for the directors to allot additional shares to themselves or their supporters in order to guarantee a majority of votes'. See *Corporate Power and Responsibility*, above n 71, 137. On the corresponding position under Delaware law, where equity dilution is essentially permitted as an aspect of directors' general fiduciary discretion over business judgments (subject to prior satisfaction of the *Unocal* doctrine in the case of a control-related scenario), see above ch 4 of this volume, pts III and IV.C.

[163] Section 551(2) of the Companies Act 2006 permits a company's shareholders, by way of ordinary resolution, to give its directors the general authorisation to allot new shares in future, or alternatively to authorise a particular future exercise of the power by directors. Furthermore, in cases where the directors of a company are given general authorisation in the above way, the shareholders may further resolve (by way of special resolution) to empower the directors to allot new equity securities in the company as if both the statutory and Listing Rules pre-emption rights requirements did not apply (see Companies Act 2006, s 570(1); LR 9.3.12(1)).

[164] Section 571 of the Companies Act 2006 (and, likewise, Listing Rule 9.3.12(1)) alternatively allows the pre-emption rights requirement to be disabled – by way of special resolution – only in respect of a specified allotment of equity securities.

say, they merely serve to reinforce rules that are determined elsewhere within the law in a largely quasi-contractual manner, and whose application would likely produce the same basic substantive outcome regardless. Most notable in this regard is the UK Takeover Code's longstanding prohibition on unauthorised share dilutions and other managerial actions that have the effect of frustrating an actual or imminent bid for a public company, and which is widely (and justifiably) regarded as an authoritative statement of investor-driven best practice in a contest-for-control scenario.[165] Accordingly, it may be concluded that shareholders' anti-dilution rights – far from representing a material regulatory intervention in the ordering of intra-firm affairs – are ultimately just a statutory affirmation of endogenous corporate governance norms, with the effect that they *reinforce*, rather than detract from, pre-existing private ordering dynamics.

In response to such arguments, though, the following important observations represent salient evidence *against* the proposition that shareholders' statutory anti-dilution rights are, at root, contractually-determined phenomena. First, whilst such rights are formally capable of being disapplied, it should be noted that disapplication of a right is *not* the same thing as reversibility or 'opt-out' in the sense described in chapter four. As I explained earlier in the book, the essential characteristic of a reversible or 'opt-out' right is its capacity to be eradicated or overridden *completely* insofar as its application to an individual firm is concerned.[166] However, in the case of both the statutory prohibition on unauthorised share allotments and the statutory pre-emption rights scheme, disapplication of the relevant provisions is expressly deemed to be possible for a specified period of no more than five years from the formal date of disapplication.[167] The effect in practice within many public companies is to establish a periodic process of dialogue between management and shareholders, whereby management is compelled to elicit reasons in support of its request for original or further disapplication of either or both the above procedural requirements.[168] The

---

[165] See The Panel on Takeovers and Mergers, The Takeover Code (September 2011), General Principle 3 and Rule 21, available at: www.thetakeoverpanel.org.uk/wp-content/uploads/2008/11/code.pdf.

[166] On this, see above ch 4 of this volume, fns 4–6 and accompanying text.

[167] See Companies Act 2006, s 551(3)(b). Strictly speaking, this restriction only applies to general authorisations of directors' share allotment power. However, since (under s 570(1)) general disapplication by shareholders of the pre-emption rights scheme is only permissible in companies where general allotment authorisation has already been given, it follows that the disapplication period for pre-emption rights is necessarily limited in accordance with the same time frame.

[168] In deciding whether to vote in approval of a disapplication request (ie where the board wishes to allot new equity securities on a *non*-pre-emptive basis), institutional shareholders will in practice be guided by the non-legally binding *Statement of Principles* (July 2008) on disapplication of pre-emption rights promulgated by the Pre-Emption Group of the Financial Reporting Council. These Principles indicate (inter alia) that: (i) disapplication requests are more likely to be routine in nature when the company is seeking authority to issue, non-preemptively, *no more than 5 per cent of ordinary share capital in any one year*; (ii) companies should

resulting process of management-shareholder communications, whilst overtly quasi-contractual in nature, is nonetheless possible only in the persisting proverbial 'shadow' of the mandatory regulatory requirement for management to renew its free allotment mandate from shareholders at specified minimum intervals.

A second observation that can be said to refute the contractarian rationalisation of shareholders' anti-dilution rights is the fact that the 'no frustration' rule in the UK Takeover Code – in addition to applying *only* in the relatively limited context of a bid scenario[169] – is *itself* ultimately reinforced, and – moreover – substantively *substitutable* in large part, by the longstanding 'proper purpose' doctrine at common law.[170] This latter principle, which is today embodied in statutory form within section 171 of the Companies Act 2006,[171] essentially dictates that it is 'unconstitutional for directors to use their fiduciary powers over the shares in the company for the purpose of destroying an existing majority, or creating a new majority which did not previously exist'.[172] According to Lord Wilberforce, '[t]o do so is to interfere with that element of the company's constitution which is *separate from and set against their powers*' (emphasis added),[173] thereby putting directors in breach of their fiduciary duty to the company *irrespective of* whether their actions in this regard were carried out in good faith for the perceived benefit of the company itself.[174] This

not normally issue more than 7.5 per cent of the company's ordinary share capital for cash other than to existing shareholders in any rolling three year period; and (iii) in determining the price of a rights issue relative to the current market price of a company's shares, *a discount of greater than 5 per cent is not likely to be regarded as routine*. See: www.pre-emption-group.org.uk/Principles.aspx. On the practical difficulties that these Principles have been prone to give rise to in some companies, including their (unintended) effect in constraining corporate financing flexibility, see P Myners, *Pre-Emption Rights: Final Report* (London, Department of Trade and Industry, 2005), available at: www.bis.gov.uk/files/file28436.pdf.

[169] Specifically, the Takeover Code's 'no frustration' rule (Rule 21) is stated to apply '[d]uring the course of an offer, or . . . before the date of the offer if the board of the offeree company has reason to believe that a bona fide offer might be imminent'. See The Takeover Code, above n 165, Rule 21.1.

[170] On the contours of this doctrine generally, see *Hogg v Cramphorn Ltd* [1967] Ch 254; *Teck Corporation v Millar* (1973) 33 DLR (3d) 288 (British Columbia Supreme Court); *Howard Smith Ltd v Ampol Petroleum Ltd* [1974] AC 821 (Privy Council); *Criterion Properties plc v Stratford UK Properties LLC and Others* [2003] BCC 50 (HL); Parkinson, *Corporate Power and Responsibility*, above n 71, 140–47.

[171] In particular, section 171(b) requires that '[a] director of a company . . . only exercise powers for the purposes for which they are conferred', although this is generally regarded as a (brief) summation of the pre-established proper purpose doctrine at common law. The continuing relevance of the pre-2006 authorities underlying this rule is expressly affirmed by section 170(4) of the Act, which provides that '[t]he general duties [of company directors] shall be interpreted in the same way as common law rules or equitable principles, and regard shall be had to the corresponding common law rules and equitable principles in interpreting and applying the general duties'.

[172] *Howard Smith Ltd v Ampol Petroleum Ltd*, above n 170, 837 (Lord Wilberforce).

[173] Ibid.

[174] As Buckley J emphasised in *Hogg v Cramphorn Ltd*, above n 170, [1967] Ch 254, 268: 'It is not . . . open to the directors in such a case to say, "We genuinely believe that what we seek

clearly establishes that the fiduciary prohibition on directorial equity dilution under the proper purpose doctrine is *logically prior* to the board's continuing possession and exercise of the discretionary administrative power vested in it under the corporate-constitutional framework.

Moreover, like any directorial duty under UK corporate law, the proper purpose doctrine is established as a mandatory and inert legal component of the equity relation, thus rendering it incapable of reversal or modification via offsetting contractual or constitutional provision.[175] It can therefore be surmised that, even if the Takeover Code's 'no frustration' principle did not exist, a fundamentally equivalent substantive outcome (ie unimpeded corporate control contests) would arise from the operation of the mandatory proper purpose doctrine at common law.[176] Accordingly, and notwithstanding the administrative convenience that the Takeover Code and Panel undoubtedly bring to the determination of control-related disputes concerning British public target companies today, it remains the case that shareholders' core anti-dilution rights – on which their continuing constitutional 'sovereignty' within the UK corporate law model can be said principally to hinge – *cannot* rightfully be regarded as a contractually-determined phenomenon. On the contrary, these pivotal corporate governance rights are for the most part attributable at root to *public-regulatory* – rather than private-contractual – initiative. This finding further underscores a revisionist conception of shareholders' corporate governance rights in the United Kingdom as existing on an exogenous and entrenched institutional basis, and thus as largely *transcending* the endogenous domain of decentralised private ordering.

to prevent the majority from doing will harm the company and therefore our act in arming ourselves or our party with sufficient shares to outvote the majority is a conscientious exercise of our powers under the articles, which should not be interfered with'''. The blunt English judicial position on this matter, rather, is that a court 'will not . . . permit directors to exercise powers, which have been delegated to them by the company in circumstances which put the directors in a fiduciary position when exercising those powers, in such a way as to interfere with the exercise by the majority of its constitutional rights' (*ibid*). In modern statutory parlance, the implication therefore is that section 171 (the proper purpose doctrine) in effect 'trumps' section 172 (the duty of loyalty) in determining the propriety of directorial conduct involving interference with the company's pre-existing balance of shareholder voting power. Notably, Parkinson has defended this lexical ordering of the two principles (albeit writing prior to their statutory codification) on the basis that the proper purpose doctrine, '[b]y invalidating takeover defences regardless of motive . . . ensures that the members are able to make their own evaluation of the merits of a bid without management interference'. See *Corporate Power and Responsibility*, above n 71, 141.

[175] On this, see above ch 5 of this volume, fns 79–81 and accompanying text.

[176] Admittedly, the (arguably semi-subjective) 'substantial purpose' test promulgated by Lord Wilberforce in *Howard Smith* (above n 170) for determining the propriety of directorial conduct allegedly in breach of the proper purpose doctrine provides a materially greater degree of substantive leeway to defendant directors than the rigid 'no frustration' rule under the Takeover Code. On this, see Parkinson, *Corporate Power and Responsibility*, above n 71, 144. Notwithstanding, the intended effect of both provisions is fundamentally similar – that is, to render attempted equity dilutions *unsusceptible* to the normal 'good faith' standard of evaluation under the director's duty of loyalty. On this, see above n 174.

IV. THE *COUNTER*-CONTRACTUAL NATURE OF THE EQUITABLE
FIDUCIARY PRINCIPLE UNDER ANGLO-AMERICAN LAW

In chapters four and five, I explained the effect of the US business judgment rule and UK internal management doctrine in establishing a strong
judicial disinclination to intervene in – or otherwise subject to questioning
– strategic and other managerial decisions undertaken at the micro (ie
individual firm) level.[177] As a consequence, the basic ex ante decision-
making primacy of the board is reaffirmed – on an ex post facto basis –
by the near-watertight immunity that directors enjoy from retrospective
judicial scrutiny of any honestly taken decisions that are conducive to
negative payoffs for the corporation and its shareholders.[178]

Notwithstanding the effect of the above doctrines, and also the various
aforementioned ways in which the liability 'sting' of fiduciary liability can
be eradicated or reduced for directors,[179] it remains the case that – on a
base level at least – the fiduciary capacity of directors is a necessary *constant* of the equity relation as it exists within any corporation. In corporate
law it is trite that directors, as fiduciary representatives of the company
(and, indirectly, its shareholders), are generally required to prioritise the
interests of the company as a whole above their own personal interests at
all times, and to seek to avoid situations that are liable to give rise to conflict in this regard. Understood in this sense, the fiduciary principle is a
structural prerequisite of the wide scope of executive discretion with
which boards, and their managerial delegates, are habitually entrusted
within the corporate constitutional framework. This is because the inalienable fiduciary capacity of directors is of fundamental importance in
establishing the basic normative inclination of the board as the company's
effective agents. As such, the board is expected to resolve the administrative discretion that it enjoys in the ultimate service of the company's interests, while using its collective entrepreneurial judgement to decide upon
the specific courses of action that are most conducive to this end.

Without the general guidepost provided by the fiduciary principle,
directors would have no broad criterion of accountability by which to

[177] See above ch 4 of this volume, pt III (on the US business judgment rule); ch 5 of this
volume, pt II.A (on the UK internal management doctrine).

[178] That is, at least where the negative payoff for the corporation involved falls short of
outright and manifest wastage of corporate resources. On this, see *Lewis v Vogelstein* 699 A 2d
327 (Del Ch 1997) 366 (Chancellor Allen): 'The judicial standard for determination of corporate waste is well-developed. Roughly, a waste entails an exchange of corporate assets for
consideration so disproportionately small as to lie beyond the range at which any reasonable
person might be willing to trade. Most often the claim is associated with a transfer of corporate assets that serves no corporate purpose; or for which no consideration at all is
received'. See also *Brehm v Eisner* 746 A 2d 244 (Del 2000).

[179] On this, see above ch 4 of this volume, fns 15–16 and accompanying text; ch 5 of this
volume, pt II.C.

determine the overall propriety of their conduct when exercising (or authorising the subordinate exercise of) their executive discretion. The likely result is that the continuing exercise of this discretion would be rendered illegitimate – and hence unsustainable – in the eyes of those who principally stand to be affected by it (namely shareholders). For this reason, it can justifiably be said that the equitable fiduciary doctrine – far from constraining the discretion that directors enjoy when making decisions with respect to the allocation and/or appropriation of the corporation's invested resources – is, contrarily, *intrinsic* to the very possession and exercise of such discretion by directors in the first place.

Although the fiduciary principle could be said to function as an influential general norm for directors (or, at least, legally well-advised directors) at all times, the situations in which directors' fiduciary duties to the company can potentially be enforced as a basis for potential liability are both limited and relatively marginal. As any corporate lawyer will testify, the fiduciary doctrine is predominantly applicable in so-called 'self-dealing' situations, where directors are typically accused either of making a personal profit out of their position in the company, or else of having a direct or indirect commercial relationship with the company that potentially compromises their supposed impartiality of commercial judgement when acting for the company.

The relevant UK and American Law Institute (ALI, whose Model Business Corporation Act has been adopted by the majority of US States *other than* Delaware) provisions on directorial self-dealing comprise tests that focus first and foremost on whether the relevant profit or transaction has been properly disclosed by the conflicted director.[180] Delaware, on the other hand, has constructed an approach that by comparison focuses more on the adjudged substantive fairness of the conduct in question.[181] I do not intend to go into further doctrinal detail on the various competing approaches, which have been more than adequately analysed elsewhere.[182] It suffices to note for present purposes that, in situations where the

---

[180] On the UK position, see Companies Act 2006, ss 175(5), 177(1) and 182(1); *Bhullar v Bhullar* [2003] 2 BCLC 241 (CA) (Jonathan Parker LJ) re the requirement for disclosure of corporate opportunities that directors intend to exploit personally: 'Whether the company could or would have taken [the] opportunity, had it been made aware of it, is not to the point: the existence of the opportunity was information which it was relevant for the company to know, and it follows that *the [directors] were under a duty to communicate it to the company*' (emphasis added). On the ALI position, see Model Business Corporation Act, §§ 8.60–8.63 and 8.70; ALI, Principles of Corporate Governance, § 5.05.

[181] See (re conflicting interest transactions) Delaware General Corporation Law, § 144; *Sinclair Oil Corp v Levien* 280 A 2d 717 (Del 1971); (re the corporate opportunity doctrine) *Broz v Cellular Information Systems* 673 A 2d 148 (Del 1996) (Veasey CJ): 'It is not the law of Delaware that presentation to the board is a necessary prerequisite to a finding that a corporate opportunity has not been usurped'.

[182] See, eg C O'Kelley and R Thompson, *Corporations and Other Business Associations: Cases and Materials*, 6th edn (New York, Aspen, 2010) 277–323; Kershaw, *Company Law in Context*, above n 138, chs 13–14.

perceived impartiality of a director is undermined by a potential positional conflict of interest, the business judgment (or internal management)
protection to which they would ordinarily be entitled lapses. At the very
least, the invocation of such protection by a defendant director in such
circumstances will be dependent on certain prior showings by him
concerning the averred transparency and/or fairness of the conduct in
question.

As noted earlier, the fiduciary principle has conventionally been rationalised by contractarian theorists in terms of a so-called contractual 'gap-
filling' mechanism.[183] From this perspective, the doctrine is understood as
a logical structural response by (informationally- and computationally-
limited) shareholders and managers to 'the impossibility of writing
contracts completely specifying the parties' obligations'.[184] This is on the
commonly acknowledged basis that '[n]o contract can cover all contingencies'.[185] Therefore, by enabling courts to render invalid or inequitable
any future directorial conduct that fails to satisfy certain broad statutory
or judicial thresholds of transparency and/or fairness, the law is perceived to have the notional effect of retroactively 'mimicking' the outcomes that the contracting parties would have reached ex ante had they
been possessed with full information and foresight at the relevant time.[186]

Moreover, since – according to this particular view – the corporate fiduciary principle is nothing more than a surrogate relational contract term, it
logically follows that this doctrine has no special legal or moral status
over and above that of other quasi-contractual provisions determinative
of a firm's internal governance arrangements.[187] Hence the normative
implication is that the fiduciary principle – like any ordinary contractual
term – should be readily reversible or alterable by private contractors at
will on an ad hoc basis, where its continuing operation and potential
enforcement is deemed administratively cost-ineffective from the perspective of the firm and its shareholders.

Although the contractarian depiction of the fiduciary principle as an
excludable contractual construct has apparently had a marginal degree of

[183] On this, see above ch 3 of this volume, fns 58, 79–80 and accompanying text.

[184] Easterbrook and Fischel, 'Contract and Fiduciary Duty' (1993) 36 *Journal of Law &
Economics* 425, 426.

[185] Ibid. Easterbrook and Fischel note that the problem of contractual incompleteness is
confounded, moreover, in situations where the contractual subject-matter is highly complex,
particularly where a transaction involves the hiring of professional or other expertise. See
'Contract and Fiduciary Duty', ibid.

[186] As Easterbrook and Fischel explain: 'When one party hires the other's knowledge and
expertise, there is not much they can write down. Instead of specific undertakings, the agent
assumes a duty of loyalty in pursuit of the objective and a duty of care in performance'.
Accordingly it can be said that the law, by applying the fiduciary principle as a general default
rule in such scenarios, is 'prescribing the outcomes the parties themselves would have reached
had information been plentiful and negotiations costless'. 'Contract and Fiduciary Duty', n 184
above, 427.

[187] Ibid.

judicial support within the Anglo-American environment,[188] the over-whelming weight of jurisprudence on this issue[189] establishes a converse view of the doctrine as being *counter*-contractual – or, perhaps more accurately, *pre*-contractual – in nature. That is to say, rather than being a consequential *product* of intra-firm contracting, the fiduciary principle actually operates *as against* – or, on an alternative view, *logically prior to* – the micro-level private ordering process. Whilst the longstanding equitable prohibition on undisclosed self-dealing by fiduciaries is often regarded to be a *consequence* of a trustee, agent, or director's duty of loyalty to his beneficiary, principal, or shareholders, the better interpretation of the

---

[188] See, eg the Commonwealth decision in *Hospital Products Ltd v United States Surgical Corporation* (1984) 156 CLR 41, 97, where the High Court of Australia (Mason J) provided that: 'The fiduciary relationship, if it is to exist at all, must accommodate itself to the terms of the contract so that it is consistent with, and conforms to, them. The fiduciary relationship cannot be superimposed upon the contract in such a way as to alter the operation which the contract was intended to have according to its true construction'. See also the dictum of Lord Browne-Wilkinson in the case of *Kelly v Cooper* [1992] AC 205 (PC), where his Lordship opined that: 'like every other contract, the rights and duties of the principal and agent are dependent upon the terms of the contract between them, whether express or implied. It is not possible to say that all agents owe the same duties to their principals: it is always necessary to have regard to the express or implied terms of the contract'. Both of the above opinions imply that the relevance of private ordering rationality is highly pertinent within the fiduciary relational context. In response, however, it should be noted that the former of these cases is a first instance Australian decision, the facts of which essentially concerned the construction of a distributorship agreement. As such, its status as a valid authority on the application of directors' duties within UK companies is – to say the least – highly questionable. Meanwhile, the latter authority – a Privy Council decision – nonetheless concerned the factually distinct question of whether an estate agent was bound – as a fiduciary – to disclose to his client the fact that he was also acting for the seller of a neighbouring property, where the same purchaser was intent on purchasing both properties (thus making this information highly material from the first client's perspective, in terms of the price that he could potentially expect to obtain for his property from the eventual purchaser). There was, furthermore, no suggestion in this case that the defendant estate agent was personally profiting by not disclosing this information to the first client, which in any event would have entailed a breach of confidentiality vis-à-vis his fiduciary relationship with the second client. Although refusing to disclose this information may have resulted in the first client obtaining a lower than possible price for his property, this outcome could not be regarded as fundamentally antithetical to the first client's interest as a principal. Consequently, it cannot be said that the estate agent fundamentally abrogated his capacity as a fiduciary at any time during his dealings with the first client, as would have occurred had he personally benefited therefrom. This renders the *Kelly v Cooper* case clearly distinguishable from corporate self-dealing cases not just on the basis that no *directorial* conflict of interest is involved, but also on the ground that the alleged conflict in question cannot be equated in any way with an orthodox self-dealing scenario. As such, the first client cannot be said to have in any way (whether expressly or implicitly) 'contracted out' of his basic fiduciary right vis-à-vis the estate agent, simply by employing the agent under circumstances where it was conceivable that such a conflict of competing fiduciary duties on the agent's part could occur. Therefore all that this authority establishes is that the precise content of a fiduciary's obligations towards his principal will inevitably vary depending on the specific factual context, *not* that the basic fiduciary duty existing between a principal and agent is *itself* contractually removable at the behest of either party. In short, then, the primacy of private ordering in the fiduciary relational context is *not* made out here.

[189] For a brief summary of some of the most prominent strands thereof, see below nn 192–93.

classical case law on the fiduciary principle[190] is that such reasoning should be *reversed*.

Accordingly, it can be said that the fiduciary's 'good faith' duty of loyalty towards his principal or beneficiary is – at least in circumstances of unequal informational access between the parties[191] – only an effective and credible constraint on the fiduciary's exercise of day-to-day discretionary administrative power *because of* the pre-existing prohibition on undisclosed self-dealing to which he is subject. The logic here is that, by curtailing the scope for dishonest promotion of personal over corporate interest by directors at source, the fiduciary principle creates effective 'space' for courts to adopt a generally liberal and non-interventionist position (under the business judgment rule or internal management doctrine) when assessing the propriety of purportedly honest decisions made in the interests of the company. Otherwise, the duty of loyalty would necessarily have to rest on an *objective* (as opposed to subjective) foundation, as honesty on the part of the defendant director could not justifiably be presumed by the court a priori.[192]

---

[190] On this, see ibid.

[191] It is noteworthy that, whilst Easterbrook and Fischel refute the significance of informational asymmetries as a justificatory basis for the fiduciary principle on the basis that such asymmetries exist also in non-fiduciary contexts, this view has been described as 'puzzling' given that 'informational asymmetries are part and parcel of the monitoring problem involved in hiring expertise' (to which the same authors argue the fiduciary relation is primarily targeted). See Easterbrook and Fischel, 'Contract and Fiduciary Duty', above n 184, 436; R Romano, 'Comment on Easterbrook and Fischel, "Contract and Fiduciary Duty"' (1993) 36 *Journal of Law and Economics* 447, 448. If (as the latter of the above views seems to suggest) the fiduciary principle in corporate law – and equity generally – can indeed be regarded as motivated by the acknowledged prevalence of informational asymmetry and consequent unilateral contractual vulnerability within such relationships, then it can arguably be inferred that the existence of this doctrine is underpinned by a *public-protectionist*, rather than private-contractualist, ethos.

[192] This important (and frequently elided) point is made by Lord Eldon in the early English case of *Ex parte James* (1803) 8 Ves 337, where his Lordship explained that: '[The fiduciary principle] *stands much more upon general principles than upon the circumstances of any individual case*. It rests upon this: that the [self-dealing transaction] is not permitted in any case however honest the circumstances; the general interests of justice requiring it to be destroyed in every instance; as *no court is equal to the examination and ascertainment of the truth in much the greater number of cases*' (emphasis added). In a similar vein, Lord Russell of Killowen emphasised in *Aberdeen Railway Co v Blaikie Bros*, (1854) 1 Macq 461 (HL) that: 'The rule of equity which insists on those, who by use of a fiduciary position make a profit, being liable to account for that profit, in no way depends on fraud, or absence of bona fides; or upon such questions or considerations as whether the profit would or should otherwise have gone to the plaintiff, or whether the profiteer was under a duty to obtain the source of the profit for the plaintiff, or whether he took a risk or acted as he did for the benefit of the plaintiff, or whether the plaintiff has in fact been damaged or benefited by his action. *The liability arises from the mere fact of a profit having, in the stated circumstances, been made. The profiteer, however honest and well-intentioned, cannot escape the risk of being called upon to account*' (emphasis added). This frequently cited dictum clearly establishes that the fiduciary obligation of directors to avoid putting themselves in a position where their interest and duty may potentially conflict *logically precedes* their corresponding duty to act honestly and loyally in the company's interests at all times. On this, see further Lord Upjohn's eloquent interpretation of Lord Cranworth's opinion in *Blaikie Bros*, as expounded in the influential case of

Indeed, it may be reasoned that the very fact of one fulfilling a fiduciary capacity *in itself* precludes the relevant officeholder from engaging in conflicted transactions or improper profiteering, at least without the authorisation or approval of his principal. Moreover, the prohibition of such activities (at least in the absence of proper authorisation or approval) can be regarded as a logical precondition of a principal (ie the company as represented by its collective body of shareholders) being able to give informed consent to executive decisions concerning the allocation of their resources. It accordingly makes no sense to excuse directorial self-dealing on the ground that it was incidental to honest pursuit of a company's interest, or because shareholders were either not materially harmed by the relevant conduct, or would likely have acquiesced in it had they known about it in advance. Rather, self-dealing in the above sense (or, at least, adjudged 'unfair' instances thereof) is, by its very nature, something that no rational principal would ordinarily agree to their agent engaging in, at least without having the prior opportunity to give direct and specific assent thereto.

Therefore, while the bulk of internal governance issues are in effect 'up for grabs' within the notional shareholder-management 'bargain', one thing is established to be beyond the contracting parties' permissible contractual reach. This is the foundational equitable concept that those persons who are appointed as the company's directors have the inalienable and irremovable responsibility of acting as the fiduciary guardians of their principal's (ie the company's) collective interests, which – in particular – includes putting their principal's interests ahead of their own at all times. Furthermore, this basic tenet of the legal relationship stands regardless of what the parties might attempt to provide otherwise in the notional governance agreement at hand.[193]

Boardman v Phipps [1967] 2 AC 46. See also *Regal (Hastings) Ltd v Gulliver* [1967] 2 AC 134, 159 (Lord Porter): '[A director's liability for undisclosed profiteering] does not depend upon breach of duty but upon the [independent and logically prior] proposition that a director must not make a profit out of property acquired by reason of his relationship to the company of which he is director'. Furthermore, the standard disgorgement remedy for self-dealing – insofar as it requires complete submission by the wrongdoer to the company of any profit made resultant upon his breach of duty (and regardless of whether or to what extent the company itself was harmed by the breach) – is arguably further counter to contractarian rationality. This is because disgorgement is apparently designed to achieve 'unconditional deterrence', thus rendering it unprofitable for directors or trustees to deviate from the non-self-dealing norm under *any* circumstances. See Easterbrook and Fischel, 'Contract and Fiduciary Duty', above n 184, 441, who consequently criticise this position on the ground that 'treating every appearance of profit taking by the fiduciary as if there were a real problem would yield far too many false positives'. Ibid, 442.

[193] The counter-contractual rigidity of this basic equitable principle, as derived in the first place from the pre-industrial English law of trusts, has famously been described as 'unbending and inveterate'. See *Meinhard v Salmon*, 164 NE 545 (1928) 546 (Cardozo J). See also *Bray v Ford* [1896] AC 44, 51 (Lord Herschell): 'It is an *inflexible* rule of a Court of Equity that a person in a fiduciary position, such as the respondent's is not, unless otherwise expressly

Thus by virtue of the fiduciary principle, there arises the general expectation that the agent's (ie director's) discretionary administrative power will be exercised in a manner that is broadly conducive to advancement of the principal's (ie company's) best interests, notwithstanding the extensive leeway afforded to the directorial 'agent' in fulfilment of this basic open-ended obligation. Consequently, the reciprocal power imbalance between management and shareholders becomes potentially sustainable, even under conditions of bounded rationality and significant informational disparity inter se.

The conclusion that can be drawn from the above discussion is that the equitable fiduciary principle in Anglo-American corporate law, far from being an object of contractual freedom in the ordering of intrafirm affairs,[194] would contrarily appear to represent a facet of counter-contractual *regulatory paternalism* in corporate governance. Accordingly, the proverbial shadow of the interventionist state – whether as manifested via judicial or statutory channels – can justifiably be said to loom large over this particular area of the law.

---

provided, entitled to make a profit; he is not allowed to put himself in a position where his interest and duty conflict' (emphasis added). Likewise, in *New Zealand Netherlands Society 'Oranje' v Kuys* [1973] 1 WLR 1126, 1129–30 (emphasis added), Lord Wilberforce reaffirmed that '[t]he obligation not to profit from a position of trust, or, as it is sometimes relevant to put it, not to allow a conflict to arise between duty and interest, is *one of strictness*'. The foundational authority that established the stringency of the trustee's (and, latterly, director's) fiduciary duty not to profit from his position is commonly regarded to be the famous English case of *Keech v Sandford* (1726) Select Cases Temp King 61, where the Lord Chancellor emphasised (in the context of a dispute concerning renewal of a lease held on trust for a minor, in the name of the trustee of the estate) that 'it is very proper that rule should be strictly pursued, and not in the least relaxed'. See also *Aberdeen Railway Co v Blaikie Bros*, above n 192, 471 (Lord Cranworth LC): 'it is a rule *of universal application* that no one having such duties to discharge shall be allowed to enter into engagements in which he has, or can have, a personal interest conflicting, or which possibly may conflict, with the interests of those whom he is bound to protect' (emphasis added).

[194] It would appear that Easterbrook and Fischel, in drawing this conclusion (see above nn 184–87 and accompanying text), erroneously conflate the duty of loyalty and prohibition on unauthorised self-dealing together as the one supposed legal doctrine, under the umbrella title of 'duty of loyalty'. For example, they explain (at 432) how '[a] duty of loyalty means acting for the exclusive benefit of the beneficiary', but then proceed immediately to state that 'the usual remedy is disgorgement of the trustee's gain'. This seems to be intermingling two lexically ordered principles. Likewise, the authors infer (at 433) that the business judgment rule only applies to duty of care cases, and consequently draw the conclusion that 'the duty of loyalty is strong but the duty of care is weak'. However, they do not acknowledge that the business judgment rule can also apply to some loyalty-based issues, such as the propriety of non-commercial business objectives (on this, see above ch 4 of this volume, fns 40–43 and accompanying text). Therefore the correct dichotomy is not so much 'strong duty of loyalty / weak duty of care' (as the authors allege), but rather 'weak *duties* of loyalty and care / strong (mandatory) prohibition on unauthorised self-dealing'.

V. SUMMARY

Readers may reasonably take umbrage at the apparent volte-face that I could be perceived as taking in this chapter, in relation to the general thrust of the discussion in the three prior chapters of this book. The discussion up to this point has sought to highlight the key conceptual elements of the contractarian paradigm of corporate governance, and the main respects in which they are manifested in the actual form and substance of US and UK corporate governance law. By contrast, in this chapter I have deliberately sought to 'muddy' the descriptive picture of the law presented so far, by illustrating the many important features of Anglo-American corporate governance law that, on initial inspection at least, appear not to conform to the dominant academic blueprint of the subject.

Such features include the significant body of mandatory (in the United States, federal) rules pertaining to the fundamental governance function of systematic corporate disclosure, and also related regulatory decrees determining the proper format of communications between shareholders and managers in and around the annual corporate meeting by means of the proxy process. In the United Kingdom, meanwhile, even the core division of decision-making power and influence between shareholders and the board of directors is determined largely on a mandatory and thus irreversible statutory basis. And, most fundamentally of all, the extensive ambit of discretion that Anglo-American law vests in corporate boards (and, indirectly, managers) is structurally *premised on* – and thus *made possible by* – the inherently mandatory status of the longstanding equitable fiduciary principle.

In conclusion, then, it can justifiably be said that the very operation of the quasi-contractual dimensions of Anglo-American corporate governance law would be rendered impossible in the absence of the foundational regulatory 'building blocks' of the subject outlined in this chapter. On the basis of this revelation, I will proceed in the following chapter to critically evaluate the principal respects in which contractarian scholars have attempted to rationalise the mandatory aspects of Anglo-American corporate governance law. In these ways, as I will show, defenders of the contractarian paradigm have sought to render their position consistent with the various 'real world' contours of the relevant legal frameworks, with a view ultimately to maintaining the validity of the key descriptive – and, in turn – normative components of their theoretical model.

I will argue, however, that the contractarian case for mandatory shareholder-protectionist rules is ultimately prone to logical explosion when subjected to close analytical scrutiny. Accordingly, in my view, this argument requires further development if it is to be capable of accounting for the significant regulatory dimensions of 'core' corporate governance law as it exists in both the United States and United Kingdom. With this consideration in mind, I will subsequently attempt to provide a revised and more nuanced theoretical explanation for the complex hybrid of quasi-contractual and regulatory rules that constitutes Anglo-American corporate governance as a legal-institutional system.

7

Rationalising Regulatory State Paternalism within an Expanded Contractarian Paradigm

I N THE PREVIOUS chapter, I sought to demonstrate that Anglo-American corporate governance law – in spite of its proclaimed predilection for facilitating private ordering – in reality exhibits a significant number of mandatory or regulatory features. Moreover, such aspects of corporate governance law – far from being peripheral or extraneous to the subject – are in fact determinative of some of the most fundamental and definitive features of the core corporate equity relation between shareholders and management.

I have already explained how, within the private ordering paradigm, mandatory rules are a difficult empirical pill to swallow. From a contractarian perspective, the purportedly problematic characteristics of mandatory corporate governance laws are two-fold. First, there is their perceived effect in undermining individual contractual autonomy, by seeking to pre-empt institutional outcomes that *can* and – thus, arguably – *should* be determined privately by contractors. Secondly, mandatory rules in private law could be said to prevent contracting parties from rationally calculating what arrangements are best suited to improve their own joint utility or welfare, instead seeking to prescribe a state-determined outcome that is likely to be unreflective of the affected parties' individually rational preferences. As such, mandatory rules are arguably detrimental on both a moral (autonomy-centric) and socio-economic (utility-centric) basis.

At the same time, though, with enough intellectual sophistication it is possible to arrive at a contrasting understanding of mandatory corporate governance rules as a *reflection of* – or, at the very least, a *response to* – individual contractual preferences, rather than as a preclusive substitute for such. Indeed, contractarian theorists, far from ignoring or seeking to cover up the difficulties that mandatory rules pose for their conceptual model of corporate governance, have contrarily opted to recognise and subsequently tackle this empirical phenomenon head on. Hence, in recent decades, an important element of contractarian scholarship on corporate governance has comprised attempts to explain the presence of the prima facie mandatory or regulatory aspects of corporate law in a manner that actually *supports*, rather than detracts from, the basic private ordering rationality behind the contractarian position.

As I will argue below, although this sub-school of 'interventionist-contractarians' deserves praise for undertaking such a seemingly intractable intellectual challenge, the main arguments that its members have advanced in support of their position are, in my opinion, ultimately of limited effectiveness in seeking to sustain the validity of private ordering rationality in its application to the regulatory features of corporate governance law. In particular, the interventionist-contractarian position encounters serious difficulties when it attempts to rationalise mandatory corporate governance rules on the basis of hypothetical bargaining rationality. That is, in the absence of *actual* contracts or private arrangements (whether expressly or implicitly) between corporate participants with respect to internal corporate governance norms, interventionist-contractarians have sought to preserve the contractual metaphor by seeking to explain prevailing features of the law essentially as a representation of 'what contracting parties (ie shareholders and managers) *would have* bargained for', had they been able to apply their minds directly to the task.

The role of the regulatory state, accordingly, is in effect to 'step into the shoes' of the contracting parties (principally shareholders) by providing the terms that they would have been inclined to negotiate for within the idealised hypothetical bargaining scenario. Furthermore, insofar as a number of such terms are perceived to be so important in nature that no (or, at least, *almost no*) rational shareholders would be inclined voluntarily to dispense with them, their constitution in concretised and irreversible legal form can be regarded as necessary for the purpose of honouring notional contractor expectations. For this reason, many corporate law rules – even those that are mandatory in form – are frequently viewed to be merely *market mimicking* in effect. As such, the mandatory regulatory imposition of these norms is largely uncontroversial on a normative level. This is because the state – in promulgating and enforcing the relevant rules – is *not* seeking to compel outcomes different from those that shareholders would ideally prefer but, for whatever reason, are unable to insist on directly under 'real world' bargaining conditions.

I will seek to demonstrate in this chapter that the so-called 'market mimicking' rationalisation of mandatory corporate governance rules is both limited and, moreover, *fundamentally paradoxical* in nature. In essence, my claim is that interventionist-contractarians *give away too much* by admitting a case for regulatory displacement or 'override' of otherwise endogenous corporate governance norms in response to systematic adverse selection by investors. As such, the interventionist-contractarian depiction of the state's appropriate role in corporate law-making strays too far over the conventionally-perceived divide between: on the one hand, the fundamentally facilitative (or quasi-*private*) state function of contractual 'gap-filling'; and, on the other, the manifestly *public* state function of 'regulatory paternalism' – that is, deciding vicariously on investors' behalf what is in their overall best interests, in the belief that investors are systematically incapable of making such judgements for themselves on a private basis. By accepting the latter function as the appropriate law-making role for the state, interventionist-contractarians – far from presenting an institutional framework for the formation of more efficient 'contracts' than those that are liable to ensue from direct private selections alone – contrarily *sacrifice* all that is 'contractual' about their model by substituting (governmentally-derived) public policy in place of (contractually-derived) private ordering as the principal institutional determinant of many core corporate governance norms.

To the extent that the above critique of the contractarian rationalisation of mandatory rules is accepted by readers, the implications for Anglo-American corporate governance scholarship and – in turn – legal practice are potentially significant. In particular, this chapter's findings call into question the continuing validity of the contractarian paradigm as a descriptive and normative characterisation of the Anglo-American corporate governance system. Moreover, they suggest that the contractarian paradigm of corporate governance is ultimately incapable of providing a valid rationalisation of the significant regulatory features of this area of law without accepting the existence of a core and irreducible 'public' dimension thereto.

Accordingly, in the final part of this chapter, I will seek to determine whether contractarian rationality is actually capable of absorbing a considerably greater 'public' or regulatory element than it does at present, without sacrificing either its analytical rigour or normative consistency. To this end, I will seek to offer a refinement of contractarianism that I believe retains the essential analytical and normative sharpness that the private ordering paradigm is known for, whilst at the same time recognising the law's inherent public-regulatory dynamic.

The roadmap for this chapter is thus as follows. I will begin in part I by examining (and also discarding) the popular contractarian argument that mandatory rules are not in fact mandatory at all, on the basis that the capacity of corporations (especially in the competitive-federalist legal context of the United States) in effect to 'migrate' to their legal domicile of choice gives them the practical capacity to 'opt out' of laws, even those that are mandatory, via inter-State re-incorporation. In part II, I will assess (and also defend) the key respects in which mandatory rules are regarded as structurally essential to private ordering dynamics, both in corporate and non-corporate law fields, insofar as they ensure the correction of inevitable market failures – including negative externalities and the systematic underproduction of certain essential 'public goods'. In part III, I will set out the main features of what is arguably the most far-reaching and also controversial justification for mandatory corporate governance rules within the contractarian paradigm: that is, the claim that such rules serve merely to 'mimic the market' by importing the terms that rational contractors would insist on under hypothesised bargaining conditions, thereby rendering the relevant laws fundamentally 'trivial' (ie *non-socially-determinative*) in nature. I will then go on in part IV to critique the so-called 'market mimicking' rationalisation of mandatory rules by pointing out the fundamentally paradoxical – and thus logically self-defeating – nature of the argument that it entails.

Finally, in part V, I will offer a revised contractarian rationalisation of Anglo-American corporate governance law premised on the concept of 'macro-accountability', which I believe is essential to understanding the significant public-regulatory dimensions of the subject today. Linking back to the core themes developed in chapter one of this book, I will argue that the mandatory regulatory protection of shareholders' constitutional status within corporate governance is essential for securing effective ongoing managerial accountability, thus enabling the continuing legitimation – and, in turn, sustainability – of managers' discretionary administrative power on a macro (ie system-wide) basis. I will subsequently highlight the principal prescriptive ramifications that follow from this position, in relation to the most controversial current and recent developments in both US and UK corporate governance. This will be followed by a summary of conclusions to the discussion in this book as a whole.

I. ARE MANDATORY RULES 'MANDATORY' AT ALL?

Before proceeding further, it is necessary to put to rest a common – but limited – argument that is advanced by some contractarians[1] to assert the

---

[1] My reference to 'contractarians' in this chapter includes both those scholars who expressly describe themselves as such, and also those who – whilst perhaps not inclined to place themselves directly within this school of thought – are nonetheless broadly sympathetic to, or at least influenced by, the basic rationality of the contractarian paradigm (and thus may be understood, for purposes of the following discussion, as 'soft' contractarians). Most prominent amongst the group of legal scholars who I believe would expressly describe themselves as 'contractarian' are Frank Easterbrook, Daniel Fischel and Stephen Bainbridge. Examples of scholars who I would situate within the 'soft' contractarian tradition, meanwhile, are Bernard Black, Brian Cheffins, Roberta Romano, Melvin Eisenberg, Jeffrey Gordon and Lucian Bebchuk. In categorising these scholars in the above way, I intend to neither cause offence nor misrepresent the views of the relevant individuals in any way. Therefore I would stress that the above categorisation is a subjective product of my own personal interpretation of these individuals' work, which stands open to challenge by readers who have developed alternative perspectives thereon. Furthermore, when I refer to an argument as 'contractarian', I do not wish to suggest that *all* of the scholars who in some way meet this description necessarily share that particular point of view.

purported 'triviality'[2] of mandatory corporate governance rules, in the sense of their fundamentally *non*-socially-determinative effect vis-à-vis private ordering outcomes. For want of a more eloquent term, this argument is best termed the 'take-it-or-leave-it'[3] rationalisation.

The take-it-or-leave-it argument basically asserts that mandatory corporate governance rules are in practice not mandatory at all, because corporations ultimately can choose to incorporate or re-incorporate in any jurisdiction offering an alternative 'menu' of regulatory choices.[4] An analogy can be drawn with a store selling only one variety of a particular product, say sandwiches for instance. Assuming that there are stores selling other types of sandwich, and that these stores can easily be accessed in the alternative to visiting the first store, the consumer's choice will in reality not be constrained at all.

By a parallel course of reasoning, one can conclude that an investor who chooses to invest her wealth in a corporation governed by a particular 'bundle' of mandatory rules is doing so at the opportunity cost of investing in a firm subject to another state's regulatory system, or alternatively putting her wealth to a non-corporate use such as real estate, commodities or unincorporated enterprise.[5] The chain of logic is that since: (a) investors will rationally seek to put their capital into those firms offering the most economically advantageous set of governance 'terms', and (b) firms will in turn seek to incorporate (or re-incorporate) in those jurisdictions offering the most investor-friendly set of terms (given that the system of corporate law to which a firm is subject is generally determined by its state of incorporation[6]); it follows that (c) state law-makers will compete with one another to offer the terms that investors (and, in turn, incorporators) find most attractive with a view to enhancing the revenues that states derive (both directly and indirectly) from incorporations carried out within their respective jurisdictions.[7]

Accordingly mandatory rules, in spite of their prima facie rigid and anti-contractual form, can be regarded in themselves as the dynamic product of a market-evolutionary process involving investors, firms and law-makers. The political implication is that mandatory corporate governance rules, just like reversible-default provisions, represent the outcome of a free private

---

[2] The concept of 'triviality' in this sense was first developed by Bernard Black in his now classic article 'Is Corporate Law Trivial?: A Political and Economic Analysis' (1990) 84 *Northwestern University Law Review* 542.

[3] In using this term I am indebted to Stephen Bainbridge, who first coined it in the phrase cited at note 8 below.

[4] For a paradigmatic statement of this general view, see FH Easterbrook and DR Fischel, 'The Corporate Contract' (1989) 89 *Columbia Law Review* 1416.

[5] See FH Easterbrook and DR Fischel, *The Economic Structure of Corporate Law* (Cambridge MA, Harvard University Press, 1991) 4.

[6] On this, see above ch 4 of this volume, fns 19–23 and accompanying text.

[7] On this, see above ch 4 of this volume, fns 26–29 and accompanying text.

ordering process in which no individual participant in the proverbial 'bargain' (whether an investor or even an entire corporation) need be compelled to conform to a sub-optimal institutional outcome. As Stephen Bainbridge eloquently puts it:

> the rights of the shareholders are established through bargaining, even though the form of the bargain typically is a take-it-or-leave-it standard form contract provided off-the-rack by the default rules of corporate law and the corporation's organic documents.[8]

Notwithstanding its conceptual elegance, the above contractarian rationalisation of mandatory rules is severely limited when considered in the context of the United Kingdom. The argument has been developed with specific regard to the competitive-federalist corporate law-making system that exists in the United States, whereby – as I explained in chapter four – incorporators have an effective 'menu' of 51 different State-level corporate law systems to choose from.[9] Moreover, in the United States there are no deliberate legal barriers either to inter-State re-incorporation or to the setting up or transfer of a company's business operations outside of State boundaries.[10]

By contrast the United Kingdom, in spite of being composed of two traditionally autonomous legal systems[11] and four separate national legislatures today,[12] nonetheless by and large exhibits a unitary corporate law system. At the wider EU level, meanwhile, in spite of the principle of community-wide freedom of establishment,[13] it remains possible for Member States to restrict companies incorporated within their national jurisdiction from having their primary business establishment in another Member State.[14] The effect of this legal position – known as the 'real seat' doctrine – is to prevent incorporators in general from deciding on a company's state of incorporation independently from the question as to where it intends to conduct its principal business operations.[15] This precludes

[8] SM Bainbridge, *The New Corporate Governance in Theory and Practice* (New York, Oxford University Press, 2008) 33.

[9] On this, see above ch 4 of this volume, fn 21 and accompanying text.

[10] Arguably the most influential and comprehensive rationalisation (and defence) of the US competitive-federal system of corporate law-making is provided in R Romano, *The Genius of American Corporate Law* (Washington DC, AEI Press, 1993).

[11] These are the formally independent national legal systems of England and Wales (as traditionally applicable also to Northern Ireland), and Scotland.

[12] Namely the UK Parliament at Westminster, the Scottish Parliament in Edinburgh, the National Assembly for Wales in Cardiff, and the Northern Irish Assembly at Stormont.

[13] The strongest affirmation of this principle in the context of cross-border incorporation/establishment disputes remains the well-known *Centros* case. See Case C-212/97 *Centros Ltd v Erhvervs-og Selskabsstyrelsen* [1999] ECR I-1459.

[14] See Case C-210/06 *Cartesio Oktato es Szolgaltato bt* [2009] ECR I-9641 ('*Cartesio*'); Case C-81/87 *The Queen v HM Treasury and Commissioners of Inland Revenue, ex parte Daily Mail and General Trust* [1988] ECR 5483 (*Daily Mail*).

[15] On this, see P Syrpis and A Johnston, 'Regulatory Competition in European Company Law after Cartesio' (2009) 34 *European Law Review* 378.

companies (and, indirectly, investors) from engaging in the type of unencumbered corporate law jurisdiction 'shopping' that contractarian theorists commonly laud as a key strength of the US law-making system.[16] By implication, it means that mandatory corporate governance rules established within an EU (including UK) context cannot readily be regarded as the product of rational free choice and are thus largely out of kilter with the private ordering hypothesis.

A further and more general problem with the take-it-or-leave-it rationalisation of mandatory corporate governance rules is that it does not on its own satisfactorily explain why, even within the parameters of an American-esque competitive-federalist system, mandatory rules are chosen by regulators in preference to the more flexible and prima facie market-responsive option of reversible-default provisions. Accordingly, some further explanation is required to account for the widespread presence of mandatory corporate governance rules within the Anglo-American environment. This is especially pertinent in the case of the United Kingdom's corporate law-making arena where, as explained above, the range of alternative regulatory choices available to incorporators (and prospective re-incorporators) remains significantly restricted in practical terms.

II. THE ACCEPTABLE AMBIT OF STATE INTERVENTIONISM IN PRIVATE ORDERING: NEGATIVE EXTERNALITIES AND PUBLIC GOODS

I explained in chapter three how, within the contractarian paradigm, the problem of negative externalities – that is, the uncompensated infliction by firms of costs on third parties (especially environmental interests) situated outside of a firm's notional contractual nexus – is appropriately dealt with via mandatory regulation extraneous to 'core' corporate law. The purported aim of such regulation is to ensure, via the imposition of appropriate civil and – where necessary – criminal liability, that the adverse social costs to a firm of its productive activities are fully (or, at least, substantially) reflected in the private cost calculus underpinning its a priori decision as to whether or not to engage in such activities. In this way, the law theoretically mitigates the scope for divergence between the private (firm) and public (third party) payoffs of a given course of

---

[16] On the potential benefits of engendering US-style regulatory competition in the EU context, see J Armour, 'Who Should Make Corporate Law? EU Legislation versus Regulatory Competition' (2005) 58 *Current Legal Problems* 369; J Lowry, 'Eliminating Obstacles to Freedom of Establishment: The Competitive Edge of UK Company Law' (2004) 63 *Cambridge Law Journal* 331; WG Ringe, 'Sparking Regulatory Competition in European Company Law – The Impact of the Centros Line of Case-Law and its Concept of "Abuse of Law"' in R de la Feria and S Vogenauer (eds), *Prohibition of Abuse of Law – A New General Principle of EU Law* (Oxford, Hart Publishing, 2010).

entrepreneurial action, without obfuscating the firm's fundamental prudential motivation.[17]

I further explained in chapter three how the contractarian paradigm, by
conceptually distinguishing such 'externalities-internalising' regulation
from the scope of corporate law as conventionally defined, succeeds in preserving the essential privity of corporate governance within its conceptual
model.[18] At the same time, though, by permitting (limited) recourse to
regulatory state interventionism in the above situations, the externalities
argument equips the contractarian paradigm for dealing with any negative
public effects of business activities (such as harm to the physical or ecologi-
cal environment) that by their nature are incapable of being incorporated
within its underpinning private bargaining dynamic.[19]

A similar basic argumentative logic supports the other common concession that contractarians typically make to regulatory state interventionism in private ordering. This is the well-known 'public goods' argument
that I set out in chapter six when explaining how the general investor
need for one such 'good' – namely widespread firm-relevant information
– establishes a strong case for mandatory (disclosure) regulation even
within the context of an otherwise facilitative-contractual framework of
corporate governance law.[20] On a broader social-institutional level, meanwhile, even scholars of a strongly contractarian or neo-liberal disposition
are in general agreement that, at the most basic level of civil society, the
fundamental structural preconditions of a market system are dependent
on extra-contractual governmental design. Thus the state is vested with
inalienable residual responsibility for establishing a reliable judicial and
legislative system for the constitution, formation and enforcement of contractual and proprietary interests between private parties, together with
the prohibition of fraud, monopoly, and other practices averse to the market's underlying structural and ethical 'rules-of-the-game'.[21]

More generally, the provision of effective policing, national defence and
basic communicative infrastructure (eg a national or inter-state road network) from public taxation revenues is regarded as similarly essential to
any functioning and sustainable market-based system of production and

---

[17] On this, see above ch 3 of this volume, fns 8–9, 16–18 and accompanying text. However,
for an influential counter-perspective highlighting the potentially wealth-*reducing* effect of
'externalities-internalising' regulation when applied in respect of productive economic
activities, see RH Coase, 'The Problem of Social Cost' (1960) 3 *Journal of Law and Economics* 1.

[18] On this, see above ch 3 of this volume, fns 8–9 and 13–18.

[19] See above ch 3 of this volume, fns 16–17 and accompanying text.

[20] See above ch 6 of this volume, pt II.B.

[21] See, eg M Friedman, *Capitalism and Freedom* (Chicago, University of Chicago Press,
1962) 27: '[T]he organization of economic activity through voluntary exchange presumes
that we have provided, through government, for the maintenance of law and order to prevent coercion of one individual by another, the enforcement of contracts voluntarily entered
into, the definition of the meaning of property rights, the interpretation and enforcement of
such rights, and the provision of a monetary framework'.

exchange.[22] This stands as a near-universal truth, moreover, regardless of one's particular political opinion about the social benefits or dangers of state interventionism beyond this base minimum level.[23] Finally, the preservation of macro-economic conditions conducive to continuing market stability – if only by the most basic governmental means of producing monetary instruments and determining the national base rate of interest – is likewise almost unanimously accepted as a legitimate state function, irrespective of one's view about the appropriate extent of governmental economic policy-making additional to this threshold.[24]

A common feature of all the above institutional phenomena is their exhibiting the aforementioned defining characteristics of a public good, namely non-excludability and non-rivalry, which will inevitably result in their systematic underproduction (and, in the most extreme case, *non-production* altogether) by private market providers.[25] However, insofar as the regulatory mitigation of negative externalities, and corresponding provision of public goods, are structurally essential for the effective functioning of a voluntary, market-based system for allocating goods and services, then they are undeniably antecedent to the neo-liberal contractarian paradigm – both of corporate law in particular, and of socio-economic arrangements more generally.

Against this background, it could be surmised that contractarians (and, indeed, neo-liberal scholars more generally), in seeking at once to admit the necessity of – but also significantly limit the permissible ambit of – regulatory state interventionism in private ordering, are proverbially 'trying to have their cake and eat it'. That is to say, acknowledging that the purportedly self-regulatory domain of private ordering (both in corporate governance matters and in citizens' socio-economic affairs more generally) is necessarily dependent on an irreducible minimum of governmentally-mandated institutional infrastructure, opens an awkward regulatory 'can of worms' for contractarians that could be said to discredit their argument against state interventionism in other – less structurally fundamental – respects.

Indeed, in a derivation of the traditional 'concession' theory of corporate law development, it may be asserted that the fundamental

---

[22] See Friedman, *Capitalism and Freedom*, ibid, ch 2 ('The Role of Government in a Free Society').

[23] At a reasonable stretch, the public goods argument can be further extended to require that social-institutional arrangements protect or embody certain intrinsic liberal values that private bargaining dynamics are incapable of reflecting; for instance race and gender equality, and non-discrimination on grounds of religion, disability or sexuality.

[24] Despite providing one of the most influential expositions of the political dangers of unnecessary governmental interference in a 'free' economy, Friedman nevertheless remarked in reference to 'the monetary system' that '[t]here is probably no other area of economic activity with respect to which government action has been so uniformly accepted'. See Friedman, *Capitalism and Freedom*, above n 21, 27.

[25] On this, see above ch 6 of this volume, fns 111–13 and accompanying text.

dependence of market-based selection processes upon an antecedent 'floor' of public interventionism (whether via regulatory or administrative means) *in itself* renders the whole notion of private ordering inherently *artificial*, and hence indefensible against further state interventionism. In other words, the fact that the state creates the structural preconditions for private ordering arguably entitles it – quid pro quo – to set regulatory boundaries to the appropriate scope of such where this is seemingly justified by public interest considerations, and *irrespective of* whether the resulting constraints align with the collective private preferences of contractors.[26]

Notwithstanding the normative appeal of the above claim to those who are intuitively sympathetic to the case for greater public-regulatory interventionism in corporate governance affairs (and indeed private ordering practices more generally), it is imperative to note a compelling counter-argument that can be raised by contractarians in defence of the deregulatory/non-interventionist position. This counter-argument proceeds from the premise that, in a liberal-democratic political economy, the collective preference of citizens to permit economic exchanges and/ or private social-institutional arrangements (including corporate governance norms) to be ordered on a decentralised basis via voluntary market processes necessitates that the state – in reflection of this general public will – effectively cedes allocative and/or regulatory sovereignty over such matters to civil society actors and groups situated outside of government.

However, in a certain range of situations – such as where 'pure' (ie non-regulatorily-underpinned) private ordering is conducive to negative externalities or macro-instabilities, or where state provision of public goods is essential to the continuing effective functioning of the market exchange system in any respect – a policy of *outright* state non-interventionism in contractual affairs will likely be rendered either self-defeating (as in the case of non-provision of an essential public good), or otherwise contrary to the central values of individual autonomy and private utility-enhancement that governmental deference to private ordering is intended to promote (as in the case of imposition by a firm of an 'uncorrected' externality on a third party). In such instances, targeted regulatory interventions in the above regards are likely to be conducive to *safeguarding* – rather than undermining – these important contractarian values. Moreover, insofar as the centralised and systematic correction of negative externalities and provision of public goods by the state are essential preconditions of decentralised and private methods of institutional ordering in other respects, the occasional targeted

---

[26] It should be noted that this argument is not just specific to corporate law, but rather could also be used as a normative basis for regulatory state interventionism in contract law, property law, and other reputedly 'private' or facilitative areas of law.

deployment of such regulatory techniques can reasonably be regarded as consistent with – and, indeed, *part and parcel of* – a more general state policy of non-interventionism in citizens' (and, indirectly, firms') voluntary contractual affairs.

There remains, however, an outstanding issue of concern for contractarians. While the deliberate regulatory intervention of the state in the above regards may ultimately be supportive of the continuing feasibility of private ordering in other respects, it may still be remarked by critics of the contractarian position that 'regulation, at the end of the day, is regulation'; and that, regardless of the specific end that a particular regulatory or administrative intervention by the state seeks to achieve, the fact still stands that private ordering has in some way been superseded by public policy (albeit in this case, a public policy designed to advance private ordering practices in the longer run). Accordingly, it may be said that any institutional outcomes that follow from such 'interference' are entirely arbitrary and artificial, with the implication that the state is no less entitled in future to regulate with a view to constraining or superseding private ordering, as it is entitled to regulate in order to enable the private ordering process to function in the first place. That is, now that the regulatory floodgates have been opened, for the interventionist state 'everything is up for grabs' regardless of the consequences for the individual autonomy or collective utility of contractors.

However, the above 'artificiality' criticism of externalities and public goods regulation is ultimately misplaced, insofar as it elides the crucial asserted fact that such state interventions *themselves* stem ultimately from quasi-contractual agreement, albeit at the macro (ie economy-wide) rather than micro (individual firm) level. The logic is that, due to the inherent incapacity of contractors to capture the full benefits of such institutional developments privately were they to be introduced by contract, contractors instead make the collective decision – in their a priori capacity as citizens – to submit voluntarily to the universal and coercive authority of the state with respect to these matters. In this way, contractors (qua citizens) are together able to make a reliable collective commitment to contribute to the maintenance of externalities-mitigation and public goods provision on an ongoing basis, notwithstanding that their individual self-interest qua economic actors (at least in the short term) would be better served by a strategy of *non*-cooperation with these overall schemes. The role of mandatory regulation, accordingly, is in effect to 'bond' the expectation of each market participant to the effect that all other participants will contribute towards maintaining the relevant institutions. This enables the participants as a group – via submission to a regulatorily-compelled system of externalities-mitigation and public goods provision – collectively to transcend the inevitable 'prisoner's game dilemma' that would otherwise preclude the voluntary formation of such a scheme (in spite of the overall benefits to the group of doing so).[27]

The above discussion thus establishes that – contrary to first appearances – regulatory or administrative state interventions in private ordering, geared to the reduction of negative externalities or provision of public goods, do not represent independent or self-standing public policies in their own right. Rather, they ultimately derive from – and are thus inextricably linked to – the initial macro-agreement between citizens under which they collectively assent to a sustainable institutional framework to govern their future economic relations with each another.[28] It follows that state interventionism – albeit as understood exclusively in the limited forms discussed above – is structurally inseparable from the initial (negative) policy decision of the state to refrain from directly regulating a given field of economic activity, instead delegating self-regulatory capacity to the relevant contracting individuals or firms.

Such methods of regulatory state interventionism are thus fundamentally *consistent* with private ordering rationality from a conceptual standpoint. Accordingly, acceptance of a limited role for state interventionism in the above ways, far from providing a normative licence for wholesale state 'override' of private ordering outcomes, contrarily *reinforces* the normative case for a (negative) state policy of regulatory non-interventionism in micro-level market affairs more generally. This pertains not only to fundamental questions of economic resource allocation amongst competing uses, but also to contingent matters of market-institutional (including corporate governance) norm design.

III. THE 'MARKET MIMICKING' RATIONALISATION OF REGULATORY STATE INTERVENTIONISM

A. The Extraordinary Scope and Controversiality of the 'Market Mimicking' Rationalisation

Acceptance of a limited licence for state interventionism in corporate governance, at least for the overtly public-regarding objectives described above, is relatively uncontroversial. This is so even within the otherwise-

---

[27] For a fuller exposition of this argument, see J Rawls, *A Theory of Justice*, revised edn (Oxford, Oxford University Press, 1999) (first published 1971) 236–37. In particular, Rawls posits that 'even among just men, once goods are indivisible over large numbers of individuals, their actions decided upon in isolation from one another will not lead to the general good'. It follows that '[s]ome collective arrangement is necessary and everyone wants assurance that it will be adhered to if he is willingly to do his part', with the result that 'the use of [regulatory] coercion is perfectly rational from each man's point of view'. See ibid.

[28] I am grateful to Andreas Kokkinis for helping me to identify this important point in personal conversation.

deregulatory confines of the contractarian paradigm. Where the permissible ambit of public regulatory initiative is restricted to the purportedly 'external' (ie extra-contractual) concerns of externalities-mitigation and public goods provision, it cannot be said to interfere with the substantive 'core' of corporate governance as it is conventionally understood.

I explained in chapter three how the contractarian paradigm seeks normatively to establish something of an 'inside/outside' dichotomy with respect to supposedly 'corporate' and 'non-corporate' concerns – the former being the proper preserve of the private law of corporate *governance*, and the latter rightfully subject to the public (or regulatory) law of corporate *effects*. And, whilst contractarians typically do not dispute the state's entitlement to wield determinative regulatory influence on the latter 'external' side of this notional divide, the former 'internal' side is – by contrast – deemed to be regulatorily 'out of bounds' except for purely facilitative measures that are designed to reflect investors' pre-existing private preferences.[29]

As my doctrinal analysis in the previous chapter of this book has hopefully demonstrated, though, this dichotomous understanding of the various laws pertaining to corporate control matters is – to a significant extent – empirically unsubstantiated within the Anglo-American environment today. Rather, it is manifestly the case that many of the most central aspects of the reputedly 'internal' side of corporate governance in the United States and United Kingdom are constituted in mandatory regulatory form. In particular, the fundamental structural features of the equity relation in these two countries (and especially the United Kingdom) would appear to be determined *at least as much* by determinative state decree as by prudential market-driven initiative. The effect of this finding is to render the aforementioned dichotomy somewhat over-simplistic as a method of conceptually categorising its subject-matter, at least in the absence of some further convincing explanation as to why the supposedly 'internal' dimension of corporate governance law should continue to be understood in principally facilitative and quasi-contractual terms.

To this end, a contractarian explanation for the widespread presence of regulatory laws pertaining to corporate governance's theoretically contractual core has been developed in the guise of the so-called 'market mimicking' rationalisation of mandatory rules.[30] Like the 'public' grounds for regulatory interventionism discussed above, the market mimicking argument is designed in recognition of – and also as a response to – the inevitable existence of market failures in voluntary private ordering mechanisms. However, there is a notable distinction between the two types of argument, by virtue of which the latter case for state interventionism sits rather less

---

[29] On this, see above ch 3 of this volume, fns 8–9 and 13–18.
[30] On the concept of market mimicking rules in corporate law generally, see Black, 'Is Corporate Law Trivial?', above n 2, 552–55.

comfortably alongside the other aspects of the contractarian paradigm of law.

As illustrated above, the negative externalities and public goods arguments for state interventionism are premised on what is best referred to as *public* market failures. The notion of public market failure denotes situations where unregulated private ordering is structurally incapable of eliciting contractual outcomes that reflect the prudential interests of third parties. The term 'third parties', as used in this context, denotes those who are situated outside of the relevant bargaining nexus (eg the firm) and thus are incapable of protecting their interests directly via contractual provision. Involuntary (ie tort) creditors and local communities stand out as conspicuous examples in this regard.

By contrast, the market mimicking case for state interventionism is predicated on the existence of *private* market failures: that is, instances where unregulated private ordering fails to produce outcomes reflective of the prudential interests of *the contracting parties themselves*. The essential logic is that, while voluntary contracting is a fundamentally efficient and desirable mechanism through which to order the bulk of society's economic arrangements (at least relative to the available alternatives), the functionality of such cannot always be taken for granted under 'real world' bargaining conditions. If, however, regulation is deployed in such a way as to 'tease out' the purportedly 'optimal' bargaining outcomes that are liable to ensue in the absence of transaction costs and other impediments to efficient contracting, then contracts can 'be made to work'.[31] That is to say, the regulatory state – via appropriately targeted interventions in private ordering – can succeed in providing 'what the parties would ideally have wanted' as the outcome to their mutual bargain, but for whatever reason were unable to arrive at – or perhaps even recognise as optimal – under the given circumstances. In other words, the purpose of regulation is in effect to 'mimic' the operation of an efficiently functioning market, whereby contracting parties are impulsively inclined towards those agreements that are best calculated to advance their respective material interests.[32]

---

[31] For instance, Jeffrey Gordon claims that: 'it is a mistake to assume that full contractual freedom in corporate law would necessarily lead to private wealth maximization. The existence of some mandatory rules may lead to *better contracts*. In other words, the mixed system of optional and mandatory legal rules that we observe may be best *even from an essentially contractarian perspective*'. Accordingly, 'any efficiency losses from the rigidity of mandatory rules may be outweighed by the gains such rules generate *by addressing defects in the contractual process*' (emphasis added). See JN Gordon, 'The Mandatory Structure of Corporate Law' (1989) 89 *Columbia Law Review* 1549, 1554, 1549. For a similar defence of mandatory corporate governance rules on fundamentally contractarian grounds, see LA Bebchuk, 'The Debate on Contractual Freedom in Corporate Law' (1989) 89 *Columbia Law Review* 1395.

[32] For example, Bernard Black argues that '[s]ome mandatory rules [in corporate law] may survive because they mimic the market', and thus 'would be universally adopted by contract, assuming the parties knew about them'. Black claims that such rules are consequently 'trivial', in the sense that they 'have no bite' (that is, no socially-determinative effect in their own right). See Black, 'Is Corporate Law Trivial?', above n 2, 552, 551.

For this purpose, the market mimicking rationalisation makes reference to the concept of a hypothetical bargaining scenario, the conditions of which are calibrated in such a way that any practical obstacles to the reaching of optimal (or, at the very least, mutually advantageous) voluntary arrangements are 'factored out' of the picture.[33] Whereas some variants of hypothetical bargaining rationality work on the basis of a notionally 'ideal' contractual forum conducive to economically optimal results,[34] others merely seek to envisage circumstances where the parties are able to direct their minds specifically to the issue (or 'term') in question.[35] Under either approach, though, the essential purpose of regulation is the same: that is, to provide for what the parties *would have* stipulated were they both able and inclined to negotiate explicitly over a given matter.[36] For this reason, the market mimicking rationalisation of state interventionism can be understood as an avowedly *counter-factual* phenomenon.

The market mimicking rationalisation is a much more controversial – and, as I will demonstrate below, logically problematic – line of argument than the publicly-oriented justifications for market failure regulation documented above. This is for two main reasons. First, there is the aforementioned fact that, in distinction from the negative externalities and public goods arguments, the market mimicking rationalisation goes straight to the heart of the core contractual dynamics of corporate governance, rather than just the indirect social impacts thereof. Secondly, and more fundamentally, at the very heart of the market mimicking rationalisation there is a prima facie contradiction. This is the apparent tendency of the argument simultaneously to both proclaim *and* deny the capacity of private contracts to produce distributive outcomes that are optimal – or, at least, broadly desirable – from the perspective of the contracting parties themselves. Indeed, of particular noteworthiness in this regard is the fact that the market mimicking rationalisation supports a relatively extensive (for contractarian standards) role for regulation – not just for the orthodox facilitative purpose of 'filling gaps' in (otherwise independently-constituted) agreements, but – moreover – with a view to effecting *outright displacement* of actual contractual outcomes, and their substitution with a regulatory embodiment of those outcomes that allegedly would have ensued within some sort of fictional alternative reality.

[33] On this, see Bebchuk, 'The Debate on Contractual Freedom in Corporate Law', above n 31, 1410–11.

[34] See, eg Easterbrook and Fischel, 'The Corporate Contract', above n 4, 1433.

[35] According to Charny, hypothetical bargaining standards deployed by different scholars vary from one another in accordance with the following two main 'sliding scale' criteria: (i) *generality* (ie how specifically geared is the deployed standard to the circumstances of the actual 'agreement' in question?); and (ii) *idealization* (how abstracted from reality are the conditions under which the hypothetical contractors are assumed to be bargaining?). See D Charny, 'Hypothetical Bargains: The Normative Structure of Contract Interpretation' (1991) 89 *Michigan Law Review* 1815, 1820–21.

[36] See Charny, 'Hypothetical Bargains', ibid, 1815–16.

In the specific context of Anglo-American corporate governance, the market mimicking argument for state interventionism in private ordering is particularly pertinent given the acknowledged necessity to protect investors vis-à-vis management's exercise of discretionary administrative power. This applies especially in widely-held ownership environments where significant informational asymmetry between contractors is – to varying extents – endemic to the corporate equity relation. I demonstrated in chapter two how, in the absence of countervailing institutional measures designed to engender effective managerial accountability, the legitimacy – and, in turn, sustainability – of the corporation's necessary reciprocal power imbalance is undermined by the sacrifice of individual (investor) autonomy that it inevitably gives rise to.[37]

Accordingly, where managerial accountability norms and other investor protections are embodied in the form of reversible or adaptable rules, the problem of reciprocal power imbalance can be mitigated in a normatively unproblematic manner insofar as the direct beneficiaries of those rules (ie investors) can justifiably be viewed as consenting to the relevant protections 'by default'. The relevant legal framework can thus be understood as a means of protecting investors' individual autonomy vis-à-vis unaccountable exercises of executive discretion, while at the same time preventing investors' actual preferences from being usurped by coercive state decree. However, where formal managerial accountability to shareholders is achieved by recourse to *non*-contractually-negotiable mandatory rules, the 'acceptance by default' argument is much more difficult (indeed, prima facie impossible) to sustain. The ensuing rules therefore come across as fundamentally *paternalistic* in nature. As such, their apparent intended effect is to dictate to investors what is publicly decreed to be good for them, rather than leaving investors to make this decision for themselves on a private basis, whether independently or with the support of facilitative (but not preclusive) default rules.

For the above reason, the market mimicking rationalisation of mandatory corporate governance rules – and, indeed, of state interventionism in private ordering generally – raises a number of significant problems for contractarians, both methodologically and logically. Before assessing these difficulties (in part IV), it is first essential to analyse the key contours of the argument at hand. As the following discussion will demonstrate, the argument in favour of regulatory interventionism in private ordering for market mimicking purposes essentially boils down to an extended scholarly attempt to answer the following question – why can investors not be trusted to bargain for protectionist corporate governance 'terms' on a private basis, unaided by the pervasive hand of regulatory state interventionism?

---

[37] See above ch 2 of this volume, pt II.A.

B. Why Can Investors Not be Trusted to Bargain for Protectionist Governance 'Terms' Privately?

Contractarian theorists in general accept that, despite the overall economic benefits of natural rule selection, there are inevitably occasions where rules will be 'mispriced' by the market: that is to say, where investors will fail to discount adequately the projected returns from a corporate equity investment to reflect latent weaknesses or inefficiencies in the relevant firm's governance structure. Rule mispricing is likely to occur in situations where the 'search' costs that investors must incur in order to ascertain the importance of any particular corporate governance 'term' are prohibitively high. This could be said to be true in respect of complex, niche or infrequently used governance rights of shareholders, such as their limited rights of intervention in corporate decision-making via the medium of the proxy process, or their entitlement to initiate or at least approve proposed amendments to a company's constitutional documents. In the absence of mandatory and universally-applicable rules setting out these rights, the arguably likely outcome is that investors will systematically fail to acquire the degree of legal awareness and understanding required to recognise: first, those cases where any such provisions are excluded under the terms of the relevant firm's constitution; and, secondly, the consequences of such exclusion for the overall balance of decision-making power between a company's shareholders and board/management.[38]

Accordingly, mandatory rules can be depicted, in contractarian terms, as theoretically guiding investors' towards those regulatory outcomes that they would be inclined to bargain for in an environment where information and legal expertise were costless (or, at least, proximately costless) to acquire. Mandatory rules could therefore be said to compensate for 'real world' inefficiencies in the private ordering process resulting from the inevitable presence of transaction costs, informational disparities and ensuing internal power imbalances.[39] The ultimate outcome is the establishment of 'better contracts'[40] that accord more closely to the purportedly 'optimal' power equilibrium between shareholders and directors/management.

A further, related factor operating in favour of mandatory rules within the contractarian paradigm is the acknowledged weaknesses in the link between the rule pricing mechanism and the various market disciplines

---

[38] See, eg Easterbrook and Fischel, 'The Corporate Contract', above n 4, 1436.

[39] Easterbrook and Fischel argue that the legitimate function of courts (within the contractarian paradigm) is that of '[p]roviding, as a public service, the rules the parties themselves would have chosen in a transaction-cost-free world'. See 'Contract and Fiduciary Duty' (1993) 36 *Journal of Law and Economics* 425, 427.

[40] See Gordon, 'The Mandatory Structure of Corporate Law', above n 31, 1554.

that are said to be acting on the firm and its management at any point in time. Therefore, even to the extent that the capital market is capable of correctly discounting a firm's equity on the basis of its apparently problematic corporate governance arrangements, it is highly questionable whether this will have any material influence on either the future running of the company's business or the status of its board or management.

Orthodox versions of contractarianism place considerable emphasis on the cost of capital as a market-based constraint on adverse managerial rule selection. The argument is that a corporation which fails to provide the governance terms that the capital market demands will ultimately struggle to raise fresh outside equity, impeding its capacity for re-investment and consequently constraining its ability to compete in product markets.[41] Such a chain of events is likely ultimately to lead to one of either two possible outcomes, namely the outright failure of the firm or, at the very least, the diminution of its share price to the extent that a hostile takeover becomes a reasonable possibility. Since both of the above eventualities entail the virtual certainty of managerial displacement, managers theoretically have a powerful negative incentive to maintain the continuing support of the capital market by, inter alia, offering investors a protective and efficient corporate governance framework.[42] And, insofar as a significant proportion of managers' compensation customarily takes the form of executive stock options and other share-price-based forms, they arguably have a further positive incentive to make pro-shareholder rule selections.[43]

At the same time, more interventionist variants of contractarianism accept that a number of factors in reality operate to reduce considerably the sensitivity of capital and product market forces to adverse managerial rule selections. Most pertinent amongst these is the fact that a company's market equity valuation is dependent on a whole range of considerations including (inter alia) its current and predicted product market performance, the general quality of its management, and any wider industry or macro-economic factors likely to impact on the future earnings potential of its business. Within this diverse range of variables a company's corporate governance arrangements are likely to have at best only an incremental impact on its share price performance and, in turn, its costs of raising equity capital. Furthermore, to the extent that a corporation is reliant on retained earnings and/or covenant-based debt finance to fund its ongoing business operations, an increase in the cost of equity resulting from the establishment of pro-managerial or otherwise unattractive (from

---

[41] See Easterbrook and Fischel, 'The Corporate Contract', above n 4, 1419–20, who consequently assert (at 1419) that 'the dynamics of the market drive [managers] to act as if they had investors' interests at heart. It is almost as if there were an invisible hand'.

[42] See Bainbridge, *The New Corporate Governance*, above n 8 at 36, 66.

[43] See SM Bainbridge, 'Director Primacy and Shareholder Disempowerment' (2006) 119 *Harvard Law Review* 1735, 1741.

the viewpoint of shareholders) governance provisions is likely to have a negligible impact on its financing flexibility. Likewise, where there is significant 'slack' in product markets as a result of oligopoly or other uncompetitive market conditions, increased capital costs will have a limited knock-on effect on the firm's prospects for competitive survival.[44]

For the above reasons, then, pro-managerial (or otherwise non-shareholder-friendly) governance norms are highly unlikely to diminish a company's capital or product market performance to an extent sufficient to precipitate a hostile takeover bid for the firm, or to increase materially the probability of business failure. And, although managerial stock options and other forms of equity-based compensation are supposed to provide a continuing incentive for efficient and pro-shareholder rule selections by managers, their effectiveness in this regard is naturally diminished to the extent that other non-governance-related variables have the effect of 'crowding out' the impact of internal rule choices on share price. In addition, whilst the involvement of specialist securities market intermediaries such as investment bankers in the initial public offering of a company's equity theoretically contributes to the 'correct' pricing of its initial governance terms, the same professional scrutiny mechanisms are not available for constitutional amendments that are proposed by management subsequently. This potentially permits opportunistic managers to initiate so-called 'midstream' opt-outs from reversible pro-shareholder governance rules during the life of an established corporation, on a substantially unchecked – and consequently unpriced – basis. Even in respect of a public company's initial governance arrangements, however, it is questionable to what extent securities underwriters will realistically have foresight of the potential market reaction (if any) to intricate structural, disclosure or fiduciary rules affecting the firm and its investors.[45]

Against this background, mandatory corporate governance rules are justified within the contractarian paradigm – on the basis of hypothetical bargaining rationality – as a method of compensating for the inevitable limitations of market-based mechanisms in pricing and disciplining adverse managerial rule selections. Accordingly, mandatory corporate governance rules can be regarded as establishing, on a universal basis, the set of governance terms that would likely be adopted by managers under fictional conditions of 'extreme capital market rule-sensitivity', where

[44] On this, see MA Eisenberg, 'The Structure of Corporation Law' (1989) 89 *Columbia Law Review* 1461, 1489.

[45] Moreover, the investment banks that are employed to set the terms of a company's IPO arguably have an incentive to acquiesce in the establishment of inefficient pro-managerial governance provisions with a view to maintaining underwriting custom from that firm's management. This arguably over-rides to a considerable extent their theoretical reputational incentive (discussed above ch 3 of this volume, fns 105–06 and accompanying text) to ensure that securities offerings are conducted on terms that are economically advantageous from an investor perspective. On this, see Eisenberg, 'The Structure of Corporation Law', ibid, 1518–19.

inefficient or anti-shareholder rule selections are likely to prompt an immediate and severe market 'punishment' for a firm and its management.

Moreover, mandatory corporate governance rules are argued to be particularly important in respect of issues on which managers' interests are likely to diverge substantially from those of shareholders, such as managerial self-dealing and other positional conflicts of interest as regulated by the equitable fiduciary doctrine and supporting regulatory provisions. The expectation is that managers, if presented with the opportunity to propose constitutional amendments that have the effect of disapplying such provisions in respect of any individual firm, will rationally be inclined to exploit their informational and positional advantages vis-à-vis shareholders in order to do so.[46] And, given the general inclination of shareholders to acquiesce in resolutions proposed by management via the proxy machinery, there is correspondingly a strong likelihood that such opt-outs will be formally approved irrespective of their overall economic effect on the corporation and its investors.[47]

Investors' search costs are further exacerbated in environments where there exists significant variability between the respective constitutional terms (including deregulatory opt-outs) offered by different firms, making it difficult to compare the overall merits of competing governance structures. Therefore an additional benefit to investors of mandatory rules is the degree of inter-company standardisation that they provide on numerous governance issues, making it easier for investors to identify any anomalous or stand-out terms on an individual firm basis.[48]

In all of the above ways, then, regulatory state interventionism in private ordering is said to have the intended effect of mimicking the operation of an efficient external market for corporate securities. This is true insofar as corporate governance law seeks to establish – on an artificial basis – the governance 'terms' that rational investors would have been inclined to bargain for vis-à-vis corporate managers under competitive capital-raising conditions. The normative implication of the claim, meanwhile, is that corporate

---

[46] On this generally, see Bebchuk, 'The Debate on Contractual Freedom', above n 31; Eisenberg, 'The Structure of Corporation Law', above n 44. Arguably a common example of such a practice in the US is the widespread classification of boards described above, which enables firms to opt out of the default 'shotgun' power that would otherwise be available to shareholders under Delaware law. On this, see above ch 4 of this volume, fns 11–14 and accompanying text.

[47] Even in instances where managers are not inclined to implement self-serving opt-outs from pro-shareholder governance rules, the very prospect of such opt-outs occurring can potentially have a negative knock-on effect on the general level of investor confidence in the firm and its management. On this, see Gordon, 'The Mandatory Structure of Corporate Law', above n 31, 1573–75, who refers to this notion as the 'opportunistic amendment hypothesis' for mandatory rules.

[48] See Gordon, ibid, 1567–69, who calls this the 'public good hypothesis' for mandatory rules.

governance law *should* seek to fulfil such a market mimicking role, at least to the extent that the market is perceived as a socially preferable means (relative to the alternatives) of allocating scarce financial capital between competing productive uses.

As prima facie sophisticated as the above line of argument is, however, its convincingness is undermined by a number of inherent weaknesses, which become apparent on closer and more critical reflection. These limitations will now be examined in turn.

IV. THE LIMITATIONS OF THE 'MARKET MIMICKING' RATIONALISATION

A. The Inherent Arbitrariness of Hypothetical Bargaining Rationality

The first problem with the market mimicking argument for regulatory state interventionism concerns the methodology of its underpinning hypothetical bargaining construct. As useful as this conceptual device is, a hypothetical bargain is ultimately what it purports to be – that is, *hypothetical*. As such, it has no innate empirical content but – rather – begins life as nothing more than a theoretical 'empty vessel' that requires subsequent 'filling' by scholars on an artificial and counter-factual basis. However, far from being an innate weakness of hypothetical bargaining rationality, the theory's characteristic counter-factuality is its most powerful feature, in that it establishes a normative case for social or regulatory outcomes different to those prevailing under (inferior) real world bargaining conditions.[49]

But given that the point of deploying the hypothetical bargaining construct is to justify desirable outcomes from purported 'first principles', everything depends on *how* – exactly – the identity of the contractors is constructed within the theory's notional 'original position' of the fictional bargaining table.[50] Absent convincing and generally acceptable reasons to justify *why* the hypothetical contractors were constructed in a given way, any conclusions that result from the deployment of such logic are likely to be rejected as invalid on grounds of their perceived arbitrariness or political partiality.[51]

The defensibility of the answers given to methodological questions such as the following are hence crucial to the validity of any particular application of hypothetical bargaining rationality: *How rational should the*

---

[49] On the counter-factuality of the hypothetical bargaining construct, and the conceptual problems that this poses, see R Dworkin, 'Why Efficiency?' (1980) 8 *Hofstra Law Review* 563.

[50] On this, see V Brudney, 'Corporate Governance, Agency Costs, and the Rhetoric of Contract' (1985) 85 *Columbia Law Review* 1403, 1415–16.

[51] On this difficulty generally, see Charny, 'Hypothetical Bargains', above n 35.

notional contractors be presumed to be as economic actors? How much awareness should they be deemed to have of their specific circumstances? And what should their presumed risk appetite be? It is my contention that none of these points of uncertainty have been satisfactorily settled by those who – consciously or subconsciously – deploy hypothetical bargaining rationality in attempting to justify regulatory interventionism in corporate governance affairs on market mimicking grounds.

With respect first to the issue of what degree of economic rationality hypothetical investors should be taken to possess, the contractarian paradigm of corporate governance is both ambivalent and somewhat contradictory. In this regard, a number of alternative constructions are possible. One approach, which could be termed the 'weak' bargaining hypothesis, queries merely what arrangement *the actual parties* (ie investors and managers) in question would have bargained for in regard to a specific aspect of their future relationship, had they been directly afforded the opportunity to do so ex ante. A second potential approach – constituted at a slightly higher level of theoretical abstraction (the 'semi-strong' bargaining hypothesis) – seeks to determine what arrangement hypothetical contractors of *the relevant type* (eg ordinary shareholders, or professional institutional shareholders) would generally favour in respect of any particular matter, irrespective of the specific characteristics, preferences or competencies of the parties in question. A final possible approach – which operates at the most abstract level of analysis (the 'strong' bargaining hypothesis) – attempts to surmise what arrangements perfectly rational contractors, exhibiting the characteristics of classical 'economic man', would tend to bargain for absent any limitations on information and foresight, or other inhibiting transaction costs.[52]

The advantage of the weak bargaining hypothesis is its more immediate relevance to the circumstances of the parties in question, which increases the likelihood of its purported 'outcomes' being accepted as valid in respect of the situation at hand. Correspondingly, the disadvantage of the strong bargaining hypothesis is its extreme counter-factuality in relation to the circumstances at hand, which renders its normative conclusions difficult to accept in the absence of convincing and generally acceptable reasons for doing so. At the same time, though, the strong bargaining hypothesis – in being positioned at a level of analysis relatively far removed from reality – is generally equipped to elicit more universally-applicable recommendations (whether for preservation or reform of existing norms or laws) in respect of a particular matter than circumstantially-sensitive approaches to the same issue.

---

[52] On these alternative possible constructions of the notional hypothetical bargain, see Charny, 'Hypothetical Bargains', above n 35, ibid, 1817.

All social-scientific analyses based at root on contractarian logic tend as a general rule to fall into one of the above three categories of abstraction, whether intentionally or by accident. However, which of these three categories the *corporate* contractarian rationalisation of state interventionism falls into it is not readily apparent. Nor is it apparently spelled out in either a clear or consistent way across the principal theoretical literature, with both the 'pure' and more transaction-costs-focused variants of corporate contractarianism making notably different presumptions from one another in relation to such matters.[53]

In addition to creating uncertainty about the degree of economic rationality to be attributed to contracting parties in the hypothetical bargaining scenario, the market mimicking rationalisation of regulation throws up a further unresolved question concerning how much awareness corporate contractors (ie investors and managers) should be deemed to have of their specific circumstances when negotiating with one another in the notional original position? Two potential theoretical methodologies stand out in this regard. In the first alternative, the negotiating parties are deemed to have knowledge of their relative starting positions, and accordingly bargain for protective governance terms with those considerations in mind. In the second alternative, the parties are regarded as negotiating for protective terms behind a fictional 'veil of ignorance', by virtue of which they are presumed to be unaware of their particular starting point relative to other contractors. At the same time, though, all parties are deemed to be in possession of general knowledge and understanding of the overall endeavour that they each form part of.[54]

In the corporate governance context, it is clearly of material relevance to the likely outcome of hypothetical bargains which of the above two theoretical approaches is deployed. In particular, a priori awareness of one's status as a manager or shareholder will undoubtedly impact on what one sees as an individually advantageous outcome of the original bargain over relative governance entitlements. This is especially so in widely-held ownership environments where there exists an inevitable scarcity of opportunities for ex post facto 'settling-up' of parties' initial contractual entitlements in the event that they prove to be insufficient.

---

[53] Whilst the orthodox or 'pure' variants of contractarianism (such as those developed by Easterbrook & Fischel, and Bainbridge) apparently seek to attribute proximately rational economic characteristics to corporate participants, the more transaction-costs-focused versions of the theory (such as those developed by Williamson and Hart) are premised on what the relevant authors perceive to be inherent limitations on the rationality of corporate participants as human agents. For a comparison of these two approaches, see G Kelly and J Parkinson, 'The Conceptual Foundations of the Company: A Pluralist Approach' in J Parkinson, A Gamble and G Kelly, *The Political Economy of the Company* (Oxford, Hart Publishing, 2000).

[54] The latter 'veil of ignorance' methodology is based on the influential work of the rationalist political philosopher John Rawls. See Rawls, *A Theory of Justice*, above n 27, 118–23.

Notwithstanding these points of concern, corporate contractarianism is in general somewhat ambivalent on this particular issue. Most leading expositions of the contractarian paradigm would appear to stop short of deploying full 'veil of ignorance' methodology, with parties to implicit corporate contracts at least presumed to know who they are in a broad generic sense (eg managers, shareholders, creditors or employees). But the same theory would appear to attribute little-to-no awareness on the part of contractors of their relative position *within* each relevant participant 'grouping' (eg whether one is an informed institutional shareholder or uninformed retail investor), which might otherwise lead parties of the same broad identity to form significantly different contractual preferences from one another.[55]

Furthermore, corporate contractarians have shown scant appreciation of the need either to articulate or justify their particular theoretical methodology of choice when resorting (expressly or implicitly) to hypothetical bargaining rationality. In particular, the theory's exponents have failed to explain why recourse to the orthodox veil of ignorance construct is apparently not merited when determining what constitutes an efficacious a priori allocation of governance entitlements between managers and shareholders. This issue is of particular concern given the general prominence of this particular method of deductive reasoning within contractarian analyses of social arrangements more generally, in both legal theory and rationalist political philosophy.

A final aspect of arbitrariness inherent in the hypothetical bargaining model deployed by corporate contractarians is the inbuilt and undefended assumptions that it seems to make about the risk appetite of contracting parties. It goes almost without saying in corporate-contractarian literature, with its heavy emphasis on orthodox law and economics reasoning, that the common guiding objective of contractors is purportedly to arrive at whichever distribution of governance entitlements is most likely to advance their overall wealth as a group – the assumption being that the bigger the resulting 'pie', the bigger the particular slice that each individual contractor will ultimately be entitled to. However, far from being an indisputably 'neutral' objective to attribute to contractors in the original position, the goal of overall wealth-maximisation implies that contractors have a predisposition towards risk that impels them to accept the possibility of adverse distributional outcomes in the sharing of the notional pie. That is to say, contractors will focus their energies on seeking

---

[55] For instance, whereas the informed institutional shareholder with relatively informal access to management may perceive detailed corporate disclosure or proxy regulation as little more than costly and unnecessary bureaucracy, the uninformed retail investor may view the same laws as a necessary and inalienable proprietary 'life line' in the absence of alternative means of access to firm-specific information or governance influence.

an overall wealth-maximising outcome, on the assumption that this will indirectly prove beneficial to them on an individual level.[56]

In short, then, corporate contractarianism envisages a firm's participants negotiating with the best (or, at least, proximately best) possible individual distributional outcome in mind, thus imbuing them with the notional psychological characteristic of 'pathological optimism'.[57] In making this significant assumption, contractarian theorists foreclose consideration of the reasonable possibility that many corporate contractors negotiate with an alternative risk appetite that impels them to forego potential further increases in overall group wealth beyond a given level, in order to ensure at least a minimal guaranteed level of sharing in the ultimate collective output. In the corporate governance context, an investor with the latter psychological make-up might consequently be likely to favour a regulatory scheme that guarantees shareholders a minimum level of guaranteed rights of intervention in corporate decision-making. Moreover, the investor's preference in this regard would likely remain the same even where it were demonstrated that the firm's overall wealth-creating capacity will probably be greater in the event that shareholders forego such rights in favour of vesting unqualified executive authority in the board of directors.

It should be emphasised that the hypothetical investor in the above scenario is no less rational than the investor who shows a disregard for such distributional concerns in the original position. The only difference is in

---

[56] Surveying the basic normative thrust of corporate-contractarian scholarship generally, Victor Brudney has observed that '[i]f the contract (under which the stockholder is said to offer his investment in exchange for managerial services) is "knowingly" and "freely" made by the parties, then on conventional assumptions, *its performance makes each of the parties better off and creates a larger pie for society* – assuming no externalities, public goods, or market failures' (emphasis added). See Brudney, 'Corporate Governance', above n 50, 1404.

[57] Indeed, this attribution would appear to be a basic characteristic of orthodox law and economics methodology more generally, from which the corporate-contractarian school of thought is ultimately derived. For instance, Richard Posner – arguably the principal progenitor of the modern law and economics movement in the US – has been a consistent critic of John Rawls's argument that individuals in the notional 'original' bargaining position would choose a set of institutional arrangements whereby inequalities in resources inter se are only generally acceptable to the extent that they improve the utility of those least well-off within the relevant group (see Rawls, *A Theory of Justice*, above n 27, 65–70). Posner has argued that Rawls attributes an excessive degree of risk aversion to his hypothetical contractors, and also that the original position – as formulated by Rawls – results in 'the choices of the unproductive' being 'weighted equally with those of the productive'. See RA Posner, 'The Ethical and Political Basis of the Efficiency Norm in Common Law Adjudication' (1980) 8 *Hofstra Law Review* 487, 499. On this basis, Posner argues that the 'efficiency' of a given contractual outcome – understood as denoting its propensity to maximise the wealth of the parties as a general group (irrespective of relative distributional outcomes) – is the criterion that 'actual' (as opposed to hypothetical) contractors would therefore tend to favour as the principal determinant of social arrangements. According to Posner, '[s]ince efficiency is a widely regarded value in our world of limited resources, a persuasive showing that one course of action is more efficient than the alternatives may be an important factor in shaping public choice'. See RA Posner, *Economic Analysis of Law* (Boston, Little, Brown, 1972) 6.

their relative degrees of risk tolerance, whereby one is led to favour the 'pure' wealth-maximising outcome, and the other is drawn towards the outcome that favours a 'satisficing'[58] degree of group wealth-creation tempered by an offsetting level of concern for individually adverse social-distributional outcomes. But the contractarian position, in automatically attributing the former risk appetite to contractors without further explanation, ultimately taints its normative conclusions with the charge of arbitrariness by failing to justify the underpinning factual assumptions of its approach. For this reason, any normative argument that is advanced for greater or lesser public regulation of corporate governance affairs on market mimicking grounds should be regarded as prima facie invalid. That is, at least in the absence of a rigorous accompanying defence of the various factual assumptions and imputations on which this claim is based.

B. Are Hypothetical Contracts Really 'Contractarian' at All?

A second and more fundamental weakness in the market mimicking rationalisation of mandatory corporate governance rules is its unintended normative effect in undermining the conceptual validity of the contractarian account of regulation in its entirety. Above all, it may justifiably be queried whether the hypothetical contracts that are forwarded in support of purportedly 'market mimicking' regulatory outcomes are really 'contractarian' in nature at all, at least in the ordinary sense of the word. There are two principal reasons to doubt the 'contractualness' of the contractarian argument in this regard: one of which concerns the basic theoretical logic of the argument, whereas the other derives from a crucial (and, I will argue, inherently self-defeating) concession that proponents of this claim have frequently made.

With respect to the former (logical) concern, David Charny has observed that '[i]t is by no means clear that individuals should be bound to hypothetical – as opposed to actual – contracts, or even that it is appropriate to call such hypothetical contracts "contracts" at all'.[59] On this basis, Charny doubts the relevance to hypothetical contracts (whether as embodied statutorily or judicially) of traditional arguments for contractual obligation based on the individual autonomy of voluntary parties to an agreement, given that no actual or explicit assent has ever been signalled by the

---

[58] On the concept of 'satisficing' outcomes as a motivating goal of economic activity generally, see HA Simon, 'Theories of Decision-Making in Economics and Behavioral Science' (1959) 49 *American Economic Review* 253.

[59] See Charny, 'Hypothetical Bargains', above n 35, 1817. Likewise, Ronald Dworkin asserts that 'a counterfactual consent provides no reason *in itself* for enforcing against me that to which I would have (but did not) consent', and indeed 'is *no consent at all*' (emphasis added). See Dworkin, 'Why Efficiency?', above n 49, 578.

notionally 'contracting' parties to the terms thereof.[60] Moreover, the fact that in such cases no actual agreement has been either promulgated or assented to means that there are no specific terms – whether express or even implied – that can be used as a working basis for constructing the hypothetical contract. This means that the relevant rule-maker (whether legislative, judicial or administrative) must in effect pluck a hypothetical agreement out of thin air by seeking to determine what the contracting parties *would have* bargained for in respect of the situation at hand.[61]

But in the absence of any concrete evidence as to what the parties themselves would have been inclined to bargain for in the circumstances at hand, the only available proxy for such are what Charny calls 'socially extant expectations of fairness or reasonableness'.[62] These expectations are inevitably derived from the rule-maker's perception of the 'general social consensus about how various types of transactions should be structured', so that there is 'little need for inquiry into variations of perceptions or preferences among individual transactors'.[63] Accordingly, in cases where individual contractors exhibit differing private preferences from one another, those individual preferences that do not align with the perceived general social consensus with respect to a particular matter can be rejected by the rule-maker a priori as examples of erroneous adverse selection.[64]

Thus by means of the above course of logic, substantive concepts of fairness or welfarism in social arrangements are effectively brought into contractarian argumentation via the proverbial 'back door'. This demonstrates the methodological inescapability of using substantive outcomes as the *starting point* – rather than end point – of hypothetical bargaining rationality. As Kronman highlights, '[t]he inference in all hypothetical bargains must . . . be *from mutual benefit to consent*, rather than the other way around, as in the case of actual agreements' (emphasis added).[65] In other words, the fact that a given regulatory arrangement is objectively judged to be mutually welfare-enhancing is *in itself* a reason for treating it as a substantive outcome of some hypothetical bargain, even though no underpinning contractual agreement to this effect has ever occurred between the parties who are subject to the rule in question.[66]

---

[60] Charny, ibid.

[61] See JC Coffee, 'The Mandatory/Enabling Balance in Corporate Law' (1989) 89 *Columbia Law Review* 1618, 1628. Coffee claims that the 'greatest defect' of hypothetical bargaining rationality is its focus on seeking artificially to provide 'what parties would have wanted', rather than attempting to compel them to bargain 'for what they do want'.

[62] Charny, 'Hypothetical Bargains', above n 35, 1838.

[63] Ibid.

[64] Ibid.

[65] See AT Kronman, 'A Comment on Dean Clark' (1989) 89 *Columbia Law Review* 1748, 1750.

[66] Atiyah has made essentially the same point in the following succinct terms: '*If* one starts by assuming that all men are rational, *if* one then assumes that they desire certain goals, *if* one can demonstrate that these goals are best reached by a certain path, and *if* one then finds

Kronman explains how, on this basis, 'the assertion that . . . [the parties] would themselves hypothetically agree to . . . adoption [of a relevant term] *adds no justificatory force of its own*, for this last claim follows automatically from – it is entailed by – the rule's welfare enhancing character'.[67] It follows that '[h]ypothetical contract arguments are not really contractualist at all', given that '[t]hey explain and justify their conclusion by an appeal to considerations of welfare alone, the latter providing their necessary and sufficient conditions'.[68] For this reason, the market mimicking rationalisation of mandatory rules – to the extent that it is premised on hypothetical bargaining outcomes – is more appropriately understood as a *welfarist*, rather than contractualist, line of argument.

Insofar, therefore, as the market mimicking rationalisation of state interventionism in private ordering does not even fit the necessary characteristics of a 'contractarian' argument at all in the accepted sense, it can justifiably be concluded that private ordering rationality is on its own incapable of accounting for the significant regulatory dimensions of Anglo-American corporate governance law as a system. With the effective breakdown of the contractual metaphor as a means of giving normative force to prevailing distributions of corporate governance rights, it arguably follows that such outcomes stand to be determined on the basis of democratic public policy debate, just like any other avowedly welfarist social outcome. In this context, continual recourse to the fictional rhetoric of the hypothetical private bargain could thus be said to obfuscate the fundamentally *public-regarding* nature of the necessary institutional enquiry at hand.

Notwithstanding the seriousness of the above revelation for the logical defensibility of the market mimicking rationalisation of regulation, there remains to be added one further nail in the proverbial coffin of this argument. This concerns a significant – indeed, *self-defeating* – concession that interventionist contractarians have made in providing an explanation for why mandatory rules are purportedly an acceptable and, moreover, essential complement to private ordering dynamics in corporate governance. In short, proponents of the market mimicking argument make the logically fatal error of arguing for (limited) regulatory state interventionism in corporate governance on grounds of systematic irrationality in private rule selection methods.

Although contractarian theorists are generally prepared to concede the inevitable existence of some 'real world' imperfections in shareholder

---

man on that path, it is a natural conclusion that man finds himself there as a result of a deliberate act of free choice'. See PS Atiyah, *The Rise and Fall of Freedom of Contract* (Oxford, Clarendon Press, 1979) 51. Writing as far back as 1979, Atiyah claimed that '[t]oday this form of reasoning is often treated as highly fictitious' (ibid).

[67] See Kronman, 'A Comment', above n 65, 1750.
[68] Ibid.

rationality and market-based pricing mechanisms,[69] the market mimicking argument goes above and beyond this by advocating the widespread invocation of mandatory rules as a structural response to the *systematic* mispricing of corporate governance norms by the capital market.[70] In making this sizeable allowance for widespread investor irrationality, the market mimicking argument arguably gives away too much by inadvertently invalidating the very assumption on which the validity of its private ordering hypothesis rests: that is, the basic (albeit imperfect) capacity of capital markets to reflect the requisite degree of relevant information about a firm, including its internal rule structure, to make possible the proximately rational selection and pricing of its securities by investors.[71]

As an unfortunate consequence of adopting this awkward starting position, the market mimicking rationalisation of mandatory rules is inevitably inclined towards contradictory normative claims. On the one hand, proponents of this view assert that corporate law rules should do no more than mimic the institutional choices that corporate participants (particularly investors) would be inclined to make themselves under idealised bargaining conditions. On the other hand, though, the same school of thought accepts that corporate participants are in reality very often incapable of making purportedly rational or efficient rule selection choices unaided.

The inevitable implication is that the interventionist regulatory state must ultimately make these calls instead by trying to ascertain what rules hypothetically rational contractors would be inclined to favour in respect of any given corporate governance problem, and also which of these rules the same hypothetical agents would deem so important and/or complex as to be rendered incapable of removal or variation under any possible conditions. But for the state to do any more than this – for instance, to promulgate rules on the basis of public policy considerations rather than majoritarian private preferences – would arguably be to overstep its permissible remit as a purportedly passive-facilitative rule-maker. Thus contractarianism at the same time both asserts and denies the deliberate policy-making remit of the regulatory state in corporate governance. In the case of mandatory rules,

---

[69] Indeed, as I explained in chapter three of this volume, the economic rationale for the principle of shareholder exclusivity in corporate governance law is premised on the (assumed) *incapacity* of corporate equity investors to draft 'complete' contracts that provide protection against all conceivable contingencies. If information were costless to acquire, enabling shareholders to make rational investment choices based on full foresight of the consequences thereof, then this purported 'incomplete contract' problem would not exist. See above ch 3 of this volume, pt III.B (i).

[70] See, eg Easterbrook and Fischel, 'The Corporate Contract', above n 4, 1436.

[71] In finance theory, this assumption is known popularly as the Efficient Capital Markets Hypothesis (or ECMH), on which see EF Fama, 'Efficient Capital Markets: A Review of Theory and Empirical Work' (1970) 25 *Journal of Finance* 383. For a critical perspective on the ECMH, see LA Stout, 'The Mechanisms of Market Inefficiency' (2003) 28 *Journal of Corporation Law* 635.

moreover, this conceptual double-bind is exacerbated by the inescapability (for corporate participants) of the institutional outcomes that result from state interventionism, especially when it comes to fundamental governance issues such as the distribution of decision-making power and influence at the heart of the corporate structure.

Accordingly, by accepting the case for state-promulgated mandatory rules on the basis of systematic investor irrationality, the market mimicking argument could be said to tread a very fine line between advocating: on the one hand, the essentially quasi-*private* state function of market correction by means of contractual 'gap-filling'; and, on the other, the manifestly *public* state function of 'regulatory paternalism'. In this sense, regulatory paternalism entails the interventionist state substituting its own (publicly-constituted) conception of what makes a purportedly effective or desirable corporate governance framework in place of those (suboptimal) structural outcomes that are likely to result from privately-driven, market-based rule selections.

The unavoidably paternalistic slant of the market mimicking rationalisation of mandatory corporate governance rules has significant normative consequences, insofar as it calls into question the purportedly endogenous dynamic underpinning the development of Anglo-American corporate governance norms. In particular, it infers that mandatory corporate governance rules rest on a fundamentally *anti*-contractual basis insofar as they represent a largely wholesale *substitute to*, rather than supplementary facilitator of, the market-driven private ordering process. On this basis, one can justifiably draw the conclusion that contractarianism is ultimately incapable of rationalising the significant, fundamental and perpetual presence of mandatory rules at the heart of Anglo-American corporate governance, at least without accepting an intrinsic public-policy-making role for the interventionist regulatory state.

The implications of this finding – with respect to the future development of both legal scholarship and corporate governance law itself in the United States and United Kingdom – will now be explored in the following, and final, part of this chapter.

V. EXPANDING THE FRONTIERS OF THE CONTRACTARIAN PARADIGM

A. The Challenge at Hand

If existing contractarian rationalisations do not fully account for the significant regulatory dimensions of Anglo-American corporate law, then it may naturally be asked whether there is an alternative rationalisation that is better equipped to explain the prevailing structure of Anglo-American corporate governance law in all of its complexities. But whilst identifying the inconsistencies and lacunae in contractarian logic is one thing, constructing an alternative conceptual model that provides a more relevant and defensible rationalisation of prevailing corporate governance rules and structures is quite another.

Indeed, besides its undoubted explanatory elegance and intellectual sophistication, one of the principal factors underlying contractarianism's continuing influence today is the simple lack of viable competing theoretical paradigms that can provide a counter-explanation of corporate governance law with a comparable degree of systematic rigour.[72] For these reasons, in attempting to construct a more defensible theoretical rationalisation of regulatory state interventionism in corporate governance law, I have tried as best as possible to stay within the broad conceptual parameters of the contractarian paradigm. At the same time, I have found it necessary to expand the existing frontiers of the contractarian position in an attempt to render it responsive to the undeniably paternalistic character of the subject's public-regulatory dimensions. The risk, of course, is that where one pushes the boundaries of this logic too far, the proverbial band will snap. At the very least, though, by evaluating my following attempt to render the existing theoretical paradigm consistent with the true underlying nature of its subject-matter, readers might develop a conclusive view on the merits of either retaining or rejecting the contractarian position in future.

With these considerations in mind, my revised contractarian explanation for regulatory state paternalism in corporate governance thus proceeds as follows.

---

[72] A notable recent exception to this trend, however, is Michael Galanis's excellent article 'Vicious Spirals in Corporate Governance: Mandatory Rule for Systemic (Re)Balancing? (2011) 31 *Oxford Journal of Legal Studies* 327. In essence, Galanis argues that contractually-determined corporate governance rules are insufficient in preventing the systematic expropriation of rents by strong parties from weak parties within the firm. On this basis, Galanis presents an argument for mandatory rules based on the need to rebalance the inter-firm contracting process in order to render it sustainable in the long run. Whilst Galanis's argument represents a valuable and progressive contribution to the field, its principal focus appears to be on (economic) power imbalances between (relatively strong) shareholders and (relatively weak) employees, with the normative implication that regulatory interventionism in corporate governance should be geared mainly to recalibrating the bargaining dynamics of this particular intra-firm relation in favour of the latter group. In contrast, my focus in the present work is on the inherent structural power imbalance between (relatively strong) managers and (relatively weak) shareholders, to which the existing body of 'core' Anglo-American corporate governance law is (for better or worse) almost exclusively geared today. Also, whilst Galanis's paper is focused on developing a normative case for greater regulatory interventionism in corporate governance in future, my (more modest) focus in this book is simply on seeking to make sense of the existing body of corporate laws, as a necessary prelude to any subsequent enquiries of a more reformist nature. Therefore, whilst I do not disagree with the claims that Galanis makes in his paper, I believe that our respective approaches are geared sufficiently differently from one another to stand up independently in their own terms, and without undermining each other.

B. Managerial Accountability as the Principal Rationale for Mandatory Corporate Governance Laws

I emphasised in chapter two that the principal and definitive purpose of corporate governance law should be understood as that of engendering an effective and ongoing process of managerial account-giving to shareholders. In this way, the law has the effect of legitimating – and thus sustaining – the necessary reciprocal power imbalance between management and shareholders at the heart of the public corporation, notwithstanding the fact that the basic structural characteristics of this relation are fundamentally averse to investors' continuing contractual autonomy as economic actors.[73]

Accordingly, the main dual function of mandatory shareholder protectionist laws is: first, to provide an appropriate formal forum for the bilateral deliberation[74] of fundamental, important or controversial issues pertaining to the corporate equity relation; and, secondly, to effect an equalisation – or, at least, moderation (in shareholders' favour) of the relative influence and resources that managers and shareholders, respectively, bring to the proverbial corporate discussion table. In these ways, corporate governance law seeks to engender more effective deliberative conditions than would be possible by recourse to management-shareholder private ordering alone. The ultimate intended effect of such extensive regulatory intervention is to secure the legitimacy – and, in turn, sustainability – of the corporate equity relation, by demonstrably ensuring its consistency with the basic liberal-democratic principle of individual (investor) autonomy.[75]

The most obvious and fundamental respect in which Anglo-American corporate governance law provides for the effective giving and receipt of accounts by management in the above sense is by mandating the annual shareholders' meeting (or, in the United Kingdom, Annual General Meeting) as the formal fulcrum for periodic management-shareholder deliberations within public companies.[76] In the Delaware case of *Hoschett*

---

[73] On this, see above ch 2 of this volume, pt II.

[74] Or, where influential investors have differing preferences from one another, *multilateral* deliberation.

[75] On this, see above ch 2 of this volume, pt II.C.

[76] Under US (Delaware) law, annual shareholders' meetings are mandatory except in cases where directors are elected by the unanimous written consent of shareholders. See Delaware General Corporation Law, § 211(b). For obvious reasons, though, such a process is highly impracticable in widely-held ownership environments, with the effect that the requirement for annual shareholders' meetings operates as a universal rule for publicly listed companies in the US. Likewise, under UK law, Annual General Meetings are a mandatory requirement for all public companies (under s 336(1) of the Companies Act 2006), notwithstanding the leeway that private companies now enjoy under the 2006 Act regime to dispense with the AGM requirement.

v TSI International Software,[77] Chancellor Allen articulated both an economic and political justification for regarding the annual shareholders' meeting – and associated corporate election procedure – as compulsory and irreducible elements of corporate governance. In terms strongly resonant of Dubnick's notion of 'presumptive account-giving' explained in chapter two above,[78] Chancellor Allen first explained the functional or economic rationale of the dual meeting and election process as follows:

> The annual election process is a structured occasion that necessarily focuses attention on corporate performance. Knowing that such an occasion is necessarily to be faced annually may itself have a marginally beneficial effect on managerial attention and performance. Certainly, the annual meeting may in some instances be a bother to management, or even, though rarely, a strain, but in all events it provides a certain discipline and an occasion for interaction and participation of a kind.[79]

Secondly – and more significantly for present purposes – the Court highlighted the important normative or political function of the annual corporate meeting and election by explaining that:

> while the model of democratic forms should not too strictly be applied to the economic institution of a business corporation . . . it is nevertheless a not unimportant feature of corporate governance that at a noticed annual meeting *a form of discourse . . . among investors and between shareholders and managers is possible* (emphasis added).[80]

Accordingly, the Court emphasised that: [t]he theory of the meeting *includes the idea that a deliberative component of the meeting may occur*' and, whilst in reality 'meetings are very far from deliberative convocations . . . a keen realization of the reality of the degree of deliberation that is possible, should make the preservation of residual mechanisms of corporate democracy more, not less, important' (emphasis added).[81]

Clearly, this deliberative logic is applicable to the basic procedure of the meeting itself including the laying of accounts and reports, and the raising of questions by investors in anticipation of reasoned answers by the board thereto. It could furthermore be said to extend to the procedure for voting on the election of directors and other issues proposed for resolution, including the rules regarding the preparation and solicitation of proxies by both management and shareholders.

Indeed, as noted in the previous chapter, the regulatory provisions concerning the proxy solicitation process surrounding the annual shareholders' meeting are mandatory for US and UK listed companies alike, thereby

---

[77] *Hoschett v TSI International Software* 683 A 2d 43 (Del Ch 2006).
[78] On this, see above ch 2 of this volume, fns 95–96 and accompanying text.
[79] *Hoschett v TSI International Software*, above n 77, 44–45.
[80] Ibid, 45–46.
[81] Ibid, 46.

260 Rationalising State Paternalism

reaffirming the above understanding of deliberation and reasoned account-giving as being integral and characteristic aspects of the Anglo-American corporate governance system.[82] Furthermore, the mandatory rights of intervention in corporate decision-making enjoyed by shareholders under UK corporate law[83] – and most notably shareholders' collective 'shotgun' right exercisable vis-à-vis directors[84] – reinforce the perceived managerial imperative of effective and ongoing account-giving to investors, both within and outside of the formal meeting environment. The intended outcome of such reasoned deliberation – from management's perspective – is to preclude the need for direct exercise of shareholders' intervention rights in cases where investor concerns are seen to go unanswered or unresolved.

Of course, the capacity of the annual shareholders' meeting and surrounding proxy solicitation process to serve as an effective deliberative forum is contingent on the extent to which investors are able to vote, speak and act on an informed basis. Otherwise, managerial account-giving is rendered impossible. Accordingly, the key purpose of mandatory disclosure requirements – especially those pertaining to the publication of ongoing firm performance and extraordinary business transactions and events[85] – is to mitigate the innate informational disparity between management and shareholders by providing an objective and credible informational floor to their common deliberations. This brings the corporate communications process closer to the hypothetical ideal speech scenario[86] by enabling shareholders to evaluate managerial proposals (including directorial nominees) in the light of information additional to that provided voluntarily by management itself.

Mandatory disclosure requirements also enhance the rigour of managerial account-giving by providing investors with the informational capacity – in appropriate cases – to initiate proxy proposals independently of those advanced by management, ranging from ad hoc strategic recommendations to calls for outright managerial displacement. Whilst such 'insurgent' proposals are usually highly unlikely to command majority shareholder support, their very (actual or potential) advancement is in itself likely to prompt the giving of reasons by management in defence of its current policies or position. And, as I explained in chapter two, such deliberative reason-giving is essential to maintaining the legitimacy of management's possession and exercise of discretionary administrative power vis-à-vis shareholders and the corresponding acquiescence of investors therein.[87]

---

[82] See above ch 6 of this volume, fn 120 and accompanying text.
[83] On this, see above ch 6 of this volume, pt III.
[84] See above ch 6 of this volume, pt III.C.
[85] On this generally, see above ch 6 of this volume, pt II.
[86] On this concept, see above ch 2 of this volume, fn 104 and accompanying text.
[87] See above ch 2 of this volume, pt II.

Arguably the most practically significant institutional determinant of ongoing managerial accountability, however, is the process of capital-raising on external markets. It was explained in the previous chapter that, in instances where a corporation has insufficient internal cash reserves to satisfy its projected investment needs, the necessity of 'going to the market' in search of new equity or debt finance compels that management pay a significant degree of deference to investor interests and concerns. In particular, management must proffer sufficiently convincing reasons and supporting data in its public offering prospectus and related communications, to convince prospective investors that the price at which new equity securities are being offered on the market is truly representative of underlying firm value.[88]

However, in cases where management is able to rely on a particular investor to purchase new securities on a selective or off-market basis, the market imperative of a priori public account-giving that would otherwise exist is removed. Accordingly, a crucial (and relatively undocumented) purpose of the mandatory pre-emption rights scheme under UK corporate law[89] – in addition to preventing uncompensated dilution of existing holdings in the firm – is to foreclose management's ability to evade the aforementioned process of account-giving to the market via selective securities allotment. The ultimate effect of this process is to check and – consequently – *legitimate* the extensive degree of discretion enjoyed by management in appropriating and allocating equity capital in the fulfilment of its internally-determined strategic plans.

A broadly similar rationale could be said to underlie the United Kingdom's prohibition of frustrative takeover defences, as established under both the Takeover Code and – to a less severe extent – by the (mandatory) 'proper purpose' doctrine at common law.[90] From the perspective of the argument at hand, the chief value of a contest for corporate control (whether instigated by way of tender offer or proxy contest) is its effect in compelling an incumbent management team, along with the outside control contestant(s), to engage in a high-level process of account-giving concerning the future strategic direction of the business. Management and prospective control-acquirers are thus each compelled to articulate their respective visions for the firm's future: in the former group's case, with a view to supporting its recommendation either to reject a tender offer or to refuse to support an insurgent proxy contestant; and, in the latter's case, with a view to convincing the target corporation's shareholders either to tender their shares at the specified bid price, or else to oppose the

---

[88] On this, see above ch 6 of this volume, fn 161 and accompanying text.

[89] On this, see above ch 6 of this volume, fns 158–59 and accompanying text. As explained earlier, the common law principle in this regard is today codified in section 171(b) of the Companies Act 2006.

[90] On this generally, see above ch 6 of this volume, fns 169–76 and accompanying text.

(re)appointment of management's directorial nominees in an upcoming election. Additionally, the incumbent management team will be expected to defend its past record in office, with the effect that managerial account-giving in a contest for corporate control is typically both a priori and ex post facto in nature.

As against this, however, frustrative takeover defences – where freely permitted – tend to preclude the above account-giving process insofar as a target company's management is presented with the opportunity to 'just say no' to a prospective control-acquirer, by refusing to remove a poison pill or other defence in the face of a hostile bid. Thus the 'no-frustration' rule in the UK Takeover Code, by prohibiting unauthorised action by a target company's board that has the effect of precluding the execution of an actual or imminent bid, operates so as to maintain the managerial imperative to articulate reasons to shareholders for recommending rejection of the bid. Shareholders, meanwhile, remain free to accept or reject those recommendations in the light of any competing representations made by the bidder(s). In this regard, the no-frustration rule is reinforced both by the specific Code requirements concerning the content of a target company board's advice and recommendation to shareholders,[91] and also by the aforementioned proper purpose doctrine – which, as noted earlier – demands articulation by a target company board of its substantial purpose for seeking to influence the balance of voting power between shareholders.[92]

Even in the United States, where both selective equity allocations and frustrative takeover responses in general are ultimately subject to the (limited) fiduciary discretion of directors,[93] the same basic deliberative logic permeates throughout this area of law. The effect of the *Unocal* doctrine under Delaware law is to compel a target corporation's board, in defence of a breach of duty action brought against them, to articulate to the court a discernible threat that the relevant bid posed to corporate policy and effectiveness – and also the purported proportionality of the board's response thereto – as a prerequisite to obtaining business judgment protection.[94]

As I explained in chapter four above, the diversity of factors that can potentially amount to such a threat, and also the ambit of judicial leeway afforded to boards who opt to defend bids in a relatively heavy-handed manner, have both been expanded progressively by the Delaware courts

---

[91] See The Panel on Takeovers and Mergers, The Takeover Code (September 2011), Rule 3.1 ('Independent advice: Board of the offeree company'), available at: www.thetakeover-panel.org.uk/wp-content/uploads/2008/11/code.pdf .

[92] On this, see *Howard Smith Ltd v Ampol Petroleum Ltd* [1974] AC 821 (Privy Council), discussed briefly above ch 6 of this volume, fn 176.

[93] On this generally, see above ch 4 of this volume, pt IV.C.

[94] On this, see above ch 4 of this volume, fns 70–74 and accompanying text.

over the past three decades.[95] Nonetheless, the basic fact remains that *some* discernible threat to the corporation must be articulated by the board, which should – moreover – be rationally related to shareholders' interests in some way.[96] In this way, the court is cast in the role of effective managerial account-recipient, charged with determining indirectly on shareholders' collective behalf whether management's response to the bid in question represented a proper fiduciary course of action.

Viewed in this conceptual light, the distinction between the UK and US approaches to regulating managerial responses to hostile tender offers is arguably not as stark as it is commonly perceived. Both involve the managerial articulation of objectively verifiable reasons for believing that the prospective bid poses a threat to the corporation and its shareholders. The key difference is that, in the United Kingdom, the validity of such representations stands to be evaluated in the last place by shareholders directly; whilst, in the United States, it is the (Delaware) courts that are entrusted with ultimate responsibility for evaluating the line of reasoning deployed by the target company's board in justification of its defensive actions. At a fundamental level, though, both approaches represent different ways of providing optimal incentives for effective managerial account-giving, whether to shareholders directly or else to the court as the vicarious guardian of shareholders' collective interests.

Furthermore, the managerial imperative of reasoned account-giving in US corporations persists even in (non-control-related) scenarios where 'straight' business judgment protection is ordinarily available. Even where the business judgment presumption applies, there remains an irreducible fiduciary requirement for defendant directors to articulate *some* rational basis on which their conduct can be regarded as conducive to the advancement of the interests of the corporation and its shareholders, no matter how indirect or tangential the asserted link to shareholder welfare may be.[97] This demonstrates that, notwithstanding the significant deference that Delaware law affords to managerial prerogative, even at the most basic level management has an inalienable residual obligation to explain itself in the sense of proffering an objectively assessable explanation in support of its conduct.

The implication is that – ultimately – the board's continuing entitlement to managerial powers is premised on the fiduciary imperative to give a reasoned account to shareholders of its exercise of those powers. The procedural necessity of managerial account-giving, moreover, persists as an unavoidable precondition of the board (and, indirectly, management)'s

[95] See above ch 4 of this volume, fns 85–96 and accompanying text.
[96] See *Revlon v MacAndrews & Forbes Holdings* 506 A 2d 173 (Del 1986), as discussed above ch 4 of this volume, fns 79–80 and accompanying text.
[97] See *Shlensky v Wrigley* 237 NE 2d 776 (Ill 1968) and *Dodge v Ford Motor Co* 170 NW 668 (Mich 1919), as discussed above ch 4 of this volume, fns 41–42 (see also accompanying text).

legitimate possession and exercise of such powers in US corporations, notwithstanding the tendency of courts to defer to the board's executive prerogative in almost all cases where the rationality of its decision-making is called into question.[98]

C. The Relationship Between Managerial Accountability and Cost of Capital

(i) Micro-Cost of Capital and the Concept of Macro-Premium

At this point, it is necessary to examine in more detail the precise link between increased managerial accountability at the individual firm level ('micro-accountability'), and the ease – or, conversely, difficulty – with which that same firm can gain access to external (ie non-retained) investment capital ('micro-cost' of capital).

In chapter two above, I explained that, in corporate organisations, the legitimacy of senior executive office-holders' possession and exercise of DAP is reflected in the firm's cost of capital – that is to say, the willingness of investors to purchase the firm's securities, and, in particular, its equity capital.[99] I further highlighted the important function of managerial accountability mechanisms in securing the legitimacy – and hence sustainability – of the central corporate power imbalance between management and shareholders.[100] It was noted that, in the presence of bounded rationality – where outside (ie non-managerial) actors operate at an innate disadvantage compared to managerial insiders as regards access to firm-relevant information – effective monitoring or evaluation of managerial conduct is rendered impracticable. Furthermore, in view of the natural inclination of investors in widely-held ownership systems towards extensive diversification of holdings, the degree of supervisory engagement between investors and investee managers is naturally limited by portfolio investors' rational propensity for passivity (at least with respect to micro-level concerns).[101]

However this fact, far from negating the value of managerial accountability mechanisms, on the contrary renders formal account-giving by management all the more important. This is because, where informational limitations render micro-level monitoring impossible or cost-ineffective from investors' perspective, the *formal accountability* of managers – that is, the extent to which managers are legally required to give a reasoned

---

[98] On this judicial tendency generally, see above ch 4 of this volume, pt III.

[99] On this, see above ch 2 of this volume, pt II.B.

[100] See above ch 2 of this volume, pt II.C.

[101] EF Fama, 'Agency Problems and the Theory of the Firm' (1980) 88 *Journal of Political Economy* 288, 291.

account of themselves to shareholders on an ongoing basis – represents an important (albeit imperfect) proxy for more directly valuable, but harder to ascertain, criteria.[102] Such generally indiscernible criteria include the overall riskiness of the firm's securities, the viability of its strategic initiatives, and the competence and trustworthiness of its senior executive officers.

The paramount value of formal managerial accountability under such circumstances derives from the fact that, in the absence of equal informational access between managers and shareholders, the latter will be inclined to regard a decision-making structure where managers are continually called to account for the exercise of their executive discretion as being preferable – all other things being equal – to a decision-making structure where managers are generally not expected to account to outsiders for their decisions and actions. In particular, an accountability-focused organisational governance framework is generally conducive to greater external trust than an unaccountable framework, with a positive knock-on effect on the legitimacy of management's possession and exercise of discretionary administrative power, and – ultimately – the cost to the firm of raising external capital. The logic is that, under conditions where senior corporate decision-makers are continually required to explain their decisions and conduct to the principal subjects of their power, one can expect that both the quality of the resultant decisions and propriety of the ensuing managerial conduct will be higher than under circumstances where such extraneous checking mechanisms are absent.[103]

A potential criticism of the above line of reasoning should, however, be noted. It may be argued that the above claims are unoriginal, and are actually just a repackaged version of the well-known 'agency costs' model of corporate governance expounded within orthodox corporate-contractarianism.[104] From this point of view, one might surmise that the various legal requirements for managerial account-giving are simply examples of the phenomenon that law and economics scholars frequently refer to as 'bonding' mechanisms. As I explained in chapter three above, the purported practice known as bonding – when carried out in a corporate governance context – essentially involves managers voluntarily giving binding assurances to investors against any future diminution of the value of the latter's capital resulting from managers' conduct.[105]

Furthermore, where certain managerially-invoked bonding mechanisms (eg majority-independent boards or performance-related compensation) prove to be popular across a large number of similarly-positioned

---

[102] See above ch 2 of this volume, fn 84 and accompanying text.
[103] On the basis of this expectation, see above ch 2 of this volume, fns 100–01 and accompanying text.
[104] On this generally, see above ch 3 of this volume, fns 86–87 and accompanying text.
[105] On this, see above ch 3 of this volume, fns 76, 90 and accompanying text.

firms, it arguably makes sense for the state – or other relevant rule-making body – to require the initiation of such mechanisms as a general rule, so as to mitigate the transaction costs that firms would otherwise incur in voluntarily establishing such processes on their own initiative. So long as the agency cost savings for shareholders resulting from the enhanced monitoring exceed the relevant mechanisms' overall 'set up' costs, it follows that the relevant bonding mechanisms are cost-effective from an investor perspective.

In such circumstances, the involvement of a centralised rule-maker – whether the state or a central securities or corporate governance regulator – in setting up these mechanisms is unproblematic from a contractarian perspective, as the rule-maker is arguably doing nothing more than mimicking the choices that investors would make for themselves if possessed with the requisite legal-institutional expertise. Therefore – if enhanced managerial account-giving provides a perceived assurance for equity investors against future loss of shareholder wealth – the state provision of formal accountability mechanisms is arguably *not* inconsistent with the basic tenets of private ordering rationality.

Setting aside for now the arguments that I raised earlier in this chapter about the logical defensibility of such 'market mimicking' explanations for mandatory corporate governance rules,[106] the above criticism can be deemed problematic for a further important reason. Since accountability mechanisms are driven by investors' rational lack of firm-specific awareness, it logically follows that even accountability mechanisms themselves – where implemented at the micro level – are in general likely to be either ignored or, at least, undervalued by investors in assessing the overall value of a firm's securities. Indeed, even in legal environments (such as the United States and United Kingdom) that are relatively permissive of micro-level private ordering in various respects, the extent to which the particular corporate governance arrangements adopted by any firm impact upon its cost of capital is a matter of much debate and frequent scepticism.[107]

At the same time, it is undeniable that the transaction costs entailed in the initial set up and subsequent administration of managerial account-giving mechanisms (especially the annual corporate meeting and surrounding formal communications) are typically considerable, and furthermore are likely to increase as a function of firm capitalisation. It is therefore natural for managers to be sceptical about the overall value of enhanced accountability

---

[106] See above pt IV.

[107] Notable contributions towards this debate include: L Bebchuk, A Cohen and A Ferrell, 'What Matters in Corporate Governance?' (2009) 22 *Review of Financial Studies* 783; PA Gompers, JL Ishii and A Metrick, 'Corporate Governance and Equity Prices' (2003) 118 *Quarterly Journal of Economics* 107; HA Skaife, DW Collins and R LaFond, 'Corporate Governance and the Cost of Equity Capital' (2004), available at: ssrn.com/abstract=639681.

in corporate governance, given that the 'up-sides' in terms of reduced cost of capital are inevitably limited by investors' bounded rationality at the micro level, whilst the down-sides for individual firms – in terms of increased bureaucratic costs – are typically extensive. Indeed, one of the most common criticisms of recent corporate governance initiatives – especially in the United States – aimed at enhancing managerial accountability to investors, is that they are cost-ineffective and therefore *unreflective* of the institutional choices that firms (or, more specifically, managers and investors) would themselves make if left to bargain over the terms of corporate governance independently of the state.[108] From a contractarian perspective, the natural conclusion that one might draw from this observation is that corporate governance law is out of kilter with private ordering, and thus is inefficient and, moreover, of doubtful bureaucratic legitimacy in the sense referred to in chapter two above.[109]

However, there is an alternative and – I would submit – more empirically sustainable explanation for the apparent plethora of mandatory managerial accountability mechanisms that seemingly pervade Anglo-American corporate governance law today. Such an explanation – moreover – does not involve a radical step away from orthodox contractarian logic, although it does nonetheless involve expanding the existing normative frontiers of this paradigm somewhat. It proceeds as follows.

As I explained above, the widespread presence of bounded rationality makes the accountability of a firm's corporate governance arrangements – including managerial account-giving mechanisms – difficult to assess on a micro basis. Moreover, the pervasiveness of diversified portfolio investment, and the associated collective action and free-rider problems, renders the micro-assessment of such factors by investors fundamentally irrational from the viewpoint of monitoring cost-effectiveness. However, if one shifts the primary point of investor focus from the micro to macro level, the determination of relative managerial accountability levels becomes a much more readily achievable and – indeed – cost-*effective* endeavour from portfolio investors' perspective.

This is because investors – even those holding heavily diversified equity positions – will have a rational interest in ascertaining corporate governance conditions on a national, exchange or other relevant system-wide basis, to the extent that an appreciable proportion of their risk exposure is dependent on corporate equity investments in that particular locality or environment. It follows that, if a particular corporate governance *system* (whether national or exchange-based) mandates managerial account-giving on a particularly extensive or rigorous basis, the equity securities

---

[108] See, eg A Barden, 'US Corporate Law Reform Post-Enron: A Significant Imposition on Private Ordering of Corporate Governance?' (2005) 5 *Journal of Corporate Law Studies* 167.

[109] On the concept of bureaucratic legitimacy in corporate governance, see above ch 2 of this volume, pt II.E.

of a firm that either incorporates or lists within that environment will likely trade at a material premium over and above their fundamental value, to the extent that the enhanced power-legitimacy – and ensuing reputational advantages – of being part of that general governance *system* are conducive to a lower micro-cost of capital for the firm. This is what may be referred to as the concept of 'macro-premium'. Firms attain a macro-premium by being part of a corporate governance *system* that is generally perceived by the market to engender especially high levels of managerial accountability, relative to other 'competing' national or exchange-based governance systems.

By way of example, the United Kingdom is generally perceived to have a strongly shareholder-protectionist system of corporate governance relative to other jurisdictions, including a relatively high frequency of opportunities for compulsory managerial account-giving. It follows that a firm which is acknowledged to be part of the United Kingdom's corporate governance system will tend be recognised as a 'high accountability' firm, and (all other factors being equal) can consequently expect to attain more ready access to external capital in comparison with firms that are not acknowledged to be part of that system.

Of course, not all component parts of the applicable corporate governance system may be suitable for the specific characteristics and circumstances of the firm in question, so that there may be some elements of regulatory 'ill-fit' or cost-ineffectiveness. However, so long as the reduction in micro-cost of capital enjoyed by the firm consequent to its perceived 'membership'[110] of that system exceeds the corresponding compliance and maladaptation costs thereof, continuing conformity with that system's regulatory framework is overall wealth-*increasing* from the firm's perspective (albeit prima facie cost-*in*effective).[111]

---

[110] In general today, 'membership' of the UK corporate governance system in the fullest sense of the term can be said to accrue to all UK-incorporated companies with an equity listing on the Main Market of the London Stock Exchange, who are consequently subject to the Companies Act 2006, the UK Corporate Governance Code, corporate governance-related listing requirements, and the Takeover Code. Whilst overseas-incorporated companies with a London listing are not subject to the Companies Act 2006, they will nonetheless be required to conform to the UK Corporate Governance Code where they opt for a Premium Listing on the London Stock Exchange (on this, see above ch 6 of this volume, fn 128). My reference to 'membership' as it relates to the US corporate governance system, meanwhile, is intended generally (but not preclusively) to apply to companies that are both registered in the state of Delaware (and thereby subject to Delaware state law) and whose equity securities are traded on a domestic public investment market (either the New York Stock Exchange or NASDAQ), thereby additionally rendering its management subject to relevant federal securities legislation and SEC rules.

[111] For a rationalisation – along similar lines – of the continuing comparative attractiveness of the US as a corporate listings venue in the post-SOX era, in spite of the relatively high bureaucratic costs burden for firms thereof, see JC Coffee, 'Law and the Market: The Impact of Enforcement' (2009) 156 *University of Pennsylvania Law Review* 229, 235–37.

(ii) Macro-Accountability as a Public Good

The above explanation could be said to provide a justification for greater managerial accountability per se at the macro level, even to a level in excess of the individual firm's prima facie optimal level of bonding. But it does not automatically explain why a significant proportion of managerial accountability mechanisms in the United States and United Kingdom are *mandatory* in nature, and thus of universal application to firms within the relevant rule jurisdiction.

In other words, would a more optimal arrangement not be for managerial accountability mechanisms to be made available on a reversible opt-out basis, so that individual 'member' firms can exploit the macro-premium consequent upon their perceived membership whilst, at the same time, opting out of those regulatory requirements that give rise to unjustified compliance and/or maladaptation costs? In this way, a regulatory system could arguably enable each of its member firms to strike an optimal compliance balance between: on the one hand, reducing its cost of capital by enjoying a significant macro-premium; and, on the other hand, reducing its bureaucratic cost burden by eliminating the necessity for cost-ineffective compliance. So long as an appreciable proportion of firms comply with an appreciable proportion of applicable regulations, the apparent 'high-accountability' characteristic of the relevant corporate governance system will be preserved, notwithstanding the fact that some firms may occasionally choose to disapply – at the micro level – some of the majoritarian-default rules that are in place.

As elegant as the above logic may be, however, it fails to consider the obvious free-rider problem that such a scenario presents. If the propensity of a given corporate governance system to be perceived as 'high-accountability' in nature is contingent on an appreciable proportion of member firms being compliant with the applicable managerial accountability rules, it follows that the member firms – in order to be confident of being able to exploit the expected macro-accountability premium – must be assured a priori that a sufficient proportion of other member firms will comply with the applicable regulatory framework so as to imbue the overall system with the 'high-accountability' descriptor.

The problem, though, is that macro-accountability is by its very nature a *public good*: that is to say – like information – it is both non-excludable and non-rivalrous in nature.[112] In other words, due to investors' limited monitoring incentives at the micro (but not macro) level, those firms which are fully – or, at least, substantially – compliant with the applicable

---

[112] On the concept of public goods generally within economic theory, see above ch 6 of this volume, fn 111 and accompanying text. On the ultimate consistency of the 'public goods' argument for regulatory interventionism with the basic tenets of the contractarian paradigm, see above pt II.

regulatory framework are unable to prevent the non-substantially-compliant member firms from free-riding on the 'high-accountability' descriptor in order to exploit the resulting macro-accountability premium (non-excludability). Furthermore, under the same monitoring conditions it is possible for the substantially-compliant member firms to exploit the macro-accountability premium without necessarily reducing the value of that premium for the non-substantially-compliant member firms, and vice versa (non-rivalry). Consequently, there will always be incentives for non-substantially-compliant member firms to free-ride on the compliance efforts of the substantially-compliant firms with the ultimate outcome that macro-accountability – as a general reputational resource – will be systematically *under-produced*. That is to say, each member firm will be inclined to generate a materially lower degree of managerial accountability than would be the case if it could individually appropriate all of the reputational benefits – and ensuing capital cost savings – therefrom.

Or, to put the issue another way: in a demand-side populous capital market where there exists a very large number of issuing member firms, an extra unit of accountability (however measured) at the micro (individual firm) level will occasion only a negligible, if any, increase in macro-accountability and ensuing macro-accountability premium for the relevant firm. Clearly, then, there is simply no incentive at the micro level for firms to invest in greater compliance with managerial accountability norms under these circumstances, unless an appreciable proportion of member firms are able to coordinate their compliance efforts to ensure that the overall rate of compliance is high enough to produce a material macro-accountability premium. Only in these circumstances will the compliant firms be compensated adequately for the corresponding increase in bureaucratic costs thereby entailed.

In a populous capital market, however, the mass coordination of member firms in implementation of a single macro-compliance strategy is highly impracticable, especially in view of each member firm's rational disinclination to invest in increased managerial accountability beyond the individually optimal level (ie the level at which the marginal cost of further micro-compliance with applicable managerial accountability norms is equal to the corresponding marginal reduction in micro-cost of capital). Accordingly, where important managerial accountability norms are subject to disapplication on a firm-specific basis, member firms will – in general – be inclined to opt out of those norms once compliance therewith becomes cost-ineffective at the micro level.[113] This is in spite of the likelihood that further mass compliance on a coordinated basis might elicit a

---

[113] For the same reason, it is impracticable to expect individual firms to be inclined voluntarily to opt into a high-accountability governance system so that regulatory arbitrage drives efficient investor protection, whilst providing economic disincentives against excessive (ie cost-*in*effective) shareholder protectionism.

macro-premium for each member firm that is *more than* sufficient to offset the marginal bureaucratic costs of extra compliance at the micro level. The outcome is that – in the given case – an overall wealth-*reducing* outcome prevails for each member firm.

It can thus be reasoned that, in the absence of mandatory rules compelling universal compliance, systematic under-compliance with managerial accountability norms will be endemic to a corporate governance system.[114] This provides a compelling economic case for the mandatory implementation of managerial accountability norms across a corporate governance system as a whole, even if the consequences of doing so prove to be prima facie cost-ineffective or otherwise undesirable in some respects for individual member firms.

In short, therefore, state regulation should *supplant* – rather than supplement – private ordering with respect to the internal governance dynamics of the corporate equity relation. Moreover, this conclusion is justified on the basis of what are essentially *contractarian* grounds.

D. Ramifications of Expanded Contractarian Paradigm for Current Issues in Anglo-American Corporate Governance Law

(i) The Regulatory Paradox: Cost-Ineffective Laws May Still be Overall Wealth-Increasing

The first notable ramification of macro-accountability theory for Anglo-American corporate law concerns the trend documented in chapter six above towards greater mandatory (especially federal) regulatory intervention in intra-firm governance affairs, as observed most conspicuously in the US law-making context.[115] In response to the common negative perception of such developments as an unwarranted intrusion into private ordering, it can reasonably be surmised that many apparent aspects of excessive bureaucracy or 'red tape' in the existing law may actually be wealth-*increasing* for firms (and, indirectly, society) in the long run, notwithstanding their apparent cost-*in*effectiveness at the micro level.

This is because the perceived value of such laws in engendering greater managerial accountability on a system-wide basis, coupled with the general desirability of formal accountability as an institutional quality *in itself* within corporations (for the reasons outlined above), has the effect of *increasing* investors' collective willingness to subject themselves to management's discretionary administrative power in firms that are subject to

---

[114] That is, at least within a widely-held corporate ownership environment such as that prevailing in the US or UK, where investors' incentives for micro-monitoring are low and firms' macro-compliance coordination costs are high.

[115] See above ch 6 of this volume, pt I.A.

the relevant laws. In such cases, the macro-premium to be derived by firms from compliance with accountability norms – where sufficiently significant – will potentially outweigh the corresponding losses to firms in the form of increased compliance and maladaptation costs.

For instance, I explained in chapter six above how the new federal 'say on pay' procedures applicable to US listed corporations have faced considerable criticism on account of allegedly being over-burdensome, formally inflexible, and largely undesired by a significant proportion of the investor community.[116] However, if 'say on pay' is understood principally as a regulatory method for compelling increased formal managerial accountability in the sense described in this book, a different perspective on its overall instrumentality emerges. It may be said that the intended long-term value of 'say on pay' inheres not so much in its propensity to engender improved standards of corporate efficiency or business performance (a claim which in itself is highly debatable), but rather in the general contribution that such procedures make towards establishing a more accountability-centric national corporate governance system. In particular, 'say on pay' can be regarded as an important institutional element of a governance framework which is broadly responsive to public concerns about managers' capacity to exercise discretionary administrative power in ways that are potentially averse to, or otherwise neglectful of, investor welfare. The overall objective is arguably to legitimate – and thereby sustain – managers' continuing possession and exercise of discretionary administrative power, with such legitimacy reflected ultimately in the cost to compliant firms of raising external capital.[117]

However, the above claim as to the wealth-increasing propensity of prima facie cost-ineffective regulation is not a universal proposition, and certainly does not establish that 'more is always preferable to less' when it comes to the regulatory compulsion of managerial accountability to shareholders. Rather, just as there exists an individually optimal level of managerial accountability for each individual firm, there can likewise be said to exist a *systemically* optimal level of managerial accountability on a macro basis: that is, the level at which the marginal bureaucratic costs to firms as a whole from any further increase in regulatorily-mandated accountability are equal to the marginal collective gains from easier corporate access to external capital. Beyond this threshold, the collective compliance and/or maladaptation costs to firms of any further mandatory regulation aimed at increasing managerial accountability to shareholders is liable to outweigh the corresponding collective reduction in firms' cost of capital.

---

[116] On this, see above ch 6 of this volume, pt I.A.(ii).

[117] Furthermore, the mandatory (and thus irreversible) status of 'say on pay', as constituted under the federal Dodd-Frank Act (on which, see ch 6, ibid), is arguably crucial in preventing otherwise-non-conforming firms from opting out and thus free-riding on the resulting macro-accountability premium.

In such instances, increased managerial accountability – at least where implemented on a mandatory (and thus irreversible) regulatory basis – tends to be net wealth-*reducing* at the macro level, even after factoring in the effect of the macro-accountability premium in increasing the systemically optimal level of managerial accountability. In other words, managerial accountability will be mandated at an economically *excessive* – and therefore inefficient – level.

Moreover, a brief survey of the recent history of US corporate governance regulation demonstrates that the extent of the applicable macro-accountability premium tends to vary over time with changing investor preferences, which themselves are conditioned by changing social attitudes concerning the value of executive accountability as a general institutional quality of corporations. Accordingly, in times of recent corporate scandal or more general financial and/or macro-economic crisis, the accountability of private sector decision-makers for their exercise of discretionary administrative power is typically cast into greater scrutiny – both by investors and the public generally – on a system-wide (and, indeed, even inter-systemic) basis. The Enron and WorldCom bankruptcies of 2001 and 2002; and, more recently, the investment bank failures and associated executive compensation scandals of 2007 and 2008, bear pertinent testimony to this.

However, when public opprobrium at such aspects of executive power-abuse or maladministration subsides, the perceived value of responsive regulatory measures from an investor (and wider social) perspective will tend to be correspondingly reduced.[118] In turn, the extent to which managerial accountability norms that are prima facie cost-ineffective on a micro level can still prove to be overall wealth-maximising when implemented mandatorily at the macro level will likewise be lower. The ultimate outcome is that perceived 'red tape' in the regulatory design of corporate governance norms will not be offset by increased managerial accountability and resultant power-legitimacy at the macro level. In such instances, alleged 'over-regulation' of the corporate equity relation hence becomes both a common and justifiable cause of investor and wider public concern. The developing public hostility to the controversial internal controls provisions of Sarbanes-Oxley discussed in chapter six above[119] is perhaps the most conspicuous modern manifestation of this phenomenon.

However such cases, far from undermining the validity of the macro-accountability hypothesis developed above, merely point to the structural limitations of the macro-accountability premium as a market mechanism for counteracting the bureaucratic costs to firms of complying with

---

[118] John Coffee refers to this phenomenon as the 'regulatory sine curve'. See JC Coffee, 'The Political Economy of Dodd-Frank: Why Financial Reform Tends to be Frustrated and Systemic Risk Perpetuated' (2012) 97 *Cornell Law Review* 101.

[119] See above ch 6 of this volume, pt I.A.

prevailing corporate governance norms. As such, in terms of the present argument they are most appropriately understood as the exceptions that prove the general point.

(ii) The Limitations of 'Soft Law' Norms: One Size Can Actually Fit All!

A second apposite implication of macro-accountability theory for current debate on corporate governance law is of more immediate practical relevance to the United Kingdom. A claim that is frequently made with respect to the design of legal rules in relation to corporate governance matters, especially in the UK environment, is that 'one size does not fit all'.[120]

As I explained in chapter five above, the United Kingdom's characteristic system of non-statist, market-invoking regulation is designed to promote flexibility at the point of firm-specific norm application.[121] This phenomenon is manifested most conspicuously in the British-originated concept of 'comply or explain', which underpins the application of the UK Corporate Governance Code.[122] In theory, 'comply or explain' promises a 'win-win' outcome insofar as it enables effective managerial accountability to be achieved without imposing an excessive compliance or maladaptation costs burden on compliant firms. In terms of the key themes developed in this book, therefore, it could be regarded as the ideal legal-institutional means for achieving corporate power-legitimacy whilst, at the same time, guarding against the risk of bureaucratic illegitimacy at the level of the corporate governance framework itself.

However, it has frequently been demonstrated over recent years that the practical operation of the 'comply or explain' principle in UK corporate governance does not always align with the above theoretical portrayal. In reality, it is rather the case that the Code's recommendations are very often followed somewhat blindly by firms in a rigid manner, whereby deviation from the prescribed norms is kept to a minimum. In the limited instances where such deviation occurs, moreover, it is often 'justified' by merely generic or 'boilerplate' written explanations in companies' annual corporate governance statements. At the same time, investors and proxy advisors have been known to adopt a characteristically unpermissive (or so-called 'box-ticking') attitude in monitoring and evaluating deviations from core Code norms, so that in practice the Code has for many firms come to be regarded as a kind of surrogate (and formally unenforced) piece of quasi-legislation, rather than a dynamic and merely indicative

---

[120] See, eg SR Arcot and VG Bruno, 'One Size Does Not Fit All: Evidence from Corporate Governance', London School of Economics Working Paper (2007), available at: ssrn.com/abstract=887947.

[121] On this, see above ch 5 of this volume, pt IV.

[122] On this, see above ch 5 of this volume, fn 131 and accompanying text.

statement of 'best practice' with respect to corporate institutional design (as has always been the intention of its promulgators).[123]

The commonality of such restrictive attitudes towards corporate governance norm appliance in the United Kingdom arguably affirms the validity of the macro-accountability hypothesis developed in this chapter. That is to say, whilst investors can be said to value the UK Corporate Governance Code in general as an influential framework of managerial accountability norms, they afford only a limited degree of consideration to the merits of specific outlying provisions at the micro level, on the basis that prohibitive information-gathering costs coupled with an inevitable 'free rider' risk render such enquiries largely cost-ineffective from an individual investor perspective. Against this background, the practical value of 'comply or explain' in encouraging the nuanced tailoring of corporate governance norms to individual firm characteristics is clearly significantly limited, with the unintended outcome that the Code risks becoming a source of bureaucratic illegitimacy *in itself.*

Moreover, to the extent that companies subject to the Code's recommendations are consequently encouraged – on a systematic basis – to render merely perfunctory and unreflecting compliance with the various principles and provisions therein, there exists the very real danger of Code compliance being perceived by boards and investors as a purely procedural and formalistic endeavour – divorced from the apparent 'realities' of business leadership and strategy-formation. To the extent that this occurs, the perceived value of the Code as a relevant and effective system of managerial accountability norms is correspondingly called into question.[124]

In such circumstances, the mandatory state promulgation and enforcement of substantive corporate governance norms may ultimately be preferable to the existing system of 'soft' (market-invoking) regulation, given that: first, no material loss of flexibility will consequently be entailed in the micro-level application of norms (as none or next-to-none can be said to exist in any event); whilst, secondly, the presence of a centralised public norm enforcement agent arguably provides a more credible 'signalling' of the commitment of the corporate governance system as a whole to engendering improved managerial accountability at the macro level – leading in

---

[123] On these issues generally, see MT Moore, 'Whispering Sweet Nothings: The Limitations of Informal Conformance in UK Corporate Governance' (2009) 9 *Journal of Corporate Law Studies* 95. On the practical limitations of the 'comply or explain' principle, see also I Macneil and X Li, 'Comply or Explain: Market Discipline and Non-Compliance with the Combined Code' (2006) 14 *Corporate Governance: An International Review* 486.

[124] This is on the commonly-held understanding that merely procedural or formalistic methods of executive accountability (such as the appointment of a specified minimum percentage of independent directors, or the establishment of an appropriately constituted board sub-committee structure) are on their own insufficient to bring about the sort of 'real' substantive accountability that, ultimately, will only result from the largely *extra*-regulatory endeavour of getting the 'right' mix of personalities on a company's board and associated decision-making forums.

turn to a likely higher level of macro-premium for those firms that are subject to the relevant norm framework. It can accordingly be surmised that – in the absence of a genuine *private* commitment by boards and investors towards maintaining flexibility in the micro-level application of non-statist (or 'soft') corporate governance norms – the regulatory compulsion of uniform (ie 'hard') accountability standards by the state on an 'across the board' basis represents an overall preferable institutional outcome from investors' collective perspective, compared to the alternative of devolving compliance-monitoring responsibilities to investors directly.

Where the above conditions apply, it can thus justifiably be surmised that – contrary to the accepted orthodoxy amongst corporate lawyers in the United Kingdom today – 'one size *can* actually fit all' when it comes to the challenge of designing and enforcing applicable governance norms across a given corporate-regulatory system as a whole. For this reason, it may curiously transpire that the United Kingdom ultimately stands to improve the comparative economic attractiveness of its national corporate governance framework by demonstrating a counter-intuitive willingness to *curtail* the theoretically 'soft' or market-invoking quality that its compliance system has become internationally renowned for.

VI. SUMMARY

In this chapter, I have explained why the widespread presence of mandatory and irreversible state-promulgated rules prima facie presents an unwelcome empirical challenge to the contractarian conception of how corporate governance norms evolve. This is not to say that contractarians are blind to the existence or even the occasional value of mandatory rules in corporate law. On the contrary, proponents of the contractarian paradigm of corporate law have gone to considerable lengths to develop the theory's contours so as to provide an account of mandatory rules that is consistent with its evolutionary, private ordering ethos. Therefore mandatory legal rules have been rationalised within the contractarian paradigm as a necessary structural means of mitigating the imposition by firms of negative externalities on third parties, and for enabling the production of certain essential public goods that are likely to be systematically underproduced in response to prudential private incentives alone.

The above two arguments are relatively unproblematic from a logical point of view, and in any event seek only to 'correct' the incapacity of market signals to reflect the interests of parties who are otherwise unable to protect themselves directly via contract. However, a much more controversial and, ultimately, indefensible rationalisation of state interventionism in private ordering has been forwarded by contractarians in the form of the 'market mimicking' argument for regulation. In essence, this argument presents socially-determinative regulation as a necessary means of compensating for contractors' practical incapacity to bargain directly for adequate protection of their interests under 'real world' informational limitations and other transaction costs. The normative implication of the claim is that regulation should be designed to do just enough so as to reflect what contracting parties *would have* done under idealised bargaining condition, but should stop short of seeking to displace privately optimal outcomes by reference to wider public policy considerations.

As I have sought to demonstrate in the above discussion, though, the market mimicking argument is ultimately undermined by the contradictory nature of the normative claims that it makes, which are especially problematic in the context of corporate governance. Above all, it may be said that contractarian theorists of corporate governance – in advancing the market mimicking rationalisation of mandatory rules in the field – in effect 'bite off more than they can chew' by inadvertently admitting a permissible case for widespread state interventionism in private ordering, supposedly as a means of preserving the efficacy of private ordering practices *themselves*. As I have argued, however, this claim is inherently contradictory and, ultimately, *self-defeating* as an intended line of opposition to increased regulatory state involvement in corporate governance affairs. In consequence, contractarian advocates of this position cannot help but admit the existence of a significantly and unavoidably *public* dimension to Anglo-American corporate governance as a system. Scholars of the subject are correspondingly compelled to accept the democratic regulatory state as a core and active determiner of many of the most fundamental components of this field of law.

On this basis, I subsequently sought to determine whether contractarian rationality is capable of absorbing a considerably greater 'public' or regulatory element than it does at present, without sacrificing either its analytical rigour or normative consistency. In particular, I enquired whether shareholder protectionism – as an aspect of regulatory state paternalism – can still be rendered consistent with the fundamental logic of the dominant contractarian paradigm of corporate governance law. I found that effective managerial accountability in widely-held public corporations, far from being a purely contractually-derived phenomenon (as contractarian 'agency costs' theory suggests), is – on the contrary – a contractually *unattainable* public good. As such, its promulgation at a socially efficient level is necessarily dependent on the active regulatory intervention of the state, even to the extent of coercively *overriding* private ordering outcomes that would otherwise be likely to ensue at the micro (ie individual firm) level.

This finding – to the extent that it is accepted by readers as a valid and defensible conceptual proposition – simultaneously both challenges and reaffirms the dominant contractarian paradigm of corporate governance as it exists in the Anglo-American environment. On the one hand, it *challenges* the contractarian position by seeking to import into its logic certain concepts – namely public policy and regulatory state interventionism – that have conventionally been viewed as averse to the theory's fundamentally private and anti-statist normative hue. On the other hand, it seeks ultimately – and somewhat paradoxically – to *reaffirm* the empirical and logical validity of the contractarian paradigm, by recourse to the widely-accepted economic concept of (non-contractually-attainable) public goods. In explaining mandatory managerial macro-accountability norms in such terms, I have tried to re-orientate the contractarian paradigm in such a way as to enable it to account for the significant public-regulatory dimensions of Anglo-American corporate governance law as a system, without requiring recourse to the logically indefensible 'market mimicking' rationalisation of state interventionism that was examined (and subsequently rejected) earlier in this chapter.

The two main practical ramifications of the macro-accountability hypothesis developed in this chapter, as outlined in part V above, may be regarded by some readers as somewhat regressive in nature. In particular, they both allude to the argument that a reversal of the dominant ideological tide in Anglo-American corporate governance over the past three decades – away from decentralised private ordering of governance norms and towards greater centralised state determinism – is now in order. However, in making these tentative insights, I seek not to deliberately 'buck the trend' of general academic opinion in this area of thought, but rather simply to highlight certain unidentified complexities and idiosyncrasies within the existing framework of the law. Indeed, this chapter is not principally intended to be a case for the radical reform of existing corporate governance norms in either the United States or United Kingdom. Rather, its motivating objective – like that of the book as a whole – is to seek to make greater sense of the key components of the law *as it currently is*. This is on the premise that, only when we – as scholars – properly and comprehensively understand the nature of the phenomenon that we are teaching and writing about, can we begin to build a sensible and informed case for its future revision or reform.

It is my hope that the various observations and arguments of the preceding seven chapters have helped to forge such an understanding in the minds of readers, notwithstanding the possibility that – as a result – some readers may have begun to think somewhat differently about corporate governance law compared to their conception of the subject prior to picking up this book. To this end, I will now conclude the general discussion of this book with a brief summary of the key insights that have been developed herein.

8

Conclusions

I BEGAN THIS book by querying the fundamental nature of corporate governance law in the United States and United Kingdom. In particular, I questioned where exactly this area of law should be positioned in relation to the notional normative fault-line between facilitative 'private' law and regulatory 'public' law subjects. Although I have sought to answer this question in detail over the course of the previous seven chapters of this book, I feel that it is only appropriate to end the book by attempting to provide a direct response thereto. Somewhat frustratingly (but perhaps not unexpectedly) for readers, the answer that I will provide to this question is neither neat nor succinct.

On its exterior, Anglo-American corporate governance law is undoubtedly a private law subject. Like other areas of private law, it exhibits a range of expressly flexible and facilitative formal features, rendering its substantive content contingent to a significant extent on the prudential preferences of corporate contractors (ie investors and managers) at the 'micro' or individual firm level. Such features of the law, moreover, are entirely consistent with the idealised model of corporate governance that is presented within the contractarian theoretical paradigm, whereby laws are designed to *reflect*, rather than determine, the pre-existing contractual choices of private parties.

On closer inspection of the legal architecture, though, a more complicated picture emerges. In spite of their prima facie endogenous and privately-determined character, the rich contractual dimensions of corporate governance law in the United States and United Kingdom are ultimately dependent for their effective functioning on an underpinning body of laws that, ultimately, are both *irremovable* and – in large part – *inadaptable* in nature. It can therefore reasonably be concluded that Anglo-American corporate governance law is, at root, an undeniably 'public' or regulatory phenomenon. To adopt a metaphorical analogy with the natural world, corporate governance law is thus best depicted as 'a garden' rather than 'a wilderness'. That is to say, whilst by nature organic and evolutionary, it can only be made to develop in a manner that is desirable to its progenitors if its evolution is allowed to proceed within parameters that are strictly controlled in advance via artificial or synthetic means.

But where, one might ask, does this ultimately take us in practical terms? In other words, what are the implications of the above understanding of corporate governance 'as artificial design' for the appropriate future development of the subject matter?

Above all, the conceptual portrayal of corporate governance law developed in this book calls for a more tolerant and progressive attitude towards regulatory state action in this field. Increasingly over recent decades, 'regulation' has come to be understood in a highly pejorative sense by many private (and especially corporate) lawyers, as a mechanism that is liable to deprive individuals of their economic freedom of action in the service of (frequently misguided) governmental 'grand plans'. The twenty-first-century federal initiatives on corporate governance and securities market regulation in the United States, and also the now-notorious UK Companies Act 2006, are typically forwarded as pertinent examples in this regard.

However, if the above discussion has established anything, it is that in the field of corporate governance, 'regulation' is not the dirty word that it is frequently made out to be. It is my belief that, rather than being seen as something that is liable to deprive individuals of their liberty as economic actors, regulation should rather be viewed – in the corporate governance context especially – as a phenomenon that can ultimately *contribute to* securing individual contractual freedom. Above all, regulatory state interventionism is structurally necessary in this environment for counteracting inherent economic-organisational power disparities, which would otherwise constrain the capacity of corporate contractors (in particular equity investors) to bargain directly for protection of their interests via decentralised 'self-help' practices.

Furthermore, on the understanding that corporate governance is ultimately an artificial and regulatorily founded phenomenon (albeit with a significant endogenous evolutionary dynamic), there would appear to be no obvious normative impediment to the regulatory dimensions of the law being used to achieve manifestly public-regarding objectives. Indeed, a key argument presented in the final chapter is that the motivating rationale for the existing framework of core corporate governance regulation in the United States and United Kingdom – that is, securing the legitimacy and consequent sustainability of corporate-managerial power by mandating its exercise on manifestly accountable terms – is in itself a contractually *unattainable* public good. As such, its effective implementation is necessarily dependent on interventionist state initiative, over and above any outcomes that private parties would otherwise have been inclined to agree on with one another privately.

On the whole, it is my hope that this book will help to inspire future academic enquiry and debate on these fascinating and relatively unexplored issues lying at the interface between corporate law, finance, and political economy. In particular – and following on from the theory of 'macro-accountability' developed in the final chapter – further empirical investigation is necessary with respect to the precise implications for public equity valuations of firms incorporating or listing within perceived 'high accountability' corporate-regulatory environments.

Of course, many readers may ultimately take issue with some of the specific normative arguments or conclusions that I have advanced in this book: such potential disagreements I accept and, moreover, welcome. At the very least, though, if this book provokes some engaged thought and discussion on issues that have until now largely been swept under corporate law's metaphorical cognitive carpet, then my efforts in writing it will not have been in vain.

It remains to be seen whether the dominant contractarian paradigm – with its innate aversion to infusing public policy considerations into corporate law's orthodox analytical spectrum – is capable of withstanding a methodological 'turn' along the above lines. In this book I have attempted – to the best of my abilities – to forge some sort of unity between the dual rationalities of private ordering and public policy within corporate law theorising, principally by seeking to understand the intrinsic regulatory dimensions of the subject in terms of traditional contractarian concepts. This is not to deny, however, the inevitable uneasiness of the conceptual marriage that exists between these two facets of the legal framework.

As unsatisfying as this notion may be for those who seek to deploy logic to make sense out of chaos, the field of Anglo-American corporate governance law – like so many complex social phenomena of its kind – is ultimately unsusceptible to being understood properly through any one single theoretical prism. Of course, whether this in itself merits abandoning the established trail of theorising on the subject to date is quite another matter. For the reasons explained earlier in this book, I would caution against such reactionary thinking irrespective of one's personal views on the overall merits of the analytical and normative orthodoxy in this field. As the history of attempted governance design in other areas of life has demonstrated, absent exigent moral reasons for abandoning the status quo in its entirety, *evolution* – rather than revolution – is ordinarily the safer and more constructive (albeit less immediately exciting) pathway to perceived progress.

Therefore, however one is influenced by the insights presented in this book it will pay to tread carefully when taking the next steps forward.

Bibliography

Alchian, AA, 'Uncertainty, Evolution, and Economic Theory' (1950) 58 *Journal of Political Economy* 211.

Alchian, AA and Demsetz, H, 'Production, Information Costs, and Economic Organization' (1972) 62 *American Economic Review* 777.

Alcock, A, 'Higgs – the wrong answer?' (2003) 24 *The Company Lawyer* 161.

Arcot, SR and Bruno, VG, 'One Size Does Not Fit All: Evidence from Corporate Governance', London School of Economics Working Paper (2007).

Armour, J, Black, B, Cheffins, B and Nolan, R, 'Private Enforcement of Corporate Law: An Empirical Comparison of the United Kingdom and the United States' (2009) 6 *Journal of Empirical Legal Studies* 687.

Armour, J, Hansmann, H and Kraakman, R, 'What is Corporate Law?' in R Kraakman, J Armour, P Davies, L Enriques, H Hansmann, G Hertig, K Hopt, H Kanda and E Rock, *The Anatomy of Corporate Law: A Comparative and Functional Approach*, 2nd edn (Oxford, Oxford University Press, 2009) 1.

Armour, J and Skeel, DA, 'Who Writes the Rules for Hostile Takeovers, and Why? – The Peculiar Divergence of US and UK Takeover Regulation' (2007) 95 *Georgetown Law Journal* 1727.

Arrow, KJ, *The Limits of Organization* (New York, Norton, 1974).

Atiyah, PS, *The Rise and Fall of Freedom of Contract* (Oxford, Clarendon Press, 1979).

Attenborough, D, 'How Directors Should Act When Owing Duties to the Company's Shareholders: Why We Need to Stop Applying Greenhalgh' (2009) 20 *International Company and Commerical Law Review* 339.

Austin, J, *The Province of Jurisprudence Determined* (W Rumble (ed)) (Cambridge, Cambridge University Press, 1995) (first published 1832).

Ayres, I and Braithwaite, J, *Responsive Regulation: Transcending the Deregulation Debate* (Oxford, Oxford University Press, 1992).

Bainbridge, SM, 'In Defense of the Shareholder Wealth Maximization Norm: A Reply to Professor Green' (1993) 50 *Washington & Lee Law Review* 1423.

—— 'Why a Board? Group Decisionmaking in Corporate Governance' (2002) 55 *Vanderbilt Law Review* 1.

—— 'Director Primacy: The Means and Ends of Corporate Governance' (2003) 97 *Northwestern University Law Review* 547.

—— 'The Business Judgment Rule as Abstention Doctrine' (2004) 57 *Vanderbilt Law Review* 83.

—— 'Director Primacy and Shareholder Disempowerment' (2006) 119 *Harvard Law Review* 1735.

—— *The Complete Guide to Sarbanes-Oxley* (Avon MA, Adams Media, 2007).

—— *The New Corporate Governance in Theory and Practice* (New York, Oxford University Press, 2008).

—— 'Dodd-Frank: Quack Federal Corporate Governance Round II' (2010) UCLA School of Law, Law-Econ Research Paper No 10-12.

Baird, DG and Rasmussen, RK, 'Private Debt and the Missing Lever of Corporate Governance' (2006) 154 *University of Pennsylvania Law Review* 1209.

Barden, A, 'US Corporate Law Reform Post-Enron: A Significant Imposition on Private Ordering of Corporate Governance?' (2005) 5 *Journal of Corporate Law Studies* 167.

Bebchuk, LA, 'The Debate on Contractual Freedom in Corporate Law' (1989) 89 *Columbia Law Review* 1395.

—— 'Federalism and the Corporation: The Desirable Limits on State Competition in Corporate Law' (1992) 105 *Harvard Law Review* 1435.

—— 'The Case Against Board Veto in Corporate Takeovers' (2002) 69 *University of Chicago Law Review* 973.

—— 'The Case for Shareholder Access to the Ballot' (2003) 59 *The Business Lawyer* 43.

—— 'The Case for Increasing Shareholder Power' (2005) 118 *Harvard Law Review* 833.

Bebchuk, LA, Cohen, A and Ferrell, A, 'What Matters in Corporate Governance?' (2009) 22 *Review of Financial Studies* 783.

Bebchuk, LA, Fried, JM and Walker, DI, 'Managerial Power and Rent Extraction in the Design of Executive Compensation' (2002) 69 *University of Chicago Law Review* 751.

Berle, AA, 'For Whom Corporate Managers *Are* Trustees: A Note' (1932) *Harvard Law Review* 1365.

—— *The Twentieth Century Capitalist Revolution* (New York, Harcourt, Brace & World, 1954).

—— *Power Without Property: A New Development in American Political Economy* (New York, Harcourt, Brace & World, 1959).

—— 'Modern Functions of the Corporate System' (1962) 62 *Columbia Law Review* 433.

—— *The American Economic Republic* (New York, Harcourt, Brace & World, 1963).

Berle, AA and Means, G, *The Modern Corporation and Private Property*, 4th edn (New York, Harcourt, Brace & World, 1968) (first published 1932).

Biondi, Y, Giannoccolo, P and Reberioux, A, 'Financial Disclosure and the Board: A Case for Non-independent Directors', Bologna University Department of Economics Working Paper No 689 (20 January 2010).

Black, B, 'Is Corporate Law Trivial?: A Political and Economic Analysis' (1990) 84 *Northwestern University Law Review* 542.

Black, B and Coffee, J, 'Hail Britannia?: Institutional Investor Behavior Under Limited Regulation' (1994) 92 *Michigan Law Review* 1997.

Blair, MM, *Ownership and Control: Rethinking Corporate Governance for the Twenty-First Century* (Washington DC, Brookings Institution, 1995).

Blair, MM and Stout, LA, 'A Team Production Theory of Corporate Law' (1999) 85 *Virginia Law Review* 248.

Blauner, R, *Alienation and Freedom: The Factory Worker and His Industry* (Chicago IL, University of Chicago Press, 1964).

Bottomley, S, *The Constitutional Corporation: Rethinking Corporate Governance* (Aldershot, Ashgate, 2007).

Bowman, SR, *The Modern Corporation and American Political Thought: Law, Power and Ideology* (PA, Penn State University Press, 1996).

Bozeman, B, 'A Theory of Government "Red Tape"' (1993) 3 *Journal of Public Administration Research and Theory* 273.

Bradshaw, C, 'The Environmental Business Case and Unenlightened Shareholder Value' (2013) 33 *Legal Studies* (forthcoming).

Bratton, WW, 'The New Economic Theory of the Firm: Critical Perspectives from History' (1989) 41 *Stanford Law Review* 1471.

Bratton, WW and Wachter, ML, 'Shareholder Primacy's Corporatist Origins: AdolfBerle and "The Modern Corporation"' (2008) 34 *Journal of Corporation Law* 99.

—— 'The Case Against Shareholder Empowerment' (2010) 158 *University of Pennsylvania Law Review* 653.

Brownlie, N, *Trade Union Membership 2011* (London, Department for Business Innovation and Skills, 2011).

Brudney, V, 'Corporate Governance, Agency Costs, and the Rhetoric of Contract' (1985) 85 *Columbia Law Review* 1403.

Bruner, CM, 'The Enduring Ambivalence of Corporate Law' (2008) 59 *Alabama Law Review* 1385.

—— 'Power and Purpose in the "Anglo-American" Corporation' (2010) 50 *Virginia Journal of International Law* 579.

Cadbury, A,*Corporate Governance and Chairmanship: A Personal View* (Oxford, Oxford University Press, 2002).

Campbell, D, 'Adam Smith, Farrar on the Company and the Economics of the Corporation' (1990) 19 *Anglo-American Law Review* 185.

Chandler, AD, *The Visible Hand: The Managerial Revolution in American Business* (Cambridge MA, Harvard University Press, 1977).

—— *Scale and Scope: The Dynamics of Industrial Capitalism* (Cambridge MA, Belknap, 1990).

Charny, D, 'Hypothetical Bargains: The Normative Structure of Contract Interpretation' (1991) 89 *Michigan Law Review* 1815.

Cheffins, BR, *Company Law: Theory, Structure and Operation* (Oxford, Oxford University Press, 1997).

—— 'Using Theory to Study Law: A Company Law Perspective' (1999) 58 *Cambridge Law Journal* 197.

—— *Ownership and Control: British Business Transformed* (Oxford, Oxford University Press, 2009).

Cheffins, BR and Thomas, RS, 'Should Shareholders Have a Greater Say Over Executive Pay?: Learning from the US Experience' (2001) 1 *Journal of Corporate Law Studies* 277.

Clift, B, Gamble, A and Harris, M, 'The Labour Party and the Company' in JE Parkinson, A Gamble and G Kelly, *The Political Economy of the Company* (Oxford, Hart Publishing, 2001) ch 3.

Coase, RH, 'The Nature of the Firm' (1937) 4 *Economica* 386.

—— 'The Problem of Social Cost' (1960) 3 *Journal of Law and Economics* 1.

Coffee, JC, 'Market Failure and the Economic Case for a Mandatory Disclosure System' (1984) 70 *Virginia Law Review* 717.

—— 'The Mandatory/Enabling Balance in Corporate Law' (1989) 89 *Columbia Law Review* 1618.

Coffee, JC, 'Law and the Market: The Impact of Enforcement' (2009) 156 *University of Pennsylvania Law Review* 229.

—— 'The Political Economy of Dodd-Frank: Why Financial Reform Tends to be Frustrated and Systemic Risk Perpetuated' (2012) 97 *Cornell Law Review* 101.

Cohen, J, 'Deliberation and Democratic Legitimacy' in A Hamlin and P Pettit, *The Good Polity: Normative Analysis of the State* (New York, Blackwell, 1989).

Collins, H, 'Flexibility and Empowerment' in Wilthagen, T (ed), *Advancing Theory in Labour Law and Industrial Relations in a Global Context* (Amsterdam, Royal Netherlands Academy, 1998) 117.

Collins, H, Davies, P and Rideout, P (eds), *Legal Regulation of the Employment Relation* (London, Kluwer, 2000).

Cooke, T and Hicks, A, 'Wrongful Trading – Predicting Insolvency' [1993] *Journal of Business Law* 338.

Cranston, R, 'Limiting Directors' Liability: Ratification, Exemption and Indemnification' [1992] *Journal of Business Law* 197.

Davies, PL, *Gower and Davies' Principles of Modern Company Law*, 8th edn (London, Sweet & Maxwell, 2008).

Davies, P and Lord Wedderburn of Charlton, 'The Land of Industrial Democracy' (1977) 6 *Industrial Law Journal* 197.

Deakin, S, 'Legal Origin, Juridical Form and Industrialization in Historical Perspective: The Case of the Employment Contract and the Joint-Stock Company' (2009) 7 *Socio-Economic Review* 35.

Deakin, S and Morris, GS, *Labour Law*, 5th edn (Oxford, Hart Publishing, 2009).

Deakin, S and Slinger, G, 'Hostile Takeovers, Corporate Law, and the Theory of the Firm' (1997) 24 *Journal of Law and Society* 124.

DeMott, D, 'Perspectives on Choice of Law for Corporate Internal Affairs' (1985) 48 *Law & Contemporary Problems* 161.

De Schutter O and Lenoble, J, *Reflexive Governance: Redefining the Public Interest in a Pluralist World* (Oxford, Hart Publishing, 2010).

De Tocqueville, A, *Democracy in America* (R Heffner (ed)) (New York, Mentor, 1956).

Dignam, A and Galanis, M, *The Globalization of Corporate Governance* (Farnham, Ashgate, 2009).

Dignam, A and Lowry, J, *Company Law*, 6th edn (Oxford, Oxford University Press, 2010).

Dine, J and Du Plessis, J-J, 'The Fate of the Draft Fifth Directive on Company Law: Accommodation instead of Harmonisation' [1997] *Journal of Business Law* 23.

Dodd, EM, 'For Whom are Corporate Managers Trustees?'(1932) 45 *Harvard Law Review* 1145.

Dubnick, MJ, '*Sarbanes-Oxley* and the Search for Accountable Corporate Governance' in O'Brien, J, (ed), *Private Equity, Corporate Governance and the Dynamics of Capital Market Regulation* (London, Imperial College Press, 2007) ch 9.

Dubnick, MJ and Frederickson, HG, *Public Accountability: Performance Measurement, the Extended State, and the Search for Trust* (Dayton OH, The Kettering Foundation, 2011).

Duxbury, N, 'The Origins of Modern American Jurisprudence, Part I: The Birth of Legal Formalism', (1991) University of Manchester Faculty of Law Working Paper No 6.

Dworkin, R, 'Why Efficiency?'(1980) 8 *Hofstra Law Review* 563.

Easterbrook, FH, 'Managers' Discretion and Investors' Welfare: Theories and Evidence' (1984) 9 *Delaware Journal of Corporate Law* 540.

—— 'Two Agency-Cost Explanations of Dividends' (1984) 74 *The American Economic Review* 650.

Easterbrook, FH and Fischel, DR, 'The Proper Role of a Target's Management in Responding to a Tender Offer' (1981) 94 *Harvard Law Review* 1161.

—— 'Mandatory Disclosure and Protection of Investors' (1984) 79 *Vanderbilt Law Review* 669.

—— 'The Corporate Contract' (1989) 89 *Columbia Law Review* 1416.

—— *The Economic Structure of Corporate Law* (Cambridge MA, Harvard University Press, 1991).

—— 'Contract and Fiduciary Duty' (1993) 36 *Journal of Law & Economics* 425.

Edmunds, R and Lowry, J, 'The Continuing Value of Relief for Directors' Breach of Duty' (2003) 66 *Modern Law Review* 195.

Eisenberg, MA, 'The Structure of Corporation Law' (1989) 89 *Columbia Law Review* 1461.

Ewing, KD and Truter, GM, 'The Information and Consultation of Employees Regulations: Voluntarism's Bitter Legacy' (2005) 68 *The Modern Law Review* 626.

Fama, EF, 'Efficient Capital Markets: A Review of Theory and Empirical Work' (1970) 25 *Journal of Finance* 383.

—— 'Agency Problems and the Theory of the Firm' (1980) 88 *Journal of Political Economy* 288.

Fama, EF and Jensen, M, 'Separation of Ownership and Control' (1983) 26 *Journal of Law and Economics* 301.

Farrar, JH, 'Towards a Statutory Business Judgment Rule in Australia' [1998] *Australian Journal of Corporate Law* 302.

Fisch, JE, 'The Destructive Ambiguity of Federal Proxy Access' (2012) 61 *Emory Law Journal* 435.

—— 'The Long Road Back: Business Roundtable and the Implications for Future SEC Rule-Making' (2012) 35 *Seattle University Law Review* (forthcoming).

Fischel, DR, 'The "Race to the Bottom" Revisited: Reflections on Recent Developments in Delaware's Corporation Law' (1982) 76 *Northwestern University Law Review* 913.

Fox, A, *Beyond Contract: Work, Power and Trust Relations* (London, Faber, 1974).

Friedman, M, *Capitalism and Freedom* (Chicago IL, The University of Chicago Press, 1962).

—— 'The Social Responsibility of Business is to Increase its Profits' in Beauchamp, T and Bowie, N (eds), *Ethical Theory and Business* (Upper Saddle River, Pearson, 2004) (first published 1979); article originally published in *The New York Times Magazine* (1970).

Galbraith, JK, *American Capitalism: The Concept of Countervailing Power* (Boston MA, Houghton Mifflin, 1952).

—— *The New Industrial State*, paperback edn (Princeton, Princeton University Press, 2007) (first published 1967).

—— *Economics and the Public Purpose* (London, Andre Deutsch, 1973).

—— *The Anatomy of Power* (Boston MA, Houghton Mifflin, 1983).

Gamble, A, Kelly, G and Parkinson, J, *The Political Economy of the Company* (Oxford, Hart Publishing, 2000).

Gevurtz, F, 'The Historical and Political Origins of the Corporate Board of Directors' (2004) 33 *Hofstra Law Review* 89.

Gewirth, A, *The Community of Rights* (Chicago IL, University of Chicago Press, 1996).

Giddens, A, *Central Problems in Social Theory: Action, Structure, and Contradiction in Social Analysis* (Berkeley CA, University of California Press, 1979).

Gilson, R, 'The Case Against Shark Repellent Amendments: Structural Limitations on the Enabling Concept' (1982) 34 *Stanford Law Review* 775.

—— 'Unocal Fifteen Years Later (and What We Can Do About It)' (2001) 26 *Delaware Journal of Corporate Law* 491.

Gilson, RJ and Kraakman, R, 'Delaware's Intermediate Standard for Defensive Tactics: Is There Substance to Proportionality Review?' (1989) 44 *Business Lawyer* 247.

—— 'The Mechanisms of Market Efficiency Twenty Years Later: The Hindsight Bias' in J Armour and JA McCahery, *After Enron: Improving Corporate Law and Modernising Securities Regulation in Europe and the US* (Oxford, Hart Publishing, 2006) 29 (first published in (2003) 28 *Journal of Corporation Law* 715).

Gompers, PA, Ishii, JL and Metrick, A, 'Corporate Governance and Equity Prices' (2003) 118 *Quarterly Journal of Economics* 107.

Gordon, JN, *The Mandatory Structure of Corporate Law* (1989) 89 *Columbia Law Review* 1549.

—— 'Corporations, Markets, and Courts' (1991) 91 *Columbia Law Review* 1931.

—— 'The Rise of Independent Directors in the United States, 1950–2005: Of Shareholder Value and Stock Market Prices' (2007) 59 *Stanford Law Review* 1465.

—— '"Say on Pay": Cautionary Notes on the UK Experience and the Case for Shareholder Opt-In' (2009) 46 *Harvard Journal on Legislation* 323.

Gower, LCB, 'Some Contrast Between British and American Corporation Law' (1956) 69 *Harvard Law Review* 1369.

Grantham, R, 'The Judicial Extension of Directors' Duties to Creditors' [1991] *Journal of Business Law* 1.

Grossman, SJ and Hart, O, 'The Costs and Benefits of Ownership: A Theory of Vertical and Lateral Integration' (1986) 94 *Journal of Political Economy* 691.

Habermas, J, *Legitimation Crisis* (Boston MA, Beacon Press, 1975).

Hannigan, B, *Company Law*, 2ndedn (Oxford, Oxford University Press, 2009).

Hansmann, H and Kraakman, R, 'The Essential Role of Organizational Law' (2000) 110 *Yale Law Journal* 387.

—— 'The End of History for Corporate Law' (2001) 89 *Georgetown Law Journal* 439.

Hart, O, 'Incomplete Contracts and the Theory of the Firm' (1988) 4 *Journal of Law, Economics and Organization* 119.

Hayek, FA 'The Use of Knowledge in Society' (1945) 4 *American Economic Review* 519.

—— *The Constitution of Liberty* (London, Routledge, 1960).

—— 'The Corporation in a Democratic Society: In Whose Interest Ought It and Will It Be Run?' in HI Ansoff, (ed), *Business Strategy* (Harmondsworth, Penguin, 1969) 266.

Hobbes, T, *The Leviathan*, Penguin Classics edn (Harmondsworth, Penguin, 1968) (first published 1651).

Hohfeld, WN, 'Fundamental Legal Conceptions as Applied in Judicial Reasoning' (1917) 26 *Yale Law Journal* 710.

—— 'Some Fundamental Legal Conceptions as Applied in Judicial Reasoning' (1913) 23 *Yale Law Journal* 16.

Honore, AM, 'Ownership' in Guest, AG, *Oxford Essays in Jurisprudence* (Oxford, Clarendon Press, 1961).

Hopt, KJ and Wymeersch, E (eds), *Capital Markets and Company Law* (Oxford, Oxford University Press, 2003).

Horwitz, MJ, 'The Emergence of an Instrumental Conception of American Law, 1780–1820' (1971) 5 *Perspectives in American History* 287.

—— 'The Rise of Legal Formalism' (1975) 19 *The American Journal of Legal History* 251.

Hoshi, T, 'Japanese Corporate Governance as a System' in KJ Hopt, H Kanda, MJ Roe, E Wymeersch and S Prigge (eds), *Comparative Corporate Governance: The State of the Art and Emerging Research* (Oxford, Clarendon Press, 1998) 847.

International Labour Organization, *Freedom of Association: Digest of Decisions and Principles of the Freedom of Association Committee of the Governing Body of the ILO*, 5th edn (Geneva, International Labour Organization, 2006).

Ireland, P, 'The Myth of Shareholder Ownership' (1999) 62 *Modern Law Review* 32.

—— 'Defending the Rentier: Corporate Theory and the Reprivatisation of the Public Company' in Gamble, A, Kelly, G and Parkinson, J, *The Political Economy of the Company* (Oxford, Hart Publishing, 2000) ch 7.

—— 'Recontractualising the Corporation: Implicit Contract as Ideology' in D Campbell, H Collins and J Wightman (eds), *Implicit Dimensions of Contract* (Oxford, Hart Publishing, 2003) 255.

—— 'Property and Contract in Contemporary Corporate Theory' (2003) 23 *Legal Studies* 453.

James, S, *British Cabinet Government*, 2nd edn (London, Routledge, 1999).

Jensen, MC, 'Agency Costs of Free Cash Flow, Corporate Finance, and Takeovers' (1986) 76 *American Economic Review* 323.

—— 'Value Maximisation, Stakeholder Theory, and the Corporate Objective Function' (2001) 7 *European Financial Management* 297.

Jensen, MC and Meckling, W, 'Managerial Behavior, Agency Costs and Ownership Structure' (1976) 3 *Journal of Financial Economics* 305.

Jensen, MC and Murphy, KJ, 'Performance Pay and Top-Management Incentives' (1990) 98 *Journal of Political Economy* 225.

Johnston, A, *The City Take-over Code* (Oxford, Oxford University Press, 1980).

Kahan, M and Rock, E, 'Embattled CEOs' (2010) 88 *Texas Law Review* 987.

—— 'The Insignificance of Proxy Access' (2011) 97 *Virginia Law Review* 1347.

Kahn-Freund, O, 'Industrial Democracy' (1977) 6 *Industrial Law Journal* 65.

Kaufman, H, *Red Tape: Its Origins, Uses, and Abuses* (Washington DC, Brookings Institution, 1977).

Keay, A, 'Wrongful Trading and the Liability of Company Directors: A Theoretical Perspective' (2005) 25 *Legal Studies* 431.

Keay, A, 'Company Directors Behaving Poorly: Disciplinary Options for Shareholders' [2007] *Journal of Business Law* 656.

——'Ascertaining The Corporate Objective: An Entity Maximisation and Sustainability Model' (2008) 71 *Modern Law Review* 663.

——'Good Faith and Director's Duty to Promote the Success of their Company' (2011) 32 *The Company Lawyer* 138.

Kelly, G and Parkinson, J, 'The Conceptual Foundations of the Company: a Pluralist Approach' in A Gamble, G Kelly and J Parkinson, *The Political Economy of the Company* (Oxford, Hart Publishing, 2000) 113.

Kershaw, D, *Company Law in Context: Text and Materials* (Oxford, Oxford University Press, 2009).

Keynes, JM, 'The End of Laissez Faire' (1926) in JM Keynes, *Essays in Persuasion* (London, Macmillan, 1931) 312.

Kraakman, R et al's, *The Anatomy of Corporate Law: A Comparative and Functional Approach*, 2nd edn (Oxford, Oxford University Press, 2009) (first published 2004).

Kronman, AT, 'A Comment on Dean Clark' (1989) 89 *Columbia Law Review* 1748.

Langevoort, D, 'The Human Nature of Corporate Boards: Law, Norms, and the Unintended Consequences of Independence and Accountability' (2001) 89 *Georgia Law Journal* 797.

La Porta, R, Lopez-de-Silanes, F, Shleifer, A and Vishny, R, 'Investor Protection and Corporate Governance' (2000) 58 *Journal of Financial Economics* 3.

Lazonick, W, 'The Quest for Shareholder Value: Stock Repurchases in the United States' (2008) 74 *Louvain Economic Review* 479.

Lippmann, W, *Public Opinion* (New York, The Free Press, 1965) (first published 1921).

Lipton, M and Rowe, P, 'Pills, Polls and Professors: A Reply to Professor Gilson' (2002) 27 *Delaware Journal of Corporate Law* 1.

Lowry, J, 'Eliminating Obstacles to Freedom of Establishment: The Competitive Edge of UK Company Law' (2004) 63 *Cambridge Law Journal* 331.

——'The Duty of Loyalty of Company Directors: Bridging the Accountability Gap Through Efficient Disclosure' (2009) 68 *Cambridge Law Journal* 607.

——'The Irreducible Core of the Duty of Care, Skill and Diligence of Company Directors' (2012) 75 *Modern Law Review* 249.

Lowry, J and Reisberg, A (eds), *Pettet's Company Law: Company and Capital Markets Law*, 3rd edn (Harlow, Longman, 2009).

MacCormick, N, *Institutions of Law: An Essay in Legal Theory* (Oxford, Oxford University Press, 2007).

——*Questioning Sovereignty: Law, State, and Nation in the European Commonwealth* (Oxford, Oxford University Press, 1999).

Mace, M, *Directors: Myth and Reality*, revised edn (Cambridge MA, Harvard Business School Press, 1986) (first published 1971).

Macneil, I and Li, X, 'Comply or Explain: Market Discipline and Non-Compliance with the Combined Code' (2006) 14 *Corporate Governance: An International Review* 486.

Manne, HG, 'The "Higher" Criticism of the Modern Corporation' (1962) 62 *Columbia Law Review* 399.

—— 'Mergers and the Market for Corporate Control' (1965) 73 *Journal of Political Economy* 110.

Marx, K, *Capital: A Critique of Political Economy*, Penguin Classics edn (Harmondsworth, Penguin, 1976) (first published 1867).

Masten, SE, 'A Legal Basis for the Firm' (1998) 4 *Journal of Law, Economics and Organization* 181.

McVea, H, 'Section 994, Companies Act 2006 and the Primacy of Contract' (2012, currently unpublished article, forthcoming).

Millon, D, 'New Directions in Corporate Law: Communitarians, Contractarians, and the Crisis in Corporate Law' (1993) 50 *Washington and Lee Law Review* 1373.

Modigliani, F and Miller, M, 'The Cost of Capital, Corporation Finance and the Theory of Investment' (1958) 48 *American Economic Review* 261.

Moore, MT, '"Whispering Sweet Nothings": The Limitations of Informal Conformance in UK Corporate Governance' (2009) 9 *Journal of Corporate Law Studies* 95.

Moore, MT and Reberioux, A, 'The Corporate Governance of the Firm as an Entity: Old Lessons for the New Debate' in Y Biondi, A Canziani and T Kirat (eds), *The Firm as an Entity: Implications for Economics, Accounting and the Law* (London, Routledge, 2007) 348.

—— 'Corporate Power in the Public Eye: Reassessing the Implications of Berle's Public Consensus Theory' (2010) 33 *Seattle University Law Review* 1109.

—— 'Revitalizing the Institutional Roots of Anglo-American Corporate Governance' (2011) 40 *Economy and Society* 84.

Moran, M, *The Politics of the Financial Services Revolution: The USA, UK and Japan* (London, Macmillan, 1991).

Morck, R, 'Behavioral Finance in Corporate Governance – Independent Directors and Nonexecutive Chairs', Harvard Institute of Economic Research Discussion Paper No 2037 (April 2007).

Myners, P, *Pre-Emption Rights: Final Report* (London, Department of Trade and Industry, 2005).

Nolan, RC, 'The Continuing Evolution of Shareholder Governance' (2006) 65 *Cambridge Law Journal* 92.

Novitz, T and Skidmore, P, *Fairness at Work: A Critical Analysis of the Employment Relations Act 1999 and its Treatment of Collective Rights* (Oxford, Hart Publishing, 2001).

O'Kelley, C and Thompson, R, *Corporations and Business Associations: Cases and Materials* 6th edn (New York, Aspen, 2010).

Parkinson, JE, *Corporate Power and Responsibility: Issues in the Theory of Company Law* (Oxford, Oxford University Press, 1993).

Pasban, MR, Campbell, C and Birds, J, 'The Business Judgment Rule: A Comparative Analysis of Company Directors' Duties and Liabilities in England and United States Law' (1997) 6 *Journal of Transnational Law and Policy* 201.

Pettet, B, Lowry, J and Reisberg, A (eds), *Pettet's Company Law: Company and Capital Markets Law* 3rd edn (Harlow, Longman, 2009).

Pigou, AC, *The Economics of Welfare*, 4th edn (London, Macmillan, 1932) (first published 1920).

Pope, JG, Kellman, P and Bruno, E, '"We Are Already Dead": The Thirteenth Amendment and the Fight for Workers' Rights After EFCA' (2010) 67 *National Lawyers Guild Review* 110.

Posner, RA, *Economic Analysis of Law* (Boston, Little, Brown, 1972).

——'The Ethical and Political Basis of the Efficiency Norm in Common Law Adjudication' (1980) 8 *Hofstra Law Review* 487.

Prosser, T, 'Theorising Utility Regulation' (1999) 62 *Modern Law Review* 196.

Rawls, J, *A Theory of Justice*, revised edn (Oxford, Oxford University Press, 1999) (first published 1971).

Ribstein, L, 'International Implications of Sarbanes-Oxley: Raising the Rent on US Law' (2003) 3 *Journal of Corporate Law Studies* 299.

Ricardo, D, *On the Principles of Political Economy and Taxation*, 3rd edn (London, Murray, 1821) (first published 1817).

Riley, C, 'The Juridification of Corporate Governance' in J de Lacy, *The Reform of United Kingdom Company Law* (London, Cavendish, 2002) 179.

Ringe, WG, 'Sparking Regulatory Competition in European Company Law – The Impact of the Centros Line of Case-Law and its Concept of "Abuse of Law"' in R de la Feria and S Vogenauer (eds), *Prohibition of Abuse of Law – A New General Principle of EU Law* (Oxford, Hart Publishing, 2010).

Roberts, J, 'The Possibilities of Accountability' (1991) 16 *Accounting, Organizations & Society* 355.

Roberts, J and Scapens, R, 'Accounting Systems and Systems of Accountability – Understanding Accounting Practices in their Organisational Contexts' (1985) 10 *Accounting, Organizations & Society* 443.

Roe, MJ, 'The Shareholder Wealth Maximization Norm and Industrial Organization' (2001) 149 *University of Pennsylvania Law Review* 2063.

Romano, R, *The Genius of American Corporate Law* (Washington DC, AEI Press, 1993).

——'Comment on Easterbrook and Fischel, "Contract and Fiduciary Duty"' (1993) 36 *Journal of Law & Economics* 447.

—— 'The Sarbanes-Oxley Act and the Making of Quack Corporate Governance' (2005) 114 *Yale Law Journal* 1521.

Rosenfeld, RA, 'An Expansion and Application of Kaufman's Model of Red Tape: The Case of Community Development Block Grants' (1984) 37 *The Western Political Quarterly* 603.

Sandel, M, *Liberalism and the Limits of Justice*, 2nd edn (Cambridge, Cambridge University Press, 1998) (first published 1982).

Schiek, D, Liebert, U and Schneider, H, *European Economic and Social Constitutionalism after the Treaty of Lisbon* (Cambridge, Cambridge University Press, 2011).

Schleifer, A and Summers, L, 'Breach of Trust in Hostile Takeovers' in A Auerbach (ed), *Corporate Takeovers: Causes and Consequences* (Chicago IL, University of Chicago Press, 1991) (first published, 1988), ch 2.

Scott, MB and Lyman, SM, 'Accounts' (1968) 33 *American Sociological Review* 46.

Sealy, LS, *Cases and Materials in Company Law* 7th edn (London, Butterworths, 2001).

Selznick, R, *Law, Society and Industrial Justice* (New York, Russell Sage Foundation, 1969).

Sharfman, BS, 'Why Proxy Access is Harmful to Corporate Governance' (2012) 37 *Journal of Corporation Law* 387.

Shiller, RJ, *Irrational Exuberance*, 2nd edn (Princeton NJ, Princeton University Press, 2012).

Shleifer, A, *Inefficient Markets: An Introduction to Behavioral Finance* (Oxford, Oxford University Press, 2000).

Simon, HA, 'Theories of Decision-Making in Economics and Behavioral Science' (1959) 49 *American Economic Review* 253.

Sinclair, A, 'The Chameleon of Accountability: Forms and Discourses' (1995) 20 *Accounting, Organizations & Society* 219.

Skaife, HA, Collins, DW and LaFond, R, 'Corporate Governance and the Cost of Equity Capital' Social Science Research Network (December 2004): ssrn.com/abstract=639681.

Skeel, DA, *Icarus in the Boardroom: The Fundamental Flaws in Corporate America and Where They Came From* (New York, Oxford University Press, 2005).

—— *The New Financial Deal: Understanding the Dodd-Frank Act and its (Unintended) Consequences* (Hoboken NJ, Wiley, 2011).

Strachey, J, *Contemporary Capitalism* (London, Victor Gollancz, 1956).

Stokes, M, 'Company Law and Legal Theory' in W Twining, *Legal Theory and Common Law* (Oxford, Blackwell, 1986) 155.

Stout, LA, 'Do Antitakeover Defenses Decrease Shareholder Wealth? The Ex Post/Ex Ante Valuation Problem' (2002) 55 *Stanford Law Review* 845.

—— 'The Mechanisms of Market Inefficiency' (2005) 14 *Journal of Financial Transformation* 95.

Syrpis, P and Johnston, A, 'Regulatory Competition in European Company Law after Cartesio', (2009) 34 *European Law Review* 378.

Teubner, G, 'Corporate Fiduciary Duties and their Beneficiaries: A Functional Approach to the Legal Institutionalization of Corporate Responsibility' in KJ Hopt and G Teubner, *Corporate Governance and Directors' Liabilities: Legal, Economic and Sociological Analyses on Corporate Social Responsibility* (Berlin, De Gruyter, 1985) 149.

Thomas, R and Cotter, J, 'Shareholder Proposals in the New Millennium: Shareholder Support, Board Response, and Market Reaction' (2007) 13 *Journal of Corporate Finance* 368.

Tsuk Mitchell, D, 'From Pluralism to Individualism: Berle and Means and 20th-Century American Legal Thought' (2005) 30 *Law and Social Inquiry* 179.

Tung, F, 'Before Competition: Origins of the Internal Affairs Doctrine' (2006) 32 *Journal of Corporation Law* 33.

Vitols, S, 'Varieties of Corporate Governance: Comparing Germany and the UK' in PA Hall and D Soskice (eds), *Varieties of Capitalism: The Institutional Foundations of Comparative Advantage* (Oxford, Oxford University Press, 2001) 337.

Walker-Arnott, E, 'Company Law, Corporate Governance and the Banking Crisis' (2010) *International Corporate Rescue – Special Edition* 3.

Wedderburn, KW, 'Shareholders' Rights and the Rule in *Foss v Harbottle*' (1957) 15 *The Cambridge Law Journal* 194.

—— *The Future of Company Law: Corporate Governance, Fat Cats and Workers* (London, Institute of Employment Rights, 2004).

Wells, H, 'The Cycles of Corporate Social Responsibility: An Historical Retrospective for the Twenty-first Century' (2002) 51 *Kansas Law Review* 77.

Wheeler, S, 'Works Councils: Towards Stakeholding?' (1997) 24 *Journal of Law and Society* 44.

Williams, R, 'Disqualifying Directors: A remedy Worse than the Disease?' (2007) 7 *Journal of Corporate Law Studies* 213.

Williamson, OE, *The Mechanisms of Governance* (Oxford, Oxford University Press, 1996).

Index

Lightning Source UK Ltd.
Milton Keynes UK
UKOW06n1518060516

273713UK00001B/26/P